# Elizabethan Secret Agent:

## The Untold Story of William Ashby

### (1536–1593)

Timothy Ashby

First Published in the UK in 2022 by
Scotland Street Press
100 Willowbrae Avenue
Edinburgh EH8 7HU

A CIP record for this book is available from the British Library.

ISBN 978-1-910895-59-7

Typeset and cover design by Antonia Shack in Edinburgh

# Contents

# Illustrations

5. George Carey 2$^{nd}$ Baron Hunsdon, miniature portrait, dated 1601, by Nicholas Hilliard 1547–1619. In a collection at Berkeley Castle, Gloucestershire.

6. Engraving of the Entry of Don John into Brussels in 1577, by Frans Hogenberg from the *Polemographia Auraico-Belgia* of theologian Willem Baudartius, published by Michiel Colijn in 1611 vol 1 p. 237.

7. A copper engraving of Johann Sturmius by Hendrik Hondius (1573 – after 1648) after an earlier contemporary portrait. Located at the British Museum.

8. Sir Francis Walsingham (1532–1590) painted circa 1589 by John de Critz (1550–1642). Original painting kept at the Yale Centre for British Art, Newhaven, Connecticut.

9. Mid seventeenth-century line engraving of Queen Elizabeth I with Sir Francis Walsingham and William Cecil, 1$^{st}$ Baron Burghley by William Faithorne (1620–1691). An original exists at the National Portrait Gallery, London.

10. A portrait of William Cecil, 1st Baron Burghley (1520/21–1598) wearing a crimson robe and riding a mule. By an unknown artist in the school of Gheeraerts, Marcus, the younger painted circa 1585. Copies of the painting exist at the Bodleian library Oxford, Hatfield house and Burghley house. Permission obtained via Alamy images website for this image, which is likely from the primary original painting at the Bodleian Library.

11. Babington's acknowledgement of ciphers used with Mary Queen of Scots. The original letters are held in the National Archives, UK. Digital image permission obtained from the National Archives and Alamy images website.

12. Elizabethan houses on Clerkenwell Close, from *The history of Clerkenwell: illustrated with nearly two hundred engravings* William J. Pinks, Edward J. Wood and A. C. Bromhead, (London 1865). Digital image permission obtained from the Alamy images website.

13. Flight of the townspeople from London into the country to escape from the Plague, from *A Short History of the English People* J. R. Green (London 1892). Digital image permission obtained from the Alamy images website.

**Picture Section 2**

1. Map of the Kingdome of Scotland (1610) by John Speed (© National Library of Scotland).

2. Scottish witches cursing travellers, from *Chronicles of England, Scotlande, and Irelande* by Raphael Holinshed (London 1577). Digital image permission obtained from the Alamy images website.

3. Portrait of James VI, and later I of England, at age eighteen circa 1585, by Adrian Vanson (1580–1601). Image courtesy of the Weiss Gallery, London.

4. Edinburgh City Plan circa 1582 engraved by Franz Hogenberg for inclusion in the *Civitates Orbis Terrarum* edited by Georg Braun.

5. 'Dowie's Tavern, Libberton's Wynd' Edinburgh, by George Cattermole (1800–1868) from Sir Herbert Maxwell, Edinburgh, A Historical Study (1916).

6. James VI of Scotland aged twenty by Alonso Sanchez Coello. Courtesy of the National Trust for Scotland, Falkland Palace.

7. Palace of Holyrood House, Edinburgh. A nineteenth-century print, digital image permission obtained from Alamy images website.

8. Galleon, copper engraving by Frans Huys after designs by Pieter Bruegel the Elder, published by Hieronymus Cock (Antwerp c. 1570). Digital image permission obtained from Alamy images website.

9. Queen Elizabeth I (1533–1603) painted circa 1588, in the style of the English school by an unconfirmed English artist, possibly George Gower or Nicholas Hilliard. Three versions of 'the Armada Portrait' were made, this image is from the one held at the National Maritime Museum, Greenwich; the 'Drake version'.

10. John Maitland (1545–1595), 1ˢᵗ Lord Maitland of Thirlestane by John Scougal (1645–1717) after an earlier painter. Courtesy of the Maitland family collection at Thirlestane Castle with Thirlestane Castle Trust.

11. Portrait of Lord John Hamilton, 1st Marquess of Hamilton, by an unknown artist c1556 of the Flemish school, the Circle of Ludger Tom Ring. Courtesy of the Hamilton family collection; Lennoxlove House.

12. Witches brewing a spell in a cauldron, woodcut c. 1508 from *De Lamiis et Pythonicis Mulieribus* (On Witches and Female Soothsayers) by Ulrich Molitor. Digital image permission obtained from Alamy images website.

13. Sir Robert Naunton, line engraving by Simone de Passe, early 17ᵗʰ century. Used as the Frontispiece from Naunton's book *Fragmenta Regalia, or Observations on the late Queen Elizabeth, her Times and Favourites, an account of the reign of Elizabeth I* (London 1641).

# *Introduction*

I knew William Ashby for many years only as an intriguing footnote in early editions of *Burke's Landed Gentry*, from a line of text therein which described him as 'Queen Elizabeth's ambassador to James VI in 1589'. I was aware that he was a distant relative, first cousin of my ancestor, Barbara Ashby of Loseby and Quenby, Leicestershire.[1] As I began researching his life and career out of genealogical curiosity, I felt a peculiar connection with him due to my personal service in government and law, and from having lived in Edinburgh.

As I delved deeper into Tudor era archives, I was astounded that William Ashby's story as an influential Elizabethan secret agent and diplomat was little known and needed to be told. He was a key figure in Anglo-Scottish relations during his tenure as English ambassador to the Court of King James VI from 1588 to 1590. As England prepared for the onslaught of the Spanish Armada, Ashby arrived in Edinburgh charged with the crucial diplomatic task of keeping the Scots 'in amity' with the English to prevent a Spanish landing in Scotland and invasion from the north.

He accomplished his objective by offering a series of inducements to the young Scottish King. After the English defeat of the Armada, Queen Elizabeth I and her chief advisors – William Cecil, First Baron Burghley, and Sir Francis Walsingham, Principal Secretary of State and Spymaster – repudiated Ashby's promises. Respected by the Scottish King and his courtiers, Ashby continued as ambassador and played an important role in the repairing of frayed diplomatic relations that led to the accession of James to Elizabeth's throne in 1603 and the union of the Scottish and English crowns.

Although Ashby died in 1593, his influence on Anglo-Scottish relations extended beyond his lifetime as well as the lives of Elizabeth, Walsingham and Burghley. His nephew and heir, Sir Robert Naunton, a near contemporary in age to King James, served as Ashby's secretary, courier and trainee secret agent in Edinburgh. After James became King of England, Naunton was knighted and subsequently appointed Principal Secretary of State, assuming Walsingham's role as one of the sovereign's chief advisors and most powerful royal officials, as well as England's spymaster.

Ashby's correspondence with Walsingham and other Elizabethan historical figures provides a wealth of information about diplomatic and political intrigues within the Scottish Court, as well as pithy observations about the personalities he interacted with. He was familiar with Scotland years before his ambassadorial appointment, having accompanied Walsingham's calamitous delegation to Scotland in 1583 when his personal mission was to recruit pro-English agents and carry reports back to Queen Elizabeth and her Privy Council. During his later tenure in Edinburgh he served as both chief of Her Majesty's diplomatic mission and – to use the parlance of today's Secret Intelligence Service – Head of Station. While often frustrated with King James VI, whom he knew as a teenager and into his early twenties, Ashby empathised with the young monarch and often risked advocating for him to the generally hostile English government.

For at least twenty years William Ashby was one of Walsingham's most trusted protégés; Sir Francis wrote that he had 'declared my mind and pleasure to master Ashby',[2] and towards the end of both men's careers Walsingham wrote to Ashby expressing 'the particular love' he had for him.[3]

Walsingham was the chief of the English intelligence apparatus that over the centuries morphed into the modern Security Service (MI5) and the Secret Intelligence Service (MI6). Queen Elizabeth I is regarded as the first monarch to have created a professional intelligence service or, more accurately, to have had one created for her by the tirelessly devoted Sir Francis, building on the organisation begun by Burghley. As Ashby's patron, Walsingham features prominently in this book. The Principal Secretary trusted him to personally brief the Queen, Burghley and members of the Privy Council, as well as to carry out sensitive foreign diplomatic and espionage missions. The latter included one of the earliest known 'black ops' (covert sabotage operations) to destroy a Spanish Armada ship sheltering in Scotland.

Prior to his ambassadorial appointment, Ashby served as an 'intelligencer' and courier between Walsingham and English diplomats and spies across northern Europe. He was involved in the rebellion of the Low Countries against Spanish rule – the 'Eighty Years War'– which was on par with Scotland as the most important English foreign policy issue during much of the Elizabethan era. Ashby often carried important messages in his mind rather than run the risk of capture and interception of written communiques, which commonly occurred in the shadow land of sixteenth-century espionage. He epitomised the Elizabethan 'gentleman spy' – well-educated, socially-connected adventurers who merged espionage and diplomacy.

William Ashby's life encompassed four Tudor monarchs and the future Stuart King, James I. From his birth in a rural corner of England that was almost unchanged since the medieval era, he lived to see his country transformed in terms of society, government, religion and culture. Ashby's career was unusually eclectic. He had degrees from both Cambridge and Oxford, spoke French, German, Italian and Latin, read and wrote ancient Greek and Hebrew, and trained as a lawyer. He was sent by Walsingham on a dangerous military intelligence operation with the Queen's cousin, repulsed an attack by enemy agents on the Rhine, and was charged with negotiating the release of an English diplomatic hostage. He twice served as a Member of Parliament.

Like Walsingham and other English Protestants, as a young man Ashby fled to the Continent as a 'Marian Exile' after Queen Mary succeeded

Edward VI to the throne. Also like Sir Francis, he was committed to use any means – including risking his life and reputation – to protect and defend Queen Elizabeth, the English state and the Anglican religion. Ashby and his colleagues believed that their country was under constant threat from 'Papists' within the British Isles and abroad, especially from powerful Continental enemies such as Spain and France, which were empowered by the Vatican to crusade against heretical England and replace Elizabeth with a Catholic monarch.

Apart from his professional endeavours, Ashby's biography provides insight into the society not only of the Tudor era but of the preceding centuries – the family connections that shaped his life and occupation. His personal background provided entrée to an extraordinary range of domestic and international connections, including leading sixteenth-century historical figures.[4] While his ancestry was an important asset in the obsessively status-conscious world emerging from the Middle Ages, William Ashby's intelligence, education and ambition were equally key to his progression as the son of an impoverished minor gentleman from a Leicestershire hamlet to the royal courts of Europe.

No known portrait of Ashby has been found, and his physical appearance is unknown. From his correspondence and observations by contemporaries, we know that he had a dry sense of humour and exhibited his classical education by liberal use of Latin, Greek and Italian tags. He was a shrewd observer of people, events and geographic features, and reflected the generally superior attitude of an Englishman of his class and era towards other nationalities and the 'lower orders'. Ashby was exceptionally well-read, relished 'philosophical' discussions, had a small circle of close friends and was intensely loyal to friends and family. He was somewhat naïve about personal relationships and occasionally melancholy. Like his patron, Walsingham, he was austere in dress and demeanour, but privately enjoyed fine wine, cuisine and the sensual aspects of the Renaissance. Unlike Walsingham, he was not particularly religious.

Many documents relating to the early decades of Ashby's life have been lost to the ravages of fires, hungry rats and decay; fortunately, a considerable body of archival materials survive to provide details of his diplomatic and intelligence work as well as his personal relationships. The diary kept by his closest friend, Sir Arthur Throckmorton, is a primary source for insight into Ashby's personality and service as an intelligencer. Wherever possible, I have used quotations from original sources, some of which are so lyrical that they seem lifted from works by Marlowe or Shakespeare.

Much of this book is focused on Ashby's service as English ambassador to Scotland during the Armada crisis and its aftermath. I have attempted to be balanced in writing about Scotland and King James VI during this period, although due to the scarcity of primary Scottish records, most contemporary sources and quotations are English and reflect a national bias that was commonplace during the era.

# Prologue
## 'The benefits conferred on us by our ancestors ...'[1]

Edinburgh, Kingdom of Scotland

Monday, 29 July 1588

The Englishman closed his tired eyes and laid aside the letter with the familiar spidery writing of Sir Francis Walsingham, his patron and chief for the past two decades. The candles in the brass candelabrum guttered from the room's numerous draughts, and the puny fire in the grate had died long ago – he didn't have the energy to wake his servant to lay another. He drew his fur-edged cloak closer, listening to the wind and rain lashing the draughty, rodent-infested lodgings in a dank close near St. Giles Cathedral, for which he was charged the exorbitant rent of 20 shillings per day.[2]

Scotland in high summer, he thought ruefully. Well, at least the rain might wash some of the ordure and rubbish down the hill to Holyrood Palace. He silently cursed the Scots – and Walsingham for cajoling him into accepting the mission. At age fifty-two, he was too old and cynical for the absurdities of diplomacy. But, after a third reading of the letter from Sir Francis received earlier that evening, he knew that his embassage in Scotland was of the utmost importance to the preservation of his Queen, country and the Anglican religion.[3]

Time was of the essence.

William Ashby, only two weeks into his appointment as Queen Elizabeth's resident ambassador in Scotland, opened his eyes, sighed and picked up Walsingham's letter warning of 'the appearing of the Spanish fleet upon the coast of the west country'.[4] His intelligence contacts had reported that the perpetually impecunious King James VI, 'greatly solicited and pressed to hearken to the large offers made to him by Spain and France',[5] and was considering bribes from England's enemies to allow them to use Scotland as a base from which to invade his country.

Shivering on this dark night in Edinburgh, capital of a country that Ashby and his peers considered savage, ungovernable and 'the old beggardly enemy', the people of which were said to have an 'aversion and natural alienation … from the English',[6] the ambassador was consumed by a dilemma that could not only end his career but result in literally losing his head. He had been verbally charged by Walsingham to promise anything to keep King James 'in amity' with the English. But he knew that he must personally take the blame for any failure, as Good Queen Bess and Walsingham could be expected to deny authority for his actions in the event of diplomatic repercussions, or if Her Majesty changed her mind, which she often did.[7]

With a deep sigh, William Ashby made his decision and rested his head on folded arms, slipping into a dream of rolling Leicestershire pastures dotted with sheep on a sunlit day.

******

Unlike Venus-Aphrodite rising as a unique personage from the sea foam, people throughout time have been moulded by their DNA, their environment and the lives of their ancestors, often unknowingly. William Ashby was a product of England's deep past, shaped by the forces of history that began on the blustery 28th day of September in 1066, when a young Norman warrior named Saffrid waded ashore on Pevensey Bay's shingle beach and watched anxiously as his struggling horse was slung over the side of a Drakkar longship.

Ashby was a fourteenth-generation descendant of Saffrid,[8] described as the 'man' (in this context, a soldier or retainer) of William Peverel (Guillaume Pevrel). Peverel was allegedly the illegitimate son of King William the Conqueror, his mother said to be Maud, daughter of the Saxon Ingleric. Whether or not Peverel was William the Bastard's bastard, he was certainly one of the King's favourites. In the years after

Hastings, he fought ruthlessly to subjugate the kingdom, and was named steward of Nottingham Castle, the Norman base in the Midlands. The Domesday Book records Peverel as Lord or Tenant-in-Chief (i.e., holding land directly from the King) of 162 manors in a dozen counties, including five manors in Leicestershire, among which was Ashby Magna.[9]

It is probable that Saffrid was one of the survivors of Peverel's *conroi*, a cavalry unit that attacked in close formation, as exemplified at the battle of Hastings. Long-serving and loyal knights of Peverel's household were given manors. Later histories of the Conquest referred to Saffrid as 'a military knight of the Norman invasion',[10] and progenitor of 'an important vavassour family'.[11] However, the earliest documentary reference to Saffrid is in Domesday, recording that in 1086 he held five manors or parts of manors in Leicestershire, Nottinghamshire and Northamptonshire confiscated from Saxons named as Edward Cild, Fredegi of Hanging Houghton, Gytha, 'wife of Earl Ralph', Alwine of Claydon and Ælfheah of Normanton. One of these manors was Ashby Magna:

'In ... Leics., Saffrid held of William Peverel in Ashby Magna sixteen carucates less two bovates'.[12]

Although Saffrid's principal seat appears to have been at Catesby, Northamptonshire, his largest feudal sub-tenancy was Ashby Magna, which comprised the equivalent of around 1,890 modern acres. Originally within the Danelaw, Ashby Magna (from the Old Norse *askr* 'ash' or the personal name *Aski* + *býr* 'farm', and the Latin *Magna* ('Big') Ashby to distinguish it from the nearby village of Ashby *Parva*, 'Little' Ashby) was listed in Domesday as having a population of one villager, ten smallholders, two slaves and thirteen freemen, with land for seven ploughlands, three lord's plough teams, four-and-a-half men's plough teams and a meadow of forty acres.[13]

In eleventh-century England, formal surnames were a rarity. Landholders would variously refer to themselves (or be referred to in legal documents) by the place where they lived. Saffrid's sons were therefore variously described as 'de' (of) Catesby,[14] Basford or Ashby. By the second generation after the Conquest, permanent surnames based on residence had become standardised for the ruling class.

Saffrid's son Phillip inherited Ashby Magna, and the legal records began referring to him as 'de Ashby' or 'de Esseby'. Located ten miles southwest of the city of Leicester, Ashby Magna was a large village by medieval standards. The Ashbys were seated at a fortified manor house, and the substantial village church of St. Mary was built by Robert de Ashby in the early thirteenth century.[15] [16]

Saffrid's descendants held Ashby Magna until 1265, when the manor and all other landholdings of William de Ashby escheated to the Crown as a result of his support for Simon de Montfort, whose rebellion was defeated by Prince Edward at the Battle of Evesham in August of that year. William de Ashby apparently remained *en situ* by arguing that he did not take part in the battle. However, in 1266 Ashby was indicted for murdering a man. Thanks to the intervention of the prioress of Catesby Priory (to which the Ashbys had donated generously during the previous two centuries, and where Saffrid was buried), William de Ashby was given a royal pardon, but decisively lost all his land.[17]

Evidently, though, the Ashby family reacquired the manor of Ashby Magna, for in 1760 Shukburgh Ashby of Quenby Hall, Leicestershire, sold the lordship of the manor to Thomas Pares.[18]

By the end of the thirteenth century, the Ashbys had recovered from the confiscation of their estates. In 1299, Richard de Ashby, grandson of the murderous William de Ashby, purchased the manor of Quenby, Leicestershire, founding the 'senior' line of the Leicestershire Ashbys, who resided at Quenby for over seven hundred years, finally losing the estate and their other properties in 1904 due to profligacy and bad debts.

Three generations later, in 1380, another Richard de Ashby married the heiress Elizabeth Burdett, only child of John Burdett, lord of the manor of Loseby, Leicestershire, thereby starting the line of the Ashbys of Loseby, from which the subject of this biography was descended.

The marriage was an enviable alliance by medieval standards, for not only was Elizabeth Burdett an heiress but she was the granddaughter of Roger de la Zouch of Lubbesthorpe (died 1350), a kinsman of the politically powerful and socially prominent Barons Zouch.[19] Elizabeth Burdett was a prize catch, but her husband had to offer something valuable in return, and the notion of romantic love was an unlikely factor. Social standing and the connections that came with it together with income-producing properties were of paramount importance in medieval matchmaking. While the Ashbys lacked the landholdings of the great nobles who were on the social rung above them, they prospered from an extensive network of family and political connections throughout the Midlands that had been earned by the sword at Hastings and expanded by succeeding generations who were seated at Loseby, a manor of 2,800 acres neighbouring Quenby, styling themselves 'Ashby of Loseby'.

In the late fourteenth century, especially in rural areas such as Leicestershire, high status marriages were still primarily between established and socially equal Anglo-Norman families. Given the fact that most people, even among the upper classes, were illiterate, elaborate written pedigrees were rare, unlike in the Tudor and Jacobean eras. Although high status families were usually vague on ancestral details, they were aware of their interwoven blood and social connections with those in neighbouring manors and nearby counties.

The Leicestershire Ashbys were adept at keeping their heads and nimbly switching to the winning side amidst the political turmoil of the fourteenth and fifteenth centuries. Considering William Ashby's diplomatic service in Scotland more than two and a half centuries later, a brief digression into the career of his forbear, Edmund de Ashby, is illustrative of the family connections that shaped his own professional life many generations later.

Edmund de Ashby of Quenby, a 'royal household knight', was appointed Sheriff of Warwickshire and Leicestershire in 1326 by Edward II, but quickly switched allegiance to his son, Edward III, following the deposition of the former in 1327.[20] In April of that year, the new king appointed him 'Keeper of the Fees' of the properties forfeited by the Earl of Lancaster after his execution for rebellion in 1322.[21] Shortly thereafter Edmund 'set out for Scotland with Henry de Bello Monte [Henry de Beaumont] in the King's service by his order.'[22] By historical coincidence, probably unknown to the future ambassador to Scotland, this delegation was sent north to negotiate the 1328 Treaty of Edinburgh-Northampton that recognised Scotland as a fully independent kingdom, with Robert the Bruce, followed by his heirs and successors, as the country's rightful rulers.

William Ashby's grandfather, his namesake, was related by blood or marriage to all the principal families of Leicestershire during the late medieval era. He was an MP in the Parliament called in 1536, which played a crucial role in Lord Chancellor Thomas Cromwell's attack on the monasteries. Cromwell cultivated MPs who 'for their worship and qualities be most meet for the purpose'. In June 1536, the elder Ashby was appointed one of the King's Commissioners to survey the monasteries of Leicestershire.[23] Leicester Abbey was surrendered to the King in 1538, and the Ashby family subsequently acquired the Abbey's lands and buildings in the village of Hungarton, adjacent to their manor of Quenby.

William Ashby senior was married twice. His first wife was Agnes Illingworth, daughter of Sir Richard Illingworth KB, Chief Baron of the Exchequer from 1463 to 1472. By Agnes Illingworth, William Ashby had several children, including his son and heir, George Ashby. After the first Agnes died, William married Agnes Pulteney, daughter of Sir Thomas Pulteney (Poultney), who was knighted by Henry VIII.[24] This Agnes was the mother of Everard Ashby, who became the father of the future ambassador, William Ashby.[25]

Everard Ashby left only faint imprints on the pages of history. He was named for his godfather, Sir Everard Digby. Despite having only a small farm and paltry income in his own right, Everard Ashby managed to make a 'good' marriage to Mary Berkeley (nee Bawde). Mary was the widow of William Berkeley of Wymondham, Leicestershire, a descendant of the first Baron Berkeley, by whom she had one son, Maurice Berkeley (1530–1600).[26] After her marriage to Everard Ashby, the family lived at the medieval manor house at Wymondham, an 1,800-acre estate nine miles east of Melton Mowbray.[27] Wymondham was inherited by the minor Maurice Berkeley along with the manors of Coston and Edmondthorpe.

William Ashby of Loseby stated rather apologetically in his 1543 will that he left the residue of his goods to his younger son Everard 'to help himself, his wife and his children, for I have no lands to give him' (although he had previously granted Everard a property called Strethill Close, part of Loseby manor). The goods included 'all the stuff bedding Implements and hangings that at time of my decease shall fortune to be in the Chamber called the knights Chamber within [Loseby Hall]'.[28]

Everard was a dutiful son, serving as an executor of his father's will and subsequently as defendant in a lawsuit against the late William Ashby's estate brought by Everard's sister, Elizabeth, seeking her inheritance.[29] He appears to have functioned as manager for his stepson Berkeley's estates, clinging to his status as 'gentleman', although local yeoman and husbandmen farmers were richer in land, livestock and cash. His half-brother George Ashby, who had inherited Loseby manor, died in 1545, less than two years after their father, and Everard's nephew John acquired Loseby through primogeniture. In 1548, Everard (identified as of 'Ashby Folville, agent') was appointed as one of two attorneys to deliver seisin (possession) of 'All the property formerly belonged to the monasteries of Owston, Kirby Bellars, Ulverscroft, Leicester Abbey and Gracedieu, and was bought … in Letters Patent, 1st March 1546, from Henry VIII'.[30]

The financial circumstances of the Ashbys of Loseby declined, largely due to the manor's dependence on sheep farming. The price of wool collapsed while grain prices increased due to scarcity caused by poor harvests. Between 1538 and 1541, England was beset by droughts. 1540 and 1541 were particularly dry – in both years, 'the Thames was so low that sea water extended above London Bridge, even at ebb tide.'[31]

Everard and Mary Ashby had three children who survived to adulthood: Elizabeth, Francis and William.

✶✶✶✶✶✶

The subject of any biography must be viewed in the context of their historical era, especially the social and cultural influences on them. Innate ambition may have been a powerful motivator, but in the sixteenth century it was very difficult to break through social barriers that were the product of previous centuries

By the time of William Ashby's birth during the latter years of King Henry VIII's reign, genealogy had become an obsession with the English gentry. A credible pedigree meant access to society. As in the case of William Shakespeare's father's grant by the College of Heralds, the right to a coat of arms might be disputed and '... some would even fight a duel'.[32] During Elizabeth's reign 'heraldry was for "up and coming merchants and gentry, people lower down the social scale" than in the past, further fuelling its popularity.' Being armigerous – descended from knights – gave men the right to title themselves 'Esquire', thereby opening the door to acceptance into society and to opportunities for marrying upwards.

The Ashbys of Loseby had been armigerous since at least the middle of the fifteenth century, and their cousins, the Ashbys of Quenby, were referred to as 'Esquire' as early as 1377.[33] The two branches of the family had distinctly different arms, although this was not unusual in the late medieval era. For example, the three branches of the Leicestershire Cave family had different arms.[34]

Making strategic marriages was considered vital for both social and economic reasons. Under the tutelage of mothers and grandmothers, daughters of the upper classes and those aspiring to higher social status became early genealogists, creating pedigrees, many of which were fanciful. Due to the strict laws of primogeniture, the only asset that impecunious male and female aristocrats had was often their pedigrees.

Fabricated genealogies became so commonplace that they were usually overlooked if the male or female social aspirant had other assets, such as beauty or significant political connections. Because tombs were considered legal evidence of ancestry, gentlemen with dubious pedigrees constructed tombs for humble ancestors that copied archaic sculptural details, and in some cases other families' monuments were appropriated and falsified 'in pursuit of a supposititious lineage'.

Sir Francis Walsingham, William Ashby's patron, pretended descent from the lords of the manor of Walsingham in Norfolk, and probably commissioned several largely fictitious pedigrees. Actually, Walsingham was descended from a humble cordwainer – a shoemaker – who founded the family fortune as a London property entrepreneur in the early fifteenth century.[35] Queen Elizabeth routinely treated Walsingham as a social inferior. The Queen initially objected to the proposed marriage between Sir Philip Sidney and Walsingham's daughter because of the disparity in rank and because she was not previously informed.[36]

★★★★★★

When William Ashby the younger entered the world, his prospects were not auspicious. The second son of an undistinguished younger son of a second marriage, he, his parents and siblings were living essentially on the charity of his half-brother, Maurice Berkeley. However, William was fortunate to have an asset that was as much prized as wealth and privilege in Tudor England – extensive blood ties, social connections and political networks dating from the Norman Conquest, which he seemed adept at exploiting. Unlike his family generally, who seemed content with the sedate lives of country gentry and lawyers, Ashby had a passion for foreign travel and intrigue, tempered as he matured with a patience for complex and often tedious diplomacy and espionage.

*Part One*
*Early Life*

# 1. Education

**1536**

The probable year of William Ashby's birth was a time of momentous events.[1] The dissolution of the monasteries gathered pace, sparking the popular uprising called 'the Pilgrimage of Grace', Anne Boleyn was executed for high treason, her predecessor Catherine of Aragon died, and the first Act of Union between England and Wales was proclaimed, laying the foundation for what would become the United Kingdom.

Anglo-Scottish animosity was perennial. Less than a quarter century after the English defeated the Scots and killed their king at Flodden, Henry VIII was trying to coerce the new Scottish monarch James V to follow his lead in breaking with the Vatican. During James's audience with the English ambassadors, 'there was a great storm and thunder, at which the Scotch King was much frightened, and, crossing himself, said he did not know whether to be more frightened at the thunder or their proposals'.[2] The Papal Nuncio to France gleefully reported 'upon the natural hatred of Scotland against England' and that 'Scotland appeared to [be] the true bridle of England'.[3]

In the twenty-seventh year of King Henry's reign, William Ashby was born into an England that had changed little since the social and economic upheaval following the Black Death nearly two centuries earlier. Rural Leicestershire, William's birthplace, was medieval in all respects.

The doctrine and rituals of Roman Catholicism continued to be practiced in village churches despite efforts of local commissioners such as William's grandfather to confiscate the Church of Rome's assets and free England from the 'Papal Yoke'.[4] Regardless of his break with the Vatican, the King maintained most features of the traditional Catholic religion. Under Henry, anti-heresy laws from previous centuries remained on the statute books and were enforced as viciously as the Inquisition in Spain. Dozens of 'Evangelical' Protestants were burned at the stake, including 'an aged father ... whose brains were dashed out with a billet of wood while being burnt',[5] 'two Dutch Anabaptists, a man and a woman',[6] who were immolated at Smithfield, 'John ... a painter', consumed by fire at St. Giles in the Fields,[7] a 'child that passed not the age of fifteen years', a 'Priest ... who leaving his papistry, had married a wife and become a player in interludes' [plays], and 'a poor labouring man' all burned alive.[8]

In Scotland, which was to feature so prominently in William Ashby's life, the Catholic Church led by Cardinal Beaton was also persecuting heretics. Henry Forrest, a Benedictine friar from Linlithgow was burned at St. Andrews for supporting Lutheranism. Norman Gourlay, a priest from Dollar, was immolated in Edinburgh with David Stratoun, the younger son of the Laird of Lauriston in Forfarshire.

With the exception of a few royal palaces and mansions, such as the Duke of Suffolk's Bradgate House,[9] most buildings dated to the middle ages. Chimneys in residences were still a rarity; in rural areas central hearths were often still used for cooking and heating. The manor house at Wymondham where William was born and spent his childhood was largely unchanged since its construction in the late twelfth or early thirteenth century.[10] The Dutch scholar Erasmus, a professor of Divinity at Queen's College, Cambridge, in the early sixteenth century, believed that the plague and the sweating sickness – 'from which England was hardly ever free' – were partly caused by 'the incommodious form and bad exposition of the houses ... the filthiness of the streets, and ... the sluttishness within doors'. The 'slutty' household interiors scorned by Erasmus were dark and smoky – glassed windows were a luxury – and floors were covered with verminous rushes in which infants crawled with pets amidst '... an ancient collection of beer, grease, fragments of bone, spittle, excrement of dogs and cats and everything that is nasty'.[11]

It had long been the custom of Leicestershire's hereditary elite to intermarry among other Anglo-Norman families, as they had for five centuries.[12] Their grandchildren of William Ashby's generation, however, began the practice of forming alliances with heirs and heiresses from the merchant classes seeking gentility in exchange for cash transfusions.

Wealth was largely measured in livestock and crops (in his will, William Ashby senior bequeathed from forty to 200 sheep to various friends and relatives).[13] Life was brutal and, in the modern sense, Darwinian. Gentry families were deeply insular and suspicious of outsiders, partially as a legacy of the Black Death, during which the Ashbys and others stationed archers around their villages and manors with a 'shoot to kill' order for strangers. Ashby kin such as the Hesilriges of Nosely, Leicestershire, took the extreme measure of burning and razing their village when the plague appeared to prevent its spread to the manor house.[14]

The imminence of death lurked for rich and poor. Average life expectancy was thirty-five years, and between a third and half of all children did not survive past the age of five. Puerperal fever, an infection caused by unhygienic conditions during birth, killed one in four women. Preparing for the next world was the primary purpose of devotional Christianity. William Ashby's forebear, Thomas Ashby (d. 1416), who survived imprisonment in the Tower of London for misdeeds as the county coroner, endowed Kirkby Priory with lands and the advowson of Twyford, Leicestershire, with the provision that the monks perpetually pray for his soul to free it from Purgatory.[15]

Ordinary people who tilled England's fields and herded sheep were especially vulnerable to weather vagaries. The summers of 1540 and 1541 – when William Ashby was a young child – were devastatingly hot across all of Europe, including the Lowlands of Scotland. Contemporary chronicles referred to 1540 as the 'Big Sun Year'. England experienced great heat and drought, with many deaths from the 'ague', which was probably malaria. The lower part of the Rhine normally flowing from Cologne into the Netherlands dried up to expose the riverbed. The drought was so severe in Italy that rain did not fall in Rome for nearly nine months. Forest and city fires flared from Spain to Scandinavia. The water level of the Seine fell so low that Parisians were able to walk across it. Thousands died from heat stroke and starvation. The following year was nearly as bad; rivers again dried up, cattle and other livestock died, and dysentery killed thousands from drinking the polluted water that was still available.[16]

With such precarious conditions, kinship ties and ancestry could tip the balance between success and failure. While social status was an important asset, education allowed William to escape from the pastures and coppices of Leicestershire and enter the shadowy world of espionage and diplomacy.

Wymondham was large enough to have a village school. William and Francis Ashby and their elder half-brother Maurice Berkeley attended it with local boys, followed by private lessons that included their sister, Elizabeth (the future mother of Sir Robert Naunton). The siblings were taught by William Gulson the elder, Wymondham's rector,[17] with religious instruction by the last chantry priest, Robert Hall, who was discharged with an annual pension of £4 13s 4d after the dissolution of the patron priory of Tutbury, Staffordshire.[18]

Latin was taught along with Greek, mathematics and religion, all of which were prerequisites for admission to Cambridge or Oxford. Less than two percent of the population could read, write and speak Latin.[19] William Ashby learned to write by copying the alphabet and the Lord's Prayer. His writings in later life were fluid and eloquent at a time when the English language and grammar were not standardised, reflecting the early influence of a learned teacher such as Gulson, who prepared his own son, William Junior, for Cambridge.[20]

Books were rare and most were printed in Latin. Gulson had a few precious volumes, including a first edition in English of the Bible, plus Latin and English prayer books and primers printed by Richard Grafton, royal printer for Henry VIII and Edward VI. William also used the Berkeleys' library and borrowed books – some of which had been expropriated from dissolved monasteries – from relatives at Loseby,

Quenby and nearby Stapleford, the seat of the Sherrards.[21] The Ashby brothers and Maurice Berkeley also learned the physical skills of young gentlemen – archery, riding, hunting and swordsmanship. William's ability to wield a sword was put to good use during a fight on the Rhine decades later.

Despite his apparent isolation in a small Leicestershire village, William Ashby was exposed to ideas and the great social and political events of his childhood. While King Henry was conservative in religious practices and ruthless in enforcing his supremacy over church and state, conversely – under the early influence of the Lord Chancellor Sir Thomas More – he encouraged the Renaissance thought and culture that was flowering across continental Europe and slowly spreading from London into other parts of England.

Family members and acquaintances were involved in local and national politics; merchants and lawyers in the nearby town of Melton Mowbray and the city of Leicester had basic intelligence networks to safeguard their own and clients' business affairs. Gentlemen such as William Ashby senior, a Member of Parliament and local Justice of the Peace, corresponded with courtiers and government officials. Peddlers carried news, gossip and crudely printed broadsheets with propaganda and ballads.[22] Approximately sixteen percent of the English population – primarily males – were fully literate in the decade of the 1540s and therefore able to read material printed in English, but news was quickly disseminated to the 'unlettered' by town criers and clerks.

Throughout William's childhood, he would have been aware of hostilities between England and Scotland. When the Scottish King James V refused to break from the Roman church, his uncle King Henry VIII launched punitive raids across the border. The Scots retaliated by invading England in November 1542, but were defeated by a much smaller English army at the Battle of Solway Moss in Cumberland. In 1544, Henry began the 'Rough Wooing' to force the Scots to break from France and form an alliance with England by the marriage of two children – Edward,

1. Armorial plaque at Quenby Hall, Leicestershire, showing the coats of arms of Ashby of Quenby, Ashby of Loseby & Zouch. William Ashby was a member of the Ashby of Loseby, Leicestershire family, which reunited with their cousins the Ashbys of Quenby on the marriage of his first cousin Barbara Ashby.

2. Henry Grey, 1st Duke of Suffolk, after a portrait ascribed to Johannes Corvus. Ashby's father, Everard Ashby, was Grey's creditor, and it is believed that the nobleman sponsored William's education at Peterhouse College, Cambridge.

A Caueat or Warening,
FOR COMMEN CVRSE-
TORS VVLGARELY CALLED
Uagabones, set forth by Thomas Harman.
Esquiere, for the vtilite and profyt of his naturall
Cuntrey. Augmented and inlarged by the fyrst author here of.
*Anno Domini. M. D. LXVII.*

¶ Vewed, examined and allowed, according vnto the
Queenes Maiestyes Iniunctions.

¶ Imprinted at London in Fletestrete at the signe of the
Falcon, by Wyllian Gryffith, and are to be sold at his shoppe in
Saynt Dunstones Churche yarde, in the West.
Anno Domini. 1 5 6 7.

3. Three prints of vagabonds and beggars. The Vagrancy Act, a statute enacted by Edward VI in 1547, permitted the unemployed to be branded with a 'V' for vagabond and enslaved for two years by whoever could capture them and bring them before justices of the peace. Enslaved vagabonds could be leased, sold or bequeathed like 'any other movable goods or chattels'. Runaways were to be enslaved for life, and could be put to death on the second escape attempt.

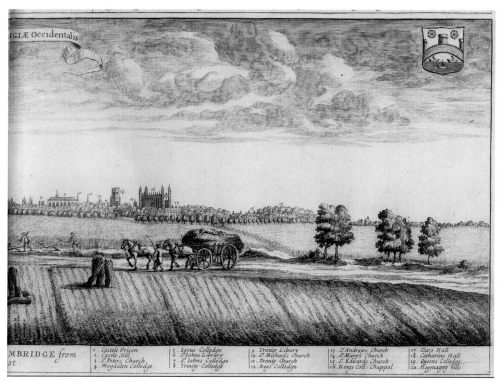

4. 'Cambridge from the West' engraving by David Loggan, from *Cantabrigia Illustrata*, 1690. A view of Cambridge that would have been familiar to William Ashby during his student years in the previous century.

5. George Carey 2nd Baron Hunsdon, a cousin of Queen Elizabeth, was Ashby´s friend and comrade-in-arms during their 1578 reconnaissance mission in the Netherlands.

6. Engraving of the Entry of Don John into Brussels in 1577, by Frans Hogenberg. Ashby was an eyewitness to Don John´s ceremonial entry to Brussels in 1577 following his appointment by Spanish King Phillip II as Governor-General of the Low Countries.

7. A copper engraving of Johann Sturmius by Hendrik Hondius (1573 – after 1648). Sturmius, considered one of Walsingham´s most important Continental intelligence assets, met with Ashby in 1576.

8. Sir Francis Walsingham (1532–1590) painted circa 1589 by John de Critz (1550–1642). Sir Francis Walsingham, Elizabeth´s spymaster and Principal Secretary of State was Ashby´s boss for a quarter of a century.

9. Mid seventeenth-century line engraving of Queen Elizabeth flanked by her principal advisors Burghley and Walsingham.

10. A portrait of William Cecil, 1st Baron Burghley (1520/21–1598) wearing a crimson robe and riding a mule. By an unknown artist in the school of Gheeraerts, Marcus, the younger painted circa 1585. Lord Burghley kept a pet mule which he enjoyed riding around his gardens at Theobalds Palace. In a twist of history, King James VI/I died there in 1625.

11. In July 1586, Anthony Babington wrote a letter in code to Mary Queen of Scots that was used as *prima facie* evidence in her trial for treason that led to her execution.

12. Elizabethan houses on Clerkenwell Close, the central building shows the house later occupied by Oliver Cromwell. The adjacent houses would be similar to William Ashby's Clerkenwell residence.

13. Flight of the townspeople from London into the country to escape from the Plague. When on reconnaisance in the Low Countries surveying major towns, the overriding concern of William Ashby and the English delegation was the plague. The town of Louvain lost half of its population. Ashby shared Walsingham's worry that the retinue was infected and doubted that they would escape without further loss.

Prince of Wales, and the infant Mary Queen of Scots. Henry declared war on Scotland and sent an invasion force to wreak rapine, slaughter and scorched-earth devastation. Fighting continued after Henry's death in 1547 until both sides were exhausted financially and by casualties.

## Cambridge

William Ashby, his brother and their cousin George Ashby of Quenby[23] were the first known members of their family to attend university, primarily because theirs was the generation that came of age after the Reformation. Formerly, the sons of landed gentry would rarely attend Oxford or Cambridge unless they were chosen by their family for a career in the Church or as clerks. While George Ashby was destined to inherit Quenby and to acquire Loseby from his debt-ridden relatives, William and Francis were keenly aware of being landless and relatively poor. The brothers needed a suitable profession to maintain their status as gentlemen, and were encouraged by their parents and other family members to become lawyers. Their teacher Gulson began preparing them for Cambridge before they reached adolescence.

Although Catholics considered Cambridge to be 'corrupted by heresy',[24] the university was actually slow to adopt the Protestant revolution despite the efforts of Bishop Nicholas Ridley and Archbishop Cranmer, the latter of whom sponsored the German protestant theologian Martin Bucer, who arrived in 1549 to assume an appointment as Regius Professor of Divinity. Resistance to the Anglican Reformation was passive yet pervasive, and while Bucer was respected by the Cambridge theology faculty and by Cranmer personally, he accomplished little before his death in early 1551. Clerical celibacy (among other conservative holdovers from the old Roman Catholic orthodoxy) remained legally compulsory until repealed by King Edward VI soon after his accession to the throne in 1547. Even after this liberalisation, lay academics could be ostracised and their careers blocked if they were married. In March 1551, the Vice-Master of Trinity caused controversy when he had to get a dispensation from the King allowing him to enjoy 'his fellowship and vicemastership, notwithstanding that he was married'.[25]

Protestants – more commonly known as 'Evangelicals' until the mid-1550s – made up only around twenty percent of London's population in 1551 and were a minority in Kent, Sussex, Essex and the city of Bristol. In most other parts of England, the new religion had barely progressed.[26] Leicestershire was one of the most reliably Protestant counties thanks to the zealous Henry Grey, Marquis of Dorset and Duke of Suffolk. William Ashby's opportunistic grandfather, who died in 1543, had cast his family's lot firmly with the Anglican Reformation by open support of Cromwell and the Greys.

The Ashbys' kinsmen and neighbours such as the Skeffingtons, Caves and Babingtons, were publicly Evangelical, although many, especially members of the older generation, privately remained communicants of the Roman church or reverted when death was imminent. The elder William Ashby, a political Protestant, stipulated in his will that 'a dirge and mass' be said for him by the 'priest clerk' of Loseby church, bequeathed 20 pence 'to the mother Churche of Lincoln', and left his son and heir 'a Chales [chalice], a Masseboke [mass book] with a vestment to be had and used as heire lomes [heirlooms] to the manor of Lowesby'.[27]

William's elder brother, Francis Ashby, arrived at Peterhouse College, the oldest Cambridge college, at the beginning of the new year of 1551 to begin his studies during Lent Term. Francis identified himself as 'Esq.' of Coston, Leicestershire, which was one of the Berkeley family's manors adjoining Wymondham.[28] He was followed by William in late September 1551 to matriculate during Michaelmas Term.

The Ashby brothers' Cambridge matriculation bracketed a summer in which the town and colleges were ravaged by the 'sweating sickness', the victims of which usually died within hours of showing the first symptoms.[29] The plague-like disease cost the lives of thousands across England and decimated the university's small academic community, killing over 200, including the teenage Brandon brothers, Dukes of

Suffolk, who died within half an hour of each other on 14 July 1551.[30] Many students fled, carrying the sickness with them.[31]

★★★★★★

The only time that William Ashby, age fifteen, had travelled more than seven leagues from his birthplace had been five years earlier when his father took him to the great city of Leicester, population three thousand, spending a day and a night on their return journey at Henry Grey, Marquess of Dorset's, new Bradgate House, an incredible example of modern architecture. William remembered the kind attention of Lord Dorset, who conversed with him in Latin and asked questions about mathematics and ancient history. The Marquess's daughter, Lady Jane Grey – at age nine just a few months younger than William – had shown him a book by Plato. He was embarrassed that unlike the girl, he was unable to read it in ancient Greek but, to impress her, promised that he would learn.

Now accompanied by his elder brother Francis, William traversed the 60-odd miles from their home to Cambridge, a five-day journey on foot. Each boy carried a fardel (travel bag) packed by their mother containing spare linen shirts, hose, manchet bread, roast mutton, hard cheese, and a leather bottle of small ale. They could not afford to hire a post horse, which anyway were rarities on the route as were the foul inns where the animals were stabled. The brothers counted themselves fortunate to beg rides on wagons and pony carts, or to join other travellers such as fellow students en route to the university. Mainly they trudged on foot along the deeply rutted and muddy roads, protected from the elements by their hooded cloaks and from vagabonds by antique basilards – long-bladed daggers from the Loseby armoury.

Travel was perilous, especially for anyone who could be readily identified as a gentleman. William had heard of the bands of desperate men, women and children, many of whom had been evicted from their cottages and livelihoods when manors were enclosed for sheep (and, at least in one instance, rabbit) farming, roving the countryside.[32] He also knew that resentment against the gentry ran deep among the dispossessed. Kett's Rebellion, a nationwide popular revolt against enclosure of land, had broken out only two years earlier. His father had told him that after the popular uprisings the Duke of Somerset observed that the rebels 'hath conceived a wonderful hate against the gentlemen and taketh them all as their enemies.'[33]

But travel was no more dangerous than being a student at Cambridge. Francis had returned to Leicestershire between terms to escape the sweating sickness. William knew that his older brother dreaded returning to university because of the deadly epidemic as well his miserable existence at the bottom of the student hierarchy. Yet Francis bore no resentment for the generosity of Lord Dorset which would make William's university sojourn more bearable.

As the Ashby brothers hurried through yet another hamlet of hovels and pinched-face inhabitants, they averted their eyes from a ragged man in a pillory, cheeks branded with a 'V', who gazed piteously at them and croaked 'water'.

*****

England was not a green and pleasant land for the destitute. The Vagrancy Act, a statute enacted by Edward VI in 1547, permitted the unemployed to be branded with a 'V' for vagabond and enslaved for two years by whoever could capture them and bring them before justices of the peace. Convicted slaves were to be fed 'bread and water or small drink, and forced to work by beating, chaining, or by any other way their master chose', and 'rings of iron could be put on their neck and legs'. Enslaved vagabonds could be leased, sold or bequeathed like 'any other movable goods or chattels'. Runaways were to be enslaved for life, and could be put to death on the second escape attempt. If a private master did not want the vagabond, the slave was to be sent to their town of birth, 'and there employed as a parish or corporation slave, the community having the same rights of selling or leasing the slave's services'.[34]

Although the Vagrancy Act was repealed in 1550, it was replaced by the reinstatement of an only slightly less heinous statute from Henry VIII's reign which did not use the terms 'slave' and 'enslaved'.

\*\*\*\*\*\*

By the time William arrived at Peterhouse, only eighteen academic residents remained, including four Fellows and the Master. Cambridge was in a sorry state in the autumn of 1551. In the aftermath of the 'great abundance of lands and goods taken from Abbeys, Colleges and Chantries' to 'serve the King in all necessaries and charges', the poor were 'bespoiled, all maintenance of learning decayed' and the rich merchants of the city 'enriched' by the 'reformation of religion'.[35]

Living conditions generally were appalling even by sixteenth century standards. Paul Fagius, the German Protestant theologian, who, with his colleague Martin Bucer, was given refuge and a readership by Cranmer in 1549, lived in an unheated room, which undoubtedly hastened his death a few months after arriving in Cambridge. Bucer survived until March 1551, helped by a gift of £20 from King Edward 'with which to buy a stove', and a cow and calf from the Duchess of Suffolk (which Bucer's Roman Catholic enemies whispered were actually two devils in animal form that inspired his lectures).[36]

A decade earlier, the Scottish Protestant Alexander Alesius was appointed by Cambridge's chancellor Thomas Cromwell as a theology lecturer at Queen's College but was soon forced out by the Papists who held sway at the university. Few other Scots were affiliated with Cambridge during the Tudor era until 1585, when Archibald Anderson matriculated as a sizar from Queens, followed by John Campbell of Corpus Christi in 1597.

In December 1550, a Fellow of St. John's college lamented that before the Reformation shook the foundations of Cambridge:

> ... there were in [religious] houses belonging unto the university ... two hundred students of divinity, many very well learned, which be now all clean gone, house and man, young toward [apt] scholars, and old fatherly Doctors, not one of them left: one hundred also of another sort that

having rich friends or being beneficed men, did live ... in
Ostles [hostels] and Inns, be either gone away or else fayne
[pretending] to creep into colleges, and put poor men from
bare livings. Those both be all gone, and a small number of
poor godly diligent students now remaining only in colleges,
be not able to tarry and continue their study ... for lack of
exhibition [scholarships] and help.[37]

Unusually, the two Ashby brothers had separate statuses as Cambridge
students, beginning a divergence that took William on a much different
professional path, although he and Francis remained close for the
remainder of their lives.

Francis Ashby matriculated at Peterhouse as a sizar – a *Scolare paupere* or
poor scholar. Sizarships were an early type of bursary system. Sizars were
granted free tuition or reduced fees and in return were obliged to act as
college servants, a humiliating situation for a young gentleman. Francis
was one of eight poor scholars benefiting from a Peterhouse ordinance
for their support. In addition to 'a weekly allowance of bread and beer to
the value of fourpence each at the Buttery', they were graciously allowed
to have 'the broken victuals left over from the meals of Master, Fellows,
Masters household, Pupils and College cooks'. In return, 'each Sunday
after dinner', Francis Ashby had to 'devoutly say *De Profundis* with the
accustomed prayers'.[38]

The social divide between sizars and full fee-paying students –
Pensioners (Commoners) and Fellow-Commoners – was stark. Francis
Ashby had to wear a different academic gown and cap and 'each day at
dinner or breakfast he must serve as directed' by the Master.[39] He could
eat meals only after serving the masters and other students. He was
required to do personal chores for Fellows and wealthier students, such as
lighting fires in their cubicles, emptying chamber pots, cleaning shoes and
running errands. His duties included 'carrying wood and earth' for the
continuous building work to construct the 'new fabric' of Peterhouse.[40]

He was obligated to sleep on a 'truckle-bed' pushed under the bed of the Fellow whom he served.[41]

Sizars led a miserable monastic existence, constantly cold, hungry and fearful of disease. They were expected to 'rise daily betwixt four and five of the clock in the morning' to attend to chores, followed by 'common prayer with an exhortation of God's word in a common chapel', and from six to ten a.m. engage in private study or communal lectures. The poor students would go to dinner at ten of the morning, where they 'had to be content with a penny piece of beef … having a porridge made of the broth of the same beef, with salt and oatmeal, and nothing else'. After their 'slender dinner' sizars would have 'learning' until five o'clock, when they would 'have a supper not much better than their dinner … immediately after the which they go either to reasoning in problems [*mathematics*] or unto some other study until it be nine or ten of the clock'. Being 'without fire', students would 'walk or run up and down half an hour, to get a heat on their feet when they go to bed'.[42]

William – identified as 'Ashby Junior' to distinguish him from Francis – entered Peterhouse as a 'pensioner' (alternately called a 'commoner'), an undergraduate whose tuition and 'commons' (room and board) were paid for privately.[43] While the identity of William's benefactor is inconclusive, there is circumstantial evidence that Henry Grey, Marquess of Dorset, sponsored him. Grey, a member of Edward VI's privy council who was created Duke of Suffolk shortly after William matriculated, was indebted to his father, Everard Ashby, for the then considerable sum of more than £240 (equivalent to roughly one hundred thousand pounds today).[44] Over the years, the Marquess sponsored Cambridge 'exhibitions' (scholarships) for a number of bright scholars, including John Aylmer, who later served as Grey's chaplain at Bradgate House and tutor to his daughter, Lady Jane.[45]

On admission, a Fellow-Commoner had to pay an *introit* of 20 shillings, and was subsequently charged 4d weekly for "firing' [firewood], spices and salt', in addition to the charge for 'bread, victuals and drink'.[46] The college butler – whose coveted position was sometimes secured through bribery – brewed 'strong ale and small beer' which was served at all meals.[47]

Cambridge's academic population was small. During the Tudor era, numbers in Peterhouse tended to vary, often from week to week depending on the plague and religious strife. The eighteen academics in residence at Peterhouse when William Ashby arrived in the autumn of 1551 declined to a total of just thirteen, including four or five Fellows, by the end of 1553 – the attrition in students due to Queen Mary's accession to the throne. Student numbers across the university tended to fluctuate wildly across the middle of the sixteenth century. There were only fifty-nine matriculants in all in 1557 – the last year of Mary's reign – rising to 527 in 1578, and then settling back to around three hundred a year.[48]

All announcements by administrative officials were supposed to be read in Latin. To maintain the Latinate theme, students wore gowns which they called togas. During the last years of King Edward's reign, which coincided with William Ashby's early studies, statutes were passed regulating subjects and lectures. In philosophy, Aristotle, Pliny and Plato were mandatory; 'in mathematics, Mela, Strabo, Pliny, Ptolemy, Euclid, Tunstall and Cardan; in dialectic, the *Elenchi* of Aristotle, the *Topica* of Cicero, Quintilian and Hermogenes; in Greek, Homer, Demosthenes, Isocrates and Euripides; in Hebrew, scriptures and grammar.'[49]

English grammar was omitted as a subject, and undergraduates such as William Ashby read mathematics, dialectic, and philosophy, as well as astronomy, 'perspective', and Greek.[50] Decades later, William sprinkled his letters to Walsingham, Burghley and other Elizabethan luminaries with Latin tags from Virgil and Tacitus and quotes by Homer and Aeschylus, the latter written in Greek. His use of classical language was not meant to flaunt his knowledge but to emphasise particular points to similarly educated gentlemen of the political and social elite.[51]

The periods of study for degrees remained much the same as in the middle ages, as was the emphasis on public disputations. The normal undergraduate came to Cambridge when he was fourteen or fifteen, or even younger, and the general course of study for the Bachelor of Arts degree lasted seven years, 'though only a minority of those who entered completed it.'[52]

Few pensioners sought a career in the church or as teachers, and it was generally uncommon to become scholars or obtain a degree. After a few terms they would leave, to travel abroad, or to enter one of the Inns of Court in London, with or without the intention of becoming practising lawyers. For some pensioners, 'Cambridge was closer to a finishing school than a university'.[53] As pensioners did not have to take university examinations, they could spend their time in Cambridge in studies directed by their tutor. 'Troublesome and disobedient scholars were to be expelled from the university, and no scholar was to dwell in the town but in a hall or hostel under a master or principal'.[54]

While William Ashby did not have to endure the humiliating regimen of his brother, his academic life was similarly gruelling. He awoke around five in the morning and hurried in his flapping gown across the muddy quadrangle to morning prayers at Little St. Mary's church, where he begged the 'Good Lorde' to deliver him 'from the tyrannye of the bishop of Rome and all his detestable enormities, from all false doctrine and heresy'.[55] After sharing the same paltry breakfast as the sizars in the refectory, William spent the next twelve hours on his studies, straining his eyes on dark winter days to read mildewed books under the weak light cast by tallow candles. After a simple supper that could be augmented by hoarded provisions bought from the butler, he went to bed in a bleak cubicle – comparable to a monastic cell – within a subdivided chamber in one of the college's two hostels.[56]

Students were no longer required to wear clerical habit and tonsure or forbidden 'to grow a beard or to wear their locks contrary to Canonical Rules', nor were they barred from wearing rings on their fingers 'for vain glorying and jetting, pernicious example and scandal of others'. However, they were still subject to strict rules of behaviour that had changed little over the previous two centuries:

> Scholars were to eschew taverns; wandering in by-ways and places of doubtful report; the exercise of crafts forbidden to clerics, drunkenness and insobriety. They were to avoid jugglers and stage-players, and the carrying of arms to the disturbance of the peace. Dice were prohibited to them, and so, too, was chess, except under special circumstances. No scholar was to keep dog, falcon or hawk in College even at his own expense...[57]

Peterhouse students were forbidden to 'pass the night in the town, nor wander aimlessly abroad even by day', and if 'for health purposes or other reasonable cause, especially after the hour of Vespers' they had 'gone far' they were required to 'return forthwith and speedily, unless they had the Master's leave'.[58] In theory, if not in practice, celibacy was strictly enforced. Women, especially young ones ('*Lotrices mulieres, praesertim juvenes*') were 'on no account allowed to enter the chamber of a Scholar', and even 'Female relations who desired converse with a Scholar' had to 'transact their business in the Hall or in some other honest place in the presence of another Scholar, or of an honest Servant of the House'. Students were even forbidden from taking their own clothing to be washed by a laundress.[59]

Like other scholars, William Ashby ignored the rules and occasionally escaped spartan college life into the taverns and dice houses of Cambridge. George Acworth, a contemporary and friend of William who matriculated at Peterhouse as a sizar, was 'time-serving and dissolute' despite that fact that he was considered a brilliant scholar.[60] William's kinsman, Everard Digby, who followed him at Cambridge several years later, was notorious for rowdy behaviour, including 'blowing a horn and hallooing in the college during the daytime, and repeatedly speaking of the master to the scholars with the greatest disrespect'.[61] William and his friends played the popular card game primero in ale houses, and joined with fellow students, drovers, whores, thieves and other town-dwellers to watch cock fights and bear-baiting in Cambridge's stinking medieval warrens.

Drunkenness was rampant, and an alarming number of inebriated students drowned while swimming in the river Cam.[62] Trade with continental Europe led to a flood of foreign wine, the lucrative sale of which was largely controlled by the colleges.[63] In March 1553, news arrived from London that Parliament had passed 'an Act to avoid the great price and excess of Wines' citing the proliferation of taverns in 'back lanes corners and suspicious places' throughout the realm. The Act decreed that prices could not exceed 8d per gallon for 'Gascoin Guion or French Wines', 4d a gallon for 'Rochel Wines', or 12d the gallon for any other wines. Cambridge was restricted to no more than four taverns, which caused an immediate outcry by the Masters of Colleges as well as thirsty academics and townsfolk. This led to the addition of a 'proviso' to the Act, exempting 'the goods or lands of any College, Hall or Hostel within the universities of Oxford and Cambridge ... or to any Master and Scholar within the said Universities and Colleges ....'[64]

By 1553, Edwardian religious reforms had become generally accepted in Cambridge, the 'intellectual heartland of the evangelical revolution'.[65] In June, the colleges were told that degrees could only be awarded to students who subscribed to the 42 Articles of Religion composed by Archbishop Cranmer, the 'most advanced systemisation of Protestant theology then in existence anywhere'.[66] The edict never came into force.

The following month, on 6 July 1553, King Edward VI died, aged fifteen. England, and William Ashby's life, profoundly changed as a consequence.

# 2. Exile

Cambridge was in tumult.

Although word of the King's death had been suppressed for two days, news and rumours spread to Cambridge as fast as a courier mounted on a sound courser could ride. Edward VI died on a Thursday, and by Sunday sermons were being preached by Bishop Ridley and other Protestants denouncing Mary Tudor.[1] The next day, Lady Jane Grey – daughter of Henry Grey, Duke of Suffolk, and daughter-in-law of the Duke of Northumberland, the late King's chief minister – was proclaimed queen.[2] On the same day, Mary began raising an army and sent a letter to the Privy Council asserting her right to the throne.

Northumberland, who was also chancellor of the university, occupied Cambridge with 1,500 troops, intending to use the town as a base from which to attack Mary's forces. He led his small army out to confront the Marianists, but widescale desertions forced him to retreat to Cambridge the following day. As a bastion of Protestantism, the university's faculty and students feared Mary and her militantly Catholic supporters. Riots broke out within the colleges and the Regent House, and the general sense of despair deepened as news came that Lady Jane and her husband had been imprisoned in the Tower and Mary recognised as Queen Regnant in London on Wednesday 19 July 1553.[3]

The following month, Mary issued a proclamation that was interpreted by some hopeful Protestants as allowing her subjects to worship as they pleased. The Queen stated that however much she wished for her subjects to embrace the Roman Catholic faith, she 'mindeth not to compel any her said subjects there unto such time as further order by common assent may be taken therein'. Mary attempted further reassurance (possibly to quell rumblings of rebellion) that any further religious changes would not be done without the consent of parliament.[4]

However, the new government acted quickly to root out heresy and restore Catholicism to the universities. On 20 August 1553, Mary wrote a letter stating that the 'disorders' at Oxford and Cambridge had been caused by 'the sensual minds and rash determinations of a few men'. The Queen nullified her late brother's Reformation laws and commanded Stephen Gardiner, Cambridge's chancellor, to reinstate and strictly observe the ancient statutes of the university and colleges. Priests began celebrating mass again soon thereafter.[5]

When William and Francis Ashby returned to Peterhouse for Michaelmas term shortly before Mary's coronation on 1 October 1553, they found Cambridge aptly described as having 'had her sweating sickness ... now began her hot sweat, or fiery trial indeed'.[6] Peterhouse, one of the most ardently Protestant colleges, was already experiencing the punitive measures of the Marian zealots. One of the Fellows, a 'Mr. Garth' was persecuted because 'he would not suffer a boy of his house to assist in saying mass in Pembroke hall'.[7]

Although the new Act repealing Edward's religious statutes allowed the Anglican service to be performed until 20 December 1534, priests who offered Protestant rites were removed, sometimes forcibly. William and his fellow students lived in fear of the 'rabble of unlearned papists' who 'used violence' against Evangelical academics such as Vice-Chancellor Edwin Sandys, whose personal property – including 'four notable good geldings' from his stable – was stolen. Sandys was sent to the Tower 'upon a lame horse that halted to the ground', and when he left Cambridge as a prisoner of the Queen's yeomen of the guard, 'some papists resorted thither to jeer him, some of his friends to mourn for him'.[8]

Within months of Mary's accession, university heads deemed to be incorrigible Evangelicals were replaced by conformists to the old religion in all but three of the colleges. In November 1553, William's tutor, the popular Ralph Ainsworth, Master of Peterhouse, was expelled for being married. He was replaced by Andrew Perne, who was mocked by scholars for his shallow, easily shifting religious allegiances. Cambridge wags nicknamed him 'Old Andrew Turncoat' and invented a mock Latin word 'perno' which they translated as 'I turn, I rat, I change often'.[9]

Like the majority of students, during Michaelmas term 1553 the Ashby brothers focused on their studies and tried to avoid drawing attention to their Protestantism. Others, especially 'Edwardian' bishops, priests and divinity students, made plans to emigrate to northern European cities that were considered cradles of the Reformation. Papists such as the Duke of Norfolk and Bishop Stephen Gardiner were appointed to Mary's Privy Council, and re-establishment of the Mass was decreed in mid-December. Any remaining hopes evaporated when it became clear that the Queen intended to restore England to Roman Catholicism and punish committed Evangelicals.

Persecution descended the academic ranks. After the Masters' expulsion, Fellows from various colleges were purged 'on account of their adherence to Protestant doctrines'.[10] Over twenty Fellows of St. John's were forced out, nine of whom fled abroad. Altogether, twenty-three Cambridge Fellows escaped to the Continent before Christmas.[11]

By Twelfth Night 1554, a wave of Evangelicals seeking refuge in Germany and Switzerland were boarding ships for the continent; after Candlemas (2 February), the flow surged as word spread of Mary's pending wedding to Prince Philip, heir to Charles V, King of Spain and Hapsburg Emperor.[12] While a return to the practices of the Church of Rome was not a great concern among the majority of common people and was welcomed by many nobles and gentry, fear of England becoming a vassal state of Spain was widespread and became a catalyst for insurrection. Whispers against the marriage became muttering, which grew to open dissent.

On 25 January, an insurrection erupted in Kent led by Thomas Wyatt. The rebellion involved a widespread conspiracy for simultaneous uprisings in Kent, Devon, Herefordshire and Leicestershire – the latter led by Henry Grey, Duke of Suffolk. The rebellion failed, and the ringleaders were executed.

Suffolk was ignominiously captured, convicted of high treason and beheaded on 23 February 1554, eleven days after the execution of his daughter, the erstwhile queen, Lady Jane Grey.

## Into Exile

After the Duke of Suffolk's beheading, William Ashby feared Marianist persecution because of his personal and family ties to the Greys. While there is no record of him actively taking part in the rebellion, his family in Leicestershire, a notoriously Protestant county, had been supporters of Suffolk. The city and county of Leicester were viewed as morasses of heresy and sedition throughout Mary's reign. In January 1555, Gardiner wrote to the 'Mayor and his Brethren of Leicester' admonishing them for breaking and abolishing 'ancient and laudable' Catholic customs and for 'being rather desirous of newfanglenes'. The Lord Chancellor ordered them to 'henceforth remain quiet and contented to follow and allow such laudable customs and revels as have always been, time out of mind, practiced among you'.[13]

A series of proclamations was issued, evidently to control what was perceived as a fractious population. The 'shooting in Hand-guns, and bearing of weapons' was forbidden. Prior to the royal wedding, 'all Victuallers, Taverners and Alehousekeepers' were ordered to 'sell no meat nor drink, nor any kind of victuals, to any Servingman whatsoever, unless he brought a testimonial to shew whose servant he was', apparently from fear of assassins posing as servants.[14]

William managed to carry on through Lent term 1554. As an eighteen-year-old undergraduate, he was not prominent enough to attract the attention of Papist zealots despite his connections. Like other Cambridge students, his decision to leave Peterhouse and England was partially motivated by Bishop Gardiner's letter of 24 March 1554 to the university's vice chancellor, John Young, commanding that 'none shall be admitted to give voice or receive degree, but only such as openly in the congregation house detested particularly ... the heresies lately spread in this realm and professed ... the Catholic doctrine now received and subscribed the same with their hands'.[15]

Youthful rebelliousness and a restless nature were also factors in choosing to become an exile. Unlike his brother Francis and cousin George Ashby, William was not willing to pretend conformity to the re-imposition of Roman Catholicism. Francis Ashby remained at Peterhouse until 1555 and left without a degree to take up a special admission to the Inner Temple.[16] In the late spring of 1554, William Ashby joined the 'large number' of young English gentlemen crossing to France, which, to the French ambassador Antoine de Noailles, seemed 'as if the half of her [Mary's] kingdom is tremulous to go there, the only difficulty being to find a safe passage'.[17]

Seventy-six of the 472 documented Marian exiles were or had been members of fifteen of the sixteen Cambridge colleges.[18] However, the actual number of Cambridge men who were émigrés – including William Ashby – was between ninety and one hundred.[19] Although William Ashby's name is not recorded among the 800-1,000 Marian exiles (about half of whom are known), his February 1556 petition for reinstatement to Peterhouse is evidence that he was in Europe for the previous two years.[20]

There were generally two streams of refugees from Mary's reign: an earlier group – largely composed of older Evangelicals – primarily driven by religious ideals who went to Germany and Switzerland, and a second group which has been described as 'frankly political, openly anti-Spanish, and only "protestant" in so far as that term covered hostility to the Queen's marriage to Prince Philip, heir to the Spanish throne'. This group of around 150 young gentlemen, a significant number of whom, like William Ashby, were Cambridge students, were ostensibly 'in a precipitate scramble for safety'.[21] However, the majority of these exiles 'would seem to have been younger sons out for adventure', who, using Mary's accession as an excuse, embarked upon a sixteenth-century version of The Grand Tour that was a rite of passage for their foppish descendants two centuries later.[22]

Most of these young men were more interested in exploring the great centres of the Renaissance in a quest for the 'new learning which runneth all the world over now-a-days'[23] rather than spending their days debating Calvinist dialectic in freezing German cities. The 'Golden Age' of Elizabeth's reign was still in the future, and the English were considered to be culturally unsophisticated by the French, Italians and Spanish. William Ashby's hunger for the 'new learning', coupled with a desire to escape from the uncertain future and dreary life of a Cambridge student, was similar to that of another young English exile, who wrote that he 'waxed desirous to travel beyond the seas, for attaining to the knowledge of some special modern tongues, and for the increase of my experience in the managing of affairs, being wholly then addicted to employ myself, and all my cares, in the public service of the state'.[24]

With his presumed benefactor dead, and his family on the edge of penury and living in fear of Queen Mary's reprisals, how was William able to survive as a teenage exile in foreign lands where he had few personal connections?

A group of sympathetic London merchants known as the 'Sustainers' had organised a 'Ways and Means' committee as early as December 1553 to support students who fled abroad to escape religious persecution. The Sustainers were twenty-six wealthy, influential men and women, some of whom were merchants involved in trade with northern European centres of Protestantism. The original purpose of this group and people affiliated with it was to provide financial support for divinity students who were expected to return to form the core of a reformed Anglican church.[25]

After Wyatt's failed insurrection, financial support was expanded to include political refugees, including university students who were not divinity scholars. In late February 1554, Peter Martyr Vermigli – a Marian exile who had been a friend and colleague of Bucer – wrote from

Strasbourg that 'English youths have come over to us in great numbers within these few days, partly from Oxford and partly from Cambridge …', and in early April a party of young Englishmen, *exules studiosi Angli*, appeared in Zurich .[26]

Considering that the entire academic population of Cambridge between the years 1551 and 1554 was probably no more than 625 (including Regent Masters and longer serving academics (Heads of House, Regius Professors etc.), William would have known many contemporaries from other colleges as well as Peterhouse.[27] These included his kinsman Robert Beaumont (Peterhouse, MA, 1550), who went to Zurich; and Matthew Carew (Trinity, 1551), a cousin of Francis Walsingham, who took part in the Devon uprising and fled to Padua.

One of the most famous of the Cambridge Marian Exiles was Francis Walsingham, Ashby's future diplomatic and intelligence chief. Walsingham, who was born around 1532, entered the university as a Fellow Commoner at King's College in 1548,[28] and had left without taking a degree by early 1551; thus there was no overlap with William Ashby's Cambridge matriculation.[29] For a year after he went down from Cambridge, Walsingham travelled in Europe, visiting 'many foreign countries whose manners, laws, languages and policies he accurately studied and critically understood'.[30] He returned in 1552 to be admitted to Gray's Inn to study law but left England again after Wyatt's failed rebellion.[31] Like William Ashby, Walsingham may have gone into exile abroad in early 1554, and was in Padua in autumn of that year.

Considering the close working relationship of both men during Queen Elizabeth's reign, it is intriguing to speculate that Walsingham and Ashby met while both were Marian exiles. While no documentation has been found to substantiate this, the Cantabrigians were a small, elite subgroup of exiles who supported one another at the various European cities where they settled.

Ashby and Walsingham had mutual acquaintances, and the commonality of their university, legal training (Ashby subsequently entered Gray's

Inn) and Protestant self-exile proved to be strong connections in later years. William's friend and fellow Peterhouse classmate George Acworth left England in 1555 despite having publicly sworn to Gardiner's edict to abide by Roman Catholicism. Like Walsingham, Acworth studied at Padua, and also at Paris, where William Ashby spent several terms as a student.[32]

Considering Ashby's later familiarity with a number of European cities, it is assumed that he travelled widely throughout the Continent during his first two years abroad, visiting fellow refugees between his studies in Paris. He acquired both courtly sophistication and personal contacts that proved to be crucial in his future professional work. It is likely that he visited Padua and Venice. Both cities were not only centres of Renaissance culture and humanist education but also harboured colonies of politically active English exiles, including Sir John Cheke, the renowned scholar and statesman, who had been imprisoned with the Duke of Suffolk but released and allowed to leave England.

Ashby's first visit to Italy as a naïve teenager may have been like the experience of a waggish young Tudor gentleman:

> I, being a youth of the English cut, wore my hair long, went apparelled in light colours, and imitated four or five sundry nations in my attire at once, which no sooner was noted, but I had all the boys of the city in a swarm wondering about me. I had not gone a little farther, but certain officers crossed the way of me, and demanded to see my rapier, which, when they found (as also my dagger) with his point unblunted, they would have haled me headlong to the strappado,[33] but that with money I appeased them, and my fault was more pardonable in that I was a stranger, altogether ignorant of their customs. Note, by the way, that it is the use ... for all men whatsoever to wear their hair short, which they do not so much for conscience' sake, or any religion they place in

it, but because the extremity of the heat is such there that, if
they should not do so, they should not have a hair left on their
heads to stand upright when they were scared with sprights
[ghosts]. And he is counted no gentleman amongst them that
goes not in black; they dress their jesters and fools only in
fresh colours, and say variable garments do argue unstaidness
and unconstancy of affections.[34]

William Ashby travelled to Paris in the autumn of 1554 and enrolled
at the Collège Royal, where he was to spend two years reading the
'humanities, dialectic philosophy, and Greek and Latin letters' ('*in
humanioribus disciplinis dialecticis philosophicis grecis latinisque literis*').[35] The
Collège had been established a quarter century earlier by King Francois I
as a Humanist alternative to the Sorbonne, which was devoted to Roman
Catholic theological studies and was militantly anti-Reformation.

Ashby found more individual and academic freedom at the Collège
than at Cambridge. The Sorbonne's Theology faculty detested the
Collège and repeatedly tried to have it closed, but it was protected by King
Henri II, probably because it was truly Humanist rather than religiously
Reformist. Henri was a patron of Renaissance culture, especially the
emerging art and architecture characterised as Northern Mannerist.

The Collège was revolutionary in comparison to other mid-sixteenth-
century European universities. Any man could attend lectures without
prior preparation or knowledge of Latin and Greek. No examinations
were given and, accordingly, diplomas were not awarded. Attendance
required no payment of tuition, which undoubtedly appealed to William
Ashby. In 1554 and 1555, the Collège's curriculum included Hebrew,
Ancient Greek, mathematics, botany, astronomy and Latin poetry.

Paris, and France generally, seems an unlikely place for a young
Englishman from a supposedly staunch Protestant background to spend
two years. Although around 150 Marian Exiles found refuge in France,
they were primarily based at the Norman cities of Rouen and Caen,
which were more welcoming refuges for English (and some Scottish)

Protestants.[36] William Ashby's motivation in studying at Collège Royal is a mystery, as is his means of financial support.

Paris was a hostile religious environment for native dissenters. Henri actively persecuted the growing number of French Evangelicals, especially the Calvinist Huguenots and Lutherans. In 1547, the King created a special judicial chamber solely to judge cases of heresy, called the *Chambre Ardente* ('Burning Chamber') by Protestants due to the number of people it sentenced to be burnt at the stake.[37] Goaded by his mistress, Diane de Poitiers, Henri's repression increased in severity, including the 1551 Edict of Châteaubriant, which empowered civil and ecclesiastical courts to detect and punish heretics and imposed draconian censorship, prohibiting the printing or importation of any books or tracts not approved by the Sorbonne's Faculty of Theology. When Châteaubriant failed to stem the rising number of Protestant converts, Henri imposed the Edict of Compiègne, which mandated the death penalty for all heresy convictions, and which has been described as no less than 'a declaration of war by the King against his Protestant subjects'.[38]

William Ashby kept a low profile during his sojourn at the Collège Royal, trying to avoid drawing attention to himself both as a Protestant and as an Englishman. Fortunately, Henri's government was not hostile to English refugees as long as they did not consort with French Evangelicals.

Ashby was on the periphery of the great power struggles and machinations in which he would later play a role. Europe – and, increasingly, the New World of the Americas – was dominated by the premier royal houses of Habsburg and Valois. Although England was a secondary player in European geopolitics, Queen Mary – daughter of the Spanish princess Catherine of Aragon and granddaughter of the revered Ferdinand and Isabella – strengthened the historical alliance with the Habsburgs.

France, considered a 'natural enemy' after centuries of warfare, was opposed to the marriage of Mary and Philip because, like the English rebels, it feared that England would become, if not a vassal state, a military and political ally of Spain. Despite a temporary cessation of Anglo-French hostilities, France was deeply distrusted. Mary's government feared that the French-born regent of Scotland, Mary of Guise, despite sharing the English Queen's devout Catholicism, could provide a base for a French invasion of England. The enmity of the Guise dynasty, and threats relating to the dark horizon beyond England's northern border, would define William Ashby's subsequent career.

Like Mary of Guise and Mary Tudor, Henri II was a staunch Roman Catholic, yet he almost flaunted his support for aristocratic English Protestant exiles plotting against Queen Mary. He exempted some of the more prominent ones from the *aubaine*, the tax on foreigners, provided financial support, allowed the freedom of the entire kingdom as long as they 'did no harm to French subjects', and even provided French warships and privateers to prey on English and Spanish shipping.[39]

Dr. Nicholas Wotton, Mary's ambassador to Henri's court, employed an extensive network of spies within the English exile community, and sent reports to London detailing their plans and support from the French. One of these double agents, the former English ambassador Sir William Pickering, was 'turned' by Wotton after his *in absentia* indictment for treason in London. Pickering told Wotton that King Henri planned to land a contingent of English rebels at Lee, in Essex, and on the Isle of Wight, who would then either fortify themselves there or march to London, raising the country against Mary *en route*.[40]

The English government took Wotton's reports seriously, and 'the threats and preparations of the exiles created the greatest alarm' at court. Summoning the French ambassador de Noailles, Mary 'loudly and indignantly demanded the extradition of the rebels, and declared that this was due to her according to the terms of a recent treaty, and was only to be expected from a power that professed to be friendly'. Henri responded by declaring his friendship for Mary, and arrogantly said that 'as for the rebels, he had heard nothing about them, his dominions were so large that he could not possibly take account of all who entered or went out of them'. The Queen's 'impatience and choler' grew, as each time she confronted de Noailles with fresh information he smoothly demurred, assuring her that his master, the King, knew nothing of the rebels. This culminated in an audience in which Mary threatened war, and when the ambassador remained imperturbable, the Queen's 'face was so transformed by anger that it lost all traces of feminine sweetness'.[41]

Ashby's name does not appear in any of Wotton's surviving intelligence reports on the exiles, which is not surprising as the English government was concerned with the rebels who schemed to overthrow Mary rather than with a young, innocuous student. William did not spend his two years at the Collège in isolation. As in other European cities, the English population was small. As well as a sprinkling of Cantabrigians (including former ambassador Pickering), William also had other social and family connections, including Dr Wotton. Wotton's sister was the mother of the executed Henry Grey, Duke of Suffolk, and the grandmother of the tragic Lady Jane Grey.

Wotton was a consummate diplomat who had served Henry VIII and Edward VI prior to his appointment by Mary Tudor as Royal Envoy to the Holy Roman Emperor Charles V (who was also King of Spain), and ambassador to France.[42]

Like William Ashby's ambassadorship more than thirty years later, Wotton functioned as both envoy and local spymaster. He was not afraid to report intelligence about Queen Mary's husband, Philip, even at the risk of arousing her wrath. In January 1554, he advised the Privy Council that the French believed that 'one of the promises made by the Emperor in connexion with the Queen's marriage is, that the Prince of Spain shall take with him to England some Spanish troops, who with the English forces, shall attack Scotland, and shall be maintained by the Emperor until that kingdom is conquered'. The French considered that this would be a serious provocation, assuming that the invasion of Scotland with the ostensible objective of eradicating Protestantism and restoring the Roman religion was a cover for Spanish imperial expansion.[43]

Wotton was adept at recruiting agents among the quarrelsome, homesick and increasingly poverty-stricken refugees by offering them pardons (which the Queen reluctantly granted) and money. Citing his success in 'converting' so many of the exiles, Wotton wrote to Mary advising that she should offer a free pardon to all the refugees, stating that he felt assured that by doing so the rebels could be turned into faithful subjects. This would have been a step too far for the vindictive Mary, and a blanket pardon was refused. However, Wotton continued to issue individual pardons and to assure English exiles that they could return home without fear of being declared traitors. It is possible that William Ashby received one of these.

Now fluent in French, the language of diplomacy, William felt confident enough about avoiding persecution that he decided to return to England. He wrote to the Cambridge regents requesting a Grace – a personal exemption from statutory requirements granted for a degree – on the basis that he be readmitted to the university due to completing nine terms 'although not in the established manner, including previous academic work at Peterhouse (which he stated was 'enough to begin his skills') plus studies in Paris. By the mid-sixteenth century, Cambridge degrees were increasingly *'gratuosi'*, that is awarded by grace, rather than *'rigorosi'*, awarded according to the rules.[44] William said that he hoped that he would not have to wait for the 'elections' – a formal meeting of the board of regents – as waiting for a decision would be 'at great living cost' for him.[45]

Ashby's petition was apparently unsuccessful as he did not return to Cambridge in 1556. Politics may have been a factor in his rejection: the Heresy Acts had been revived, hundreds of Protestants were being imprisoned, tortured and burned at the stake, and the Cambridge regents – under the arch-Catholic chancellors Bishop Gardiner and his successor Cardinal Reginald Pole – were hostile to Marian Exiles such as William even if they escaped persecution.

# 3. Return to an unhappy land

William Ashby returned to an unhappy homeland after two years abroad. Although England had been afflicted by health and economic crises during the previous decade, the 1550s were years of pestilence and tribulations of biblical proportions.

Economic malaise swept the British Isles from the greatest estates to the meagre smallholdings of the lowest husbandmen. Inflation and depression in the cloth industry caused increased unemployment and poverty. Weather extremes exacerbated peoples' economic misery, and rich and poor prayed for divine deliverance while fearing religious persecution. Bad portents had appeared soon after Mary settled uncomfortably on her throne. The *Great Harry*, the 'goodliest Ship in England', burned at Woolwich, through accident or mischief. Days after the quelling of Wyatt's Rebellion there 'appeared in the Sky a Rainbow reversed, the Bow turned downward, and the two ends standing upward; also two Suns shined at one time a good distance asunder'. To a population steeped in superstition, these and many other events were 'taken for ill signs', a display of divine displeasure.[1]

1555 had been extremely wet, ruining harvests across England. Westminster flooded after a great storm of wind and rain in October. But 1556, the year of Ashby's return from exile, had the worst weather in living memory. A deadly drought that caused springs to dry up and crops to fail was followed by incessant rains and flooding. One chronicler noted that 'all the corn was choked and blasted, the Harvest excessive wet and rainy'.[2] The quarterly price of wheat increased six-fold, and an estimated eighty percent of a common man's earnings was spent on food, even though debasement of the realm's coinage meant that pennies, groats and shillings were worth sixty percent less than half a century earlier.

Thousands starved to death across northern and western Europe. In Holland the desperate poor ate ox manure and pig dung.[3]

'Hot burning Agues and other strange Diseases took away much People'.[4] A disease colloquially called 'Jack Fisher's Flu' that ravaged England nearly as badly as the Bubonic plague was probably a combination of typhus, enteric fever and other diseases resulting from malnutrition, although deaths among the better-nourished gentry may have resulted from a virulent strain of influenza. Due to a combination of epidemic disease, bad harvests and a sharp decline in birth rates, the population of England fell by approximately sixteen and a half percent during the decade of the 1550s, with Leicestershire and Warwickshire suffering the sharpest declines of around twenty-eight percent.[5]

Both of Ashby's parents died during this decade, probably from disease as Everard Ashby died intestate, suggesting that he did not have time to make a will.

After his petition for readmission to Cambridge was rejected, William Ashby went to London, following his brother's footsteps to the Inns of Court. Leaving the old city walls, crumbling from lack of maintenance, he walked up Holborn, a country road bordered by open fields, accompanied by a man with a pushcart carrying his few belongings. Passing the 'lonely, almost forsaken, church of St. Pancras', he could see the Hampstead and Highgate hills.[6] He turned down Gray's Inn Lane towards the gardens and medieval buildings of Gray's, 'a goodly house', where for the next seven years he would be expected to spend '… some time in studying upon the first elements and grounds of the law, and … continuing by the space of seven years, or thereabouts'; he would 'frequent readings, meetings, boltings,[7] and other learned exercises, whereby growing ripe in the knowledge of the laws, and approved withall to be of honest conversation …' he would be 'selected and called to the degree of Utter Barristers, and so enabled to … practise the law, both in their chambers, and at the Bars'.[8]

A standard prerequisite for Gray's was undergraduate study at Cambridge or Oxford (usually without taking a degree), or training at one of the Inns of Chancery. It is possible that William Ashby's petition for reinstatement at Cambridge was a means of certification for his admission to Gray's Inn, which usually required a full three years at university. Although little is known about the years he spent at Gray's, it seems that, like his elder brother, he intended to have a legal career.

In the 16th century, training in the common law at Gray's Inn was secondary to making contacts that would help ambitious young men forge careers in public life and government service.[9] William Cecil, subsequently Lord Burghley, who was admitted in 1541 and elected an 'Ancient' in 1547, affectionately recalled Gray's Inn as 'the place where myself came for the unto service'.[10] Gray's was considered superior in social status to the other Inns of Court such as the Inner Temple, which William's brother Francis joined in 1554, and young men rarely were admitted without important social or political patronage. The Inns can be compared to modern North American fraternities, elite societies the members of which, old and young, provide a supportive network throughout lives and careers.

### 'Bloody Mary'

> '... innocent, harmless, and right godly men and women,
> whom she hath most cruelly roasted and fried in flames'.[11]

Writing in 1563 after Elizabeth came to the throne, Sir Thomas Smith stated that 'in the last two years of her [Mary's] reign so many of her subjects were made away, what with the executions of sword and fire, and what by sickness, that the Third part of Men in England was consumed'.[12]

While William Ashby was abroad, the persecution of Protestant heretics had risen to a level of terror that shook the foundations of English society. Mary's version of the Spanish Inquisition was a social leveller, as it burned those at the very bottom of Tudor society as well as those who had once been at the apex, although the number of working class people who were killed was disproportionately higher than those in higher social strata. In the year of the climatic and economic misery that characterised 1555, the burnings and arrests began in early February just after the Catholic holy day of Candlemas. Between February and Christmas, seventy-six people of all ages, gender and rank were burned at the stake, while hundreds of others were imprisoned and tortured.[13]

When Ashby entered Gray's Inn in early 1556, the smell of burnt human flesh and victims' ashes drifted across the old city from the livestock market and fairground called 'Schmyt Fyeld' [Smithfield] a half a mile away. January and February 1556 were especially busy months for the incineration of men and a larger than usual number of women at Smithfield and other places. Joan Lushford, a young maid, screamed piteously as the flames consumed her, as did various widows and wives. Thomas Cranmer, former Archbishop of Canterbury, was immolated outside Balliol College, Oxford, while being cursed by a pair of Spanish friars. Illiterate tailors, bricklayers, weavers, fullers and sheep shearers were burned, often for nothing more than being accused of heresy by people who bore grudges or owed debts. On 15th May, a lame painter, a simple bricklayer, and a blind man and blind boy, suffered horrific deaths.[14]

On a sunny June day, a mass burning at Stratford-le-Bow, a village on the eastern outskirts of London, attracted a large, boisterous crowd eager to be entertained by the slow deaths of thirteen heretics, including a merchant, a sawyer, two blacksmiths, a brewer, a serving-man, a pair of labourers and a pregnant woman. Cheerful sellers of apples and ale circulated while bookies solicited bets on which heretics would take the longest to die and how many would scream. The men were tied to three stakes, and the two women were forced to huddle at their feet while faggots were piled around them to stoke a single large fire, which the sheriff thought was an economical way to dispose of the sinners. Some of the bettors were disappointed that the brawny smiths succumbed before the women.[15]

★★★★★★

Of the four Inns of Court, Gray's was considered to harbour the strongest Protestant sympathies, and the 'old Liturgy' was 'grudgingly restored' in the chapel along with 'the Church furniture appropriate to it' after Mary's accession. However, the Inns of Court were largely immune from the Marian persecutions, partially because older members – the Treasurer, Readers and Ancients who comprised the 'Grand Company' – sympathised with 'the old learning', and among younger ones such as William Ashby there was 'a strong disposition to conform to whatever happened at the moment to be the law of the land'.[16] Also, influential judges and Members of Parliament such as William Cecil who kept their offices during Mary's reign remained closely connected to the Inns.

During his time in Paris, Ashby had learned the art of discretion – a requisite skill for a future diplomat and intelligence operative. Like most of his fellow students and their superiors at the Inns of Court, he refrained from involvement in words or acts that could be considered heretical or seditious.

The question remains as to how William (and Francis) Ashby were able to support themselves and finance their further education. While they may have received small bequests from their deceased parents, social and family connections were still strong during the mid-sixteenth century, and wealthy relatives could be expected to open their purses to promising young men who sought careers in law and government. William's half-brother, Maurice Berkeley, and cousins, the Ashbys of Quenby, are likely sponsors, as four decades later he left substantial bequests to their children in gratitude 'for the pains taken with me'.[17] Some of his Leicestershire kinsmen prospered under Queen Mary; William Skeffington and George Sherard were elected to Parliament in, respectively, 1555 and 1558.

Student life at the Inns of Court, while disciplined, was less strict than Cambridge, and was described as 'of a varied and attractive character', a 'sort of academy or gymnasium, fit for persons of their station'. In addition to 'courtly manners', aspiring lawyers learned 'singing and all kinds of music, dancing and such other accomplishments and diversions, which are called revels …. At other times … the greater part apply themselves to the study of law'.[18] The Inns were then proudly xenophobic, shamelessly boasting that, unlike law schools on the Continent, 'in our Inns of Court … only the natives are admitted'.[19]

Sixteenth-century English people were inured to the brutal fickleness of life. Reminders of the thin line between life and death were omnipresent, from the fat and flesh-stoked fires of burning heretics, to fatal diseases that struck down loved ones with little warning, to wretched skeletal women outside the gates of London, hoarsely begging alms beside the rotting bodies of their starved children. Young men like William Ashby were not necessarily callous by nature, but they pursued pleasure amidst the suffering around them knowing that their own lives could be cut short with no warning.

The seventh Baron Berkeley, a contemporary in age of William and cousin of his half-brother Maurice Berkeley, was a protégé of Queen Mary. Lord Berkeley, who lived with his mother at Kentish Town and on Shoe Lane,[20] hunted daily in 'Gray's Inn fields and all those parts towards Islington and Heygate [Highgate]' and had 'the company of many gentlemen of the Innes of Court, and others of lower condition that daily accompanied him' attended by one hundred and fifty servants in livery … wearing 'tawny coats'.[21] Cockfighting was so popular among the students that a round building was purposely built for it on Gray's Inn Lane, featuring rising benches circling the cock pit.[22]

In contrast to student hedonism, provision was made 'for the better relief of the Poor in Gray's Inn lane'. The 'third Butler' was made responsible for 'the carrying forth from the buttery, and also at the distribution of the alms, thrice by the week at Gray's Inn Gate, to see that due consideration be had to the poorer sort of aged and impotent persons'.[23]

In 1557, Ashby's second year of training, an attempt was made to curtail student clothing and grooming extravagances. The Inns of Court issued a 'united Order' that all lawyers and students, with the exception of 'Knights, or Benchers'[24] were:

> ...forbidden to wear in their Doublets or Hoses any light
> colours, except Scarlets or Crimsons; or wear any upper
> velvet cap, or any scarf or wings in their gowns, white jerkins,
> buskins or velvet shoes, double cuffs on their shirts, feathers or
> ribbons in their caps, upon pain to forfeit, for the first default,
> 3s 4d, and the second expulsion without redemption.[25]

Ashby and his fellow students were also forbidden to 'wear their Study-Gowns into the City any further than Fleet Bridge, Holburn Bridge, or to the Savoy', and when they were in the Commons [dining hall], they could not wear 'Spanish Cloak, Sword and Buckler, or Rapier; or Gowns and Hat; or Gowns girded with a Dagger upon the back.'[26]

Concern about overly hirsute young men and their attire was a perennial problem. In order to 'check the grievance of long beards', during the final year of Henry VIII's reign, the Treasurers of the Inns of Court were directed to confer regarding a 'uniform reformation in the length of beards and extravagance of apparel.'[27] The Order of 1557 included the decree that 'no one, under the degree of Knight ...' could 'wear any Beard above three weeks growing, upon pain of 40s, and so double every week after monition [warning]'.[28] The cause of the 'grievances' seem to have been ignored by students; in 1574, Queen Elizabeth specially ordered that every man of the society of Gray's Inn

> ... should reform himself for the manner of his Apparel
> according to the Proclamation [of 1557] ... that none ...
> should wear any Gown, Doublet, hose, or outward garment,
> of any light colour.[29]

This proclamation was separate from the 1574 Sumptuary Act, which was a largely unsuccessful attempt to regulate the wearing of clothing for the entire country, based on social status. By then, apparently, beards were no longer considered a problem.

Similar to the Cambridge colleges, fraternisation with the opposite sex was actively discouraged, at least on the Gray's Inn premises. No 'laundresses or women called "victulers" under forty years of age ...' were allowed to 'come into the chambers of the gentlemen of ... Grays Inn; and they shall not send their maids, of whatsoever age ... into the said gentlemen's chambers, on pain that the gentleman acting to the contrary shall for the first offense be out of commons, and for the second out of the Inn.'[30]

With the exceptions of the Steward, the Chief Butler and the Chief Cook, the Inn's servants (who were apparently all male) were to keep themselves 'sole and unmarried'.[31] Some instructors, such as Readers in Divinity, were also required to be unmarried, following the example of a statute of St. Paul's Cathedral governing vergers which stated that 'because having a wife is a troublesome and disturbing affair, and husbands are apt to study the wishes of their wives or their mistresses, and no man can serve two masters, the vergers are to be either bachelors or to give up their wives'.[32]

1558 was another year of misery for England. In January, the country suffered a national humiliation when the French captured Calais and its environs, the last English possession in continental Europe. In March, 'a most destructive hurricane' flooded towns and swept away hundreds amidst the debris of destroyed hovels and cottages. A lethal influenza pandemic which began the previous year intensified, with an especially high mortality rate among pregnant women.[33] The population's suffering was intensified by yet another torrid summer that prostrated London and the south, while the midlands and north were raked by severe thunderstorms and tornados that uprooted massive oaks and shattered church towers, flinging bells ringing as if by the hands of demons:

> ... within a mile of Nottingham, was a grievous tempest with
> thunder which, as it came through beat down all the houses
> and churches, cast the bells to the outside of the church-
> yards, and twisted the sheets of lead like a pair of leather

gloves and threw them four hundred foot into the field ... a
child was taken forth of a man's hand and carried two spear's
length high, and then let fall two hundred feet off, of which
fall it died. Five or six men thereabouts were killed yet had
neither flesh nor skin hurt. They were slain by the storm,
during which, hailstones fell measuring fifteen inches in
circumference.[34]

England and Scotland were in a state of low-intensity war. George
Buchanan, the Scottish Protestant theologian, observed that there 'seem'd
rather to be no Peace, than a War' in 1558, while his Papist antagonist,
John Lesley, Bishop of Ross, recalled that 'During this hoill symmer, the
warris continowit still betuix France and Flanders verey hoit, and lykwyse
betuix Scotlande and Inglande'.[35]

The bitter, barren and depressed Queen Mary died in the early hours
of Thursday, 17 November 1558. Her last five victims, including an 'aged
woman', had been burned at Canterbury two days earlier.

That morning, in Westminster and the City of London a euphony
of trumpets proclaimed twenty-five-year-old Elizabeth Tudor the new
Queen. Protestants emerged from the shadows to celebrate, while
Catholics mourned Mary's demise and bleakly anticipated the pendulum
of religious persecution swinging against them. Generally, the country
felt too debilitated to rejoice in the new monarch. As one contemporary
chronicler observed: 'The Queen poor. The realm exhausted. The
nobility poor and decayed. The people out of order. Justice not executed.
All things dear.'[36]

Elizabeth's accession increased the prospect of open war with Scotland.
Mary Stuart, whose arms were quartered with those of England in an
aggressive symbolic assertion of her dynastic right, was backed by the
French in asserting that she had a more legitimate right to the English
throne than Elizabeth. Within weeks of the new Queen's enthronement,
heavily armed Scots were raiding deeper into England in what was feared
to be a prelude to a Franco-Scottish invasion. The English responded

by laying waste to the countryside around Eyemouth, Berwickshire, where hundreds of French troops were quartered. While the immediate threat was diffused the following year by the Peace of Cateau-Cambrésis, mutual hostility continued.

## Ashby's Return to University

Soon after Elizabeth's accession, Cambridge again welcomed Protestants. The parliament that was seated in January 1559 passed a renewed Act of Supremacy. No degrees were conferred unless the candidate took a public oath acknowledging 'the Queen's Highness' as 'the only Supreme Governor of this Realm ... as well in all Spiritual or Ecclesiastical Things or Causes as Temporal, and that no foreign Prince Person Prelate State or Potentate' had any jurisdiction or authority in England. Furthermore, students and faculty had to 'utterly renounce and forsake all foreign Jurisdictions Powers Superiorities and Authorities'.[37]

The Supremacy Oath had the desired effect of rooting out Roman Catholicism in a more benign way than the brutal Marianist persecutions. The Masters of various colleges were 'deprived' and in some instances replaced by those who had been ousted during Mary's reign. The new Queen took a personal interest in Cambridge and Oxford, and 'to the intent that learned men may spring the more' a series of reforms were enacted. Holders of church benefices valued at more than £100 per annum were required to give £3 6s 8d as an exhibition for one scholar at either university. Elizabeth also granted 'privileges' to 'scholars and students and their servants' exempting them from 'musters ... and for sending men to the wars' and forbidding the taking of their horses for any royal purpose.[38]

William Ashby seems to have been a restless soul as he did not remain at Gray's Inn long enough to be selected as an Utter Barrister. On 20 November 1562, the eighth week of Michaelmas Term, he returned to Peterhouse as a Fellow-Commoner – 'with seniority amongst the Fellow-Commoners' – paying 20 shillings as his *introit* fee.[39]

Ashby apparently spent the next four years at Cambridge, receiving his M.A. degree in 1566. The same year on 21 June, he was 'incorporated M.A.' at Oxford University and became a member of Christ Church.[40] Incorporation was a process by which members of one university could have their degree status transferred to another. However, Joseph Foster's *Alumni Oxonienses* also mentions that Ashby was 'created M.A'. Here, the term 'creation' means that this was an honorary M.A., and not one earned by studying. Foster is unclear as to whether Ashby received this honorary status at Cambridge and then incorporated it at Oxford, or if Oxford conferred the status on him.[41] By the standards of the day, Ashby's receipt of M.A. degrees from both universities was rare, especially as there is no record of him pursuing an academic career subsequently.

During Ashby's years at Gray's Inn and during his second round of university studies he also pursued redress for the Duke of Suffolk's debt to his father, a lengthy process through the courts for those lacking powerful patrons, which evidently Ashby had.

On 25 April 1567, the Crown granted William Ashby a lease for twenty-one years of 'portions of the tithes of corn and hay, lands and a tithe barn in Leicestershire and Yorkshire, as well as the Manor of Bishop's Fee' with reservations, including the courts and 'profits of court of the Manor'.[42] The latter was a valuable property as, prior to the Dissolution of the Monasteries, it was a large estate owned by the Bishop of Lincoln, valued at £17 4s 0d in the *Valor Ecclesiasticus* of 1535, where the bishop held a manorial court ['Court Leet'].[43] The grant was made:

> In full satisfaction of a debt of £241 5s owed by Henry, late
> Duke of Suffolk, attainted of treason, at the time of his death
> to Everard Ashebye, William's father, as appears in several
> bills and a schedule signed by divers officers and servants of
> the Duke bearing witness to the debt, produced by William;
> Queen Mary, in consideration that the Duke's possessions
> came into her hands by his attainder, was minded to have paid
> the debt or otherwise made satisfaction for it, and Everard,

while he lived, intended to bestow the £241 5s on William for

his better support and education in letters.[44]

The grant is intriguing in that it states that Queen Mary was 'minded'-meaning inclined or disposed – to pay Suffolk's debt to Everard Ashby, but never did so. This means that the Crown recognised the debt as valid, as supported by the evidence provided by the Duke's officers and servants. The petition (which was probably drafted by William Ashby given his legal training) also mentions that the funds were intended to support William's higher education. The document is further evidence that Suffolk may have been William's patron, and that the younger Ashby seems to have been recognised as a scholar and singled out for academic support in preference to his elder brother, Francis.

William Ashby is missing from the extant documentary record until early in the year 1573, when he appears in Paris as an agent of the English ambassador, Francis Walsingham. During the intervening years, he began his career as a freelance courier and intelligencer on Her Majesty's Service.

*Part Two*

*On Her Majesty's Service*

# 4. Walsingham's Intelligencer

Francis Walsingham arrived in France on New Year's Day 1571 as the English ambassador to the court of the weak, tubercular Charles IX and his domineering mother, Catherine de Medici. At this time, Walsingham was little known outside of Elizabeth's inner circle, where he was favoured for his role in uncovering an extensive conspiracy to overthrow the Queen and replace her with Mary, Queen of Scots.

There is evidence that Walsingham was working in some capacity for the English government by September 1566, and was engaged in secret work for Sir William Cecil by August 1568.[1] He proved his worth as an intelligence officer by 'turning' the Italian banker Roberto Ridolfi – a senior agent and paymaster for the Pope, Spain and France – into a double agent.[2] Walsingham's knowledge of the Ridolfi plot and Mary Stuart's role as its nucleus convinced him at an early stage that the only way to safeguard England was to eliminate the Scottish Queen.

Walsingham was a witness to the massacre that began on the eve of St. Bartholomew's Day, 23 August 1572, during which between five thousand and thirty thousand Huguenots and other French Protestants were brutally murdered. Walsingham feared for his and his family's lives while besieged in the ambassador's residence and, like other Protestants, the mass slaughter imprinted on his mind 'the indelible conviction that Catholicism was a bloody and treacherous religion'.[3] His enemies, foreign and domestic, hated and feared him. The Spanish ambassador in London described Walsingham as 'a devilish heretic that ... constantly favours those like himself and persecutes the Catholics'.[4]

On 11 March 1573, one month before the end of his ambassadorship, Walsingham sent Burghley a letter by 'the bearer, Mr. Ashby',[5] who he said '... can acquaint him with the circumstances' of a major assault on

La Rochelle by Catholic royalist forces led by the Duke of Anjou (who succeeded to the French throne as Henri III in 1574).[6]

La Rochelle, essentially an autonomous city-state, was the most important Protestant base in France. After the St. Bartholomew's Eve massacres, the city's population was swelled by Huguenot refugees, many of whom moved on to settle in England. The city had been besieged since November 1572, and by early February twenty-eight thousand Catholic troops, a number of whom were dying from disease and foul weather, were encamped outside the walls. A series of assaults were launched, none of which succeeded. The attack which Ashby was sent to report on took place on 3 March 1573, during which the Duke of Aumale was slain by a culverin shot.

Aumale, uncle of Mary Queen of Scots, had been an English hostage in 1550 and was considered an important Papist foe by Walsingham, who rejoiced that 'the Duke of Aumale was slain and Chavigny[7] sore hurt, the two chief contrivers of the mischiefs which have here happened, and therefore have received their deserved payment'. Walsingham, still consumed with fury from his personal experience of the massacre six months previously, wrote that he hoped 'that the rest of the bloody murderers may have like punishment extended to them'.[8]

This is the earliest known documentation of Ashby's relationship with Walsingham. It is highly probable that they had been acquainted for some years. Ashby's sojourn as a student in Paris and fluent French would have made him a valuable asset to Walsingham at a time when few Englishmen, especially reliably Protestant and socially acceptable ones, had experience abroad and fluency in the languages of continental Europe.[9]

No record has been found of when, or how, William Ashby was first employed by Walsingham. As in succeeding centuries up to the present day, during the Elizabethan era the two great English universities – as well as the Inns of Court – were recruiting grounds for the diplomatic and intelligence services. Walsingham and Ashby had mutual acquaintances,[10] and if the two men did not meet during their self-exile as Marian refugees, they are likely to have done so after both returned to England; possibly prior to Ashby's 1567 compensation grants for the beheaded Duke of Suffolk's debt to his father, which may have been a form of payment for his government service.

Gentlemen diplomats and 'intelligencers'[11] – espionage agents – were not paid salaries, only expenses, and were generally remunerated with rents and other income from Crown properties. However, most such gentlemen servants of the Queen had to dip into their own purses to cover expenses, and their demands for reimbursement were a chronic source of frustration for Walsingham in his relationship with Elizabeth, who, he complained, was 'very stingy'.[12] A significant portion of foreign service expenses was for 'certain extraordinary and secret causes' including to 'the masters of ... ships hired for espial [spying] service'.[13]

During Walsingham's term as ambassador in Paris, he went heavily into debt in order to fulfil 'the condition of obedience and commandment' as the Queen's representative. He was forced to sell one of his properties in England to sustain his embassage, and borrowed a large sum from an agent of Catherine de Medici, the militantly Catholic and Machiavellian Queen mother who infamously said 'a false report, if believed during three days, may be of great service to a government'.[14]

Ashby's name does not appear in the terse entries of Walsingham's *Journal*, but neither does mention of much other correspondence recorded elsewhere.[15] It is clear from surviving documents dating from the following dozen years that Walsingham often relied on Ashby to relay crucial intelligence orally, as both a supplement and substitute for written communiques. Ashby may have accompanied Walsingham to France on a diplomatic mission in August 1570, and was certainly working for him during his term as ambassador.

It is also possible that Ashby and Walsingham were part of Sir Nicholas Throckmorton's delegation to Edinburgh in 1567, as both evidently had familiarity with Scotland prior to the Secretary's diplomatic mission in 1583, which included Ashby.[16] Throckmorton was the father of Arthur, who would become Ashby's dearest friend. Elizabeth sent Sir Nicholas to Scotland to intercede for Mary Stewart after the Scottish Queen was deposed and imprisoned by rebellious lairds. In a foreshadowing of Ashby's diplomatic mission in Scotland over two decades later, Throckmorton was given contradictory instructions which aroused the wrath of his Queen.

William Ashby is absent from the historical record during the three years following his return to London in March 1573 to brief Burghley. He reappears on 6 March 1576, when he was granted special admission to the Inner Temple at the request of his brother, Francis Ashby, who had been called to the bar as an utter barrister in 1571.[17]

Ashby did not stay long at the Inner Temple. Four months later, he was again on the Continent, at Strasbourg serving as Walsingham's intelligencer and courier. His motivation for being admitted to the Inner Temple for such a brief period is a mystery, as he is not known to have qualified as a lawyer and was to spend the remainder of his life serving Her Majesty as a spy, diplomat and Member of Parliament. As the Inner Temple functioned like a present-day gentleman's club, it seems likely that Ashby sought admission to use the premises as a base between his travels abroad, living there and using its dining hall.[18]

Ashby must have had a good reason for not returning to Gray's Inn, where he had been a law student twenty years previously. There is no record of his being sent down or otherwise leaving under bad circumstances. Given his good relationship with his elder brother, Francis, a likely explanation is that he simply desired to spend time with a family member in addition to needing habitation. Throughout his life, Ashby maintained close ties with relatives.

In Strasbourg, Ashby met with John Sturmius (Johannes Sturm). Sturmius, described by the Spanish as 'one of the heresiarchs of Germany', was a leading Protestant humanist educator and theologian as well as the chief English agent in Germany.[19] A 'high grade' source of intelligence information and influencer who corresponded with the

Queen, Burghley and Walsingham from the earliest weeks of Elizabeth's reign, Sturmius was also a respected diplomatic intermediary, having been instrumental in negotiating peace between England and France in 1545.[20] He received payments from the English government and was considered such an important asset that he was personally managed by Walsingham, who manipulated him with flattery and declarations of shared zeal for Protestantism. Walsingham was described as 'a man exceeding wise and industrious ... a most sharp maintainer of the purer Religion, a most subtle searcher of hidden secrets, who knew excellently well how to win men's minds unto him, and to apply them unto his own uses'.[21]

Walsingham would send Sturmius requests for specific information, seeking his opinion about various German rulers, asking for example whether 'they would unitedly continue ... to the advancement of the gospel and of the general peace'. He told Sturmius that '[i]f you will write upon these matters, and inform us whether any thing of the kind is to be expected, and by what ways and means it may be guarded against, you will do a most welcome service both to ourselves and to the whole Christian world'.[22]

In 1575, the French ambassador to England, Gabriel-Jacques de La Motte advised King Henri III that 'it would be good if your Majesty had Mr Sturm watched by someone in Strasbourg, for he is now the Queen's Agent in Germany'. Although de La Motte considered Sturmius 'a very learned man of letters ... in affairs of state he is simple and has little understanding, and someone close to him could discover most of their decisions'.[23] Walsingham was aware of the elderly educator's susceptibility, and it is likely that he sent Ashby to ascertain if he had been unwittingly turned by French or Spanish agents.

On 27 October 1576, Walsingham wrote from Hampton Court Palace to '[m]ost learned Sturmius' that he had 'earnestly requested' the English ambassador to France, Sir Amias Paulet, 'to interest himself as much as possible in the arrangement of the money matters between you and the friends of the true religion'. Sturmius was evidently concerned about the security of his reports to Walsingham, who assured him that as 'to the means by which you should procure your letters to be forwarded to us, I have declared my mind and pleasure to master Ashby, which I know he will explain to you; lest hereafter any of you who shall entertain a desire of writing to us, whenever any occasion may arise, may find any difficulty in this respect'. Walsingham ended by entreating Sturmius 'again and again, to write more frequently'.[24]

Trained as a lawyer, Walsingham took care with the semantics of his writings. In the context of this letter, his use of 'us' was meant to be understood by Sturmius as representing the Queen and her government, rather than him as an individual. Similarly, 'any of you' refers to the members of the Protestant network throughout Europe that Sturmius had cultivated since the reign of Henry VIII.

William Ashby's role as Walsingham's agent from at least the early 1570s is not easily defined in modern terms. He was far more than a mere courier, but not yet formally accredited as a diplomat. He served as both a freelance intelligencer and a senior agent of influence. Most importantly, though, employed by a chief who placed great value on loyalty and diligence, Ashby had Walsingham's trust.

At this time, Walsingham (who would not be knighted until the following year) had recently become Principal Secretary of State, a job encompassing foreign relations as well as serving as the country's chief administrator. In modern terms, Walsingham's combined governmental role was equivalent to that of the UK's Secretaries of State for Foreign Affairs, the Home Department, International Trade, and Defence, plus serving as Chief of the Secret Intelligence Service ('MI6'), Director General of the Security Service ('MI5'), and head of the Counter Terrorism Command of the Metropolitan Police Force. His staff and budget were comparatively minuscule, yet his responsibilities were vast and varied.

In matters of foreign affairs, Walsingham dealt with everything from pretending to orchestrate the Queen's marriage to the Duke of Anjou, to undermining the Spanish occupation of the Netherlands, to bemusedly contemplating how to respond to the French ambassador's invitation to 'Warm yourself up … a little with the grace and beauty of this fair Queen [Mary, Queen of Scots], and make yourself a suitor to make her position in [Elizabeth's] good graces a little better than it is at present'.[25]

Responsibility for managing the minutia of domestic matters ran the gamut from clearing the Lord High Admiral's servant of 'suspicion of being an aider of pirates', petitioning Lord Burghley and Lord Sussex, the Lord Chamberlain, 'that a third voyage to the North-west parts should be made by Mr. Furbisher',[26] and ruling on the rates of wages paid to 'spinsters of yarn'.[27]

Walsingham's 'secret service'[28] blended his foreign and domestic responsibilities. William Cecil, Lord Burghley, Secretary of State until 1572, began developing an active state intelligence apparatus soon after Elizabeth's accession.[29] There is evidence that Walsingham had become *de facto* chief of the intelligence service by the time he was appointed joint Secretary of State and Privy Councillor in December 1573.[30]

Walsingham was a more zealous Protestant than Burghley. He believed that the continental Roman Catholic powers and Papists throughout the British Isles were engaged in a never-ending war to subvert the realm, depose his Queen and restore England to orthodox Catholicism 'by fire and blood'.[31] He was mindful that England was still a peripheral European power, militarily and economically weak, and a country where a majority of the population still preferred the old Roman religion even if they were opposed to Papal domination.

At the time of Ashby's meeting with Sturmius, the English government was closely watching the third revolt of the States-General – the Seventeen Provinces comprising the Low Countries – against Spanish rule.[32] As part of the Holy Roman Empire, which had its capital at Brussels, the States had enjoyed a degree of autonomy, and in 1549 the Emperor Charles V (who was born at Ghent and therefore considered a Netherlands native) decreed the provinces to be an integral territory, separate from the

Empire and France. This served to unify the States into a single political entity within the Empire, under nominal Hapsburg rule but largely self-governing. Charles' edict was intended as an enlightened, pragmatic means of centralising the administrative units of the Holy Roman Empire and strengthening Hapsburg rule by streamlining the succession.

In 1556, two years before his death, Charles V divided the Hapsburg dynasty into two branches – a royal Austro-German house headed by his brother Ferdinand I, who became Holy Roman Emperor, and a Spanish house under Charles' son, Philip II, King of Spain. The Seventeen Provinces became part of the Spanish Empire, and Philip, who had inherited a virtually bankrupt kingdom, began a series of confrontations with the States when he sought to impose taxes and expand the power of the Roman Catholic church. These were accompanied by economic and political crises, followed by successive revolts which were sparked by Philip's determination to strictly enforce existing anti-heresy laws.

Concerned that a conciliatory approach would lead to rebellions elsewhere in the Spanish Empire, Philip resorted to increasingly brutal suppression, sending in troops which escalated the unrest. For example, in an atrocity resembling the 1944 Waffen-SS massacre at the French village Oradour-sur-Glane, Spanish soldiers entered the undefended town of Naarden and massacred almost the entire population – some three thousand inhabitants – before razing every building to the foundations.[33]

The States were loosely divided between Protestants in the north and Catholics in the south, but the people were united by a common hatred of the Spanish and a determination to rid themselves of oppression. 'William the Silent', Prince of Orange, a former ward and favourite of Charles V, emerged as the leader of the armed resistance against the Spanish.

The Spanish occupation and its accompanying atrocities were widely publicised throughout England as a warning of what could be expected if Spanish – and French – backed Catholicism was reimposed. Walsingham and his colleagues on the Privy Council saw the popular rebellion as a means of weakening Spain's position as the dominant European power and bolstering Protestantism. Although urged by Walsingham and Leicester to take an active role in the struggle, including funding the rebel forces and possible English military intervention, Elizabeth vacillated. After the authority of Spain was formally renounced by Holland, Zealand and Utrecht, the sovereignty of the three unified states was offered to Elizabeth, which she turned down, not wanting to offend Philip. This caused widespread antagonism towards England. William of Orange reportedly told one of Burghley's agents that he had 'no affection for the English, who are not trusted'.[34]

Orange was 'in great perplexity', claiming that the Queen pretended to believe disinformation – probably by Spanish agents – as an excuse not to intervene. The Prince wrote to Elizabeth declaring 'that all the reports of arrests and ill-treatment of her subjects in Holland and Zealand are false ... These accounts are spread by those who seek [England's] ruin'.[35] However, the Queen was incensed by the operations of 'certain sea captains calling themselves Flushingers' – Dutch pirates operating from the port of Flushing under Letters of Marque issued by the States-General – that preyed on English shipping. English merchants complained to Elizabeth that their ships and over £200,000 of goods (£60 million in 2021) had been impounded on the Scheldt River on Orange's order.

While Orange probably had no control over the Flushingers, he contended that the impoundment was justified in retaliation for acts of piracy perpetrated by English privateers on Dutch ships. Desperate to raise revenues for the struggle against Spain, the Prince was aware that it gave the States a strong diplomatic bargaining chip because the Netherlands were England's largest trading partner, and the English Merchant Adventurers of London, who owned the ships, were the most powerful trade organisation, with vast political influence within Elizabeth's government. Orange also issued a thinly veiled threat that he would be forced to seek an alliance with France if English aid failed to materialise.[36]

While Scotland also traded with the Netherlands, the volume of exported goods – wool and woollen cloth, cow hides, pitch and timber – was a fraction of the amount shipped by English merchants. Dutch and Flemish traders were reluctant to be paid for their goods in Scots pounds, which had been at parity with sterling in the fourteenth century but was worth only one-sixth of a pound in the 1570s and continued to depreciate through the remainder of the century. Soldiers were one of Scotland's most important exports to the Low Countries – as many as thirty thousand Scots fought on both sides during the Low Countries rebellion against the Spanish.

One week after Ashby and Sturmius met, mutinous Spanish forces (which had a contingent of German mercenaries) sacked Antwerp. Over eight thousand men, women and children were slaughtered, and a third of the city was destroyed, precipitating a wider popular insurrection. Walsingham was deeply troubled by intelligence reports that the Spanish were considering what today would be called genocide to pacify the Low Countries by 'extermination of the whole race, both males and females, and the destruction of their towns'.[37] The Duke of Alba and fellow Spanish officers 'boasted that they would so ruin Antwerp and Brussels that not one stone should remain on another', and that 'they should like to cut open the bellies of the women and thrust the men's heads in them, and smother them with the blood'.[38]

Walsingham had a 'love-hate' relationship with Queen Elizabeth – love in regard to her as the corporeal representation of England and supreme head of the Anglican church, yet enduring chronic frustration with her ill treatment of him as well as her parsimony and capriciousness. Under immense stress, which he sometimes blamed for his chronic poor health, he regularly threatened to resign and 'with the leave of God to convey myself off the stage and become a looker-on'.[39] Yet a deep-rooted sense of duty led him to endure government service nearly to the end of his life.

During 1577, William Ashby travelled frequently between London, the Low Countries and various German cities. His work was focused on helping to foster the formation of a 'league of the princes of Germany, professing Christian religion, against the Pope' to counter a Catholic league.[40] The Earl of Leicester and his nephew Sir Philip Sidney were strong proponents of the Protestant League, and supported John Casimir, Count Palatine, as its de facto leader. Elizabeth, often lukewarm about religious conflicts, also favoured a strategic alliance with the German princes who 'had come out of the darkness and filth of Popery', although not at the risk of war with Spain or France.[41]

In Scotland, James Douglas, 4th Earl of Morton, wielded dictatorial power as Regent. The Kirk approved of his strong stance against Papists but disliked his perceived support for a Scottish version of Anglicanism. Morton quickly won the backing of the English by letting 'Elizabeth know, in short, that she must make up her mind ... and aid him with money, a pension, and artillery, or he would look elsewhere'.[42] During Morton's regency, Protestantism became entrenched in southern Scotland while the Catholic north was generally left to its own devices.

Throughout this time, Ashby was also developing his 'tradecraft' – the techniques, methods and early technologies used in espionage. He was also recruiting a network of agents and informers. In April, he was in Frankfurt where he met with Frederic, Baron von Ruissingen, who was ostensibly an English agent. Ruissengen wrote to Walsingham saying that he would use 'the opportunity of the coming over to England of Mr. Asheby' to carry his letter, and that he had 'communicated all matters of importance' to Ashby, who would provide a 'full report'.[43] It is possible that Ashby carried a cypher back from Ruissingen to Walsingham; the German nobleman referred to this in a 1584 letter in which he asked if Walsingham 'still has the duplicate of the cipher which he sent to him ... six years ago, in which case he can write freely'.[44]

Cryptography had been advancing as a science since the beginning of Elizabeth's reign, pioneered as an important espionage tool by Burghley at the instigation of John Dee, the Renaissance polymath who was one of the Queen's favourites. Walsingham expanded its development and practical application. For a number of years, codes used by all the rival European powers were simple, easily broken substitution ciphers with a small code set. The English Secret Intelligence Service gained a major strategic advantage in 1578 when Walsingham hired twenty-two-year-old Thomas Phelippes as a forger and cryptographer. Recognised in his time as a brilliant mathematician and linguist, Phelippe's genius was on a par with that of Alan Turing nearly 400 year later. Like Turing, Phelippes was a Cambridge man, which was probably a factor in his employment by Walsingham.

Ruissingen had been in London in 1575 when he wrote to Burghley to pass on 'intelligence' about the flight of the Duke of Anjou, Elizabeth's future suitor, to join Protestant rebels including 'a legion of French footmen and Burgundian harquebussiers', and other information of a military nature.[45] Ruissingen seemed ideally placed as an intelligencer, described in 1576 as 'the Governor of Ypres, who is of good house, and well friended, and who follows the humours of the Spaniards'.[46] He was acquainted with the Privy Council faction dominated by Walsingham and Leicester which wanted England to intervene militarily in the Low Countries.

However, Walsingham knew that Ruissingen was a double agent, having reports that he was 'a suspected man with the States for that he was secretly two days in the Spanish Ambassador's house in France ... and that he should have in pension 8,000 crowns of the King of Spain'.[47] Considered one of the 'suspected nobility', Ruissingen was arrested in the Netherlands in January 1577 on suspicion of 'the different matters on which he has given the King of Spain and Don John advice prejudicial to the interests of the Low Countries', but was released the following week after intervention by the powerful Duke of Aarschot, an arch-Catholic and favourite of Philip.[48] William Ashby was also aware of Ruissingen's duplicity, but like his chief found the baron's information had sufficient value to continue contact with him.

After leaving Frankfurt, Ashby travelled to London via Brussels, where on 6 May he met with Dr Thomas Wilson, who was then in his final weeks of serving as Special Ambassador to the Low Countries, charged by the Privy Council with finding a peaceful solution to the chaotic political and military situation in the Netherlands. A few days earlier, Don John of Austria, an illegitimate son of the Emperor Charles V, and therefore the half-brother of Philip II, arrived in Brussels to serve as Governor and Viceroy of the Low Countries.

The government and people of the States, including the Prince of Orange, were optimistic that Don John would restore order to the rebellious States via a policy of peaceful compromise rather than oppression. In February 1577, he signed the 'Perpetual Edict', which provided for the removal of Spanish troops and recognised a form of union among the squabbling States in return for their agreement to accept Philip as their sovereign and Roman Catholicism as the dominant religion.

Wilson, however, was deeply suspicious. Saying that he was 'grieved and spoke his mind somewhat plainly', he told Walsingham that Don John had 'a farther fetch[49] in his head after the [Perpetual Edict]', that he believed the peace was pretended, and said that his agents reported that Don John's 'full intention was by this peace to undo the Prince and overthrow [Protestant] religion'. Wilson warned of an assassination plot against Orange 'by some Frenchmen about him', and was 'certain that the only life of the Prince is an hindrance to all the designs and purposes of Don John'. If the Queen failed to understand the Prince of Orange's key role, he said, 'England shall feel the smart of it in time'.[50]

Wilson gave Ashby a note to Walsingham stating that Ashby 'is of himself instead of a large packet' and would provide a detailed report about Don John's reception in the Netherlands. Coded communications could be purloined and deciphered by enemies, and couriers were murdered for the diplomatic 'packets' they carried. Walsingham considered Ashby's retentive mind the most secure means of transmitting sensitive information. A further benefit was provided by the fact that Ashby attended meetings and personally met with senior foreign officials, including heads of state.

Thomas Wilson's career presents a good example of the interlocking relationships among English diplomats and intelligence operatives during Walsingham's tenure as Principal Secretary. The two men matriculated at King's College, Cambridge, and although Wilson was a decade older than Walsingham, their academic careers overlapped. It is likely that Ashby and Wilson also became acquainted at Cambridge, as Wilson remained at the university, on and off, until 1553, and was considered to be within the political circle of the Dudleys and Greys (Wilson was a tutor to the two young Dukes of Suffolk who died of the Sweating Sickness in 1551).

Wilson was also a Marian Exile, and studied in Padua before moving on to Rome, where he was imprisoned by the Pope and tortured for his outspoken Protestantism. The experience scarred him, and throughout the rest of his career he was an unrelenting foe of Catholicism, known as 'a remorseless torturer' and 'officious priest-catcher' who personally tortured Papist conspirators in 'the prison in the bloody Tower'.[51]

Like Walsingham and Leicester, Wilson was a proponent of an English alliance with Protestant princes on the Continent, thus explaining Walsingham's urgent request to Sturmius for information about 'various German rulers'. Wilson returned to London a month after his meeting with Ashby, and was appointed as a Privy Councillor and deputy Secretary of State under Walsingham. Like the Principal Secretary, he considered Mary Stuart a traitor and had advocated her execution since at least 1572. He shared Walsingham's frustration with Queen Elizabeth's indifference to Mary's plots against her, saying that he doubted 'whether she so fully seeth her own peril' and that 'foreign princes' thought that her apathy in this regard was a sign of weakness, considering that the

Scottish Queen's 'offences being so great and horrible, the Queen's Majesty suffereth her to live'.[52]

William Ashby witnessed Don John's ceremonial entry to Brussels. Wilson told Walsingham that Ashby 'is able to declare of the receiving of Don John with great solemnity' and the inhabitants' general thankfulness 'for common quietness'. Without reiterating his profound cynicism about Don John's true intentions (known and shared by Walsingham and Ashby), Wilson reported that many people were saying *'fuit homo missus a Deo cui nomen erat Johannes'* (a man named John was sent from God).[53]

Dr Wilson's suspicions proved to be well-founded. The 'man sent from God' had a secret mandate from King Philip to forcefully bring the States back under Spanish control and suppress Protestantism. The Spanish mounted a propaganda campaign to lull the English and counter the Privy Council faction which distrusted them. In early July, Don John complained that 'sundry ill reports are spread touching his good intentions, which he has shown in act sufficiently to remove all distrust', and stated that these 'evil rumours probably emanate from malignant spirits, restless foreigners, and heretics who only want to introduce distrust and disorder'.[54]

Don John also attempted to charm the Queen. Wilson (who had reluctantly returned to Brussels to verify that the Spanish were abiding by the terms of the peace treaty) sarcastically told Walsingham that 'He heaped up so many good words of his affection to our Sovereign as it was marvellous', adding 'I fear that great troubles will shortly grow in this country'.[55] When Don John met with Wilson, he declared his affection for Elizabeth, saying 'indeed God had done much for her, not only to call her to the place of a Queen and so represent himself, but also to give her such a shape fit for any Queen, and therewithal a mind endued with such several and famous virtues as therefore she is had in admiration and a chief spectacle to the whole world'.[56]

Wilson passed these endearments on to Elizabeth, warning that when Don John, like other foreign princes, 'cannot prevail by open and apparent actions they will work by *convert a' doulce* means intermingling honey and sugar with their drugs of poison and destruction'. Don John's 'speech tends to this end' Wilson wrote, and cautioned the Queen to be 'very circumspect how to trust and never to believe words but the effect of words'.[57]

The following month, Walsingham presented to the Queen and Privy Council indisputable evidence from intercepted letters 'with seals and signatures' between Don John, Philip and other senior Spanish officials that the Spaniards' intent was 'not to maintain the peace'. The letters showed that Don John's 'designs are to conquer England' and that the strategic plan was 'that the [Frisian] isles being taken, England will the easier be conquered, and thinks it to be a harder matter to obtain the isles than to conquer England'.[58]

Despite the evidence of threats against her person and realm, Elizabeth was stubbornly indecisive, throwing tantrums when pressed by her councillors. When a response became imperative, she usually took a neutral position with 'a policy of pseudo-mediation between Philip II and his subjects',[59] which many considered folly. [60]

Don John and Philip were buying time because the Spanish treasury was nearly empty and they did not have the financial resources to launch their campaign to reassert domination of the Low Countries. This changed in the summer of 1577 when the long-awaited Spanish treasure fleet arrived at Seville from Havana with two million ducats worth of gold, silver and jewels. Philip's 'Royal Fifth', a twenty percent tax on the treasure, enabled him to pay off loans and borrow funds from Venetian bankers to begin the *reconquesta* of the Low Countries. As soon as a courier from the royal court at Madrid reached him with the news, Don John recalled his army from Italy, left Brussels and began taking a series of towns and castles.

Elizabeth responded grudgingly, sending Casimir £40,000 to recruit mercenaries and lending the States £20,000 with another £28,757 promised.[61] The Queen's vacillation maddened Walsingham. He wrote that 'Such as are evil affected and inclined to Spain take great hold [of

Elizabeth], to the grief of those who are best devoted to her Majesty's service and foresee the peril of her relying on so vain a hope'. Sir Francis (who was knighted in December 1577) was obliquely referring to himself as one devoted to Elizabeth's service. He subsequently gave vent to his frustration by complaining that he had 'received many a 'repuse' [refusal]' and 'as many as are called to public service, so that all men grow weary of the matter. No one has more cause to complain than myself, being decayed rather than advanced by my long and painful service'.[62]

After returning to London, Ashby reported to Walsingham at the Secretary's house on Seething Lane, near the Tower of London. There is no record of his activities during the remainder of the year, although it seems likely that he was sent back to the Continent to manage Walsingham's network of agents in the Low Countries and Germany. He was to play an important role in an intelligence collection operation the following year.

# 5. The Queen's vacillation

Don John's annihilation of Orange's rebel army near the village of Gembloux on 31 January 1578 shattered Queen Elizabeth's complacency about the Low Countries. After news of the defeat reached Hampton Court early on the freezing morning of 4 February, the Queen sent Walsingham into London to call an emergency Privy Council meeting for early the following morning at York House, on the Strand, residence of the Lord Keeper, Sir Nicolas Bacon.

Equivocation again raised its royal head. Next day, before the London meeting began, Elizabeth changed her mind (probably because of the raw weather) and ordered her government councillors to 'repair hither' to Hampton Court instead, which only five of the total number of seventeen – including the ailing Walsingham and Burghley – were able to do. Wrapped in furs, some were rowed up the Thames amidst ice floes, others endured jolting carriages over rutted roads frozen iron hard.[1] The Privy Council met late that afternoon without Leicester and others who favoured military intervention. Debate was heated, but the Queen clung to neutrality, and 'nothing was resolved'.

Elizabeth used various excuses not to commit herself, among them rumours 'that some of the States had combined with the French, while others had secret intelligence with Don John'. Elizabeth was concerned that the States were a lost cause, not worth sending English forces or lending money to.[2] Her caution was justified, as Orange's forces were scattered after their defeat, and the Prince had fled to refuge in Holland.

Walsingham was 'very ill at ease' about the true reason for the Queen's temporising. The newly knighted Sir Francis believed unnamed persons close to Elizabeth who 'incline more to the faction of Spain than to her Majesty's safety and the quiet estate of the realm, have persuaded her that she cannot in honour do anything to help the States'. This, he said, 'has wrought such a coldness in her ... that she can hardly be moved from that Spanish persuasion'.[3] Walsingham was suffering from another bout of chronic poor health and distracted by the deteriorating political situation in Scotland, where the pro-English regent, the Earl of Morton, would soon be ousted.

As Walsingham and Leicester feared, Elizabeth's dithering led to the French offering to provide the assistance so desperately sought by Orange. Within days of the Privy Council meeting, the Duke of Anjou (referred to by the Queen and her ministers as 'Monsieur' and later by Elizabeth as her 'frog', who would begin determined courting of her the following year) told the States that 'to shew his sincerity towards them he would offer them *la charte blanche*, and to accept their conditions'. Although the Protestants in the States distrusted the French after the brutal oppression of the Huguenots, and the Catholics had no interest in become a vassal state, 'their hatred to the Spaniards is such, that rather than be forced under the yoke of their insupportable tyranny, they will run any fortune, be it never so desperate, especially that of France'.

Elizabeth was running out of time to intervene and gain a strategic advantage for England. William Davison, chief English envoy in the Netherlands, who would later become Elizabeth's scapegoat for the execution of Mary Queen of Scots, warned Walsingham that:

> ... the long suspense and uncertainty of her Majesty's resolution, considering the hope with which she had entertained them, making them reject the former offers of the Duke and neglect other means ... has begun such a jealousy and alteration in some of the greatest who were before enemies to the French side, that, fearing lest her Majesty's long delay will bring forth an absolute denial, they are now the first to persuade that course; and, indeed, some

of the wisest here expect such a desperate resolution, if her
Majesty abandon them.[4]

There was a growing rift within the Privy Council over England's response to the revolt in the Low Countries. Walsingham and Leicester led the 'war party' that shared Davison's belief that overt intervention would actually result in an earlier end to the fighting, as it would compel Philip to sit at the negotiating table rather than face a full-scale war with England instead of the proxy war with the States' forces and various mercenaries (which included thousands of English and Scottish soldiers). Sir Francis was driven by a degree of Protestant zealotry bordering on Puritanism, undoubtedly shaped by his experience in Paris. He favoured intervention as a means of defending Protestantism on the Continent, which, he believed, was a first line of defence against the powerful forces that sought to restore England to the Papist religious terror of Mary Tudor's reign.

The 'peace party' led by Burghley and The Earl of Sussex was, in a modern sense, characterised by *realpolitik*. While avowedly Protestant, they were less militantly so (and some, such as Sussex, were suspected of being sympathetic to Catholicism). Elizabeth usually followed the advice of this faction because it was closer to her personal inclination towards conservatism, insularity and parsimony. Burghley and his colleagues told the Queen that if she sent an army to the Netherlands 'under a person of quality' such as Leicester, it would 'draw her into an open war against both the Kings of Spain and France, one for the injury received, the other for jealousy of our neighbourhood' [i.e., overt English influence in a continental territory].[5]

Walsingham, Leicester and their colleagues saw war with Spain as inevitable and knew that the Queen's penny pinching rendered England's poorly equipped and trained armed forces, and therefore the realm, highly vulnerable. Appealing to the Queen's frugality, Davison articulated the interventionists' opinion, reminding her that it was imprudent to lend large sums to the States-General to 'serve themselves with other nations'

– mercenaries from France, Scotland and other foreign nations – while keeping her own subjects unemployed. Isn't it much fitter, he argued, for her to succour the States 'openly with her own men, under a person of quality to keep them in good order, than either to send a few troops by stealth, which is ill, or to assist them with money without men, which is worse?'[6]

Walsingham and Leicester viewed the world through what today would be labelled a geo-strategic prism. They believed that aiding the rebellion in the Low Countries would tie down the Spanish and buy time to prepare England's defences for the invasion that Sir Francis knew was coming. To those timid advisors who cautioned Elizabeth that her forces must be kept at home in 'apprehension of an invasion in England or Ireland', the Privy Council 'hawks' replied that 'there is no doubt that the King of Spain, so long as he has his hands full in the Low Countries, will be an enemy more terrible in opinion than in effect; and as for France, how safely she might have them occupied at home, every man acquainted with the state of that country can tell'.

As a last resort, the war party appealed to the Queen on moral grounds:

> …it will be less honourable to her Majesty, having already
> passed her promise, in performing which she will show zeal
> in the cause of her poor neighbour; resolution, steadfastness,
> and magnanimity; the contrary of which may perhaps be
> 'noted and condemned' in her, if she should do otherwise.[7]

In conclusion, Walsingham and his cohorts urged, 'if her Majesty's safety, honour, and profit may move her, she will go forward with her promise to assist these countries'.

As a halfway measure, Elizabeth reluctantly agreed to lend Casimir, the German mercenary leader, £20,000 to raise 'a larger force than hers would have been', and to guarantee £100,000 (to be raised by the States or by Casimir), and if necessary, loan Casimir another £20,000 if he could provide security for repayment.[8]

The Privy Council's hawkish faction had evidently succeeded in persuading the Queen to adopt a rhetorically harder diplomatic line towards Spain. Walsingham's intelligence reports were providing proof 'from many quarters' that Philip, the Pope and Henry III of France 'were in league to destroy her, and troops are being raised for this purpose in all countries'.[9] During her first audience with Bernardino de Mendoza, the newly appointed Spanish ambassador to England, Elizabeth curtly said that she had been told (by Walsingham) that the purpose of his coming to England 'was to plan many things to her prejudice'.[10]

Mendoza reported to Philip that he found Elizabeth and most of her ministers 'quite alienated from us, particularly those who are most important', although Burghley was allegedly opposed to helping the Netherlands rebels. While some unnamed Privy Councillors were 'well disposed' towards Spain, Walsingham was the key enemy, and Leicester's 'spirit is Walsingham'.

In mid-April 1578, Mendoza again met with the Queen, who was testy to the point of belligerence. Elizabeth declared that if her demand for a 'Perpetual Edict' (a truce) in the Netherlands was not accepted, she 'would help the States with all her strength, and this she said in a loud voice, that it might be heard by everyone present' (evidently Walsingham and other Privy Council members). The ambassador responded by saying that his master, King Philip, 'had very long arms, and that if need arose, their strength would be felt in any country upon which they were placed' – a threat that the Queen reportedly 'swallowed with rather a wry face'. Overcoming her shock at Mendoza's arrogance, Elizabeth retorted that she was well aware of the 'League' between the Pope and the kings of Spain and France that had been 'hatching' for a number of years, and that she knew very well that Don John 'was on the look-out for a kingdom that belonged to her.' Now in a rage, she loudly repeated herself, 'swearing three times in the name of God that if the perpetual edict was not granted she would help the States whilst she had a man left in England', whereupon she swept out of the audience chamber.[11]

Despite Elizabeth's threats to Mendoza – which he thought to be vain posturing – her Privy Council and England's enemies, the Spanish and French, knew she was unwilling to send an English army to the Netherlands and risk what could escalate into a major war with Spain. Mendoza was disparaging of the volatile Queen, her government and what he saw as their little island, telling Philip 'as things change here so rapidly and continually, it is difficult to keep pace with them …. These people are so fickle and wavering that they are indeed insular'.[12]

Mendoza's reports should be read with scepticism, as his sources were often court gossip and innuendo, and he invariably portrayed himself positively to his King. Nonetheless, his accounts of meetings with Elizabeth and her councillors can be checked for accuracy against other sources and are generally credible.

The Queen's vacillation continued for weeks. She found various excuses 'to stay the sending of forces', such as a report that Casimir could not be counted on to commit his cavalry (which was true to the extent that he needed English loans to pay them) and 'She understood that if her forces went into the Low Countries the French King would openly send forces to aid Don John'. This was unlikely as the French strategic objective was to counter Spanish power, and they preferred that English blood and treasure be shed in doing so rather than their own.[13]

Elizabeth grudgingly conceded that 'She will be forced to aid them [the States] rather than see them overcome by Spaniards or by French', but wished to avoid this because 'The causes are too many and too apparent for avoiding inevitable danger to herself and the Crown'. She increasingly favoured Burghley's advice to send to the Low Countries 'some persons of value, credit and wisdom to move both parties to peace, and first to a surceance of arms'.[14]

Always short-tempered, stress increased Elizabeth's irascibility. She detested warfare, considering it usually inconclusive and expensive. The Queen believed that diplomacy between her peers such as Philip and Henri was the best means of resolving conflicts. She therefore tended to agree with Burghley's advice, which was often at odds not only with Walsingham but with her favourite, Leicester.

Usually, Elizabeth could supress her volatility and observe diplomatic and courtly protocol, but her control seems to have snapped in the Spring of 1578. The French envoy Albert de Gondi was in London seeking a passport to travel through England to Scotland. He sought an audience with the Queen, who kept him waiting for ten days before summoning him to vent her hatred of Mary Queen of Scots in a tongue-lashing that reverberated around the diplomatic community.

> She told him loudly in the audience chamber that she knew
> very well he had come to disturb her country and to act in the
> favour of the worst woman in the world, whose head should
> have been cut off years ago.[15]

Unable to control his own temper, the French envoy did not deny France's support for Mary, saying that 'the Queen of Scotland was a sovereign, as she was, and a kinswoman of her own, who was a prisoner, and it was not surprising, therefore, that efforts should be made on her behalf'. In a fury, Elizabeth shouted that Mary 'would never be free as long as *she* lived, even though it cost her *her* realm and her own liberty'.[16]

Others fell victim to the Queen's wrath. Gilbert Talbot, the future Earl of Shrewsbury, was strolling under the gallery at Westminster Palace when he happened to look up to see Elizabeth 'looking out of the window, my eye was full towards her, she showed to be greatly ashamed thereof, for that she was unready, and in her night-stuff'. That evening, the Queen, notoriously self-conscious about her appearance, saw poor Talbot again as she went for a walk, gave him 'a great fillip [a sharp blow] on the forehead', and 'told the Lord Chamberlain, who was the next to her, how [Talbot] had seen her that morning, and how much ashamed thereof she was'.[17] Talbot probably counted himself fortunate not to be living in Henry VIII's time, when such a transgression could have led to losing his head rather than a mere clout on it by the monarch.

During the second week of May 1578, Walsingham went with Elizabeth on a 'short progress' away from London, which included several nights at Burghley's country house, Theobald's. While accompanying his Queen on her hunting jaunt through Middlesex, Hertfordshire and Essex, Walsingham had to juggle profound affairs of state with mundane matters, the latter including an offer from a cash-strapped French duchess to sell Elizabeth a unicorn's horn. Sir Francis rejected the offer, replying that Her Majesty was 'not ... so much affected to buying jewels as her father was'.[18]

By this time, without consulting Walsingham, the Queen had decided to send a peace mission to the Low Countries instead of an English expeditionary force. Sir Francis seemed to anticipate Elizabeth's decision, writing to Davison from Copt Hall, Essex, that '... I find some disposition in her Majesty to send out of hand some personages of quality to the States to deal effectually with them in devising some good way for their safety, wherein I see some inclination in her to use my services ...The Earl of Leicester doth labour greatly to be employed in this journey, and is not without hope to obtain it'.[19]

Leicester was to be sorely disappointed.

At Burghley's urging, Elizabeth decided to make 'every effort to tranquillise the States'.[20] She decided to send Walsingham and Lord Cobham, the Warden of the Cinque Ports, as co-ambassadors to the Low Countries, a 'finely balanced duo of Protestant and near-Catholic'.[21]

The Queen's instructions to the ambassadors were threefold:

> ... first, that you travail [toil] for a peace and good agreement
> to be made betwixt the States and Don John by all means
> possible; second, that failing of the first you learn to
> understand the state and force of the country; third, that you
> enter into consideration of M. d'Anjou, how far and in what
> matter it were meet for him to deal in favour of the States.[22]

Elizabeth hoped that Walsingham and Cobham had the international stature to orchestrate a peace between the States and their Spanish overlords, but the Prince of Orange and the people of the Netherlands had made it clear that they expected Leicester to lead the initiative. Should the peace negotiations fail, the envoys could embark on an intelligence mission to assess the mood of the population, including their religious leanings, and their military capability to continue armed resistance, with or without English monetary and military support. They were also to warn the States against allowing Anjou to bring too large a French force into the territory, fearing that the Netherlands, especially the southern provinces, would become client states of France to England's detriment.

As with many of Elizabeth's other diplomatic schemes, Walsingham thought the mission was a waste of time and effort. He was 'otherwise overladen with business' and sought excuses for not going, writing '[f]or myself, I am moved upon very great causes to seek to rid my hands from the voyage.'[23] He was dealing with pressing security issues at home, such as growing evidence that the Spanish were planning to free Mary Stuart and 'trouble the quietness of her Majesty's realm'.[24]

The Queen was unmoved by his grumbling, and on 15 June 1578, Sir Francis went to Greenwich Palace to take leave of her majesty, hopeful that if, as he expected, he and Cobham failed to make 'a good peace' then Elizabeth would accept that 'a just war' was necessary.[25] On 17 June, the ambassadors took ship from Dover on the thirteen-gun Royal galleon *Achates*, with an entourage of 'six score and odd persons in number' – half of whom were gentlemen – mountains of baggage, carts and horses for the carriages of Walsingham and Cobham.[26]

William Ashby was among the more than 120 gentlemen, intelligencers, soldiers and servants aboard the warship.

# 6. Low Countries
## reconnaissance operation

Thursday, 26 June 1578.

William Ashby reined in his horse and looked across the fields at the spires of Arras shimmering in the haze of the sweltering afternoon. He was joined by his companions, Captains Carey and Malby, while their three servants hung back, one dismounting to fetch water in a leather bucket from a nearby stream for the thirsty horses.

At thirty-one, Sir George Carey was the youngest member of the party, a veteran warrior and close kinsman of the Queen, whose father, Lord Hunsdon, was rumoured to be the son of Henry VIII on the wrong side of the blanket. Sir Nicholas Malby, six years Ashby's senior at age forty-eight, was a professional soldier-of-fortune, grizzled and scarred, as tough as a blacksmith's ox-hide apron. As a seventeen-year-old, he had started out as a victualling clerk during the siege of Guisnes in 1547, was subsequently condemned to death for counterfeiting money, and was saved from the noose by the Earl of Warwick – Leicester's elder brother – to serve under him in France before taking the Queen's shilling to slaughter rebellious Irish. When sober, Malby was an amiable companion, a fount of tall tales of adventures and conquests of castles and women. He could turn from bonhomie to murderous rage at the drop of an Italian bonnet. Malby had forgotten how many men, women and children he had butchered, and Ashby had barely restrained him a few days earlier from killing a pair of monks who had cursed the Englishmen as they passed on the dusty highway. Such a murder deep inside Papist Flanders not only could have led to savage retaliation, but would have outraged Sir Francis Walsingham, whose orders were to be as innocuous as possible on their reconnaissance mission.

Due to the summer heat, the two soldiers had left their body armour at Dunkirk and were now dressed in peascod-style jacks of plates over leather breeches and jackboots.[1] Although they wore flat caps, their open steel helmets jounced on the packhorses led by their servants, readily accessible in the event of an attack. Under a padded doublet Ashby wore a fine white linen shirt with a small starched ruff. His breeches were of fine wool, over stockings tucked into riding boots. A brimmed tall hat covered his thinning hair and shaded his eyes.

Although their orders were to avoid conflict, Ashby and his companions were acutely aware that they were in a war zone, where bands of soldiers of a dozen nationalities roved, as well as brigands with no allegiance to religion or lords. All six of the Englishmen were heavily armed with riding swords and firearms; the servants with wheellock petronels, while Ashby and the two captains had handgonnes with the latest snaphance lock mechanisms, slung from holsters across their mounts' withers. Each packhorse carried a pair of arquebuses wrapped in oiled leather sheets.

Ashby's eyes narrowed as he looked at Malby, who was quenching his thirst from a silver flask that he doubted contained water.

'We must be on our guard in Arras,' he said, pointing to their destination. 'Remember that its governor favours the French and hates us. His sport is hanging Protestants. We are riding into the lion's den'.[2]

\*\*\*\*\*\*

Walsingham's secondary instructions from Elizabeth and her government were to 'learn to understand the state and force of the country' if they failed to mediate 'a peace and good agreement … betwixt the States and Don John', yet Sir Francis decided to pursue intelligence collection in parallel with diplomatic efforts. This was premeditated disobedience of his and Cobham's orders, which had specified that 'the second part of your charge' was to be undertaken only 'If you see no likelihood of agreement'; Walsingham's entourage landed at Dunkirk on 21 June, and he lost no time in 'sending abroad' his handpicked 'certain gentlemen' on reconnaissance expeditions.[3]

There were six intelligence operatives in total, five of whom were seasoned officers of unquestioned loyalty to Walsingham. In addition to Ashby, Carey and Malby, another team comprised Henry Killigrew (a fellow Cambridge alumnus and Marian exile), and Sir Francis's kinsmen William Pelham and Guildford Walsingham, the latter a young man who was a member of the Secretary's staff.[4] Aside from the younger Walsingham, William Ashby was the only member of the group who did not have a military background. As such, he served as Walsingham's 'eyes and ears' for the crucial social and political aspects of the expedition, whereas the soldiers focused on military matters.

In an era when the average lifespan was forty-two years, and only eight percent of the population lived past seventy, it is notable that some of the men on the reconnaissance missions were old by the standards of the day. At fifty, Pelham was the eldest, while Ashby and Malby were, like Walsingham, in their forties. The mission was dangerous, and each man had been personally asked to serve by Sir Francis.

Before setting out to Antwerp from Dunkirk, Walsingham issued written orders to Ashby and his other 'gentlemen':

> Of all cities and towns that you come into which are of any
> account you shall observe the strength, both by situation and
> by fortification and by 'furniture of garrison' [armaments].
> There, and in other places you pass through, you shall inform
> yourselves of the inclination of the inhabitants to peace or
> war; What party Don John has in them and how they stand
> affected to him or to the States; How they stand affected in
> religion, and whether there is any disposition to tolerate
> both; What willingness is in them to pay the taxes already
> imposed, and how they could endure to have them continued
> or increased if the war grows in length; What union there is
> among them and what likeliness of its continuing, whether
> the countries you pass through and the towns you come

into are well-affected or not; How they are affected generally towards her Majesty, and towards France; How the gentlemen dwelling out of the towns in the country that you pass are affected.[5]

Killigrew and Guildford Walsingham made a five-day loop through the Flemish cities of Poperinge, Ypres, Armentires, Messines, Lille, Oudenarde, Tournay and Ghent, before linking again with the main entourage at Antwerp. With their two servants they travelled by wagon and were reimbursed £7 by Walsingham for their 'diet' and lodging.[6]

Ashby and his comrades took a wider circuit through what is now French Flanders, surveying St. Omer, Hesdin, Arras, Douai, Cambrai, Mons and other cities and towns. Their journey was considerably more dangerous; the loyalties and religious affiliations of the populace were sharply divided – 'some Don Janists,[7] some *bons patriotes*; the most bent on papistry'. At Arras, the warlord Seigneur de Capres, 'suspected to favour the French', had '200 harquebusiers lying about the town in villages; they be on horseback', while a captain sent by the Prince of Orange was outnumbered with only fifty mounted harquebusiers.[8]

The party's report on military dispositions and religious and political inclinations was meticulous. Many of the towns and cities were 'well watered' (moated), while others were 'deeply ditched but dry'. The two captains carefully noted the weakest parts of city walls, the number of gates, and whether the defenders were professional soldiers or militia composed of local 'burgesses'. In some places, the burgesses would not let the Englishmen inspect the fortifications out of fear that they would 'suffer much extremity before the Spanish government'.

They visited 'The Camp at Enghien' in Hainaut where the 'States' Forces' were recovering from their mauling in January. Among more than fifteen thousand foot soldiers were two regiments of Scottish mercenaries. Turning north, Ashby's team bypassed Brussels and Antwerp to locate another States' army camped outside the walls of 'Boisleduc'[9] in Brabant, where they found three thousand disgruntled Englishman and an equal number of 'Almains' (Germans).

Ashby observed that while a majority of the population, especially in southern Flanders, were for 'the most part given to papistry', the people generally were 'utterly misliking the French' and yet 'no way affected to Don John' despite their Catholicism. Even though most people were all '*bons patriotes*', they were not disposed to tolerate any other religion. He told Walsingham that '[t]hey desire and hope for English aid; we might judge their good affection toward her Majesty by the courtesy they used to us'.

Those who were supporters of the States were willing to sacrifice their goods and life for liberty from Spanish rule, but the 'Don Janists' were strong, and 'it is doubtful how the present 'state' will be gathered [united]'. Ashby found that a majority seemed to be '[r]ather affected to her Majesty than to France'. Yet, as the team got closer to the French frontier, they found greater support for French aid against the Spanish. At Mons they encountered a French ambassador 'from the Duke of Alençon' who had 'perused all the frontier towns of those parts' on a similar mission to theirs.[10]

The report of Ashby, Carey and Malby verified what Walsingham knew from other intelligence sources: the States preferred Queen Elizabeth and English assistance for their struggle, but if this was not forthcoming, they would turn to France, which was preparing for an incursion into the Low Countries. Only a week after Ashby's visit to Mons, Anjou occupied the city and made it his headquarters.[11]

The military assessment of the States army and its capabilities concluded that although it could not match the Spanish in strength, its leaders were competent, and its native soldiers were committed to resisting Philip regardless of the cost in lives or the time required to gain independence. The role of Count Casimir and his German cavalry, plus English, Scots and other mercenaries, was crucial if the Netherlanders were to defend themselves and ultimately prevail, but they could not hope to do so without significant financial support, if not military assistance, whether from England or France.

After receiving Walsingham's message of the English delegation's arrival in Antwerp, Wilson responded from London with a despairing account of the complacency gripping Elizabeth's court: 'I write nothing but that we do nothing here'. The Queen and many of her councillors seemed oblivious to lurking threats, which 'do so lull us in security that we do not fear any danger at all', to the point that most royal warships were ordered to be decommissioned and their crews discharged. Wilson prayed that 'trial be never made within this realm, either by foreign or 'domestical' people, either of the courage, constancy, or loyal faith amongst us'. Regarding the mission to the Low Countries, Wilson warned Sir Francis: 'Do your endeavour for a peace, and you shall have thanks on your return. If you tell us of the necessity of war, I tell you plainly that we cannot abide to hear of it'.[12]

Within days of their arrival, the ambassadors and their staff were pessimistic about their chances of success. Cobham wrote to Burghley that although their meetings with Orange and the States' representatives had been amicable, the Netherlanders 'did not think Don John would hearken to such a peace as was secure for them, and they found by experience that all treaties of the peace have brought them danger'.

If Walsingham replied to Wilson's bleak warning not to send bad news, it was either through secret channels or it has been lost. However, his series of letters on 5 July, the same day that Cobham wrote to Burghley, suggests that he was responding to its contents.[13] Sir Francis wrote to Lord Hunsdon, his brother-in-law Sir Walter Mildmay and other allies that he was 'tired with the writing of over many letters, and the setting down of our long negotiation here. It is hard to judge what success it will take, especially touching the matter of peace'.[14]

Walsingham seemed more concerned with the deteriorating situation in Scotland, warning Hunsdon about a Scottish envoy being sent to Elizabeth's court with a 'commission to make some overture for a contract of closer amity between the two Crowns', expressing his frustration that her Majesty 'has doubtless shown herself more backward than stood with her safety', and imploring Hunsdon to 'deal effectually with her Majesty in that behalf'.[15] Robert Bowes, English ambassador to Scotland, urged the need to 'quench the fire of sudden sedition' that was arising, adding that if unchecked, the 'dissembled quietness' in the kingdom 'may burst into a greater rage than it could at this present'.[16]

By mid-July, Walsingham and Cobham had mutually concluded that their peace mission would be fruitless. Cobham told Burghley that there was no hope that Don John would yield to the proposed terms, and '[n]ow that there is no great cause of our stay, it may please your Lordship to help us home'.[17] In a similar vein, Walsingham wrote to Burghley that he hoped 'when you are thoroughly informed that there is no further cause for our stay, you will stand so much our good lord as to further our return'. The ambassadors reported that the States were gathering their forces for continuation of the rebellion, but were handicapped 'by great want of money'.[18]

Both ambassadors warned that Orange and the States government were close to a formal alliance with the French, having 'a general disposition, rather than be under the tyranny of the Spaniards, to seek a new master; rather than 'fail masters'– the latter seemingly a slap at the English for Elizabeth's tepid support. Walsingham and Cobham were affronted that 'Monsieur' had not responded to their requests for a meeting, which was the third objective of their mission, Sir Francis complaining that they were being 'dallied with by M. d'Anjou's deputies'.[19] Although rarely in agreement, the ambassadors concurred that England must take the initiative before the French could do so.

Anjou was playing for time while conducting his own negotiations with Orange and the States. Assuring them that he only desired 'the prosperity of [their] affairs', he had levied forces 'through almost all the provinces of France, with the view of aiding you to execute your enterprise of freeing your country from the tyranny of the Spaniard, according to the request which you made to me'. Anjou assured them that his army 'will soon be here in such numbers that when joined with yours they may, with the help of God, check the insolence of the enemy'.[20]

Walsingham was a grand strategist with the rare ability to envision how the conflict in the Netherlands was pivotal to the future of not only English but European politics and religion. He deeply resented others, including his sovereign, who lacked his vision. Now he was approaching the limit of his frustration. He wrote to Burghley that because of the perception of England's 'cold and uncertain dealing' towards the States and the fact that he and Cobham had been sent 'with so slender matter' [authority] to provide material assistance, their mission served only to benefit 'Monsieur' to the detriment of England.

Sir Francis reiterated the warning that although the Netherlanders 'have no great affection to the French' they were resolved 'never to return to the Spanish obedience, and seeing no assurance of English help, standing as it does always upon doubtful terms, and being ready to alter upon every cross accident, it is to be feared they will be driven to throw themselves into the French protection'. Skirting the edge of criticism of the Queen, he said 'Her Majesty's delay in' approving the loans 'has bred a marvellous discontent at this time when for lack of payment of their soldiers their whole army might be thrown into disorder by mutiny'. Ever mindful of his country's honour, he stated that Elizabeth's uncertain policy was 'a very dishonourable and dangerous course by the alienating of these countries'.[21]

Walsingham's imploring letter and new instructions from the Privy Council, written on the same day, 18 July, crossed at sea. With Elizabeth's blessing, the Privy Council seemed agreeable to allowing the ambassadors and their staffs 'to forthwith return home again', with the caveat that if they were engaged in negotiations with Anjou and his representatives, they had the option to 'abide there some time longer for that purpose, and proceed therein to such effect as may tend to help the States against the forces of their enemies, without danger of making the French, under colour of aid, a possessor of the Low Countries'.[22]

However, Walsingham and Cobham were dismayed to read that Elizabeth had decided not only against providing direct financial assistance to the States, but to demand collateral for existing and future loans by pledging the towns of Flushing and Sluys. Furthermore, the Queen stipulated that funds raised by new loans should be used to pay off previous debts rather than to sustain the States' army. Walsingham and Cobham were ordered to 'only give them [the States] comfort by offering your own endeavours, without making any promise in her Majesty's name' – in other words, they could say or do anything on their own, unofficial, initiative to mollify the Netherlanders, but the Queen wouldn't back them up.[23] Hinting at Elizabeth's foul mood, the Councillors advised that if the ambassadors returned with written agreements to pledge the towns, 'you will be the more able to deal with her Majesty for the further enlarging of her favours'.[24]

Burghley sent a personal letter in the same packet addressed to both ambassadors, seeking to ameliorate their expected distress at the Council's instructions. He tactfully described the toxic environment at court. When Elizabeth 'perceived that the States required more money' she exploded in rage, which 'fell sharply in speech upon' him when he tried to calm her. She subsequently accused the Lord High Treasurer of 'great oversight that there was no security for the money already lent' to the States. The Queen brushed aside Burghley's calmly reasoned explanation, as he admitted '[b]ut this advice did not content her'.[25]

Elizabeth resented Walsingham for opposing her policy of pacification of the Low Countries. She ordered his and Cobham's return, no doubt to vent her wrath on Sir Francis. Although Burghley was not Walsingham's close friend and often opposed him on policy, he considered him vitally important to England's security and a loyal subject even if the Queen often seemed oblivious to his enormous contributions. The Lord Treasurer succeeded in countermanding the recall order, most likely to spare Sir Francis from a confrontation that could lead to his resignation, dismissal or worse. He warned 'how sharp her Majesty has been with some of us here as Councillors', adding that Walsingham 'was not free of some portion of her words'. Betraying his exasperation with Elizabeth, Burghley wrote:

> Yet we all most dutifully bear with her offence, not despairing
> but that however she mislikes things at one time, at another
> she will alter her sharpness, especially when she is persuaded
> that we all mean truly for her safety, though she sometimes
> will not so understand.[26]

The gist of Burghley's message was that however much Walsingham and Cobham chafed at being in the Netherlands on a mission that neither believed in, it was to their best interests to stay there until the royal temper cooled. The Lord Treasurer hinted that they could use what amounted to foreign exile productively by seeking dialogues with 'Monsieur' and Don John. Betraying an uncharacteristic peevishness at the Queen's treatment of him, Burghley ended his letter 'From Havering[27], where I am kept only to receive some chidings upon daily debate of these matters'.[28]

Other correspondents warned Walsingham that he was in grave disfavour with Elizabeth, who was fixated on loans to the States and blamed him for mismanaging negotiations. Through an intermediary, Sir Christopher Hatton[29] tried to explain to him what must have seemed the irrational 'causes of her discontent and mislike of your doings in this service'.[30]

Leicester, who arrived at Havering Palace several days after the Council dispatched its instructions to the ambassadors, was furious to learn of its contents and the insult to Walsingham. He immediately confronted Elizabeth 'to remind her how dangerous a course this resolution might take for her, how manifest a loss she would bring not only to her friends utterly by her foes (*sic*), but to make her friends her utter enemies'. To avoid the 'great discredit' not only to England but to 'her own hurt, never to have any trust again among strangers', he begged her to reconsider assistance to the States. But the Earl 'found her earnestly resolved not to change her mind'.[31]

Saying that he 'cannot leave this part of friendship undone', Leicester told Walsingham how he defended him to Elizabeth, saying that by sending a man of such stature and respect as her representative, no one could doubt that Sir Francis was 'doing anything but what was commended by her, or having such authority to deal for the advancement of this service that what you did might be held as in a manner concluded from herself'.[32]

The Queen was unmoved. Leicester wrote '[b]ut all this would little prevail howsoever the matter goes. I am not acquainted with any particular cause, but methinks by Mr Secretary Wilson some dealing there has been not good'.

Was Leicester suggesting a conspiracy within the Court? He lamented that the situation he found and Elizabeth's behaviour "makes me afraid, and the more I love her the more fearful I am to see such dangerous ways taken …. for never was there more need, nor stood this Crown ever in like peril, I mean this our only Queen whom God alone must now defend and uphold by miracle. Other ordinary helps are almost past hope'.[33]

The Spanish ambassador, Mendoza, had a mandate from Philip to subvert the English government if possible, or at the least to influence the Privy Council's 'peace' faction. Writing to Gabriel de Zayas, Philip's Secretary of State, Mendoza reminded him that the king had ordered him 'to try to gain over some of these ministers', and he 'made some steps towards doing so with the earl of Sussex, Lord Burleigh, and James Crofts, the Controller' and '… it has been necessary to give them some hopes of reward'. The ambassador boasted that Elizabeth 'gives me audience freely and I have her now in an excellent humour, thank God, whilst the Englishmen in general are not bad friends with me, as they think that I shall not do anything against them in the event of disturbance'.[34]

Evidently, some Privy Councillors accepted Spanish bribes. At the time of Elizabeth's summer progress, Mendoza told Zayas:

The Queen has been very suspicious of me hitherto, as she has been assured that I was coming to perform I know not what bad offices, but she is being undeceived and is turning her eyes now more towards his Majesty [King Philip]. The same may be said of some of her ministers, who have begun to get friendly with me, and I can assure you that, if his Majesty wishes to retain them, I see a way of doing it. It has been a good deal to bring them so far; seeing how distrustful they were ... because, as they themselves tell me, no account was made, even of their mistress, much less of them. Any money that may be given to them will not be wasted. God knows the trouble I have had in getting her and her ministers even so far as this towards the condition which you mention, as they always want to see something substantial beforehand, which is the natural character of their countrymen.[35]

In the same secret report, Mendoza wrote: 'I am dealing with one of Walsingham's officers and a great man in his office. He is entertaining my advances, and is giving me some information already, from interested motives, in the hope also that his payment will be regular if I stay here'.

A grandee, decorated military commander and competent spymaster, Mendoza had a high opinion of himself and probably embellished his intelligence activities to maintain favour in Madrid. However, in the shadow land of Elizabethan espionage he was certainly able (or thought he was able) to obtain important information from courtiers and occasionally privy councillors by greasing their palms. Conversely, Walsingham and Burghley were often happy for their operatives to feed him snippets of information or misinformation as well as trivial intelligence under the guise of becoming double-agents.[36] This probably explains Mendoza's boast that he was dealing with one of Walsingham's officers and 'a great man in his office', presumably while Sir Francis was abroad. This man's identity is unknown.

It is clear from the writings of Burghley, Leicester and others that government policymaking was in a state of chaos during the summer of 1578, and the Queen was at her most erratic and vindictive.

# 7. *Purgatory in the Low Countries*

The military and political situation in the Low Countries was deteriorating to England's disadvantage even before Walsingham and Cobham received their new instructions. The States responded to Anjou's overtures positively while still clinging to the prospect of unequivocal English support. From the earliest days of the rebellion, its leaders had been under no illusion that they could win freedom without military and financial assistance from other European powers.

Despite expressing their gratitude for what was perceived as Monsieur's 'readiness as a pledge and assurance of your desire to set us at liberty' from 'the tyranny of the Spaniards', the Netherlanders were wary of Anjou's intentions, 'being as unwilling to accept him as fearful to reject him; and which were the less dangerous is a question hard to discuss'.[1] They found excuses for delaying acceptance of his assistance. At this time, Orange and the States deputies were becoming aware that Walsingham and Cobham had no authority to approve a treaty with Anjou, or anything else for that matter. The Netherlanders were buying time in the hope that Elizabeth might intervene in their favour.[2]

Walsingham was distraught after receiving the messages describing the Queen's anger and condemnation, which he felt was cruelly unjustified. He was aggrieved 'to receive so hard measure at her majesty's hands' and – writing in the third person as he often did when responding to her personal tirades – was 'chiefly sorry to see her deal so unkindly with those that serve her faithfully'.[3] Although inured to Elizabeth's lack of appreciation and tantrums, the new charges dealt a severe emotional blow at a time when he was beset by frustration with his diplomatic mission and concerns about subverting England's national security from within. He was suffering from recurrence of his chronic illness, no doubt exacerbated by depression and stress. In a letter to Burghley, Sir Francis said that his 'few lines' were 'being written by an indisposed body, but a more indisposed mind'.[4]

The Queen ordered him to meet with Anjou to 'know as much as you may the very secret of his mind', ostensibly for strategic purposes but also to confront him with a rumour that he planned to spurn her to marry Orange's daughter.[5] Sir Francis responded that he would obey Elizabeth's order to meet Monsieur, even though he could only anticipate receiving 'some flourishes of great goodwill towards her, to make her the less suspect his intentions', after which, 'seeing no hope of doing good here, and that we begin to grow in contempt (though the people here still hope in her Majesty)', he planned to return to London, where he expected to 'receive a very hard welcome'.[6]

Some historians have claimed that Walsingham was being whimsical[7] or unreasonably paranoiac when he wrote to his wife's uncle, Thomas Randolph, 'It is given out, both there and here, that we shall be hanged at our return, so ill have we behaved ourselves here. The worst is, I hope, we shall enjoy our ordinary trial, my Lord to be tried by his peers, and myself by a jury of Middlesex. The most heinous matter they can charge us with is that we have had more regard to her Majesty's honour and safety than to her treasure'.[8] However, Sir Francis believed that his enemies were conspiring against him and gaining influence with Elizabeth to the exclusion of her most devoted counsellors, including Leicester. Having been instrumental in sending enemies of the state to the Tower – and the Executioner's Block – the Secretary knew that he was vulnerable to fabricated charges, especially because he was being kept away from the seat of power for months.

Elizabeth's mistreatment of Walsingham was legendary throughout court and diplomatic circles. She publicly called him 'a knave and a Puritan'. On one occasion she took offense with the Secretary over a petty matter, 'after which she threw a slipper at Walsingham and hit him in the face, which is not a very extraordinary thing for her to do, as she is constantly behaving in such a rude manner as this'.[9] Sir Francis told the Queen how 'infinitely grieved' he was 'to be so greatly crossed' by her, venting his bitterness that 'being at home' he was 'always subject to sundry strange jealousies, and in foreign service to displeasure'.[10]

The Queen nicknamed him her 'Moor' because of his swarthy complexion and habitual black clothing. On rare occasions, Sir Francis fought back with acerbic wit, which Elizabeth may have appreciated as he managed to keep his head and position. After an undeserved criticism, he wrote to her that 'The laws of Ethiopia my native soil are very severe against those that condemn a person unheard... to take that way of counsel that may be most for your honour and safety'.[11] Ethiopia was a generic term for the home of 'Moors' or Black Africans.

During the Queen's summer progress, the opposing Privy Council factions were united in frustration with her increasingly erratic behaviour and irresolution over England's two most important, and analogous, foreign policy issues, the Low Countries and Scotland. As a traditional ally of France, Scotland had for generations been a strategic threat, now greatly expanded by Spain's rising power and ruthless support for the Counter-Reformation. The revolt in the Low Countries served to undermine the Spanish Empire and tie down forces that could otherwise threaten England through Scotland, as proved to be the case a decade later.

The large number of Scottish mercenaries fighting on the rebel side in the Netherlands could otherwise have served in a Scottish invasion army or wreaked havoc by raiding across the Borders. Ironically, the Scottish troops were unwittingly serving as English proxies, and a portion of their pay – which was often scarce – originated from Elizabeth's treasury.

Scottish mercenary soldiers included Alexander Whishart, who received a commission as a cavalry captain in March 1596 for 'his good service at the dyke of Kowenstyen'. Following his return to Scotland, Whishart got into a fight at Leith with Sir William Balfour, another veteran of the Netherlands Wars, after Balfour 'struck him with a rod'.

After Whishart broke his sword in the altercation, he 'shot a pistolet' at Sir William but missed. Both men were imprisoned at Edinburgh Castle before being 'formally reconciled by the Privy Council' to prevent 'distraction and factions among the Scottish captains and commanders in the Low Countries'. Bartholomew Balfour, a kinsman of Sir William, served as colonel of the 'old Scots Regiment' from 1585 to 1594. Other Scottish officers included captains named Sir William Murray, John Dallachy, William Nesbit, Alexander Melville and William Waddell. The latter two officers were killed in action fighting the Spaniards.[12]

While languishing in the Low Countries, Walsingham received complaints from Burghley that the Sieur de Bacqueville, the envoy sent to Elizabeth's Court by Anjou, and the French ambassador, Michel de Castelnau, Seigneur de Mauvissière (who Burghley, with uncharacteristic wit, called 'Backvile' and 'Malvesire'), had 'more credit' [influence] than her most senior advisors.

Burghley – who had reassumed his role as domestic spymaster in Walsingham's absence – had heard that the 'errand' of the French envoys was 'to break again into the matter of marriage'. Bacqueville and another of Anjou's representatives, de Quissy, were guests of the Queen in August and September, sometimes meeting with her privately to the annoyance of Burghley and fellow counsellors. The envoys reportedly asked Elizabeth to loan Monsieur 300,000 ducats but, true to her penny-pinching nature, the Queen baulked, even though the Frenchmen asserted that King Henri would 'be surety for his brother and that certain personages would come hither shortly to represent him and his brother to treat of the marriage'.[13]

The Lord Treasurer was unhappy that Elizabeth was conducting personal diplomacy with the French without consulting him or other Council members. Burghley was concerned that the Queen was not only discussing marriage, but was also undermining Walsingham and Cobham's diplomatic efforts, telling Sir Francis that 'Monsieur says he has warrant from her Majesty, though to me unknown, to come thus hastily into the Low Countries.... to me this course is strange; what other Councillors know of it, I am not inquisitive'.[14]

Elizabeth was keeping all of her advisers in the dark. Leicester told Walsingham that regarding 'her marriage, no man can tell what to say, as yet she has "imparted with" no man, at least not with me, nor for aught I can learn with any other'.[15] At the Queen's behest, de Quissy was provided with 'horses and shipping to pass over the seas into the Low Countries with his company and servants with the Queen's Majesty's good favour' to meet with Anjou 'to know his resolution in all things'. Unlike Leicester, Burghley and Sussex perceived Monsieur as the last best hope of a royal husband for the Queen, and sought to prevent a complete breakdown in his revived marriage suit both for dynastic reasons and to keep him from assuming England's protective role in the Netherlands that she had spurned.[16]

On 1 August, the States won a battle against Don John's forces, in which English and Scottish mercenaries played a significant role. Ashby's friend Arthur Throckmorton fought in this engagement and wrote to him how 'our men brought in a booty of kine [cattle], mares and horses from the enemy; five spies were taken and put to death in our camp'.

People throughout both England and Scotland rejoiced at news of the victory; Spaniards who had boasted of their invincibility had been beaten by untested and ill-trained English and Scottish troops. Cognizant of the national mood, Elizabeth fleetingly reconsidered assistance to the Low Countries. Burghley wrote to Cobham and Walsingham that the Queen was 'greatly perplexed to think that the Low Countries may become French; and while she is in fear of this, she seems ready to hazard any expense. It is now determined that if upon your answer necessity shall induce her to send forces, Lord Leicester will come over without delay and the army shall follow'.[17] Ever mindful of Elizabeth's mercurial nature, Burghley ended by cautioning that while her message was 'at present earnestly meant, I can assure nothing, but only this, that I am uncertain of much'.[18]

An enclosed letter from the Queen chided the ambassadors for not yet meeting with Anjou, who was making himself unavailable while negotiating a treaty with the States. Not mentioning her interest in marriage with Monsieur, she told them that 'we are still more and more moved to doubt of his doings to prove very dangerous', and suggested that if they uncover evidence that Anjou was planning to 'become Lord of the countries, or, which may be as evil in the end, incline to the side of the King of Spain, the danger of either of which our Crown and State cannot endure', she would consider 10,000 to 12,000 men or advancing money to the States'.[19]

During that summer's progress, the Queen's conferences with Leicester – who was often ill – were 'seldom and slender', and his influence was eclipsed by his long-term opponent, the Earl of Sussex, who Leicester, Walsingham, Wilson and probably Burghley suspected of being an informant for Mendoza.[20] However, even Sussex, the Lord Chamberlain, felt Elizabeth's sharp tongue. During a feast in honour of Monsieur's envoys, she publicly humiliated him over a trivial matter, telling him 'to hold his tongue, that he was a great rogue, and that the more good that was done to people like him the worse they got'.[21] The Queen's self-directed marriage diplomacy was causing a widening rift with even her most sycophantic councillors.

While the Spanish doubted whether a marriage between Elizabeth and Monsieur would take place, they didn't discount it entirely. Although probably an act of disinformation designed to sabotage the match and increase the Queens' insecurity, Philip used diplomatic channels to let the English know that he would offer his second daughter Catalina as a child bride to Anjou with a rich dowry that included parts of the Netherlands.[22]

Whether or not Elizabeth was serious about sending an English army and financial aid, or merely piqued at Monsieur's possible rejection of her in favour of a ten-year-old *princesa*, she had left things too late. On 13 August, Anjou's representatives in Antwerp concluded a treaty with the States to assist them 'with men and means for their deliverance from the insupportable tyranny of the Spaniards, and from the wicked invasion of Don John and his adherents', allowing Monsieur to maintain an army of ten thousand foot and two thousand horse at his expense for three months, and thereafter with a smaller army if the war was not ended.

In consideration for his assistance, the States granted Anjou the title of 'Defender of the liberties of the Low Countries against the tyranny of the Spaniards and their adherents' together with certain more substantial advantages. Although the treaty offered an alliance with Elizabeth, it implied that she was no longer the foremost ally; England would be on an equal footing with any other princes or commonwealths that desired to join them. In a further insult to the English Queen, the States agreed that if they ever decided to have another sovereign, they would elect Anjou. Monsieur was also allowed to take any town he wished outside of the Low Countries, thereby acquiring *de jure* title to some places he had already occupied.[23]

Knowing that the treaty was signed and sealed, Anjou finally found time to meet with Walsingham.[24] Sir Francis travelled to Mons with his staff, including William Ashby, who was the only remaining member of the delegation familiar with the city.[25] While Walsingham's report on the meeting has been lost, it seems from other correspondence that it was inconclusive. Following his return to Antwerp, he and Cobham met with Orange, who, to their great chagrin, was now 'inclined to the French'.[26]

With their protracted mission on the verge of complete failure, Walsingham and Cobham requested a meeting with Don John to make a final attempt at 'pacification'. While it is doubtful that the now thoroughly cynical ambassadors, especially Walsingham, believed there was any hope of mediating peace, their approach was to use the treaty with Anjou to make 'demands' on behalf of the States from what was a spurious position of strength. It was like playing Maw, one of Elizabeth's favourite card games, with a very weak hand.

Traveling through a plague-blighted countryside to Louvain, the ambassadors and their entourage met with Don John's agent, Jean

Marmier de Gastel, the day before their formal meeting with the Governor-General. If the surviving message is to be believed, the English envoys sent Gastel to his master with extraordinary threats, although Walsingham claimed that he merely 'exhorted' the States to propose more reasonable conditions.[27] They told Gastel that despite what Don John may have heard to the contrary, Anjou had the backing of his brother, King Henri, who would unhesitatingly commit French forces. Cobham and Walsingham warned that:

> The wisest counsellors of France were of opinion that this opportunity of possessing the Low Countries was not to be neglected, being so many ways beneficial to the Crown of France.... It being apparent that France would in the end enter openly into the action, Don John would do well to consider the inconveniences that might follow; as that France, which before was equal to Spain, would become superior. 'The King of Spain shall lose the best cow of his dairy,' if it be considered what incredible sums the Low Countries yielded to him and his father towards their wars with the French King.[28]

Therefore, Don John 'would do better to grow to an accord than wilfully to hazard the loss of the Low Countries; which would open a gap for further defection and alteration in the King's dominions, where no little discontent reigned'.[29] The bold implication was that the Spanish Empire could collapse if Don John failed to agree to their terms.

To continue the gaming metaphor, the communication seems like a last desperate cast of the dice, for the Spanish knew that the French had no intention of going to war with them to conquer the Netherlands. Don John must have been bemused to read that 'the present state of his force' was 'much inferior to the enemy's and likely daily to decay by reason not only of the plague, but for lack of victuals'. While his own forces were indeed suffering from the plague, he was aware that Orange's army – although numerically superior – was decimated by desertion and sickness. The mercenary 'English soldiers ... are driven to great straits by lack of their pay',[30] and less than 1,500 men were left out of a force of over 3,400.

The Scots were 'all shot, without pikes, and so of themselves not able to make head against the enemy'. Duke Casimir had lost over a third of his 'lanceknights', and the starving German, English and Scottish soldiers had pillaged the countryside to the extent that all villages within a mile of Antwerp were abandoned. Cobham described the States' forces as 'an army of discontented persons',[31] and Casimir told Elizabeth that without her promised funding, his 'whole army will vanish to the great disadvantage of your reputation and the confusion of the common cause'.[32]

Anjou's army was small and plague-ridden, while Don John had twenty thousand experienced soldiers. Monsieur was so desperately short of funds that he was forced to ask not only Elizabeth but other princes and money-lenders for loans. There was also a suspicion by Walsingham and Davison that the French were colluding with Don John.[33]

Predictably, Don John rejected the peace proposals. As the deeply discouraged ambassadors and their shrunken entourage were preparing to leave for Antwerp, they were inexplicably asked by the Governor-General to stay for several more days at Louvain, which, as Walsingham wrote, they did 'in hope of some good fruits to follow our travail'.[34] The Englishmen were terrified of catching the pestilence; the town where they were housed by Don John was 'all infected by the plague, two or three houses only excepted, in one of which [the English] were lodged'.[35] As it soon became clear that there would be no further meetings with Don John, 'having concluded nothing, and having as it seems little hope of doing good', they returned to Antwerp.[36]

In Antwerp they felt beleaguered by hostility from their hosts, disease and lack of funds to sustain their diplomatic mission. Walsingham implored Wilson to get the Queen's permission for his and Cobham's 'return as soon as you can'. His argument that '[o]ur abode here is no less unprofitable to ourselves than chargeable to her, and therefore the less we stay, the more profit it will be both for her and us' was intended to have a double meaning, as Sir Francis was appealing to Elizabeth's miserliness as well as the damage to all their reputations which he now regularly expounded on.

******

The overriding concern of William Ashby and the English delegation was the plague. One of Cobham's servants died soon after returning from the ten-day mission to Louvain, which Ashby learned later had lost half of its population that year. He shared Walsingham's worry that the retinue was infected and doubted that they would escape without further loss.[37] Every ache and bowel upset was feared as a harbinger of vile death. Ashby and his colleagues tried various nostrums to ward off the contagion, including drinking 'nothing but Rhenish wine ... the best physic you can find for your body'.[38] The surviving servants refused to go out, so victuals were left at their door by the few vintners, bakers and butchers still in business. A miasma hung over the city from bloated corpses in streets and gutters which were torn apart by feral dogs. The Englishmen huddled in the sweltering chambers of the ancient house in which they were quartered, some praying while others, such as Ashby, numbed their terror with wine.

******

Sir Francis was deeply dispirited, revealing his bitterness and fears for England and its sovereign in letters to friends and colleagues. His peace mission had turned out to be 'illusory and vain', and Elizabeth's decision to withhold aid would 'breed ... great peril' to her and create 'great mistrust to the whole realm'; he likened its consequences to a dangerous storm drawing closer. Careful not to criticise the Queen directly, he blamed her misguided policy on 'authors of the advice' who were more interested in private profit than her well-being and England's security.[39] Walsingham lamented that 'God has closed up her heart from seeing and executing what may be her safety; which we who love her and depend on her fortune cannot think of but with grief'.[40] His sentiment was shared by Leicester, who told him he was 'sorry in my soul to see the slack determinations here, fearing they must come in the end to her Majesty's utter harm'.[41]

The Secretary was convinced that he was being undermined by his enemies at court; the 'home malice', he wrote, 'has wrought me no small grief of mind to be so unkindly dealt with.'[42] He and Cobham would 'return home the most discontented ministers that ever were employed on foreign service'. His melancholy enhanced by the spectre of the plague, Walsingham told Thomas Heneage that if 'God send me well to return … I will hereafter take my leave of foreign service'.[43] He signed his correspondence 'with a weary hand and a wounded mind'.[44]

Her Majesty was not ready to allow Walsingham to return. He was instructed to wait in the event that Monsieur might wish to consult him about reviving his half-hearted marriage suit, which had become Elizabeth's preoccupation to the neglect of important foreign and domestic issues. Burghley was exasperated, telling Walsingham '[t]his marriage matter occupies heads here, so that it is the more hardly digested, because it is both earnestly followed and readily heard',[45] to which Sir Francis responded, '[h]e is worthy to be deceived who will trust to French promises'.[46]

Walsingham resented having to tarry at the whim of Anjou amidst the deadly epidemic. He told Burghley 'I am sorry to stay here to entertain a cause from which by former experience I have so little hope of good result', but he and Cobham remained at Antwerp until 25 September, fretting at the expenses while fruitlessly waiting for a summons from Monsieur which never came.[47] The ambassadors and their staff returned to a similarly plague-ravaged London on 7 October 1578.

There was rejoicing at the Court when news came of Don John's death on 1 October, probably from the plague, but reported as 'partly as some think of very grief and melancholy, partly of a disease they call *les brogues*[48] by which he was extremely tormented, but chiefly, as it is given out, of the French sickness, whereof in the opening [autopsy] he was found to be inwardly wasted and consumed'.[49] Walsingham was not among those who celebrated. Although Don John was an enemy, Sir Francis had developed a rare respect for him despite their brief acquaintance. He told Burghley that he 'never saw a gentleman for personage, spirit, wit, and entertainment comparable unto him. If pride do not overthrow him, he is like to prove a great personage'.[50]

After his return to court, Walsingham was not hung; nor did he 'convey [himself] off from the stage ... to become a looker on'.[51] He was, however, subdued from what he felt was his unfair chastisement while abroad, the machinations of his enemies at court, and consuming frustration with the Queen's marriage negotiations while neglecting vital state affairs. He told Hatton:

> I would to God her Majesty forbear entertaining any longer
> her marriage matter. No one thing hath procured her so
> much hatred abroad as these wooing matters, for that it is
> conceived that she dallieth therein.[52]

The Secretary's bitter experience proved to be a sobering lesson for William Ashby, who experienced similar repudiation during his own service as England's ambassador to Scotland a decade later. In the interim, the Netherlands' struggle for independence from Spain continued haphazardly, punctuated by savage bloodlettings.

# 8. Brigands on the Rhine

Saturday, 20 August 1580

They came at night, ten or a dozen marauders armed with snaphance pistols and swords, some so drunk on cheap Rhenish that a pair fell into the river during the attack. But William Ashby and Arthur Throckmorton were ready for them. [1]

The Dutch-built Aak had been slowly voyaging up the Rhine hauled by teams of dray horses plodding along the tow path. Before leaving Nijmegen, Ashby had received intelligence that King Philip was offering bounties to freebooters to take English gentlemen hostage. The Aak's captain, a grizzled Dutchman who wore his hatred of Spaniards like a black cloak, had seen a band of shifty-eyed ruffians in a gasthaus the previous night. The same group had been observed throughout the day, riding spavined horses and following the boat along the river road at a leisurely pace.

Ashby was aware that they were outnumbered, just two Englishmen and three Dutch crewmen who had an ancient sword, a pike and a brace of harquebuses loaded with bird shot. But Ashby and Throckmorton had been trained in swordplay since childhood and were each armed with rapiers and peverels. Ashby knew that their advantage lay in the fact that the attackers' aim was to take them alive – there would be no Spanish escudos for dead Englishmen.

The attack was easily repelled. The brigands paused on the riverbank, trying to gauge the distance to leap to the boat's deck. On Ashby's order, the crewmen and Throckmorton fired into the men, scattering them, while their comrades in the river struggled ashore in panic as Ashby and Throckmorton slashed at their heads and shoulders with their swords. As Ashby later told Walsingham, 'it was our good haps to repulse them, and so, by God's help, avoided their fingers'.[2]

\*\*\*\*\*\*

The best source of primary information about William Ashby's personal life and professional activities can be found in the diaries kept by Arthur Throckmorton from 1578 to 1595, which have been aptly called 'the fullest ... most extensive and revealing of all Elizabethan diaries that remain'.[3]

Despite the twenty-year difference in their ages, Throckmorton (who was probably born in 1556) was one of Ashby's closest friends and confidants. Described as an 'impulsive and hot-blooded youth', he was another of Walsingham's protégés, who subsequently became a courtier, married one of the Queen's ladies-in-waiting, and whose sister secretly wed Sir Walter Raleigh. As with most Midlands gentry, the Ashbys and Throckmortons were distantly related.[4]

In May 1579, Throckmorton recorded that Ashby was to go to France with Henry Middlemore, Groom of the Queen's Privy Chamber, who served as a courier and emissary.[5] During this period, Ashby worked for Walsingham as a freelance intelligencer, spending his time between missions in gentlemanly pursuits. After returning from France, he was in Leicestershire during the summer of 1579, staying at Loseby and often visiting Beaumanor, the nearby home of Throckmorton's mother.

The following year, Ashby and Throckmorton left London in late July on a lengthy continental tour which combined pleasure with intelligence collection. The wealthy younger man covered all the expenses, letting the relatively penurious Ashby manage transportation, lodging and meals. Careful notes were made, and reported to Walsingham, of military capabilities and defences as well as political and religious affiliations. For example, the island of Walcheron was said to be able to 'set forty ships of war to sea and levy twenty thousand men for service', was soundly Protestant, and governed by the Prince of Orange, whereas Dusseldorf was 'wholly Romish' with a garrison of one hundred men-at-arms. Traveling by boat, wagons and rented post-horses, they meandered through places that would soon be revisited by Ashby. Throckmorton kept meticulous accounts of their expenditures: fifteen meals in Cologne cost eighteen rix-pennies, and their beds at the hostelry of the 'Holy Ghost' cost twenty-four of the same coins. They were returning to Cologne from Dusseldorf when attacked by the brigands. After fending off the assault, both men bought large horse pistols to augment their smaller petronels.[6]

Now joined by Throckmorton's servant, who had been sent to Nijmegen to get their baggage, they progressed up the Rhine through Bonn, Andernach and Coblenz, stopping in Frankfurt for the autumn fair, where Arthur bought books, including a German-Latin-French dictionary which he shared with William. Ashby used the large stock of paper brought in their baggage to write to Walsingham, reporting that Frankfurt was 'a free town of the Emperor's, standing in champion country, with liberties a mile about, the town ditch [moat] forty paces broad with plenty of fish, and with its double walls'.[7]

In Nuremberg they lingered for several weeks, having met with a group of other Englishmen of Arthur's generation, including Robert Sidney, who would visit Ashby in Edinburgh with Throckmorton eight years later, and the future diplomat Henry Neville. In November, Throckmorton and several of his newfound companions moved to Prague, where they decided to winter. Ashby remained in Nuremberg for another two weeks, probably on Walsingham's orders, before joining Arthur in Prague. The Englishmen boarded with 'Signor Scipioni of Ferrara ... paying 20 dollars a month' between them.

Throckmorton recorded that at the end of November Ashby wrote to Walsingham railing against Mary Queen of Scots, and was corresponding with Giacopo Castelvetro,[8] Horatio Palavicino and 'Dr. Willes, English envoy to Venice'. Ashby's correspondence is evidence that he was communicating with – as well as recruiting and managing – other members of Walsingham's international intelligence network. Castelvetro was an Italian exile who had begun employment in Edinburgh as Italian tutor to King James a few months earlier.[9] He served

as a spy within the Scottish court for four years and subsequently became
a Continental courier for Walsingham and Burghley. Ashby probably
became acquainted with him in London, and was to meet him again in
Scotland in 1583.[10]

Horatio Palavicino was a Genoese merchant and banker who was
a 'bagman' for Walsingham, distributing funds to intelligencers in
Northern France. He was 'a collector of political intelligence' from
'numerous commercial correspondents' and was 'often employed ... to
furnish intelligence from abroad'. Palavicino provided information to
Walsingham about Sir Edward Stafford's treasonous dealings with the
Spanish.[11]

Ashby and Throckmorton quarrelled over William's belief, shared with
Walsingham, that Mary Stuart should be executed, which was opposed
by Arthur. In December, Throckmorton noted that he wrote Ashby 'a
letter of Re : con : sil : ly: and received another of him'. Despite the harsh
winter weather, Ashby travelled between the Continent and London at
least twice during the early months of 1581. He carried letters between
Sir Francis and the resident ambassador to France, Henry Brooke (who
preferred to be known as 'Henry Cobham'), a younger brother of Lord
Cobham, co-ambassador on the blighted peace mission to the Low
Countries two and a half years earlier. The messages were innocuous,
relating to ongoing negotiations for the Queen's marriage to Anjou
(which neither the English nor the French governments seem to have
taken seriously) and other trifling diplomatic intelligence.[12]

After a mission to Paris in March, Ashby returned to the lodgings he
shared with Throckmorton in Prague, but further squabbling ensued. On
18 March 1581, Arthur wrote that 'W.A. jarred', a week later William
was 'sick', and on 27 March the Diary states 'W.A., A.T., unconstant, not
secret, quarrelsome, flatterer, envious, etc'.[13]

Seen from the perspective of modern eyes, the closeness of Ashby and
Throckmorton might suggest a homosexual relationship, with occasional
lovers' tiffs. But there is nothing in the diary or their correspondence to

support this. On the contrary, Throckmorton records his assignations, including a passionate affair in Florence with a woman he referred to as '*la camilla capraia*' [Camilla the goatherd]. In the sixteenth century, men preferred each other's company for travel and cultural pursuits, and enjoyed loving, non-sexual friendships. Throckmorton often mentions 'laying with' various male relatives and friends, meaning that they shared a bed. It was commonplace for travellers to sleep with multiple strangers at inns. For example, the Great Bed of Ware could accommodate as many as twelve people at once.[14]

Throughout the winter, both men punctuated intelligence gathering about Jesuits, the Emperor Rudolf and foreign envoys with reading and sampling local cuisine and wine. Throckmorton was an avid collector of books, which were generally unaffordable to Ashby. Arthur purchased a three-volume set of Suetonius's *Lives of the Emperors*, Vitruvius' *on Architecture*, and works by Euclid, Piccolimini and Horace, all of which were devoured by William.

In early April, Throckmorton left for Vienna, while Ashby remained in Prague for several more weeks before returning to London. Their friendship had been restored, and Throckmorton continued to correspond with Ashby during the remainder of William's life.

Ashby may have accompanied Walsingham to France for nearly two months from July to September 1581 in another of a series of foreign diplomatic missions which the Secretary considered wasted time and effort. Elizabeth sent Sir Francis 'over the seas' to negotiate an offensive/defensive Anglo-French league while trying to keep the nearly extinguished flame of the royal marriage alight. However, the French wanted the marriage agreed before a treaty, which was contrary to Walsingham's instructions. Burghley was advised that 'we have nothing to do here, the league without marriage being now utterly broken off',[15] and the Secretary told another colleague that he would 'labour by all the means I can to break the journey off. You yourself can tell how hardly I was used in my last voyage, and as this is a matter of more danger than that, I have cause to fear to be served with harder measure than I was'.[16] He returned to London having once again failed in what he had considered to be a futile mission even before it began and, fearing the wrath of the Queen, begged Burghley to 'stand to his defence'.[17]

Ashby's status within the diplomatic and intelligence apparatus changed in 1582. Since the inception of his service for Walsingham at least a decade earlier, his role had been amorphous, inhabiting what has been described as 'the grey area between diplomat, agent, intelligencer and spy'.[18] In June, Sir Francis sent him to Augsburg to gather intelligence during the Imperial Diet, the *Reichstag* or deliberative body of the Holy Roman Empire, presided over by Emperor Rudolf II and attended by the Germanic empire's leading nobles.

As a result both of his knowledge of northern Europe and connections at Elizabeth's court, William Ashby's role had been upgraded from a courier and agent who knew Walsingham's 'mind and pleasure' to that of an accredited diplomat. During the Diet's two-months convocation, Ashby sent Sir Francis a series of detailed reports, ranging from an analysis of the Empire's policy towards 'the Turk', which Ashby called 'a mighty and puissant enemy of theirs and all Christendom', to descriptions of imperial banquets, where he said there 'was plenty of dainty dishes, plate curiously wrought, and heavenly music during the feast, but no drinking *alla tudesca*' [in the German manner].[19]

His letters to Walsingham contain pithy observations about his hosts which would seem familiar to later diplomats. Ashby warned that the Hapsburgs, due to 'hatred to the French, as their ancient enemies and competitors', would 'favour the cause of Spain', but could be relied on to support whichever ally offered the most money, 'for the German is indifferent on what side it falleth, readiest to help the party that is best able to entertain him, and mercenary in all causes without respect of religion'.[20] The German states were hostile to the French from concern that they 'should grow so great, for that in time they will be unquiet neighbours, as always, they say, it hath been the humour of that nation'.[21]

After the Imperial Diet concluded, Ashby reported that the German Electors had decided not to intervene in the Low Countries 'because it was not material to them whether the French or the Spanish enjoyed those provinces, so as the homage and duty to the Empire were satisfied'. This was a blow to English diplomacy, as the Privy Council had hoped that the German Protestant princes and dukes would materially support the Netherlanders. The only positive intelligence was 'that the Spanish government had been more troublesome and prejudicial to Germany than the French', therefore hope remained that a wedge could be driven between Spanish and Germans.[22]

At the beginning of August, Ashby received a letter from Walsingham asking him to negotiate the release of Daniel Rogers, an abducted Anglo-Flemish diplomat. Rogers, a former student of Johannes Sturmius, had been on Walsingham's staff in the Paris embassy.[23] Like his colleague Ashby, he was engaged in coordinating a Protestant League and played an important role in diplomatic and intelligence operations in the Netherlands. In 1577 Rogers had forwarded secret information to Walsingham about a Spanish plot to invade England using the subterfuge of seeking haven from a storm. Rogers was described as 'an evil tool' by the Spanish, who considered him a particularly troublesome enemy agent.[24]

In October 1580, while *en route* to a meeting in Nuremburg with the Imperial Diet and Emperor Rudolf, Rogers was captured by irregular forces commanded by 'Colonel Schenk', a warlord in the pay of the Spanish who was described as what in modern terms would be a psychopath 'led by such furies'.[25] Despite showing his 'passport, signed and sealed with the Queen's hand and seal', Rogers was taken to Schenck's castle, which was 'full of freebooters, and a company of rakehells', where he was 'searched to the very skin, and whatever money, writing, or thing of value we had, they took'. Rogers was carrying confidential letters with the Queen's seal, which, along with letters from the Prince of Orange, Schenck opened 'in the presence of soldiers and rash heads'. Schenck accused him of being sent 'to levy new forces for use against the King' [Philip], and threatened to send him to the rack if he refused to confess about 'a league which her Majesty had made with the Protestants of Germany'.[26] Ever the mercenary, Schenck probably thought he could extract information from Rogers to sell to Alexander Farnese, Duke of Parma and nephew of King Philip, who had succeeded Don John as Governor-General of the Netherlands in 1578.

When Rogers held firm, Schenck bade him 'to be of good cheer; he would do no hurt to my body, but would make the Queen ransom me with 5,000 crowns'. No ransom was forthcoming, and although Rogers was not tortured, he was kept under close and humiliating confinement and 'threatened to be sent into Spain'. He described how 'the men that took me played at dice for all that I had. Some had my chain, some my money, some my rings, and my apparel was distributed among them. What they have done with my five horses, pistols, and petronels, swords, &c., I cannot tell. Nor have they left me one farthing in my purse'. Three of his companions, including his brother, were kept in fetters, and a fourth died of a gunshot wound suffered during their capture. In his letter begging Elizabeth to effect his release, Rogers told Walsingham that 'were it not that my keeper were drunk at this time with Rhenish' he would have been unable to write.[27]

The kidnapping escalated to a major diplomatic row. At Walsingham's urging, Elizabeth wrote to Parma. The Duke did not respond, but ordered the Baron van Anholt and Schenck, one of whom was holding Rogers captive (even the Duke was unsure about his whereabouts), in King Philip's name to free the English diplomat.

Sir Francis and Leicester twice voted for a motion before the Privy Council to arrest Mendoza and imprison him in the Tower until Rogers was released. Burghley opposed the motion, arguing that there was great diplomatic and social inequality between the Spanish ambassador and Rogers, as Mendoza was an accredited resident ambassador (and a nobleman), whereas Rogers was 'only a servant of the Queen sent with letters'.[28] Burghley prevailed, but Walsingham continued his efforts.

Although Rogers' capture was originally mischief-making by the Spanish, it had now damaged diplomatic relations to the point that Philip and Parma were genuinely attempting to free him. Schenck, however, cared nothing for great power diplomacy. Rogers reported that Schenck, in a rage, told him that 'if the Prince of Parma should command me to be set at liberty, rather than I should get away free, he would thrust me through ... his meaning was but to have money for my ransom'.[29]

Ashby replied to Walsingham's letter that his 'diligence shall not be wanting' in trying to free Rogers, 'being desirous to see him delivered out of this purgatory, which the poor gentleman hath suffered so long'. He told Sir Francis that he would seek out Rogers on his way back to England later that month, and hoped that he would obtain his release so that they could 'cross the seas together'. Ashby recounted his attempted abduction 'in the same country' less than a month before Rogers' capture, describing how he and Throckmorton repulsed the attackers.[30]

Ashby spent the next few weeks conferring with his counterpart in Augsburg, George Gilpin, a seasoned diplomat primarily involved in negotiations regarding the Low Countries. Gilpin was, unlike Ashby, a salaried English government agent, who had been operating for several years under cover as Secretary of the Merchant Adventurers.[31] The two agents decided to use their extensive network of diplomatic and intelligence contacts to accomplish the task of freeing Rogers, enlisting the venerable Johannes Sturmius to write to various royal commissioners. They were able to procure letters from the Emperor Rudolph to Parma, and to William, Duke of Cleves,[32] the latter because the abduction had occurred within his dominion. The Englishmen were disappointed with the Emperor's letters, which they considered 'not so effectual as was desired'.[33]

Traveling by boat along the Rhine by way of Cologne, Ashby went to the Duke of Cleves' summer court at Hambach Castle, a massive fortress in the midst of a sweet chestnut forest on a mountain overlooking the river, where 'he delivered to the Duke the Emperor's letter, requesting in his Majesty's name that he would vouchsafe his good favour and help for the delivery of the gentleman taken from Schenck'.[34] He was courteously received by Duke William, who told him that he would do anything in his power to help because of his affection for Queen Elizabeth. The Duke was an important member of the Protestant League and was evidently acquainted with Ashby from his work on Walsingham and Leicester's behalf in this regard.

Despite the annulment of his sister's marriage to King Henry VIII over forty years previously, Duke William was friendly towards England. He sent Ashby with a letter to his chancellor at Schwanenburg Castle in Cleves, 'recommending' (Ashby's word) that he assist according to the obtuse text of the Emperor's letter. By now, Ashby was aware of the tangled web of politics and venality that ensnared Rogers, and therefore had 'small hope that any good will be done in this cause'.[35]

The political and military situation in the Low Countries was chaotic, with only nominal imperial and ducal jurisdiction over dozens of lawless petty barons and warlords whose allegiances changed more often than their under-breeches and hose. Roger's captor Schenck had fought under William of Orange before joining the Spanish Army of Flanders, and a few years later returned to the banner of the Dutch Republic. Although Orange claimed political and military rule over all seventeen provinces, he effectively controlled only two.[36]

Ever mindful of the attack that he had fought off and the one that cost Rogers his freedom, Ashby set sail on the Rhine again with the hope that 'with God's help [to] make such haste as this dangerous passage will give me leave; for what betwixt the States and the Malcontents these parts were never more dangerous to pass'.[37] The Malcontents (among whose leaders was the young Baron van Anholt) were predominately Catholic soldiers employed by the States who mutinied due to lack of pay, and who then ostensibly went to war against Calvinist Ghent. In reality, many became freebooters, roaming the countryside looting, raping and taking hostage anyone who appeared ransomable. When Spanish finances improved enough to pay them, the Malcontents were absorbed into Parma's forces as he launched the reconquest of Flanders and Brabant. However, their depredations continued as they swept ahead of the main Spanish army.[38]

Ashby was unsuccessful in freeing Rogers; however, the captive diplomat praised him for persuading the Duke of Cleaves to arrest and execute Andreas Kirckhout, one of Schenck's lieutenants. Kirckhout 'was beheaded in the marketplace at Cleves, and afterwards his head and body put upon a wheel' outside the town, an execution meant more to appease Queen Elizabeth than to punish the miscreant.[39] Schenck would have suffered a similar fate if he had not been imprisoned and held for ransom in another nobleman's castle, while the Baron van Anholt had recently died from wounds received at the Siege of Lochem.

Subsequently replying to Elizabeth's letters (drafted by Walsingham), the frustrated Duke told her sharply that she must 'clearly understand that Rogers was captured by robbers, not by reason of any fault in us or ours, but by his own carelessness and temerity; because he heedlessly scorned the present danger (the army of the Spanish King being in our neighbourhood and his soldiers running here and there in our dominions)'.[40]

Rogers, 'the poor gentleman, fast bound with chains', was held in a castle by 'a very tyrant' for four years until the English government paid the local equivalent of £200 for his release in October 1584.[41] Schenck met a fitting end: while leading an assault on Nijmegen, his force was repulsed, he leapt into the Waal river to escape, and drowned. When his bloated body was found a few days later, they decapitated the head and put it on a pike, quartered the body and exhibited it above the city's four gates.[42]

Although Ashby's immediate mission was to attempt to negotiate the release of Rogers, his meetings at Hambach and Cleaves were detours on his journey to London carrying letters from Emperor Rudolf to Queen

Elizabeth.[43] This correspondence concerned growing hostility between merchants of the Hanseatic League, who complained that the English were monopolising what had heretofore been free trade, and the Merchant Adventurers, who sought greater access to the German markets.[44] The Hanseatic League (called 'Hanse' in English diplomatic correspondence) was a commercial and defensive confederation of merchant guilds and market towns in northern Europe that had once dominated Baltic trade but was in decline in the 1580s. Ashby continued to carry letters between Elizabeth and Rudolf through the first half of the following year, 1583.

William Ashby's personal circumstances also changed in the early 1580s. He no longer needed to lodge like a student at the Inner Temple, having taken up residence in the village of Clerkenwell, a mile north of the Thames. His house had been recently built on the eastern part of the south side of Clerkenwell Green, the choicest part of the village favoured by 'persons of quality'. The house was of medium size, narrow-fronted and timber-framed with a plastered front. Its three floors, reached by a central staircase, had two rooms per level, each with the luxury of a fireplace.[45] Sheep grazed on the Green, and were welcomed, unlike the worn-out horses, hobbled without water, champing a last turf meal while waiting their turn for the knackers' yards behind Cowcross Street.[46]

******

Accompanied by his manservant, Peter Haye, Ashby would walk down Turnbull[47] and Cowcross Streets to the Holborne Bridge, then along the footpath bordering the noxious stream misnamed the Fleet River. Like most Londoners, they ignored the decomposing carcasses of cats, dogs and human infants, as well as the occasional adult human corpses. Fending off the beggars infesting the wharves near the former monastic house of the Black Friars, Ashby would hail a wherry and pay thruppence to carry him to Walsingham's country house, Barn Elms, up the river at Barnes, Surrey, or downriver under the houses clustered on London Bridge to the pool of London to take ship to Antwerp or Calais.[48]

\*\*\*\*\*\*

The journey was perilous at any time of day or night. After the dissolution
of Clarken Well's Augustinian priory under good King Henry nearly half a
century earlier, the area south of the Green had become a warren of poverty,
crime and prostitution. Ashby kept a hand on the hilt of his rapier, and Haye
carried a cudgel in addition to a dagger as they passed The Cock on the east
side of Turnbull Street, eyed by masterless men, cutpurses and bleary doxies
hovering outside the inn. Clarken Well was within the parish of St. Sepulchre,
which Ashby knew was part of a wider district known as the 'Rules of Fleet',
where Fleet Prison debtors could get lodgings. Their desperate circumstances
augmented the area's degeneracy, yet Ashby habitually wondered how these
wretched men managed to come up with a farthing or two for the price of
a cockfight, a bear-baiting or a flagon of ale. He knew how the strumpets
earned their tuppence.

Sometimes when Ashby passed the great hall of the old Dominican
monastery named after the friars' black robes, he would pause to listen to the
angelic voices of the boys of the Chapel Royal as they practiced or performed
there. He had enjoyed the revels at Gray's Inn whilst a student of laws, and
on rare occasions when he was not abroad, he paid four pence to watch the
plays staged in the cavernous hall by the child choristers. Ashby hoped that
his duties for Walsingham would not keep him away from London during the
coming month, when he hoped to see the new comedic play Campaspe by
John Lyly, which was to be performed by his troupe of boy actors called The
Children of Paul´s. He had taken Lyly's book, *Euphues, or the Anatomy of Wit,*
with him to the Imperial Diet in the summer of '82, and after reading it had
agreed with the author that it was 'Very pleasant for all Gentlemen to read,
and most necessary to remember'.[49]

Ashby had considered giving the book to Walsingham, who had a library
surpassing most noblemen's, but decided that the austere Sir Francis would
consider the work frivolous. He always secretly smiled when remembering
the Secretary's remark that he would rather stay in England 'with a piece of

bread and cheese' than be based in France with 'all their best [delicacies] and entertainments', a sentiment with which Ashby privately disagreed.[50]

★★★★★★

Evidently, Ashby's financial situation changed around the same time that his status within Her Majesty's diplomatic and secret intelligence services improved. Whether he had a new source of income or lived off the tithes from properties in Leicestershire and Yorkshire, as well as the former Bishop of Lincoln's manor, is unknown. Like many other gentlemen, including Walsingham, he borrowed money from lenders in London and from his Ashby and Berkeley relatives.

*Part Three*
*Scotland*

# 9. Anglo-Scottish animosity

By mid-summer 1582, relations between England and Scotland were at a nadir. Scotland was perceived by most English, including Elizabeth and her Privy Council, as barbarous and ungovernable.[1] Ashby's contemporary the highly influential English author William Camden wrote that the Scots:

> ... drank the bloud [blood] out of wounds of the slain: they establish themselves, by drinking one anothers bloud [blood] and suppose the great number of slaughters they commit, the more honour they winne [win] and so did the Scythians in old time. To this we adde [add] that these wild Scots, like as the Scythians, had for their principall weapons, bowes and arrows.[2]

While Camden's commentary was gross anti-Scottish propaganda, the kingdom was riven by wild, murderous lairds constantly changing fealty for political and financial gain. The authority of James VI was constantly undermined, the penniless yet extravagant teenage King arguably a mere figurehead, literally seduced by a succession of unscrupulous and corrupt noblemen. Although Scotland had undergone a Protestant Reformation a generation earlier, by the early 1580s religious affiliation was secondary to domestic politics, much to the frustration of the three great powers vying for strategic influence – England, France and Spain.

Generally, the Scots equally despised the English as their 'auld enemies'. Over the past three centuries, English armies had invaded Scotland numerous times, including the pillaging and burning of Edinburgh and nearby villages in 1544, which Scots remembered with deep animosity. In April 1581, a proclamation was made across Scotland 'that no Scottish man have any dealing or intercourse with any Englishman, and that no

Scottish man or woman bring any victuals to Berwick on pain of death',
and that any Englishman entering into Scotland was to be arrested and
imprisoned.[3] The Queen's cousin, Henry Carey, first Baron Hunsdon,
commander of the English border forces, recommended to the Privy
Council that in retaliation a 'like proclamation' should be made along the
Borders and throughout England.[4]

Robert Bowes, Elizabeth's resident envoy to Scotland from 1577 to 1583
(who preferred to be safely based across the border at the heavily fortified
frontier town of Berwick), reported that 'It is now thought as dangerous
in Scotland to confer with an Englishman, as to rub on the infected with
the plague, and most men openly flee the English company...'.[5]

Despite their contempt, Elizabeth and her government recognised
Scotland's vital geo-strategic importance, representing threats as potential
military bases for enemies such as France and Spain, as well as Counter-
Reformation forces committed to replacing Elizabeth with the Catholic
claimant Mary Stuart. Walsingham called Scotland 'the postern-gate to
any mischief or peril that may befall to this Realm'.[6]

English policy towards Scotland was based on five policy objectives:
- Keep James VI under Queen Elizabeth's influence by any means
necessary;
- Counteract and neutralise the influence of France and Spain; ·
- Weaken the King's natural affection for his mother;
- Dampen the Scots' popular hostility for their queen's imprisonment;
- Unite and secure the fractious nobility into a stable, pro-English
confederation.

England's enemies also secretly viewed the Scots with contempt; the
Spanish, who were committed to restoring the British Isles to dogmatic
Catholicism, thought that Scottish Papists lacked appropriate religious
zeal. Mendoza told Philip that 'small trust can be placed in Scotsmen,
who moreover are people of notoriously weak faith'.[7]

Elizabeth's Privy Council was increasingly concerned about the
dominant influence of Esmé Stuart, the half-French, Catholic, Sieur

d'Aubigny, who after meeting the thirteen-year-old James in 1579 '...
quickly became master of his grace's person ... [and] laboured to alienate
the King's mind from the amity of England, and to draw him to that
which should proceed from the Papists in France.'[8] In March 1580, the
King forced his cousin Robert Stuart, Earl of Lennox, to relinquish his
title, which was promptly awarded to d'Aubigny. In the same year, the
formal establishment of a royal household marked the beginning of
fiscal recklessness and mounting debts. The new Earl swiftly consolidated
control over James and assumed an active role in government as Lord
Great Chamberlain and First Gentleman of the Bedchamber, roles which
he created for himself with the King's blessing.[9]

D'Aubigny, the newly created Earl of Lennox, immediately began
plotting against the pro-English Earl of Morton, the last Regent, whom
he saw as an impediment to his growing authority despite the Earl's
retirement. After Morton's execution on 2 June 1581, allegedly for
participating in the murder of the King's father, Lord Darnley, the English
saw their hope of controlling James slipping away.[10]

Upon hearing of Morton's beheading, Elizabeth was initially furious
with James, reportedly overheard musing, 'That false Scotch urchin, for
whom I have done so much! to say to Morton the night before he arrested
him, "Father, no one else but you has reared me, and I will therefore
defend you from your enemies", and then after this, the next day, to order
him to be arrested, and his head smitten off! What can be expected from
the double dealing of such an urchin as this?'[11] However, the Queen soon
reverted to her habitual temporising about James and Scottish policy.

James had little choice in acceding to Morton's execution. He was not
yet fifteen years old and in thrall to Lennox and other enemies of the
Regent. Even as a young teenager, James was aware that his survival was
at stake. He had no close family to turn to, his reprobate father, Lord
Darnley, having been murdered when he was an infant, and he never
knew his mother. His early life contrasted sharply with William Ashby's,
who seems to have had a happy and even indulgent childhood plus a

strong and supportive family network even after his parents' death. James had been raised under the harshly Protestant tutelage of the intellectual George Buchanan, who routinely beat James yet succeeded in inspiring an enduring passion for literature and learning. While his classical education was as comprehensive as Ashby's, James did not have the benefit of attending university to learn social skills and develop crucial personal relationships. As a result, he stood isolated from his own council, some of whom, such as John Maitland, the Lord Chancellor, attended the University of St Andrews.

Hunsdon, Elizabeth's cousin, expressed his pessimistic feelings to Walsingham: 'What hope her majesty may have that the King of Scots in any respect will be ruled by her so long as this Council is about him, he leaves to wiser than himself, but for his part he looks not for it'.[12] He subsequently warned Sir Francis that Elizabeth would find that James's 'fair speeches and promises will fall out to be plain dissimulation', that any amicable overtures from the King and Lennox would prove to be nothing but 'French promises and Scottish false practices', and that 'no trust [could] be had to any of them, but to serve their own purposes'. In Hunsdon's prejudiced opinion: '... her majesty will do best to let them alone with their own doings, who shortly will devour one another, and to cause as little favour to be shown in any respect to any of that nation in any part of England as may be, and to be utterly forbidden to have any traffic in England, which is the only way to bring down their pride and insolency'.[13]

Although Lennox staged a public display of conversion to the Church of Scotland, Walsingham's agents provided intelligence that the Duke was, if not a crypto-Catholic, actively conspiring with the French, the Spanish and Papist Scottish lairds. Lennox was reported to have drawn 'the King to carnal lust'[14] (sodomy was a mortal sin and punishable by death) and to be facilitating the overthrow of the Protestant religion 'by seeking to seduce the King by filling his ears with wicked devices and speeches and withdrawing his residence to places frequented by Papists, full of traitorous persons to his estate, and overflowing with whoredom and all kinds of insolences'.[15] This opinion was generally shared by the conservative Kirk and by the Protestant lairds.

After news of the April 1581 edict barring Englishmen from Scotland was received in London, the Privy Council – at Walsingham's insistence – blamed Lennox, agreeing that he would not have taken such a 'violent course' without 'some expectation and hope of timely maintenance from foreign parts, which were better prevented than let run on'. The Council agreed that it would be 'best for her majesty to have nine thousand or ten thousand men put in readiness to enter Scotland for removing of d'Aubigny from thence, on the first occasion offered'.[16]

Elizabeth forbade military intervention, suggesting instead that the fourteen-year-old James be asked for an explanation for 'this new and strange course they have begun to take'.[17] The Queen probably took seriously French King Henri's threat that if 'she settled things in her own way in Scotland' then he would prevent this 'with all his forces' and that 'for every soldier she sent thither he would send four, and all other assistance in a like manner'.[18]

Walsingham found that King James' intercepted letters, and devotion to Lennox – who was assigned the code number '32' by the English Secret Intelligence Service – demonstrated 'of what rare towardliness [*capability*] that young prince is, and how dangerous an enemy therefore he would prove unto England if he should happen to run to any other course'.[19] Diplomatic alarms in London reached a crescendo when, in August 1581, James raised Lennox to a Dukedom, highest rank in the Kingdom of Scotland, second only to himself.[20] Lennox and the Earl of Arran – 'the worst thought of, and accounted the falsest that is in Scotland'[21] – who were uneasy partners at the head of Scotland's government and rivals for James's favour, were notorious for their corruption, systematically extorting money, land and goods from a wide variety of nobles, merchants and the Kirk (the Presbyterian church).[22]

English and Scottish apprehension about the course of James's government was relieved by the 'Ruthven Raid' on 22 August 1582, when a group of lairds launched a *coup d'etat*. The King was lured to Ruthven Castle, home of the Earl of Gowrie, and effectively placed under house arrest. Gowrie led a faction known as the Lords Enterprisers, Protestant noblemen who, while not sycophantic anglophiles, believed that alignment with England was strategically necessary to end the resurgent threat of Roman Catholicism.[23] The coup was motivated by suspicion that Lennox was planning to assassinate Gowrie, Mar and other Protestant lords, as well as the corruption and oppression of Lennox and Arran, outlined in the Kirk's 'final supplication' to James, that – probably more than coincidentally – was issued on the day of the Ruthven Raid:

> We have suffered now about the space of two years such false accusations, calumnies, oppressions and persecutions, by the means of the Duke of Lennox and him who is called the Earl of Arran, that the like of their insolencies and enormities were never heretofore born with in Scotland....Which wrongs ... have entered plainly to trouble the whole body of this common wealth.[24]

A government was formed, headed by Gowrie, with the King as its nominal figurehead. The new regime sought to bring fiscal order out of the economic chaos caused by Lennox's corruption and financial incompetence as well as James' uncontrolled spending – a marked change from the years of Morton's regency (1572–1578), when political stability and financial surpluses were maintained.[25] Gowrie, the royal treasurer, was personally owed £45,376[26] by the King for expenditures including livery for the royal household, tennis equipment, James' hats, and various sundries.[27]

The new regime forced James to banish Lennox, ostensibly by showing him evidence of the 'craft, subtilty, and treason' of the Duke and his accomplices as well as his alienating of the King's 'mind from the amity of England and to think nothing pleasant but that which proceeded from the Papists in France'.[28] James – taken under heavy guard to Holyrood Palace in Edinburgh – was probably persuaded to issue a royal banishment order by a threat to arrest and execute his favourite, who was to be 'pursued with fire and sword as a traitor' if he did not leave Scotland.[29] Lennox plotted to overthrow the Ruthven regime and reinstall James as his puppet king.[30] He delayed his departure from Scotland using various excuses while organising supporters in strategic positions around Edinburgh who could be called up at short notice. His plan was to enter via a door in the palace's long gallery and free the King, then 'kill and stik and hang all them that they micht have apprehendit of the [Lords Enterprisers] and their followers'.[31]

The King resisted attempts by the Ruthven lords and the English to turn him against Lennox. After receiving safe conduct passes, Sir George Carey (son of Lord Hunsdon and Ashby's comrade-in-arms on the 1578 Netherland's reconnaissance operation) hurried to Scotland with Bowes to meet James. When the English envoys expounded on the Duke's 'evil intent', James went red in the face and passionately defended Lennox, muttering that he did not believe the allegations against him. Carey told Queen Elizabeth that James' 'great affection' for Lennox 'seems not to be quenched'.[32]

To dissuade Lennox from raising forces to rescue James, the Ruthven lords told him that 'if he did not at once retire to France, they were resolved to carry through what they had commenced', threatening to 'send the King to England, or put him out of the way by some other method'. While the first threat was probably hollow (the English did not want James to add to the many problems caused by his imprisoned mother), Lennox was made aware that James was 'so strictly guarded … that all chance of [the Duke] doing anything advantageous was frustrated, and … his Majesty exposed to evident danger' – a clear threat that James could be assassinated if a rescue attempt was launched.[33] Lennox dropped his rescue plan after it was betrayed by his 'houndsman' the day before it was to commence.[34]

Lennox's pleading letters to James were intercepted and went unanswered,[35] yet the young King managed to secretly send a confidant to him on the day of his departure to say that 'he hoped soon to get rid of these people who were detaining him against his will ... and assured him that he would soon have him back, and would never change in his kind feelings towards him, nor rest until he had been avenged on the traitors'.[36] The Duke was ignominiously forced to travel to France via England using a safe conduct pass from Queen Elizabeth. In London, he met with Elizabeth, who publicly chastised him, accusing him, among other things, of going to Scotland at the order of the Duke of Guise and issuing a proclamation ordering that no person should trade with England.[37]

Fearing plots to rescue James not only by Lennox and Arran, but also from the French, the new Ruthven regime recruited 200 foot soldiers and an equal number of cavalrymen, ostensibly to serve as a guard for the King, but in reality to keep him captive. While the guard's role was to also protect the Ruthven 'noblemen presently resident with his majesty', most of the regime's lords had their own armed retainers. The King's Guard, commanded by Colonel William Stuart,[38] cousin of the Earl of Arran, were essentially mercenaries, willing to give their allegiance to whoever employed them (or turn against those who no longer could pay their wages).[39]

Although the Spanish believed that the kidnapping was an English plot, Elizabeth and her counsellors did not instigate the *coup* even though they welcomed it.[40] Carey and Bowes conveyed the Queen's 'approval of their action, and disapproval of their methods' to Gowrie and his fellow Lords Enterprisers.[41] Walsingham knew that the Ruthven regime was fragile and required significant financial and political support if it was to survive. Carey brought £1,000 with him from London, which he gave to Bowes as 'Part of the money paid to the King of Scots' guard',[42] but this amount fell short of the 2,000 marks promised to the Ruthven regime.[43] Months passed while Walsingham received reports of a new French embassy in Edinburgh extending its tentacles – and bribes – into the opposition now led by Arran and his cronies. Elizabeth reluctantly approved £200 to purchase gold chains for Gowrie and Colonel Stuart but continued to balk at sending more funds to pay the King's Guard.

Frustrated by the Queen's neglectful, parsimonious, attitude towards Scotland, Walsingham confided his fears to Burghley, stating that French and Spanish subversive efforts were unabated and that he 'holds Scotland for lost unless God be merciful to this poor island'.[44] Fearing that it might already be too late to save the Ruthven regime from collapse, in March 1583, Sir Francis met with Burghley and fellow Privy Council members and got their support (with ample use of his intelligence reports) to form a united front in persuading Elizabeth to appropriate £10,000 per annum for Scottish 'pensions'. Half of this would be used to buy James' cooperation, and the remainder divided between trustworthy noblemen and the upkeep of a permanent English embassy in Edinburgh. Walsingham thought that this amount would guarantee the survival of the Ruthven regime and lead to a new treaty for a Protestant Anglo-Scottish league. The Queen immediately vetoed the proposal on the grounds that she 'utterly misliked ... the casting of her into charges' [expenses].[45]

By May 1583, the King's Guard had gone from grumbling over lack of pay to a trickle of desertions to seek better employment. John Colville, the Scottish envoy and English agent,[46] wrote to Walsingham, begging him on behalf of Bowes to send funds to prevent the guards 'dissolving', quoting the English ambassador that 'Indeed the life of our cause consists in them'.[47] Bowes managed to pay the guards £300 out of his own pocket (which Elizabeth refused to reimburse). Shortly afterwards, the English government received the welcome news that Lennox had died in Paris, apparently from natural causes.

Sir Francis, the consummate spymaster, had good reason to fear for England and his Queen, who sometimes seemed maddeningly unconcerned about the intelligence he shared documenting plots against her. Leicester had complained to Walsingham that Elizabeth was slow to believe that the great increase of Papists was of danger to the realm, adding that he prayed that 'the Lord of His mercy open her eyes.'[48] English Jesuits adopted a change of policy from simply ministering to Roman Catholics to actively promoting sedition against Elizabeth and her government. Some became willing agents of the continental powers, reporting to their French, Spanish and Papal contacts that many Catholics 'were anxious to see the deliverance of England from its Protestant yoke and would even go so far as to join an army sent to depose Elizabeth.'[49]

The Duke of Guise (code-named 'Hercules') was plotting the assassination of Elizabeth with the knowledge and backing of Philip II.[50] Lennox had been conspiring with Mary Stuart – and through her with Guise –and was only waiting for the political environment in Scotland to be 'in a fit state for our forces to go thither and begin the enterprise in accordance with the plan proposed last year'.[51] Letters intercepted from Henry III, King of Navarre, and the Prince de Condé, were evidence that Lennox had asked Guise to send 500 French soldiers to form a garrison in Edinburgh.[52] Sir Francis considered Guise, head of the Catholic League, to be England's most implacable enemy, instigator of the St. Bartholomew's Day Eve massacres which haunted him for the rest of his life.

The 'enterprise' was a bold plan to liberate King James, reunite him with his mother, and gather Catholic forces for an invasion of England.[53] Juan de Tassis, Spanish ambassador to the French court from 1581 to 1584, reflected a hard-line shift in Spanish foreign policy from his predecessor who believed that the 'English problem' (i.e., Protestantism and Mary's claim to Elizabeth's throne) could be solved by diplomatic means. Tassis believed that an open war against England, through Ireland or Scotland, was needed to reassert Spain's hegemony in Europe.[54] A landing was to take place at the port of Dumbarton, on the Clyde River, and Tassis gave 5,000 crowns as a bribe to the captain of Dumbarton Castle to support the invasion.[55] To give the 'enterprise' the appearance of a Catholic crusade, there would be 'soldiers of various nations', including Italians and German Catholics', and equal numbers of French and Spanish men-at-arms. The hope was to land between 3,000 and 4,000 troops, or 'a much larger force, almost a regular army.'[56] After months of negotiations, the Pope promised 50,000 crowns towards the cost of the enterprise, which Philip thought was too little, as the Spaniards estimated that the entire expense would be around 400,000 crowns.[57]

Mary Stuart was seen as the key to 'banish the jealousy which may exist between Spain and France if each nation for itself yearns for the conquest of England'. Mendoza, the Spanish ambassador, pointed out to Philip 'the many advantages ... to your interests by the elevation of the Queen of Scots to the throne after England has been converted, and for many reasons France will equally benefit'.[58] Walsingham and Burghley were keenly aware that Spain's strategic objective was not just to restore Roman Catholicism across Britain, but to make England and Scotland vassal states within the Spanish empire.[59]

Nominally acting for the King, in May 1583, the Ruthven regime sent a special delegation to London jointly led by Colonel Stuart and John Colville to ask for an alliance, for money, and to propose marriage to the Queen or to have her advice on an alternative marriage partner for King James. Stuart, cousin of the Earl of Arran who had been Lennox's rival for James's affection and favour, served as the King's personal ambassador (and Arran's agent), whereas Colville represented the Ruthven regime.

Walsingham knew that James was desperately in need of financial help either from France or England, and that the King had assured de la Mothe,[60] the French ambassador, that 'although he had two eyes, two ears, and two hands, he had but one heart, and that was French'.[61] James had decided however, before giving further encouragement to France, to try come to an understanding with Elizabeth, both for financial assistance and out of hope to be named her successor.[62] The Ruthven lairds wanted to cultivate James as a strong Protestant monarch, and hoped that with adequate political and monetary support from England, their beleaguered government would survive.

Queen Elizabeth was amused by the seventeen-year-old James' marriage proposal, drolly responding that 'with respect to the King's marriage, she thanked them much for placing into her hands a matter of such great importance .... As for herself, she had decided to decline, as she thought she was better without a husband ... she would say no more but that there was no person in England with the necessary qualifications for the purpose'.[63]

When the Scottish ambassadors had a second audience with the Queen, they did not pursue the marriage proposals, focusing on 'the importance of an offensive and defensive alliance' with the Ruthven regime, to help the Protestant religion become more firmly established, and to obtain a 'loan' for the King. Colonel Stuart threatened that 'if these points were not accepted, they would be obliged to seek alliance with other princes, which, up to the present, they had avoided' so as not to offend the Queen.[64]

Elizabeth was indignant, sharply telling Stuart that she had expected to preserve her friendship with James because of her kindness to him during his childhood, as well as their relationship and shared Protestant religion, but now she saw that it was only a question of money with him, which 'was the lowest form of pledge'. Stuart argued with her, saying that 'friendship was proved by the readiness with which help was given in time of need'.[65]

Afterward, the Queen complained resentfully to Walsingham and Burghley about the 'importunity' of the Scots, 'who were always asking for money, and using their religion as a pretext for despoiling her, which she would never allow'. Burghley agreed with her, but Walsingham – ever mindful of Scotland's vital strategic importance and knowing of French and Spanish machinations – counselled further discussions with the Scottish envoys.[66]

The following day, Stuart met with Walsingham, bringing 'great pressure' on him to persuade Elizabeth to help James, reiterating the threats of being forced into alliances with England's enemies. That night,

Walsingham briefed the Queen. Across the vast gulf of nearly four-and-half centuries, Elizabeth's reply to her Principal Secretary still strikes a plaintive chord. She told Sir Francis 'that her own servants and favourites professed to love her for her good parts, Alençon[67] for her person, and the Scots for her Crown, three entirely different reasons, but they all ended in the same thing, namely, asking her for money. The one object was to drain her treasury, but she would take care to defend it, as money was the principal sinew and force of princes'.[68]

When Walsingham repeated this to Stuart, he flew into a rage, again threatening that 'the Queen would repent of it, when perhaps it would be too late to remedy the evil that would befall her'.[69] Stuart was probably deliberately provocative, either to engender a diplomatic break that would lead to a French alliance, or to play a high stakes game that would compel the English to open the royal coffers to Scotland (and to himself).

His game of bluff partially succeeded. Stuart and Colville returned jubilantly to Scotland with proposals for a 'league' between the two kingdoms and a yearly pension of 10,000 crowns for James. The Colonel was adept at playing all sides; he was a key conspirator in the French plot to free the King, which 'had so far ripened that nothing was waiting for its completion except Stewart's (*sic*) presence and assistance'.[70] Stuart's hatred for the English was at a boiling point, for the ship carrying his and Colville's personal goods from London to Scotland was taken by English pirates off Yarmouth and 'a great part of their apparel and much stuff, plate, silks, and furniture' was stolen.[71]

# 10. Walsingham's failed
diplomatic mission

Consternation over Scotland returned to London in June 1583. As expected, 'the guard finding no surety of pay' scattered,[1] James regained his freedom, and the Gowrie regime collapsed.[2] The King promptly banished the Earls of Angus and Mar with their supporters, and 'the especial favourites of the King's mother' were reported to 'triumph' at court.[3] Mary was overjoyed at her son's deliverance 'out of the hands of the traitors who held him', and wrote to the Spanish and French ambassadors in London to 'advance the execution of our enterprise' at least to the extent of protecting James from any attempt by the English to return him to the Ruthven lords.[4]

The 'pension' reluctantly offered to James by Elizabeth was now used to drive a deeper wedge between the two countries. Colonel Stuart told Bowes that the 'portion' granted to the King was so insultingly small that James could 'not with honour' accept such a 'trifle'. Bowes thought that either Stuart was trying to get a larger payment or – more likely – sought to enhance the quarrel with the Queen.[5] The ambassador made what he termed 'loans' from his personal funds to the King, Colonel Stuart and others to buy continued access to the court (and the intelligence that he relied upon for his mission). When the Scots defaulted, Bowes was hounded by creditors and begged Walsingham to intercede with Elizabeth to pay his debts.[6]

James hoped that he could continue to lull the English with promises of 'amity' and professions of 'our special liking and goodwill before all Princes in the world' to his 'dearest sister' Elizabeth while courting the French for financial and political support.[7] Soon after the King returned to Edinburgh from St. Andrews, where he had escaped, Bowes confronted him about various alleged deceits, which James denied. The ambassador told him that he was authorised to state that if the King did not stop collaborating with those who were 'evil affected to the Crown of England', Elizabeth would view him as an enemy rather than a friend. The ambassador heavily stressed that Elizabeth's forces were much stronger than his, and in the event of an English invasion, the King would not be able to resist 'without the succour of strangers' (the French and Spanish), and suggested that this could lead his own people to take up arms to defend Scotland from the Papists rather than go to war with England. Friendship with, and even obedience to, Her Majesty, Bowes said, offered the best means of maintaining 'the religion, King and nation in safety'.[8]

Although James promised that he would faithfully maintain Elizabeth's friendship and follow her guidance, Bowes was accustomed to his dissembling, and knew from his spies that the determined King would say and do anything to advance his and his country's interests. James and his putative allies greatly underestimated the vast espionage apparatus conceived and managed by Walsingham. Bowes ran an intelligence operation that had deeply penetrated the Scottish government. His agents within the Scottish court were identified in his coded reports to Walsingham by numbers to protect their identities. Due to his reports, sometimes embellished by Walsingham, Elizabeth's illusions about the young King had largely vanished, having 'cause to doubt that the professed devotion towards her cannot long continue'.[9]

By early August, Elizabeth had resolved to send Walsingham to Scotland to 'endeavour to stay the dangerous effects' of the King's return to power before it was too late.[10] Walsingham refused to go, believing that Anglo-Scottish relations were so bad that the diplomatic mission would be a failure, for which he would be blamed, as had been the case in previous diplomatic missions. His colleagues admonished him for refusing an order from the notoriously vindictive sovereign, to which he reportedly replied: 'He saw no good could come of it, and that the Queen would lay upon his shoulders the whole of the responsibility for the evils' which would occur. He said she was 'very stingy already, and the Scots more greedy than ever, quite disillusioned now with regard to the promises made to them; so that it was out of the question that anything good could be done'.[11]

Summoned to Greenwich Palace, Walsingham threw himself at Elizabeth's feet and swore by 'the soul, body and blood of God that he would not travel to Scotland, even if she ordered him to be hanged for it, as he would rather be hanged in England than elsewhere'.[12] Taken aback, Elizabeth considered sending Hunsdon instead. Although Hunsdon had considerable experience in Anglo-Scottish relations, he demurred on the grounds that he had just been appointed Lord Chamberlain. Privately Hunsdon told Walsingham that he declined to interfere further in Scottish affairs, since his advice was usually ignored.[13]

While the Privy Council dithered and debated the Scottish crisis, Leicester wrote 'a letter of advice on the state of affairs' to the Queen, postulating whether it would be better for Her Majesty to deal with James and the imprisoned Mary Stuart 'by way of pacification and compromise, or else by a more absolute way' (by which he meant military force). Although the Earl advocated 'peaceable means' as more plausible and less dangerous, he urged Elizabeth to support her own position by warlike demonstration. He also advised 'the passing of an Act of Parliament, that if by any practice of the King or the Queen of Scots any danger should grow to Elizabeth they should forfeit absolutely all right or title to the crown of England'.[14]

Increasingly incensed by reports of what James naively thought were his secret dealings with England's foreign enemies and the growing influence of the anti-English faction, the Queen reportedly told a confidant that 'she could never be secure whilst that boy lived.'[15] On 7 August, Elizabeth wrote a letter in her own hand to James, opening with a thinly veiled accusation of duplicity, before letting her ire flow:

> It moves me much to 'moane' you [*lament his behaviour*]
> when I behold how diversely sundry wicked spirits distract

your mind and bend your course to crooked paths, and, like
all evil illusions wrapped under the cloak of your best safety,
endanger your estate and best good. How may it be that you
can suppose an honourable answer may be made when all
your doings gainsay your former vows? You deal not with one
whose experience can take dross for good payment, nor one
who easily will be beguiled.[16]

Reflecting Walsingham's reports that James intended to imprison
and execute the Ruthven lairds for treason at the behest of his 'craftiest
counsellors', Elizabeth urged him not to stain his honour by taking action
against them until the King received her confidential offers of 'honour
and contentment with more surety to yourself and State.'[17] She hadn't
given up on him, excusing what she saw as his 'bad behaviour' on his
youth. Elizabeth returned to her idea that a high-level diplomatic effort
might succeed in bringing Scotland's teenage king back into the English
fold, or at least bribe him into genuine neutrality.

Her patience exhausted, the Queen commanded Walsingham to go to
Scotland. Fearing the loss of his head, Sir Francis prepared for the journey,
although he wrote to Bowes that his mission would 'be with as ill a will as
ever he undertook any service in his life' because the Scots' resentment
had 'grown into so bad terms that he fears he will be able to do little good
there, and therefore would most willingly avoid the journey if by any
means he might do it without her majesty's extreme displeasure'.[18] The
Secretary was also ailing and feared that an arduous trip by land would
further damage his health.[19]

******

Ashby was in his Clerkenwell house on a sweltering day in early August
1583 when he received a note from Walsingham summoning him to Barn
Elms the following morning at ten of the clock. At their meeting, Sir
Francis told him that the Queen had ordered him to lead a delegation to
Scotland to bring the wayward young King James back into the English

fold and stymie the growing influence of the realm's many enemies within the northern kingdom. The Secretary confided that he thought the expedition would be as fruitless as the 1578 mission to the Low Countries, but as Her Majesty had ordered it, he must go, and he wanted Ashby to accompany him.

For an agent who had spent much of his career in continental northern Europe, being asked to join a diplomatic entourage to Scotland may have seemed anomalous. But Ashby had Scottish intelligence connections, including Castelvetro, 'the Scottish King's schoolmaster for the Italian tongue'.[20] Ashby was later described as a 'particular friend' of Archibald Douglas, 'Parson of Douglas', a woefully inept intriguer who was involved in a wide variety of plots, including the murder of Lord Darnley, husband of Mary Queen of Scots, during which he left his shoes behind. Douglas (not to be confused with Archibald Douglas, Earl of Angus, who Ashby also knew), was one of Walsingham's agents, and was living in exile in England from 1579 to 1586.[21]

Whatever Walsingham's motives, he obviously valued Ashby's abilities – and loyalty – enough to ask him to become a member of his reluctant delegation to the court of King James.

✶✶✶✶✶✶

On Tuesday, 13 August, Walsingham went to Oatlands Palace in Surrey to take leave of Elizabeth and receive her signed instructions, dictated to Burghley, before departing for Scotland. Sir Francis was authorised to tell James that if he would 'alter' what the English deemed 'the wrong course lately begun', Elizabeth's government was prepared to 'augment' his 'pension', and to 'offer, and to give, some reasonable sums by way of reward' to key Scottish nobles who were reliably pro-English and Protestant. However, if the 'young Prince' could not be persuaded thus, Walsingham should warn that Elizabeth had 'no cause of further dealing with him', and if the 'adverse faction' (the anti-English nationalists led by Arran and Colonel Stuart as well as the Catholics) was not 'overruled' to her satisfaction, it could be at his 'own peril and to the ruin of his State'. Should Walsingham fail to intimidate King James into restoring 'amity' with England, the Secretary was to threaten that the Queen would lose no time in pursuing a 'last remedy', and that 'she will not neglect any means ... to further it' – an unambiguous threat of an English invasion.[22]

In a private meeting with Sir Francis that evening, Elizabeth gave him a 'verbal commission' to take any steps he deemed 'most advisable' in accordance with what he knew to be her wishes. Walsingham had permission to promise James that if he would 'not marry out of the island' (to a foreign Catholic princess) and would 'bind himself to England' then Elizabeth would declare him her heir and hold out 'great hopes' for 'the release of his mother'.[23]

Although the source for the private instructions to Walsingham is the secret correspondence of Mendoza, the Spanish ambassador in London, with King Philip, it is credible. The Spanish and French intelligence services were scarcely on par with Walsingham's organisation, but nonetheless had sources throughout Elizabeth's court, her government, and her military. Walsingham had agents inside all foreign embassies in London, and it is possible that he deliberately leaked the private conversation with the Queen as a warning to James and his allies via another communication channel.[24]

For decades, the English government dangled the succession in front of James to keep him in line, particularly in times of crisis such as the aftermath of the King's liberation from the Ruthven regime, and during the Armada threat half a decade later. Despite compelling evidence that Mary was conspiring to depose the English monarch, in the summer of 1583 Elizabeth was undecided about her cousin's fate, apparently considering it more useful to keep her as a hostage – a diplomatic pawn – than to execute her.

Sir Francis delayed his departure, resting to regain his strength at his country estate, Barn Elms, which was also the headquarters of his international intelligence agency and had a stable of nearly seventy horses which were used by his couriers and agents. The Secretary waited for his retinue to gather until it totalled nearly eighty, including William Ashby.[25]

******

Early on the morning of 17 August, Walsingham's retinue departed, fording the Thames by the church of St. Mary the Virgin at Putney. At Ashby's urging, the delegation had been joined by Arthur Throckmorton with the promise that he 'would only need ride as far as it pleased him'. They were concerned about Walsingham's fragile health. Sir Francis was too sickly to 'endure the post' (riding post horses) so was 'carried in a coach or chariot'.[26] The two men rode on either side of the coach, trying to raise the Secretary's spirits with wry commentary about places and people they passed, and discussions about books such as the newly published *De Emendatione Temporum* (Study on the Improvement of Time) by the French Calvinist Joseph Justus Scaliger, who Ashby knew was greatly admired by Walsingham.

The entourage made its slow way towards Scotland along the Great North Road with frequent stops at villages along the route because of Walsingham's severe 'wind colic' and 'distemper of his body.'[27] Torrid weather added to his misery, and Throckmorton impatiently complained that the post horses he rode were crowbait unfit for the arses of gentlemen. After a miserable night at the Bell Inn in Stilton tormented by bed bugs and Walsingham's groans through the thin walls, Throckmorton took his leave, pleading 'urgent family affairs' at Beaumanor. Ashby watched him ride away, envying his ability to escape the dark mood afflicting the group, which seemed more like a funeral cortège than a diplomatic mission.

******

The delegation was made to wait at Berwick for several days due to problems with the issuance of a safe-conduct pass, including restrictions on the number of people allowed to accompany Walsingham.[28] While at Berwick, Sir Francis continued to receive intelligence reports, including ones detailing that 'All the hopes of the Papists are in Scotland' and 'The

Papists chiefly rely on the aid of Scotland'.[29] His bleak mood deepened when he was advised that he had personally been tricked into providing a passport to a Catholic agent who, secretly writing in orange juice, conspired to 'have every preacher and minister in England hanged in the church with the bell ropes'.[30] During this time, Walsingham struggled with an 'extreme pain in his right side' which kept him awake. The pain was compounded by 'an unaccompanied faintness, and a disposition altogether subject to melancholy'. Expressing the frustration and stress that exacerbated (if not caused) his sickness, he told Sir Christopher Hatton that he hoped he would 'enjoy more ease in another world than I do in this'.[31]

While he lingered at Berwick, Walsingham wrote to Burghley that Colonel Stuart 'hath made a shipwreck both of conscience and honesty. He guideth altogether the King his Master, (as it is now reported), and therefore there is small hope of his recovery when misrulers become guiders'.[32] Walsingham saw the delay in issuing a passport as another provocation by Stuart, now *de facto* head privy counsellor and intelligence chief, and his cousin, the Earl of Arran, of whom it was said 'for impudent audacity he probably had no equal'.[33] The English believed that Arran, like the late Duke of Lennox, controlled James by manipulating his affections, .

Walsingham feared that he and his entourage would be in danger without a comprehensive safe-conduct pass because of Scottish suspicion that he was on an intelligence collection mission (which was true to a certain extent), and due to the recent arrest of Scots working as English agents who were 'very straitly examined [tortured] what intelligence they had with the ministers of England'.[34] Bowes reported that James may have been led to think that the large English delegation intended to kidnap and take him to England to be imprisoned like his mother.[35]

Bowes told Walsingham that the King would not discuss any 'matters of weight' with him and had therefore appointed Arran as his surrogate 'who will offer himself and his whole power right frankly to [Sir Francis]'.[36]

Wagers were laid in Edinburgh that Walsingham would be indefinitely kept from the Scottish court as a further insult.[37]

Walsingham crossed the border into Scotland on 28 August and was kept waiting in Perth for over a week for his audience with James. His intelligencers such as Ashby and Bowes were busy collecting information, always with the awareness that they were in a hostile land and vulnerable to capture. Using their reports, Sir Francis wrote to Leicester complaining about the confusion caused by the 'misgovernment' of Arran and Stuart and stated that he would not deal with them. He suggested that English forces be sent to the border 'until it were seen what would become of this weltering State'. This was a suggestion which was not taken up, fortunately, as such an aggressive move would have itself precipitated a hostile reaction in the turbulent country.

When Walsingham, dyspeptic and impatient, finally met who he perceived as the 'ungrateful and conceited' King at Perth,[38] he 'showed him how far forth his regality stretched, and that his young years could not so well judge what appertained to matters of government'. Sir Francis accused James of rejecting Elizabeth's 'so good and sound advice' and threatened that 'Her majesty means to live in good peace with her neighbours, yet hath she not her sword glued in the scabbard, if any wrong or dishonour be offered unto her', adding that 'her majesty is as able to live without the amity of Scotland as any of her progenitors'. James responded with what Walsingham described as a 'distemperature' (a disordered mental condition), stating, 'with a kind of jollity', that as an absolute king he could do whatever he liked with his subjects, and Elizabeth had no more right to question his choice of councillors than he had to question hers,[39] in fact a reasonable enough response to Walsingham's condescending manner.

Immediately after the last of two short audiences, Walsingham rudely refused to speak to Arran or Colonel Stuart, both of whom he claimed sought to 'run a course' (side with England in exchange for bribes) with him.[40] Sir Francis' cynicism was so deep that he believed, as another of his intelligencers, Gilbert Gifford, would subsequently tell him, that 'England will find Scotland, old Scotland still, and traitorous in the greatest need', an attitude that was hardly likely to be conducive to diplomatic resolution.[41]

Walsingham hurriedly returned to his quarters to write an impassioned letter to Burghley, enclosing his more muted report to the Queen and asking for the Lord Treasurer's 'friendly and careful defence' for what he expected to be 'the greatest blame' that would be laid on him for the failure of his mission. Sir Francis said 'that there is no hope of recovery of this young Prince, who, I doubt [not] – having many reasons to lead me so to judge ... will become a dangerous enemy ... unless there may be some good means found to prevent the same.'[42]

Walsingham sent William Ashby, who accompanied him to the first audience with James, to London with the reports for the Queen and Burghley, explaining to the latter that Ashby 'can show your lordship the state of this Court, the manner of their proceeding in the government, and in what sort we were entertained'. He ended his dispatch to Burghley:

> This day I hope to take my leave of the King, and so mind
>
> to draw homewards with as much speed as my health will
>
> permit, which is not presently in the best state by reason of a
>
> great pain in my head, accompanied with a fever, whereof I
>
> have had two fits since my coming to this place.[43]

Ashby was given written instructions from Walsingham to make an oral report to Elizabeth, strategically exaggerating 'Certain observations of the King's behaviour at the time of my audience'. These included taking little interest in 'the Queen of England's well-doing', James' failure to make 'any great reckoning' of her advice, ignoring her letters, and generally appearing ungrateful for Elizabeth's 'benefits'.[44] Sir Francis knew how to play on the Queen's mistrust and irritation with James, hoping to deflect her expected blame for the failure of his mission to the 'young prince'.

The Court was still seated at Oatlands, a 'little castle, eighteen miles from London, [which] lies on a slope and commands the most glorious view'.[45] Accompanied by his servant, Peter Haye, and a pair of men-at-arms, Ashby made good time, changing post horses often as he covered the 460 miles from Perth across the drought-stricken landscape beyond the border in just four days.

The Scots engaged in a crude form of psychological warfare to bait the Englishmen. James was to become known for his obsession with quashing witchcraft and black magic, so it was most likely Arran who:

> ... hounded out a low woman, called Kate the witch, to assail
> [Walsingham] with vile speeches as he passed to and from
> the King's presence. She was, it is alleged, hired by Arran for
> a new plaid and six pounds in money, not only to rail against
> the ministry [clergy], his majesty's assured and ancient
> nobility, and lovers of the amity [English alliance] but also
> set in the entry of the King's palace, to revile her majesty's
> ambassador at Edinburgh, St. Andrews, Falkland, Perth, and
> everywhere, to the great grief of all good men.[46]

Kate was fortunate to be on the government payroll as in Scotland witchcraft and consulting with witches were capital offences. Following complaints by the English entourage, she was imprisoned 'for a fashion [pretence], large allowance was made for her entertainment, and she was relieved as soon as Walsingham had departed'.[47]

To add insult to Walsingham's cursed headache, the Earl of Arran prepared 'a scornful present for him at his leave-taking, to wit a ring with a stain [stone] of crystalline, instead of a rich diamond, which his Majesty had appointed for him'. The Earl 'did what he could to displease him, and to make his commission in all points unprofitable'.[48] It is likely that Arran and Colonel Stuart were retaliating against Walsingham for snubbing them, as well as for the theft of Stuart's goods by pirates and an attack on a member of the Scottish delegation at Durham during their return trip to Scotland. Conspiracy theories were as rife in the 1580s as in latter centuries, and the Scots probably thought that Sir Francis was behind the latter incidents.

Walsingham left Scotland on 15 September, ill, melancholy and fearful of Elizabeth's wrath. The following day, Lord Seton, a devout Roman Catholic who conspired with the Spanish, wrote to Mary Stuart: 'at the departure of the ambassador Walsingham, your son certified to me that he is determined to send me to [France] with all speed.[49] I perceive that he is thoroughly determined to continue the friendship and league of this kingdom, and to follow in everything the advice of Monsieur de Guise, and to complete the treaty commenced between you and him'. Knowing Mary's hatred for the Secretary, Seton sought to brighten her spirits by adding that 'Walsingham has been very ill received and entertained here'.[50]

Walsingham's fear that he would be castigated proved to be groundless, possibly because of the intervention of Burghley, Leicester and other courtiers. Bitter about his mission, which he thought, correctly, had further damaged relations with Scotland, the Secretary refocused on the omnipresent threat from English Catholics and their foreign supporters. Berating Sir Francis was forgotten as Elizabeth belatedly realised that her life was endangered. She told the French ambassador Michel de Castelnau 'that she has discovered, and was discovering every day, great conspiracies against her; and that there were more than 200 men of all ages who had conspired...to kill her...and that several of the conspirators were in this city, and sometimes at her court'.[51]

Soon after his return to London, Walsingham's melancholy was dispelled by the eradication of a conspiracy by Francis Throckmorton to overthrow the Queen.[52] Confessing under torture personally supervised by Walsingham, he implicated Mary Stuart, Guise, Ambassador de Mendoza and numerous English Catholics in a plot to invade England, free Mary, assassinate Elizabeth, and restore the Church of Rome. Sir Philip Sidney, who to the Queen's great displeasure, had married Walsingham's daughter soon after the Secretary's return from Scotland, wrote that Her Majesty was 'troubled with these suspicions which arise of some ill-minded subjects towards her...The Ambassadors of Spain and France be noted for great practisers [plotters]'.[53] Mendoza, the 'great practiser', was expelled from England in January 1584.[54]

Much to his relief, Bowes was recalled as ambassador. Diplomatic relations were strained to the breaking point. Cross-border raids by 'loose men' – with the blessing of some Scots lairds if not officially by James and his council – wreaked 'murders and spoils upon her Majesties subjects', while pirates from both countries operated with seeming impunity.[55] Walsingham was especially incensed that Elizabeth would not spend enough to maintain the crucial network of spies in Scotland, telling Bowes – who had been paying agents from his own pocket – 'you shall do well to spare your further charges and expenses in procuring ... intelligence'.[56]

Officially, for the Queen and the Privy Council, Walsingham concluded that despite James' promises to 'run hereafter a more milder and more temperate course', he was 'still possessed by those ill instruments [anti-English lairds and Papists] which have led him onto this dangerous course', and therefore he 'greatly doubted the performance of what he now promised'.[57] Recovering from a fall from his horse on the return journey, possibly attributed to the witch's curses, Sir Francis would have gladly cast Scotland adrift if it were not a vital part of the strategic threat from England's enemies. Privately, he 'returned greatly dissatisfied with the King of Scotland and those who are at present of his Council, and ... all was owing to the intrigues of the Queen his mother'.[58] Walsingham's 'dissatisfaction' with the King of Scotland was presumably reciprocated: James was likely outraged by the Principal Secretary's arrogance and the fact that he had now 'redoubled his hatred' of Mary Queen of Scots, the 'bosom serpent', and was determined to see her dead, either by legal means or by foul play.[59]

Despite the total failure of Walsingham's mission, it changed the course of William Ashby's life and career. The contacts made and intelligence gathered during his short time in Scotland, plus the introduction to King James, would prove invaluable during his diplomatic appointment to Edinburgh five years later. Already known and favoured by powerful members of the English court, including the Queen, and respected for his foreign diplomacy and intelligence operations, he was now being positioned for what would be the culmination of his service to Her Majesty's government.

# 11. Universal miscontent in the country

After Walsingham's return to London, Scotland continued to drift along what the English thought a politically chaotic and financially disastrous course, its lairds seeming to be embroiled in a broth of treachery, deception and vengeance, while the teenage King dallied with his favourites. Although the Earl of Arran's influence increased, James (known as '91' by the English intelligence service) was 'wholly governed by '23' [the Queen of Scots]' and her 'friends' and sought 'to advance all things to the prescribed and wished desires of '23'.[1] James was reportedly now 'inclined to pardon' the Ruthven kidnappers, having taken Elizabeth's advice, yet Gowrie and his fellow Lords Enterprisers were aware that Arran was working 'very busily to persuade and draw him to the contrary', and they feared it was only a matter of time before the King would 'readily hearken to Arran in this behalf' and crush them.[2]

A new coup *d'etat* was fomented, if not planned by Walsingham and his agents at least known and supported by them. The Hamiltons – who had sought refuge south of the border – served as London's proxies, supporting the 'English faction' with 'money and musters of men'.[3] Although Walsingham knew that Arran and James were aware of the planned rebellion, his secret intelligence service was crippled by a lack of resources in Scotland. There was no resident ambassador in Edinburgh, and Robert Bowes, serving as chief English agent, was huddled within the bastion of Berwick and weary of his role as combined diplomat and Scottish 'chief of station'. He told Walsingham that he questioned 'whether it shall be good to deal any further in intelligence' and thought that a successor should be named. His agents inside Scotland believed they had been compromised, despite being 'known only to himself', and were 'thereby afraid to continue their offices'. Bowes asked Sir Francis to 'procure his discharge' but was willing to wait until the outcome of the 'bycourse'– the planned coup by the Lords Enterprisers.[4]

Distrust between the nations deepened. Although James had 'professed, to continue in good friendship with her Majesty', on the basis of hearsay Walsingham reported that the King 'heretofore had little regard to the like promises and is still possessed by those ill instruments which have led him into this dangerous course', and therefore he 'greatly doubt[ed] the performance of what he now promises'.[5]

While James professed 'amity' with his 'loving sister and cousin' Elizabeth, Walsingham's agents documented his overtures to England's enemies.[6] The King seems to have been considering that his optimal path to the English throne was via a Spanish invasion to depose Elizabeth and install his mother in her place. He was boldly playing a dangerous game, keeping his options open for the flow of funds from England, France and Spain, so as to stave off insolvency and hoping to be on the winning side of whichever great power emerged victorious in the war between Papistry and Protestantism. In his youthful naiveté he may have been unaware that the English, Spanish and French were all wise to his machinations but chose to cultivate him for their national interests, or he may have been quite aware and ready to align his nation with the best backer, playing them off against each other.

Early in 1584, James wrote to the Duke of Guise that he had abandoned 'the English faction' (Gowrie, Angus *et al.*) and now perceived 'that the strength of my enemies and rebels is growing daily, with so many means and aims of the Queen of England for the subversion of my State, and the deprivation of my own life, or at least my honour and liberty'. He begged Guise to use all his influence with the Pope and 'the princes who are your friends' to obtain 'prompt and speedy help' which would allow him 'with the support of a good number of adherents that I have, both in Scotland and in England', freedom to follow Guise's 'advice in all things, both in religion and State affairs'. James signed his letter 'Your affectionate cousin Jacques R'.[7]

On the same day, 'Jacques R' wrote to Pope Gregory XIII in a similar vein. An ally of Guise and Philip, the Pope was similarly dedicated to eradicating Protestantism and dethroning Elizabeth in favour of Mary Stuart. James told Gregory that he particularly esteemed 'the house of Guise' for being the 'nearest and most faithful to me', stating that he 'was beginning to open my eyes' to recognise the evil behaviour of those (presumably Protestants) who had 'banded themselves against me with the aid and countenance of my neighbour the Queen of England, who has always held out her hand to all their bad enterprises undertaken with the object of utterly ruining me'.

James wrote that he was in imminent danger 'from the designs of my greatest enemies and yours', required 'some help from abroad', and because of his 'extreme need', beseeched His Holiness for 'aid and succour' to free his mother and assert their 'right to the throne of England'. Referencing the Enterprise of England, James said that he had written to his 'dear cousin the duke of Guise', and that he hoped 'to be able to satisfy your Holiness on all other points, especially if I am aided in my great need by your Holiness' – a strong hint that he was willing to adopt Catholicism. Concerned about defending himself against Scottish 'rebels and the Queen of England', James implored the Pope to 'please to keep very secret the communication I thus open with you, and let no one know that I have written this, as my interests would otherwise be retarded, and perhaps my state utterly ruined'.[8]

The King feared that Walsingham was plotting with the Scottish rebels to depose him, 'either through poisoning or some other violent end'.[9] It was no secret that Sir Francis, Leicester and other councillors sought the execution of Mary, but rumours were rife in Edinburgh and abroad that James was to be included in the regicide plans.[10]

Philip and, evidently, the Pope, took James' offers seriously. Spain's ambassador to France, Juan de Tassis, developed a detailed plan for what he called 'the English design' – the invasion and subjugation of England. The strategic objective was 'to subdue England, and liberate the Queen of Scotland, both on her own account and [so] that she may be an instrument for the permanent submission of England'. The landing of Spanish troops would be made 'among friends' in Scotland, but they would march into England under cover of 'a Catholic rising in our favour, of which the English who have the arrangement of the matter are very sanguine, and even believe that whole counties and towns will declare for us'. The Earl of Westmoreland and other exiled Papist nobles who had led the 1569 Northern Rebellion would 'return to their territories and raise their partisans to revolt'.[11]

Tassis suggested that a landing in England could be a better option for logistical reasons and because:

> ... any army which might approach England from Scotland might be generally misunderstood amongst English people to be a Scots army, and as there exists a natural hatred between the two nations, this might cause, even amongst our friends, a certain coldness, and lead the Catholics themselves to defend their country, under the impression that the Scots with foreign aid were coming to conquer it.[12]

The ambassador advised that the best way to achieve a quick conquest would be to assassinate Elizabeth and 'to suddenly set her house aflame, both with a foreign force and a rising of her own subjects, and to put the whole country at once in a blaze and turmoil'.[13]

Guise (known as 'Muzio' to Philip and his envoys) and others involved in invasion planning disagreed with Tassis, asserting 'that the best course will be to enter by Scotland'. It was said that the English had a dread of the Scots, and

> '... would not like being dominated by Scotsman, and if the crown of Scotland is to be joined to their empire, they, the English, want still to be cocks of the walk, as their kingdom is the larger and more important one. On the other hand, the

> Scots may be unduly inflated with the opposite idea, so that
>
> imperfections may exist on both sides.'[14]

A cavalry unit 'might also make an attempt at a dash from Scotland' to rescue Mary from her incarceration.[15] This was considered risky due to the distance to be travelled and the unknown strength of English forces. The best option would be for Mary to buy her escape 'which she had arranged, and for some time past has been asking for 12,000 crowns to pay for'. If Philip could provide this sum, Elizabeth could be deposed and Mary, being 'a woman of such good sense', would 'not fail to show proper gratitude … by aiding in the settlement of affairs in Flanders, and in ordering all other things to your Majesty's pleasure'.[16]

If King James converted to Catholicism, he would be 'allowed' to lead the army into England, where hopefully English Papists would flock to its banners. The Spanish were unhappy that James had not yet 'declared himself a Catholic', but were confident that 'Muzio' would work on his conversion. Judging by the Scottish King's letters to Philip, Guise and the Pope, 'great hopes may be entertained that he may come round to the Catholic religion'. However, James was to be a minor player in the post-invasion vassal government, because it was necessary to 'keep all eyes fixed on the mother, in order that she may be sought out and made mistress of the empire which is to be won, and not allow any other idea to be countenanced whilst she is alive'.[17]

Sir James Melville, one of James' courtiers and diplomats, wrote, '[t]here was at this time an universal miscontent in the country, and a great rumour of an alteration … These rumours and advertisements made his Majesty be upon his guard, and to use means to get intelligence'.[18] Riddled with Arran's spies and poorly organised, the Lords Enterprisers, led by the Earls of Mar and Angus, launched their 'alteration' by seizing the royal residence of Stirling Castle on 17 April 1584. Forewarned, James and Arran led an army of twelve thousand men that quickly recaptured the castle but missed the Lords, who fled to England. Gowrie, who had taken only an indirect role in the aborted rebellion, was apprehended and quickly beheaded.

A fresh Anglo-Scottish diplomatic row erupted as James demanded the extradition of the rebel lairds and Elizabeth refused. Walsingham, who along with Davison conspired with the exiles to return to Scotland and seize Edinburgh Castle,[19] assured them that Her Majesty would 'have a princely care both to provide for their safety during the time of their abode in England ... in respect of the zeal and good affection she has ever noted to be carried by them to the crown of England'.[20]

While James was 'kept immersed in the pleasures of the chase and of the table, and in other pleasures in which his youthful majesty took delight', Arran expanded his dictatorial power, confiscating the estates of the exiled lairds to reward his supporters, and expelling dissident leaders of the Kirk.[21] The English seemed to accept that Arran was the true power behind the puppet throne, Hunsdon telling Burghley that 'the King beareth the name, but he [Arran] beareth the sway' [power].[22]

Believing that an English-backed invasion was imminent, and equally fearful of the French and Spanish, Arran sought to lull Elizabeth with diplomacy to allow time to consolidate his regime.[23] Now Lord Chancellor of Scotland, he met with Hunsdon to renew negotiations for an Anglo-Scottish peace treaty. The meeting was opposed by Walsingham, who was in no doubt that Arran and James were duplicitous. But Burghley and the Queen favoured negotiations in the hope that diplomacy could cool simmering hostility between the two nations and negate the strategic threat.

Hunsdon felt that Arran's promises of amity could be trusted 'unless he be worse than a devil', and kept a straight face when the Earl vowed that there was no association with Mary, and that James had never corresponded with the Pope, Guise and the Spanish.[24] Walsingham knew these to be blatant lies. Elizabeth and Burghley seemed to concur, the latter telling Hunsdon that the Queen:

... could perceive no such ground of matter worth your meeting with the earl whereupon to build any certainty with the Scottish King or to give faith to Arran. For she says that his answers to most part of your articles of charge are either so general that they contain no certainty, or are so manifestly untrue in divers points that either she has cause to think that Arran cares not what he says to serve his purpose, or else is made more ignorant of the King's actions than he would seem to be, and so is abused himself, or that he is appointed to abuse her majesty.[25]

Nonetheless, the English were receptive to Arran's offer to isolate James from Mary's influence and provide intelligence about Catholic conspiracies to depose Elizabeth (some of which were already known to Walsingham, but useful as additional evidence to convict the Scottish Queen). Walsingham's cryptography expert Phelippes had recently deciphered a letter from Mary complaining that James had only received 6000 of the 10,000 ducats promised by Philip, and she was impatiently waiting for 12,000 ducats to procure her escape. She expected the Pope and 'the Catholic King' to execute their invasion plan in the spring of 1585, warning 'if that fail they shall see the complete overthrow of their whole cause, never to be again set on foot in their days'. Mary said that James 'was not a little grieved' that he had not received the full amount of money promised to him, but was 'still well inclined to their design, and will direct his course as she advises'. She closed by writing that James was sending 'a Catholic gentleman of his called Gray to the English Court, who may visit her, and impart by mouth his [James'] resolution in all their affairs'.[26]

The 'Catholic gentleman', Patrick, Master of Gray, was emerging as a new favourite of James. Described as 'a young man of great beauty', he was steadily eclipsing Arran, whose influence over James and personal power base were eroding.[27] The Earl and, and especially his wife, were despised by all levels of Scottish society for their 'insolency, cruelty, bribery, extortion, and other vices intolerable'.[28]

Gray, who was no improvement on Arran, was a master of political intrigue, treachery and deviousness. He could have been a model for Machiavelli's *The Prince*, and he may well have read the book during his self-imposed exile in France in the 1570s. Named as a Privy Councillor to James, with Arran's endorsement, Gray was dispatched to London in October 1584 to negotiate the release of Mary. Walsingham, Leicester and Davison distrusted him, knowing that Gray was complicit in various plots against Elizabeth on behalf of the Scottish Queen, and considered to be one of her leading agents. He was in the pay of a host of enemies, having 'received extraordinary favours' including 6,000 marks gifted to James by Guise. Gray had 'tasted of the Pope's bounty' and been given 'a cupboard of plate valued at 5000 or 6000 crowns' by Bernardino de Mendoza, who was appointed Spanish ambassador to France after his expulsion from England at the beginning of 1585. Acknowledging his Machiavellian talents, which were extraordinary even in an era of grand Renaissance intrigue, Davison told Walsingham that Gray could prove useful due to 'his ableness in some degree to discover '*le pot aux roses*' [to uncover plots and state secrets]'.[29]

Expediency was Walsingham's operational watchword. He had no qualms about working with treacherous foreign agents if it supported his tireless defence of Queen and country. It took little time and effort to 'turn' Gray during his embassy in London, which almost certainly fit his own agenda. Gray had written secretly to Walsingham offering his services.[30] He was added to the English payroll, receiving 'gold, angels and rose nobles to the value of 5,000 crowns'.[31]

Arran, who was as much an enemy of Papistry as he was of the Kirk, wanted to sever Mary's influence over James to bolster his faltering control of the young King. Gray was to be the instrument for this despite his professed mission to secure the Scottish Queen's freedom. His real directive was to negotiate an alliance that would safeguard Scotland from

France and Spain under the umbrella of English power while maintaining independence.

The timing of Gray's arrival in London was opportune as the government was consumed with national security concerns due to the Throckmorton Plot, the assassination of the Prince of Orange and a plethora of other conspiracies against Elizabeth, both real and fabricated. Gray fed the fires of fear and suspicion, and supported Walsingham's mission by providing evidence against Mary and Arran.

Walsingham and Burghley were writing the final drafts of the 'Bond of Association', which pledged its signatories, in the event of an attempt on Elizabeth's life, to execute not only the assassins but also the claimant to the throne in whose interest the attempt had been made. The Bond, passed into law by Parliament in March 1585, was designed to compel James to cut off ties with Mary, and to begin the legal process for her eventual execution, which Walsingham believed was key to the realm's security. In this regard, Arran was in step with English policy as he appeared to be succeeding in turning James against his mother. However, this may have been a survival subterfuge between mother and son, and Gray may have continued to play all sides for much longer than his various paymasters suspected.

Shortly before Gray's embarkation for London, Mary wrote to him that she had no doubt that Elizabeth was feeding both James and her 'with the hope of the succession' to the English crown, that this was 'but an artifice to hold us in leash', and was done only for her own security because she was 'more resolute than ever not to declare an heir while she lives'.[32] Mary had written to her son that while she could not 'entirely approve of this artificial demonstration of a discontent and new division between' them, it was understandable because their enemies such as Walsingham and Davison sought to prevent the treaty that would have freed Mary. It was doubtful, she wrote, that Elizbeth would believe the royal rift was genuine, and she would probably 'take it as dissimulation of a game designed on purpose between' Mary and James. She was worried though, that her impressionable son could be 'persuaded, either by the good promises of England or elsewhere to show himself separated from me', and would 'secretly obtain from [Elizabeth] better conditions'. If James chose this course, he would eventually be disappointed. Beware of *'la crocke en jambe'* [being tripped up], Mary warned, knowing from bitter experience that Elizabeth rarely delivered what she promised.[33]

In May 1586, Elizabeth sent Edward Wotton, 'a creature of Walsingham's', to Edinburgh to "beguile" James into agreeing to a defensive and offensive alliance that she hoped would neutralise Scotland. Wotton's patronising instructions were to 'not trouble his Majesty with business or country affairs, but with honest pastimes of hunting, hawking and horse-riding, and with friendly and merry discourses ...' and to assure him of 'his title and right to the crown of England'. Upon being told of Wotton's worldliness, in contrast to his boorish courtiers, James 'was ravished to love him before he did see him'.[34] Wotton succeeded in persuading James to the English perspective somewhat, but not ultimately to conclude the league.

Walsingham's frustration with Elizabeth's lackadaisical attitude towards Scotland was undiminished. He grumbled to Leicester (who was then in the Netherlands on what was proving to be his own misadventure) 'how hazardously her majesty dealeth in causes of Scotland ... I find it a very hard matter to conserve the amity of that country in the course now held here, and what danger may grow from the loss thereof .... [The Queen] greatly presumeth fortune [luck], which is a but a [very] weak foundation to build upon'.[35]

As evidence from Walsingham's intelligencers increased about Philip's plans for an invasion of England, the interventionist councillors were adamant that the 'contest in the Low Countries was the greatest, if not the only, obstacle in the way of Philip's meditated expedition, for, great as was the power of Spain, it seemed insufficient to maintain at one time a crusade against Protestantism in England as well as in the Netherlands'.[36]

Tying down Parma's army in Holland would buy time for ships to be built and men trained to repel the expected Spanish invasion.

The death of Elizabeth's erstwhile suitor Anjou in June 1584, followed by the assassination of the Prince of Orange the following month left the States without a leader and seemingly on the retreat everywhere from the Duke of Parma's *reconquesta*. A string of military disasters suffered by the States forces enabled Walsingham, Leicester and Davison to gain the support of Burghley and most other councillors in convincing Elizabeth that the Netherlands would be lost without direct English intervention and significant financial assistance. Delegates from the States-General travelled to London to beg for English military aid, offering sovereignty to Elizabeth, which she repeatedly rejected.

On New Year's Eve 1584, a secret treaty was signed at Joinville, France, by the Catholic League. The treaty united the powerful House of Guise with the Spanish, the Papal States, the Duchy of Savoy and German Catholics in an escalation of the Counter-Reformation. Its goal was the eradication, by fire and sword if necessary, of all Protestants in France and strict enforcement of the decrees of the Council of Trent, which codified the doctrines of the Church of Rome. The treaty was a *de facto* declaration of war against heretics anywhere. Philip agreed to finance the League by giving 50,000 crowns to each member.

Few confidences could be kept for long from Walsingham. He received 'secret advertisements' detailing the Treaty in March 1585.[37] Following her usual pattern, Elizabeth was shaken when Walsingham showed her the treaty's terms, believing like her ministers that its true purpose was to form a Papist alliance against Protestants throughout Europe that would become a crusade to crush England under the Catholic heel.[38]

The Queen soon returned to her havering, even after fresh intelligence of Philip's seizure of English shipping that he intended to use for an armada against England.[39] Sir Francis wearily told Stafford, 'how her Majesty will yield is yet uncertain ... so loath is she to enter into a war'. Despite the rare concurrence of her entire Council that it was 'a dangerous course for her and that it is impossible that she should long stand unless she enter openly and roundly into the action', the Queen continued to oppose direct English military intervention in the Low Countries, refusing 'to enter into the action except underhand'.[40] Although Elizabeth was eventually persuaded to send 4,000 men-at-arms to relieve the siege of Antwerp, the city fell before the force could be dispatched, infuriating Walsingham.

Throughout July 1585, Walsingham and Burghley led negotiations with the Netherlanders which resulted in the signing of Anglo-Dutch treaties at Nonsuch Palace, near Hampton Court, in August. Although Elizabeth had grudgingly supported the negotiations, she made a last-ditch effort for mediation 'to try to draw the wars to the end', hoping that Philip would 'enter into some treaty with the United Provinces for compounding their differences with the King, respect of their liberties and freedom of conscience'.[41] But the line was drawn, and war with Spain was now inevitable.

The fourth in a series of Anglo-Scottish 'Treaties of Berwick' was signed on 5 July 1586 after incidents including the murder of a young English nobleman by a henchman of Arran and an invasion by the exiled lairds, who led an army to Stirling Castle and coerced James to strip Arran of his titles and power and force him into internal exile. The 'Offensive and Defensive alliance' bound both parties to defend the Evangelical religion in their respective countries, to mutually defend one another in the event of a foreign invasion, and provided that Elizabeth would 'not derogate in any degree from the claims of the King of Scots to the English crown'.[42]

As his mother feared, James chose Elizabeth's 'good promises' in return for a pension of £4,000 per annum and other emoluments, including thirty bucks from the Earl of Northumberland's deer park. Elizabeth and the Burghley faction believed that James was even more fully ensnared when word came that Mary had revised her will, disinheriting him if he remained a Protestant and naming Philip as the 'legitimate heir to the crowns of England, Ireland and Scotland, in whose favour she abdicated any right she might have to those crowns'.[43] Burghley rather smugly told

Leicester that 'in Scotland, to all outward appearance, things proceed well'.[44]

The 'amity' of the most recent Treaty of Berwick was short-lived. News of Mary's beheading on 8 February 1587 'swept over Scotland' in the following weeks, from Glasgow to the Western Isles, 'a vociferous and dangerous veil to trouble the South'. James' cousin the Earl of Bothwell declared that chain mail was the only mourning wear and pressed for an invasion of England to avenge Mary. The Hamiltons offered to burn Newcastle, while the Papist lairds renewed their intrigues with King Philip. The 'Borders became alive with silence and spears', and Robert Carey, Elizabeth's envoy who was sent north to plead her innocence in the beheading, was stopped at the frontier and warned that his life was at risk if he ventured into Scotland. Scottish men-at-arms interrogated travelers at the border and confiscated correspondence, cutting off Walsingham's painstakingly reconstructed intelligence network. 'Outlaws and loose persons' resumed raids into Northumberland and Cumberland, burning English homesteads, killing farmers and stealing livestock.[45]

Gray was tried for treason and a host of other charges, including forging the King's signature using his stamp, 'consenting to the death and murder of [Mary], the Queen, his majesty's dearest mother, for the sumptuous gratitudes and rewards which the said master had received in England', and writing 'to the Queen of England … bearing in effect that if the Queen of England could not perceive her own security in taking his majesty's mother's life' then Mary should be quietly put to death '*quia mortui non mordent*' ['as the dead do not bite'].[46] Gray was imprisoned at Edinburgh Castle before being banished from Scotland, but allowed to return less than two years later due to James' undiminished fondness for him.

Elizabeth had been lulled into believing that James possessed a venality that would make him indifferent to his mother's execution as long as he received his £4,000 annual pension and believed that he was the English Queen's anointed successor. This was a dangerous assumption, as in fact the King was as outraged as his nobility (including the nominally pro-English Earls of Mar and Angus). The regicide actually was a catalyst for uniting the fractious Scots, albeit briefly. Walsingham was told by one of his agents who had escaped before the border was sealed that 'the King taketh the death of his mother most heinously'. It was also now more certain than ever that James 'giveth ear [listened receptively] to foreign nations, and namely to France', and that he was open 'to undertake the Catholic cause' in return for their aid if it resulted in setting 'the Crown of England upon his head.'[47]

In the following months, rancorous Anglo-Scottish relations subsided to an uneasy détente, although hatred of the English burned strongly. An Act was passed 'that no Scots man shall marry an English woman without licence under the great seal'.[48] Communications were restored, yet the exchange of diplomatic messages as well as personal ones between Elizabeth and James were rife with accusations and recriminations. James demanded proof of Elizabeth's 'innocency' for the death of his mother, driving Elizabeth to declare in frustration that as 'a Queen and a Prince Sovereign, she was answerable to none for her actions ... but the Almighty God alone'.[49]

As reports from Walsingham's intelligencers confirmed, Philip's invasion plans were finally coming to fruition. Elizabeth accused James with Scottish Catholics of having 'secretly assented ... to allure strange forces from Spain and other places ... to make invasion into England'.[50] Philip offered to lend James 'the wage of 30,000 soldiers for three years or longer if he would make war with the Queen of England; with further promises' that hinted at putting him on the English throne as a surrogate of the Spanish emperor.[51] Papist lairds offered to hand over to Philip 'one or two good ports near the English border to be used against' Elizabeth.[52]

Quite literally as the sails of the Spanish Armada appeared on the horizon, William Ashby was sent as Her Majesty's resident ambassador into what his compatriots considered a savage land beset by 'often mutinies and other disorders', with a mandate to keep James in amity with England whatever the cost.[53]

# 12. The Armada cometh

William Ashby was a curious choice for resident ambassador in Scotland. Although he previously travelled to Scotland at least once on a diplomatic mission, he had spent most of his career in northern continental Europe, primarily in Germany and the Low Countries, with considerable time in Paris. Between 1584 and 1586, Ashby continued serving on the Continent in his amorphous intelligence and diplomatic role. During this period, the historical record offers only brief glimpses of him. The last known account of his work outside the British Isles was in March 1586, when he was at the English embassy in Paris. He may have been clandestinely investigating Sir Edward Stafford, who Walsingham believed was a traitor serving the Spanish.[1]

In October 1586, Ashby was named Member of Parliament for Grantham, Lincolnshire, as remuneration for his unpaid government service. Grantham was a parliamentary seat controlled by the 3rd Earl of Rutland, who owned a majority of 'burgage tenements', whose occupants had the right to vote in parliamentary elections of the borough. In the eighteenth century, such seats would be called 'pocket boroughs', but they were equally notorious in the Tudor era. Ashby's immediate predecessor as MP, Arthur Hall, a 'reprobate', brought a writ against the citizens of Grantham for wages 'for his service done for them … for attendance at sundry parliaments'. However, a parliamentary committee found that Hall 'hath not given any attendance at Parliament at all'.[2]

In the sixteenth century, MPs were paid by local constituents whether or not they had voted for the Members, a practice favoured by the government as there was no cost to HM Treasury. As Ashby maintained Leicestershire and Lincolnshire connections throughout his life, his appointment was not wholly gratuitous and, unlike Hall, he took his seat at Westminster and attended Parliament.

No direct relationship between the Earl and Ashby has been found, although – given his experience and personal connections in Scotland – it is probable that he accompanied Rutland (and Thomas Randolph) to Berwick in June and July 1586 to conclude the 'League of good amity' between the two crowns.[3] Regardless of a relationship with Rutland, Ashby was nominated for the parliamentary seat by Walsingham.[4] He reluctantly resigned shortly after accepting his ambassadorial appointment.

Scotland was critical to England's national security, and never more so than in early July 1588 when the Spanish invasion fleet was approaching southwest England. A skilled diplomat was needed, with the gravitas and finesse necessary to quickly reweave the badly frayed alliance. Ashby was the choice of Queen Elizabeth (implying that others were under consideration), and he was certainly recommended for the ambassadorship by Walsingham.[5]

A possible explanation for his appointment could be that more experienced, and higher ranking, diplomats simply did not want to endure the frustration, expense and danger of the ambassadorial appointment. Randolph barely escaped assassination in Edinburgh in 1581, Wotton had been discredited, and Hunsdon, Knollys and Bowes hated serving as envoys to Scotland.

Robert Carey claimed that 'he should have been then sent ambassador to the King of Scots' in 1588, but was unable to go due to illness.[6] As Elizabeth's cousin, he may have been the first choice as resident ambassador. In addition to his aborted mission to mollify James after his mother's beheading, Carey served as special ambassador to Scotland at the beginning of 1588, where he spent two weeks at Dumfries with James being 'nobly entertained' and succeeded in restoring diplomatic relations.[7] In June, he made a second visit to Scotland, accompanied by one of Walsingham's agents named Robert Carvell, who carried £2,000 in gold coins, which he left with Bowes in Berwick to be collected by the King's 'bagman', Sir John Carmichael.[8] At that time, Carey told Carmichael and the chancellor, John Maitland, that, because he had been injured falling down stairs, he had informed Elizabeth that he was unable to be the resident ambassador, and that the Queen 'means to send some other' whom he was sure would be equally acceptable to James.[9]

Walsingham may have groomed Ashby for the appointment. He considered him a trusted and competent subordinate, known as a 'follower' of Sir Francis rather than of Burghley.[10] Despite his austere and cynical nature, Walsingham had his favourites. In a letter written to Ashby shortly after assuming his diplomatic post in Scotland, the Secretary mentioned 'the particular love' he had for him.[11]

Ashby was acquainted with Scottish courtiers and government officials, as well as with English policy towards Scotland.[12] Prior to his arrival in Edinburgh, Ashby mentioned 'my friends' in Scotland, some of whom may have become contacts during the 1583 mission, while others were noblemen such as the Hamiltons, who fled to England in 1584 after their attempted coup and returned to Scotland the following year.[13]

Elizabeth entrusted Sir Francis with the management of Scottish affairs, although Burghley pursued his own diplomacy, which was occasionally at odds with Walsingham's.[14] The Secretary mistrusted Carey, suspecting him of being too close to the conspiratorial Earl of Bothwell, whose 'gentlemen gave most great and high commendations of the Spaniards, and what worthy men they were'. During his June visit to Scotland, Carey and his entourage were invited to Bothwell's house, 'with an attention to make them drunk', after which Lady Bothwell 'seeing he had enough and fit for her purpose', reportedly seduced him into 'revealing state secrets'.[15] Sir Francis understood that Bothwell 'may be won with money' and reputedly 'hath borrowed of the King of Spain'.[16]

******

The history of the Spanish Armada has been examined in great detail elsewhere, but as it was a key part of William Ashby's life story – in fact, the primary reason for his ambassadorship – a recapitulation as it relates to his diplomatic career in Scotland is fitting.

The Spanish had been planning an invasion of England for years, although the implementation was delayed due to financial and political concerns, as well as Leicester's expedition from 1585 to 1586, which although unsuccessful militarily, did tie down Alba's forces. The execution of Mary Stuart galvanised the Catholic League, especially as Philip claimed the right to the English throne both by blood (as the descendant of English King Edward III) and by Mary's Will. Bypassing James (who the Spanish thought would be the pawn of the French Guise faction if he assumed the English throne), Philip suggested to the Pope that his daughter, the *Infanta* Isabella, would be the appropriate compromise candidate to succeed Elizabeth. Understandably, this was not well-received by James, but he maintained a cautious neutrality while courting Spanish support.

By October 1587, Elizabeth and her ministers were left in no doubt that 'a mighty army' was in preparation in Spain and the Netherlands and that an invasion via Scotland was probable. An intelligence asset in Holland reported that '... the talk goeth it [the Spanish fleet] is meant towards Scotland, and I think the Scot will not deal against England except [with] great assistance of outward friends. I hope you trust them not and then they shall not deceive you. There goeth an old speech . . . which is

> That he that England will win
>
> At Scotland must first begin.'[17]

In late January 1588, the Spanish offered to resurrect stalled peace negotiations that had been irregularly taking place for several years. Lord Howard of Effingham, Lord Admiral and a Privy Council member, believed these were a sham and expressed his dismay in a letter to Walsingham:

> I have made of the French King, the Scottish King, and the
>
> King of Spain, a Trinity that I mean never to trust to be saved

by; and I would others were, in that, of my opinion. Sir, there was never, since England was England, such a stratagem and mask made to deceive England withal as this is of the treaty of peace. I pray God we have not cause to remember one thing that was made of the Scots by the Englishmen ....[18]

In late January, Walsingham, Burghley and Leicester separately wrote to Howard, alerting him to 'the great preparation in Dunkirk for Scotland' of Parma's invasion army. The Admiral's fleet was tugging at its moorings in the Medway, eager for action. It was clear, Howard replied to Sir Francis, 'that we may assure ourselves that Scotland is the mark they shoot at to offend [injure] us', and it was therefore of the utmost importance to prepare a defence. For his part, the Lord High Admiral said, he 'would rather be drawn in pieces with wild horses than that [the Spanish] should pass through for Scotland'.

Walsingham expected the invasion to take place in April or May, and Howard was instructed to be prepared to repel either an invasion of southern England or Parma 'going with forces into Scotland', or possibly both attacks simultaneously. The Lord Admiral urged Walsingham to 'cut off this matter of Scotland', that is, to mitigate the Spanish threat with a pre-emptive invasion of Scotland.[19] Sir Francis was aware that Robert Bruce, an emissary of the Catholic lairds, had been sent back to Scotland with 10,000 crowns to purchase 'a number of small boats at Leith and send them to Dunkirk for Parma's troops' with the promise of 150,000 crowns when they joined the invasion of England.[20]

Howard, Drake and the other English captains wanted to make a pre-emptive strike at the Spanish before the Armada could arrive in English waters. However, they were restrained by Elizabeth, who did not want to jeopardise the peace negotiations. As a result, Howard complained, 'they now make but little reckoning of us, for they know we are like bears tied to stakes, and they may come as dogs to offend us, and we cannot go to hurt them'.

The Lord Admiral shared Walsingham's belief that the Spanish were simply buying time with the negotiations, telling Sir Francis that he 'was looking every hour to hear from you of more mischief coming by this disputation of peace than any good that ever shall come of it'.[21] The beliefs were well-founded: Philip had issued secret orders to Parma to keep up the negotiations deception as long as possible as a distraction while actively readying his army for the invasion.[22]

In early May, an agent in Edinburgh reported that the Scottish Papists

> ... begin to lift up their heads by reason of the Spanish army
> which threatens England intending to land on the borders of
> Scotland. The King of Spain has sent Semple[23] to the King of
> Scotland (the traitor who delivered Lier up to the Spaniards),
> to procure his aid and favour, making him many fair promises.
> We do not yet know what will come of it.[24]

The jaded Cobham, one of the peace commissioners, had warned against the futility of the negotiations before they commenced. He wrote to Burghley that the Spanish preparations for invasion 'are great, their army increaseth daily, they threaten much and assure themselves of great aid when they land. In Scotland they say they have a great party. This shows how far their actions differ from their negotiations'.[25]

Walsingham's agents reported that the Spanish flagship left Lisbon on 28 May and the entire Armada was at sea by 30 May, yet Elizabeth seemed bafflingly unconcerned. Walsingham, confined to his bed 'waiting for the recurrence of his fit', wrote to Burghley that he was 'sorry to see so great a danger hanging over the realm so slightly regarded and so carelessly provided for. Would to God the enemy were no more careful to assail than we to defend'.[26] Sir Francis was equally frustrated with Burghley, who thought that his attending court was often a waste of time, and seemed more interested in suppressing a 'roaring hellish bull' written by the exiled Roman Catholic Cardinal William Allen, 12,000 copies of which were printed for distribution in England following a Spanish victory. The Lord Treasurer took the time amidst the crisis to draft a proclamation for the Queen calling the tract 'but a blast or puff of a beggarly scholar and traitor ... intended as a traitorous trumpet to wake up all robbers and Catholics in England against their sovereign'.[27]

Admiral Howard, an old sea dog who was less circumspect than Walsingham, fulminated to Sir Francis that he was 'sorry Her Majesty will not thoroughly awake in this perilous time'.[28] He implored Elizabeth 'for the love of Jesus Christ, to awake thoroughly and to see the villainous treasons around about her', and begged her to 'trust no more to Judas's kisses, but to defend herself like a noble and mighty prince, and to trust to her sword rather than to the word of her enemies'.[29]

While the vast fleet was making it ponderous way towards Britain, Cobham told Walsingham that the possibility of peace was 'beyond all reason'. In the same letter he warned that two Spanish ships 'were ready to go to Scotland, well-appointed [armed and crewed] but to what place I cannot learn'.[30]

In mid-June, Sir Francis received credible intelligence that Papist lairds in the north of Scotland had united 'to receive the Spaniards looked for to come into Scotland by Lammas [1 August] at the furthest'. They had approached James to allow the landing and stand aside for the drive south into England. The King 'altogether denied them, but they hope[d] in the end to persuade him'. Failing that, they believed that their forces combined with the Spanish would be able to defeat the small royal army. The Catholic lairds made careful intelligence estimates of 'who will take part with the King, and who join with them'. They concluded that 'the borough and corporate towns and ministry will be on the King's side, but most of the gentlemen, householders and commons they count on their side, which will exceed the King's party by far'. The lairds were confident that James would have only two choices: to ask Elizabeth for English military support 'or else be no party to withstand their proceedings' (remain neutral during the invasion).[31]

Would James have acquiesced to a Spanish base in Scotland and supported an invasion of England from the north? Walsingham and his colleagues considered it likely. As late as early July, an intelligencer in Lisbon reported that, although the recently departed Armada was said to be bound for England, 'it is thought for certain they go for Scotland, and that the King of Scots hath promised them entry and help in his country'.[32] The Spanish seemed to think that James' loyalties could swing either way. Upon receiving a report from a Scottish Catholic bishop, Parma wrote to Philip that despite James being 'a confirmed heretic' and his government 'in the interest of the Englishwoman', if the Catholics were 'well supported' by the Spanish, 'whilst the English had their hands full elsewhere', the King would join the Catholic party and turn against the English. Parma's agent said that James had confided that, for the time being, he was 'obliged to act in an exactly contrary way, and persecutes the Catholics rigorously'.[33]

James may have been wisely holding his cards close to his chest, unwilling to commit to the powers courting him until he saw which way the wind carried the Spanish forces. However, he often blew hot and cold, passionate at one moment while disinterested the next, notorious for his preoccupation with hunting and other pleasures. Contemporaries said he played Maw, his mother's favourite card game, in the same way he conducted 'affairs of State – in an indolent manner, requiring in both cases someone to hold his cards, if not to prompt him what to play'.[34] While James never wavered from his ambition to succeed to Elizabeth's throne, he was a survivor and therefore open to options by which to achieve it.

★★★★★★

By June 1588, the decision had been made to send William Ashby to Scotland as Elizabeth's resident ambassador. Archibald Douglas, personal envoy of James VI to London and double agent, wrote to his nephew Richard Douglas at the royal court in Edinburgh informing him of Ashby's appointment. Immediately after receiving the letter,[35] the younger Douglas met with James to inform him. Expressing his frustration at what he considered a succession of empty English promises, James said that he saw no point in sending 'any gentleman upon a sudden' to him from England, unless the new envoy 'was a man of great calling' who could arrive 'fully instructed to satisfy him in all points as he expected and as was promised him'.[36]

Although the younger Douglas assured James that Ashby had impeccable credentials, was a 'particular friend' of Archibald Douglas, and 'near kinsman to Mr. Fowler, his Highness's servant, & c.', he could offer no reassurance about the overdue English promises.[37] The 'points' James expected were those propounded to other English envoys over the past several years: a substantial pension, 'some name of dignity' (i.e., a dukedom) and, most importantly, 'that nothing should be done hereafter prejudicial to his title and right to the [English] crown'.[38]

James knew that Ashby was being hastily sent to Scotland because of the panic in London at the approach of the Spanish fleet, and the long-standing English fear of Scotland serving as a base for invasion, which now seemed close to becoming reality. The King, who had met Ashby during Walsingham's 1583 mission, told Douglas that he was 'contented' with Ashby's appointment as ambassador, but that his 'coming hither' to Edinburgh should be delayed until 16 July, on the excuse that he would be away for a wedding. The King was probably prevaricating to see the outcome of the Spanish invasion attempt.[39]

Ashby travelled to Berwick during the first week of July. The towns and villages he passed through were convulsed by uncertainty and near panic as rumours spread of the pending invasion. The Spaniards were said to be 'bringing cargoes of scourges and instruments of torture, all adults were to be put to death, and seven thousand wet-nurses were coming in the Armada to suckle the orphan infants'.[40] A somewhat contradictory report stated that the enemy 'meant to carry off the English women to Spain and that the King's commission instructed them to massacre everyone they met in England, even the children'.[41] Spanish noblemen were reported to be casting lots for confiscated English estates.[42]

Men of all ages, including household servants, were mustered, although the 'number of shot, corslets, bows and bills' was alarmingly limited. Andrew Perne, the Dean of Ely, who William Ashby and his fellow students had mocked at Cambridge, promised to provide 'one demi-lance, one light horse, a petronel, a pikeman, and a billman'.[43] In Surrey, 1,500 men were reported to be 'trained and furnished with arms', while another 300 could be available if armed with bows.[44] The Privy Council ordered that prominent recusants be imprisoned in the Tower. One of Walsingham's spies, who had been 'racked and tormented' by the Spanish, escaped to bring bad news that the Armada had been augmented by 'ships of Italy with five thousand sailors'. However, the good news was that the Italian mariners were said to be 'very simple and feeble creatures'.[45]

Ashby lingered at Berwick for several days waiting for a Scottish passport. He spent the time being briefed by Robert Bowes, who in his new role as Treasurer of Berwick continued to serve as Walsingham's most important intelligencer and expert on Scotland and the Borders. Bowes related his meeting with Sir John Carmichael (during which he gave him the gold brought by Carey) the day before Ashby's arrival at Berwick. Carmichael warned that James was being 'greatly solicited and pressed to hearken to the large offers made to him by Spain and France, which by sundry in Scotland were esteemed to sound to the King's great benefit and advantage', and that the King was being urged by his councillors to accept the offers. Although 'the King's good mind and affection' were '*presently*' (emphasis added) with Elizabeth, James expected certain rewards so that he 'might be timely embraced and bound fast to her majesty'.[46]

Carmichael told Bowes that James was unhappy that 'the particularities of his desires' had not been addressed, he was tired of empty English promises, and 'trusted that her majesty would grant to him' what he wanted without further delay. Although dressed in diplomatic language, the Scot made it clear that to 'bind the King to her majesty's course' and disregard England's enemies, James required the promised 'pension of £5000 by year, to bestow upon him the title and dignity of some dukedom in England, to honour him with the order of the Garter, and at some time to present him with some jewel or other acceptable token of favour'. While not stated directly, it was implied that in the near future James wished to have confirmation of being Elizabeth's successor.[47]

Bowes equivocated, telling Carmichael that in his previous dealings with James he had expressed Elizabeth's good will and readiness 'to satisfy him in all convenient requests'. However, the velvet glove was briefly removed from the mailed English fist when he countered with a warning of the danger to the King if he pursued 'matters inconvenient either in their own nature or yet to himself, his honour or estate'. Unable to respond to James' demands, Bowes told the Scottish envoy that for 'the King's good contentment in these and all other things ... her majesty had made choice and sent Mr. Ash[by] to the King, with such acceptable matters as I trusted should be right well received, and that the sufficiency and good will of this gentleman employed should do all good offices to ... the effects desired'.[48]

Carmichael returned to report to James that he understood that Ashby would arrive with authority from Elizabeth to grant his wishes. Bowes told Ashby that during his 'long discourse' with the Scot, he had outlined the principal points of the new ambassador's negotiating position, which evidently had substantial latitude. Revealing his own sense of relief at no longer being responsible for dealing with the Scottish King's demands, Bowes wrote to Walsingham and Burghley that he left 'the travail of all these things to Mr. Ashby'. In 1588, the word 'travail' meant the same as it does today – work of a painful or laborious nature.[49]

Walsingham had given Ashby written instructions that have been lost, possibly deliberately. These contained the ambassador's broad mandate for negotiations to placate James. However, the inscribed instructions apparently differed from the Secretary's verbal orders. After his first meeting with Bowes, Ashby wrote to Sir Francis asking him to 'add anything more then by your good instructions I have already received I shall be the better able to satisfy the Lord Chancellor or the King if occasion be so offered'.[50]

Considering his long experience at the service of a mercurial Queen, as well as his crafty patron, it is not improbable that the newly appointed ambassador's request hints at worry that the outcome of his negotiations could be repudiated. Ashby was a trained lawyer, and the adage 'get it in writing' was as true in the Elizabethan era as in the twenty-first century.

As a result of Ashby's hurried departure from London, he was 'ill furnished with money', having only £30 'to carry into Scotland'. He asked Walsingham for a loan of £100, saying that '[i]t shall be repaid within six months at furthest, for I have so much of mine own to receive in London in September next'. Ashby expected to be charged an outrageous amount for lodging in Edinburgh, but hoped that some of his friends there would help find cheaper accommodation.[51]

William Ashby arrived in Edinburgh on 15 July with a staff of 'eight or nine' which included his 'man servant' Peter Haye, the intelligencer Robert Carvell (who joined him at Berwick), two clerks (who also served as intelligencers), two other servants, and a pair of body guards.[52] Ashby had no illusions about his diplomatic post: the 'state of Scotland' was described by Walsingham as resembling 'a diseased body, that one day yieldeth hope of life, and another utter despair of recovery'.[53] Ashby had dealt with numerous challenging foreign assignments during his career, but he knew that his tenure in Scotland would be the most important and difficult.

Hostility against England, and Elizabeth's representative, was palpable. Scottish resentment for the murder of their queen simmered. On the morning after Ashby's entourage arrived in Edinburgh, a crudely hand-lettered broadsheet was found nailed to the door of the lodgings which served as the English embassy:

> To Jezebel that English whore,
>
> Receive this Scottish chain,

As presages of her great malheur [misfortune]

For murdering of our queen.

A small cord of hemp, tied like a hangman's noose, was attached to the bottom of the paper.[54] A similar 'libel' had been affixed to the door of Ambassador Thomas Randolph in 1581.

# 13. Ashby's ambassadorship to Scotland

William Ashby, like many privileged English visitors to Scotland, thought Edinburgh was a primitive hell-hole, infested with savages.

Although dirty and crime-ridden, London and Paris were salubrious havens compared to Edinburgh. The Scottish capital had only one main thoroughfare, running for a mile from the King's palace at Holyrood to the Castle. The closes and wynds spiralling off the High Street were 'narrow, filthy and with six-story houses ... poorly built' and 'inhabited with very poor people .... poverty and misery seem to peep out of the open hatches which normally serve as windows'.[1] Unwanted infants were routinely 'exposed in streets and at doors'.[2]

The 'multitude of beggars' became so 'very troublesome to the neighbours of the burgh' that the city's burghers proclaimed that 'none of the said beggars be found begging through the streets and High Gate upon the Sundays, under the pain of imprisonment in the thieves hall [and be kept] forty-eight hours without meat and drink'.[3] Prostitutes infested the unfinished Trinity College Kirk, servicing workmen repairing the church and students at the new University of Edinburgh to the extent that the town council decreed a law to 'suppress the vice of fornication'.[4]

Foreign visitors described Edinburgh as 'one of the dirtiest cities ... ever seen'.... 'an accursed, stinking, reeky mass of stones and lime and dung'. A former resident of Blackfriars Wynd, a stone's throw from the English embassy, remembered that 'in the slums, dunghills and raw sewage blanketed the crowded space with a sticky black glaze'.[5] An Englishman who lived in the city wrote that 'no smells were ever equal to Scotch smells. It is the School of Physic; walk the streets and you would imagine that every medical man had been administering cathartics to every man, woman and child in town'.[6] Several months earlier, the plague had been 'very grievous in Leith, and many houses infected in Edinburgh'.[7]

Edinburgh was a dangerous place for its inhabitants but especially for Englishmen and women. Ashby's embassy was in the same dank, multi-storied house that had lodged Thomas Randolph. The former resident ambassador fled Scotland after a harquebus was fired at him through the 'window of his chamber, in the place where he is wont to sit and write … which struck through the window hard by him, and made two great holes through the wall on the far side'.[8] A previous English ambassador's wife was attacked and injured by a ruffian who was punished by being 'bound to a gibbet, his tongue pierced and banished from the town'.[9]

The embassy was in 'a mean, narrow' and fetid street near the 'High Kirk' of St. Giles, where 'the houses stand so one upon the other that none of the smoke wastes itself upon the desert air before the inhabitants have derived all the advantages of its odour and its smuts. You might smoke bacon by hanging it out the window'.[10]

There was 'no system of lighting for the streets of the city … after twilight all was sunk in Cimmerian darkness, saving for the occasional light of the moon and stars'. The dark streets became the domain of 'Night-Walkers' – 'idle and debauched persons who went about the streets during the night, in the indulgence of wild humours, and sometimes committing heinous crimes'. The Night-Walkers, believed by some to be evil spirits, indulged 'in all kind of excess, riot and drunkenness', perpetrating 'sundry enormities upon his majesty's peaceable and guid subjects', not sparing the 'ordinar officers of the burgh, who are appoint to watch the streets … some have been cruelly and unmercifully slain, and others left for deid'.[11]

Blood feuds and robberies – called 'Spuilzies' by Edinburghers – were common. A laird's agent was attacked by 'two young Hamiltons of Prestoun' whilst at evening prayers in St. Giles. Breaking 'his head with the pommels of their swords, they chased him out by the west porch … and cut off two fingers of his left hand'.[12] St. Giles became so perilous that

1.Part of the Map of the Kingdome of Scotland (1610) by John Speed, the
Kingdom of Scotland during Ashby´s service as ambassador.

2. Scottish witches cursing travellers, from *Chronicles of England, Scotlande, and Irelande* by Raphael Holinshed. During Walsingham's ill-fated diplomatic delegation to Scotland in August and September 1583, the Englishmen were hounded by 'Kate the witch', who 'assailed them with vile speeches.'

3. Portrait of James VI, and later I of England, at age eighteen circa 1585, by Adrian Vanson (1580–1601). The teenage King James VI/I in appearance as Ashby would have known him during his first diplomatic mission to Scotland in 1583.

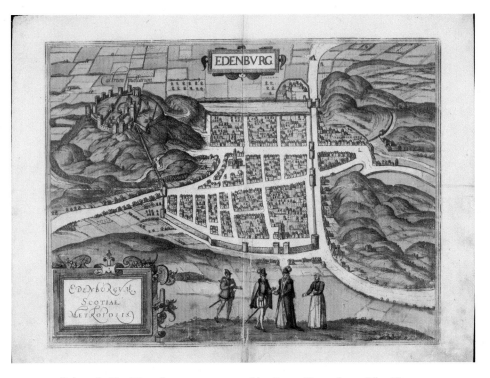

4. Edinburgh City Plan circa 1582 engraved by Franz Hogenberg. The City of Edinburgh during Ashby's visit with the 1583 English delegation and as ambassador from 1588–1590.

5. An Edinburgh street scene which would have changed little since Ashby's ambassadorial service. 'Dowie's Tavern, Libberton's Wynd' Edinburgh, by George Cattermole (1800–1868)

6. James VI of Scotland aged twenty by Alonso Sanchez Coello, as Ashby would have known him from 1588 and 1589.

7. Palace of Holyrood House, Edinburgh, as it would have appeared in the late sixteenth century.

8. Galleon, copper engraving by Frans Huys after designs by Pieter Bruegel the Elder. The San Juan de Sicilia, an Armada carrack of 800 tons with twenty-six guns and a complement of sixty-two sailors and 287 soldiers, was blown up by Ashby's agent John Smollet in Tobermory Bay on 5 November 1588.

9. Queen Elizabeth I (1533–1603) painted circa 1588, in the style of the English school by an unconfirmed English artist. The Queen's tempestuous nature frustrated Walsingham, who nonetheless served her faithfully until his death.

10. John Maitland (1545–1595), 1st Lord Maitland of Thirlestane by John Scougal (1645–1717). John Maitland was Scottish Chancellor and Ashby's principal diplomatic counterpart during his ambassadorial service in Scotland.

11. Portrait of Lord John Hamilton, 1st Marquess of Hamilton, by an unknown artist c1556. Lord John Hamilton was Ashby's closest friend in Scotland; the ambassador was godfather to his son James, second Marquess of Hamilton.

12. Witches brewing a spell in a cauldron, woodcut c. 1508 from *De Lamiis et Pythonicis Mulieribus*. The fierce storms that drove Princess Anne's fleet back to Norway were blamed on 'numerous poor Danish women' who were burned as witches for brewing 'the tempestuous winds'.

13. Sir Robert Naunton, line engraving by Simone de Passe, early seventeenth century. Naunton, Ashby's nephew and heir, was appointed by James I as Principal Secretary of State in 1618.

a city ordinance was proclaimed to punish malefactors because 'wicked people has in times past made their turbulences within the High Kirk of this burgh, by injuring their neighbours, drawing of swords and shooting of pistols, and thereby abusing that place'.[13]

Shortly after Ashby's arrival, the Earl of Bothwell's gang fought with William Stewart's on the High Street after Stewart told Bothwell to kiss his arse. Known as 'William the Sticker', Stewart lost his rapier in the melee and fled into Blackfriars Wynd where Bothwell 'strake him in the back and out the belly, and killed him'.[14]

The breakdown of law and order was partially due to the successive waves of plague that had devastated Scotland during the previous four years. No one could approach King James without a certificate proving they were disease-free. In May 1585, the Edinburgh council issued ordinances against 'beggars and filth' and evacuated the law courts and other branches of government to Stirling. Government had broken down to the point that 'vigilance commissions' were empowered to impose the death penalty for plague ordinance violations and to carry out general administration.

★★★★★★

Maitland, the Lord Chancellor, sent Ashby the King's passport on 10 July with a note leading him to believe that James would return to court around the middle of the month. The new ambassador timed his travel to Edinburgh to arrive a day or two before the King. However, in what was suspected as a diplomatic slight, he was only received by Carmichael, 'left here of purpose to entertain me, and one of the Douglases sent from the King out of Fyffe to the like effect', whereas according to normal protocol Ashby would have been met by the Chancellor.[15]

But these were not normal times, and the Scots' intent was to remind the English of their independence and ability to control the 'portal' for a northern invasion.

Ashby was kept waiting, receiving assurances on the 20th that 'the King is expected here this day: the Lord Chancellor sendeth me word that I shall have audience the 22 at the furthest'.[16] Ashby knew that James had returned to Edinburgh to attend the wedding at Holyrood of his favourite the Earl of Huntly on the 20th, for which the King composed 'a poetic entertainment with speeches from Mercury, a group of nymphs, Agrestis, and some comedy'.[17] Days passed without an invitation to present the new ambassador's credentials at Holyrood and deliver a letter from Queen Elizabeth. Unlike Walsingham during his visit, Ashby was unruffled by such slights.

The Scots were playing for time; they had their own intelligence sources and, with a time lag of a day or two, were just as aware of the progress of the Armada as were Elizabeth and her Privy Council. It was known that the Spanish fleet had been 'distressed' (delayed) by 'great storms' but had left Corunna en route for England, and possibly Scotland.

While Ashby waited for his audience with the King, he put his time to good use gathering intelligence about the domestic state of Scotland. He was 'feasted' at the house of Sir William Read (a self-professed admirer of Walsingham and double agent who was, in modern terms, an 'agent of influence'). Sir William gave him 'a fine Galloway nag' because, Ashby told Sir Francis, he 'was accounted a follower of yours, which brings me credit and profit'.[18] The ambassador was keenly aware of the undercurrents of treachery swirling around him. Like another English diplomat who preceded him, Ashby had been forewarned:

> The espial [surveillance] which will be set over him will settle
> him in sufficient acquaintance; access to court and acceptance
> with the best may be effected by noting those who first
> address themselves to him, who will be spies appointed by
> the King, his Council or some nimble head of the Papists or
> Protestants. He shall well consider their qualities, professions
> and speeches. Of this number of spies your host is likely to
> be one.[19]

Archibald Douglas had given his perspective on the political situation in Scotland when he met with him in London. Many of the nobility were divided between Protestant and Papist, while a number of the rest, usually 'indifferent' in religion, had been loyal to the late Queen Mary and considered England an enemy. Their enmity was exacerbated by 'the infinite number of piracies' committed by English mariners, which Elizabeth seemed unable or unwilling to suppress.[20]

As a result, the 'indifferents' had joined with the Catholics, which made 'that party both greater in number of nobility and stronger in force'.[21] They continued to support revenge for what they considered to be Mary's murder and an alliance with Spain or France. Although politically allied with the Papists, they would be satisfied with 'liberty of conscience' – freedom of religion – and did not seek the conversion of James to Roman Catholicism.

The King 'as yet' had not taken sides and 'gave equal favour to both parties'. But he was beginning to reach a decision and believed he had less reason to fear domestic rebellion than did Elizabeth. James was also on friendly terms with all foreign princes except her, and England stood alone against the great European powers that sought her downfall. There was widespread expectation that the 'forces of unfriends' were 'to be landed in Scotland'. Nonetheless, it was not too late to resolve James' ambiguity about supporting England and Scottish Protestants if a 'timeous remedy' could be provided by Elizabeth.[22]

James was a 'Prince grieved in mind', suffused with bitterness that the English had 'so slender regard of him, and take no better resolution for his satisfaction after so great injuries' (foremost of which was the execution of his mother). Elizabeth and her government had 'no respect nor regard unto him', and sought 'to abuse him with fair words till they have him embarked upon the same sea of troubles that they are in themselves'.[23]

He was profoundly frustrated with the Queen's vacillation, which was all too familiar to those who served her. She had agreed to give him lands in northern England that had belonged to his father Lord Darnley, as her gift rather than as a right of succession, but changed her mind and made the inheritance litigious between James and his rival for the succession, Lady Arbella Stuart.[24] The King had resolved that he would no longer delay 'to take the best course for his own surety and state of his country' and therefore could no longer be relied upon to ally with England 'for holding away of strangers to the common benefit of this isle' – a threat which was to galvanise Ashby.[25]

The 'apparent remedies' were unchanged from those propounded consistently by James, who now accepted that because Elizabeth could not 'publicly declare him second person' (her successor), he would be satisfied if she 'would privately do so under her own hand writ'. He also wanted 'a letter under the Great Seal, and the handwriting of those that were upon the jury' (which had convicted his mother of treason), 'concerning Her Majesty's innocency in that procedure'. Such a document would help to quell the outcry for revenge, and make an alliance with England more politically palatable.[26] The young King remained unwavering in his demands for an English dukedom, a £5,000 annual pension, and other rewards so that he could commit to 'enter into whatsoever sort of strait amity shall be thought convenient to be performed'.[27]

Ashby was aware that the Scots were using various means to alarm his government and pressure it to grant James' wishes. However, both the ambassador and Walsingham took seriously the threats of a Catholic insurrection in support of a Spanish invasion headed by Huntly, leader of the faction of northern Papist lairds that included the Earls of Crawford and Montrose.

Huntly was 'a great favourite' of James,[28] who was sometimes seen to kiss the Earl in public 'to the amazement [and amusement] of many'.[29] A notorious seducer of women and men, Huntly was yet another in a long series of favourites who cynically manipulated the King's affections. One contemporary wrote:

> ... to the Earl of Huntly's lying in his majesty's chamber
> and preaching Papistry, truth it is I think he be a Papist, but

not precise as he had not rather lie in a fair gentlewoman's
chamber than either in the King's, or yet where he might have
an hundred masses. [30]

On the afternoon of Sunday, 24 July, Ashby had his first audience
with King James at Holyrood Palace. Mimicking Walsingham's austerely
formal attire, the new ambassador wore a black satin doublet with a linen
cambric ruff, breeches over silk long stockings, all topped by a blocked
felt tall hat. He was immediately struck by the slovenly dress of the
King and the shabby appearance of his court and household.[31] The floor
of the audience chamber was littered with dog turds and other debris,
flies darted around an overflowing piss pot in a corner, and the smells
competed with the strong scent worn by the men to conceal their long-
unwashed bodies and clothes.

The twenty-two-year-old monarch was a very complicated and, in
modern terms, an emotionally damaged young man. Having been
'nourished in fear' of his life since infancy, he often dared 'not contradict
the great lords' and obsessively wanted to be 'considered brave and to
be feared' while desiring affection, loving 'indiscreetly and inadvisedly',
which was code for his homosexuality.[32]

James hated 'dancing and music in general, as likewise all wantonness
at Court, be it in discourses of love or in curiosity of habits', which
included men wearing earrings. The sophisticated Ashby, who had spent
years in various Continental courts as well as in London, thought the
young King crude. He was 'very rude and uncivil in speaking, eating,
manners, games, and entertainment in the company of women. He never
stops in one place, taking a singular pleasure in walking, but his gait is
bad, composed of erratic steps, and he tramps about even in his room'.[33]

James had a loud voice and spoke pompously. The King's greatest
pleasure was hunting, preferring to spend 'at least six hours together
chasing all over the place with loosened rein' to the tedium of court.
He was said by English critics to be 'too lazy and too thoughtless over

his affairs, too willing and devoted to his pleasure', which included male favourites as well as hunting.

Although James had 'a weak body', he 'was in no wise delicate'. One observer described him as an 'old young man'. English detractors said his 'ignorance and lack of knowledge of his poverty and his little strength, promising too much of himself and despising other princes ... were very bad for the preservation of his state and the government of the same'.

He could be alternately arrogant and paranoid, boasting that 'no affair of importance ever happened of which he did not know'. Although he distrusted his courtiers and nobility, claiming that 'nothing was done secretly by the lords that he did not know, by means of having spies at the doors of their rooms morning and evening, who came and reported everything to him', he nonetheless believed that his throne was safe despite numerous conspiracies against him, past and present.[34]

James was 'a true son of his mother in many things, but principally in that he is weak in body and cannot work long at his affairs, but when he gives himself to it' he could admirably 'keep himself six days continually at accounts, but that immediately after he never fails to be ill'.[35] Twenty-first century medical researchers theorise that the King suffered from an attenuated variant of Lesch-Nyhan disease, probably from inbreeding. He exhibited symptoms such as lifelong difficulties with walking due to delayed motor development, his speech was reportedly abnormal, he experienced difficulties with swallowing and was said to be clumsy and restless. James was prone to bouts of deep melancholy and liable to unpredictable outbursts of anger.[36]

Ashby gave James Elizabeth's official letter of introduction, written in her own hand, in which she said 'I have sent you this gentleman, as well to declare my good agreement to send some finischars [finishers or completion] of our league, as other matters which he hath to communicate unto you, if it please you to hear him'.[37] The King handed the letter to Maitland, the Chancellor, to be read later.

Although Elizabeth pretended to accept James' professed enmity towards the Spanish and desire for an 'offensive and defensive' league with England, her letter left no doubt that she did not trust him, thus further antagonising the Scots. The Queen prefaced her introductory letter disavowing responsibility for the execution of James' mother the previous year, although no one in either country believed this. She followed by reminding him that although he professed 'constant defence' of Scotland as well as England against 'all Spaniards and strangers', she had heard 'from both our enemies' that his reputation was being blotted 'with assurance of double dealing, as though you assured them underhand to betake you to their course'.

While Elizabeth stated that she would trust James' word until she could be 'so sure of the contrary', she issued a warning in a lyrical dictum:

> Right well am I persuaded that your greatest danger shall
>
> chance you by crossing your straight paths, for he that hath
>
> two strings to his bow may shoot stronger but never straight;
>
> and he that hath no foundation cannot but [come to] ruin.
>
> God keep you ever therefore in your well-begun path. [38]

As befitting an ambassador's first audience with a monarch, *pro forma* courtly pleasantries were exchanged, James asking after Elizabeth's health and her preparations to defend against the Armada (which James called 'the league', apparently meaning the Catholic League). The King promised to support Elizabeth, 'accompting her majesties foes his foes', before bluntly asking Ashby if he 'had anything to say in particular'.

Concealing his frustration, the ambassador replied with the same noncommittal platitudes as his predecessors, telling James 'how acceptable to her majesty was his well disposed mind, signified by Mr. Robert Carey, and also his letters preferring her amity before all other'. This was not what the King wanted to hear. He beckoned Maitland to his side, had a whispered exchange, then told Ashby that the Chancellor would confer with him and that he stood ready to meet again whenever the ambassador desired. The audience was ended. Ashby bowed and was escorted out by Maitland.

Ashby felt that his hands were tied by conflicting instructions and rivalry within the court in London. Burghley was again pursuing his own diplomatic initiative on behalf of Elizabeth, sending his agent Richard Wigmore to Edinburgh shortly before Ashby's arrival.[39] The Queen seemed obsessed with declarations of her innocence in Mary's execution, pinning the blame on Davison. Wigmore's instructions referred to 'some kind of pretended title as he [James] may make after our death as successor to this crown'. Elizabeth authorised Wigmore to tell James that he would 'receive some public instrument' certifying that 'such right as he may any way pretend can in no sort be weakened or prejudiced by the sentence of treason against his mother', harshly adding that this was 'as much as we can yield for his contentment touching that point'. The use of the terms 'pretended' and 'pretend' was deliberate, implying that James' claim to Elizabeth's throne was not recognised.[40]

The Queen's response to James' request for an English dukedom was equally dismissive: 'touching some ancient [title] of dukedom or earldom which the said King seems to affect within this our realm,' Elizabeth reminded him that Robert Carey had recently 'utterly dissuaded' James from continuing to raise the subject, especially because 'at this time [it] might breed an unnecessary jealousy between us'.

Ashby was increasingly concerned about ambiguities and missing parts of his written instructions from Walsingham. He wrote to Sir Francis three days before his first audience with the King, apparently in reference to James' renewed demands for legal proof of Elizabeth's innocence regarding Mary's death, which were anticipated. The instructions evidently contained guidance on what Ashby was permitted to offer the King in the likely event that he did 'not rest satisfied therewith'. Elizabeth's exculpatory testimony, apparently referred to in the secret instructions, was never delivered to the ambassador. Considering it 'requisite' for his negotiations, he asked Walsingham to include it in his next packet of letters.[41]

Ashby told Sir Francis that he had 'great hope of the King's faithful mind' and that he was scheduled 'to confer with the Chancellor, and afterward to the King again' the following day, Monday, 25 July. However, James was unavailable, having gone to Falkland Palace in Fife. Rumours of a Spanish victory against the English fleet had begun circulating, and panic spread among Presbyterians who feared a Catholic rebellion. 'Terrible was the fear, piercing were the preachings, earnest, zealous, and fervent were the prayers, sounding were the sighs and sobs, and abounding were the tears'[42]. James was playing for time, hoping that his friendship with Huntly and other Papist lairds would save him if the Armada prevailed, while striving to avoid a break with the English despite what he and his councillors considered Elizabeth's imperiousness.

On Friday, 19 July, five days before Ashby's first meeting with James, the Armada was sighted off the Scilly Isles. Beacons flared in Cornwall, quickly spreading along the coast and inland, alerting London. Next day, Lord Admiral Howard's fleet worked out of Plymouth harbour against prevailing winds. On Sunday, Howard's ships closed with the Spanish and at long range fired the first shots of the Battle of the Narrow Seas.

As news of the sea battles trickled into London, the Scottish envoy Douglas wrote to Walsingham on the 26th saying that Ashby had not as of the 19th 'gotten audience' with James and imploring him to give some answer 'in this perilous time' to satisfy his master.[43] Amidst the uncertainty and turmoil gripping the court, Sir Francis took the time to reply, telling Douglas that if he would send a formal confirmation that James was 'ready with his person and forces to do what he may for the advancement of the general cause', he would ensure that the Council would consider it as quickly as possible. No mention was made of the 'concessions' that Douglas had consistently sought.[44]

★★★★★★

Just past eleven of the clock at night on Monday, 29 July, the staff of Her Majesty's embassy in Edinburgh was awakened by someone hammering on the front door with the pommel of a sword. One of the ambassador's men-at-arms, wheellock pistol raised, unbarred the door to admit a drenched courier, white-faced and anxiously glancing over his shoulder. He was escorted up the stone staircase to Ashby's chamber, where he was recognised as one of Walsingham's couriers based at Barn Elms. The man handed the ambassador a leather pouch, lead-sealed with the Royal Arms.

Ashby dismissed the courier, promising a mug of ale and a dry pallet for the night. He broke the seal and removed a single letter addressed to him in the Secretary's distinctive handwriting. The letter, dated 24 July, was terse, seemingly written in haste: The Spanish fleet – 'to the number of eight score and two sail' – had appeared on the coast of the West Country and was 'bending their course' up the Narrow Seas.[45]

The ambassador sat up until the witching hour, listening to the wind and rain, interspersed with the demonic cries of the Night Walkers and their victims in the street outside the embassy. Well aware of the consequences, Ashby weighed his decision and determined to act on it in the new day that was dawning.[46]

******

There is no record of Walsingham responding to Ashby's request for clarification of his instructions, or sending the missing documents. The Secretary's letter to Ashby has been lost, but it is doubtful that it contained orders specifying how the Ambassador was to proceed with the news of the Armada's appearance. It was left to Ashby to decide what action to take, based on his written instructions and guidelines that Sir Francis did not wish to commit to paper.

Unbeknownst to Ashby, during the previous night, 28 July, Howard directed fire-ships at the Armada anchored near Calais. On their approach, panicked Spanish sailors cut or let slip their anchors and cables, and hurriedly raised sails. Some of the great ships collided as the fleet scattered. On the 29th, the day Ashby received Walsingham's letter, the decisive Battle of Gravelines began between the nimble English warships and the ungainly galleons and merchantmen of the *Gran Armada*.

# 14. Offers from Ashby to James VI

Early on the morning of Tuesday, 30 July, bleary-eyed and feeling the weight of his fifty-two years, William Ashby hastened to the nearby house of Chancellor Maitland, the King's chief advisor. He demanded to see Maitland and waited impatiently while he was roused from his bed. After the Chancellor shuffled downstairs, Ashby gave him Walsingham's news and told him that he 'meant to go to the King the same day, passing the Firth to Falkland, to impart to him the approach of the Spanish fleet'. Maitland discouraged this, asking the ambassador to return to his lodging and wait until he consulted with the Lord High Treasurer, Thomas Lyon, Master of Glamis, and Sir Lewis Bellenden, Lord Justice Clerk.[1] Ashby knew that Lyon and Bellenden, conspirators involved in the Ruthven Raid and in deposing Arran, were proponents of the League of Amity with England.[2]

Later that day, Carmichael came to the embassy, telling Ashby that he had been sent by Maitland and the other councillors and would go to Falkland to 'fetch the King back to Edinburgh'. The ambassador reported to Walsingham that Carmichael was 'an earnest favourer of the course of England', who assured him that James was devoted to Elizabeth and would 'be ready to withstand all her majesty's enemies'.

However, Ashby knew that the King's 'devotion' was contingent on fulfilling his demands.[3] In a postscript to his letter to Walsingham, he wrote '[t]ouching the charge committed to me, my next shall inform you how the answers for the satisfaction of the King are allowed of [received]'.[4]

James hurriedly returned to Edinburgh on the 31st, bypassing Holyrood to go straight to Maitland's house on the Canongate, probably to avoid untrustworthy eavesdroppers at the palace. After conferring with the

Chancellor, he sent for Ashby, who recited the details of Walsingham's letter. The ambassador concluded that the King depended on Maitland for policy decisions regarding the relationship with England, subsequently telling Sir Francis that 'the Lord Chancellor strikes the stroke, [and] on that runs the course of England above all men'.[5] 'While [t]he best sort are well affected and safe to run the course of England', he wrote, Maitland 'above the rest is the man wholly addicted' to a strong alliance.[6]

Many lairds, both Papist and Protestant, were enemies of the Chancellor because he had a countervailing influence over James and was considered to be pro-English. This was especially true of Huntly. Maitland was in a very dangerous position; Walsingham secretly corresponded with him, writing that he understood from Ashby and others 'how desirous you are to entertain mutual good intelligence with me, for the better service of both our sovereigns'. The Chancellor was probably not an English agent, *per se*, although he evidently received payments from Ashby and Bowes.[7]

Ashby knew from his extensive briefings and perusal of Walsingham's secret papers that the King and his Chancellor did not trust Elizabeth or her government, including himself, a sentiment mirrored on the English side. Hunsdon voiced the cynical opinion of Walsingham and other councillors that if Elizabeth expected 'amity or kind dealing' from James she would find herself 'greatly deceived' because he was 'maliciously bent' towards the Queen, and England generally.[8]

The diplomatic foreplay began, with the Chancellor and the ambassador aware that the exchange of courtly bromides barely concealed an issue of vital security importance to their respective countries. Both men also knew that time was of the essence. A Spanish landing in Scotland, linked with the forces of the Papist lairds, was probable, especially if the Armada failed to gain a beachhead in southern England. On the other hand, the King and his Protestant advisors knew that if the 'Enterprise of England' succeeded, the Catholics would dominate Scotland and, at best, James would be 'bridled'– allowed to serve as a puppet king of both England and Scotland.[9]

Maitland told Ashby that although James would 'hazard his life and crown against her majesty's enemies both for the advancement of religion and the safety of her person', he was nonetheless tempted by the great 'offers of the Spaniards ... to give him pay for twenty thousand footmen and five thousand horse, and what strangers [invaders] he will admit at the Spaniards' charge'.[10] James nodded while Maitland repeated the King's *quids pro quo*, which Ashby was familiar with.

First, while James was 'thoroughly satisfied' with Elizabeth's letter 'concerning her majesty's innocency touching the death of the late Queen his mother', he required 'some public note of the judgment given in the Star Chamber ... signed with the hand of the officer of that Court,' delivered to him without further delay. In addition, the Scots needed a second 'public instrument, signed by all the judges of' England, stating in unequivocal language that James' rights to the succession 'hath not or cannot in any sort be weakened, impugned, or prejudiced by' Mary Stuart's sentence of treason.[11]

Ashby thought that James' other, oft-repeated, demands were secondary to the legal instruments necessary to protect his right to succeed Elizabeth. Maitland 'still continue[d] in the thread touching the title of a dukedom or earldom', and because of his penury, the King required a yearly pension of £5,000, which had not been fully paid despite English promises in preceding years. Hinting at the threat of rebellion, the Chancellor requested funds for a royal guard of 'fifty gentlemen of Scotland and their commander'. As a final concession, and an acknowledgment of English anger at never-ending depredations in northern England by Scottish 'outlaws and borderers', Maitland asked for 'one hundred horsemen and one hundred footmen to be maintained at her majesty's charge' to stop border incursions.[12]

Ashby told the King and Maitland that it was not within his authority to agree to the pair of 'public instruments', but promised to urge Walsingham to procure these as a matter of the greatest urgency. It was agreed that 'a gentleman of credit' – a high-ranking envoy – should be dispatched from London to satisfy James on these requests.

The ambassador believed that due to the 'great danger ... considering the approach of the enemy and the faction he hath in these parts', there was no time to seek further instructions from London, which would have consumed ten days at a minimum. He 'thought it best' to agree to the demands for an English dukedom with 'reasonable revenue thereto', an annual pension of £5,000, funding for a King's guard plus 100 horsemen and an equal number of footmen 'to be employed on his borders'. An addendum to the agreement stated 'These offers to be performed during her majesty's life', probably because of the Scots' distrust that Elizabeth would find excuses for delaying performance.[13]

Although Ashby personally gave James the 'offers ... subscribed under his hand as Ambassador',[14] from subsequent correspondence with Walsingham, it seems that he backtracked somewhat, evidently advising Maitland that his 'agreement' would be contingent on authorisation from London.[15] The Scottish Chancellor may have thought that he and his king had over-reached in their demands, and informed Ashby privately that more limited concessions would be acceptable.

After this meeting, James wrote to Elizabeth hinting at his hopes for the succession by promising 'to behave myself not as a stranger and foreign prince, but as your natural son and compatriot of your country in all respects'. He appreciated her ambassador's 'offers' for his 'satisfaction' without detailing them, and urgently requested that 'commissioners' be sent to ratify the agreement so that her 'adversaries w[ill] have ado not with England but with the whole Isle of Britain'.[16] As a good faith gesture, the King 'declared himself, by open proclamation at the market crosses ... through[out] this country, to be party to all foreign enemies against this Island, has ordained all this country to be in arms, and all the descents [landing places] and ports of this coast side to be fortified in case of descent of any strangers'. This was considered a mistake by many of James' advisors, who thought he had been 'too sudden to declare himself before being assured of that he craved', but perhaps characteristic of his affectionate nature and innate desire to please.[17]

******

At this time, no one in Scotland was aware that the Armada had been thwarted in its planned invasion of southern England. With the loss of a few ships, the Spanish fleet was standing away into the North Sea, having bypassed Parma's poorly organised invasion force. Sir Francis Drake wrote that God had given the English 'so good a day in forcing the enemy so far to leeward as I hope to God the Prince of Parma and the Duke of Medina Sidonia shall not shake hands'.[18] The English naval commanders did not believe that the Spanish had been defeated, and they expected the sea battles to continue. Howard reported to Walsingham that the Spanish 'force is wonderful great and strong, but yet we pluck their feathers by little and little'.[19] The scattered Armada had reformed and, with over twenty thousand sailors and soldiers, still posed a major threat if it made a landing in Scottish territory controlled by its Catholic allies.

Although the Armada was 'dogged' by the English fleet as it sailed northwards, Howard and Drake hoped that they would not have to engage again as their 'powder and shot was near all spent', and sickness was decimating their crews. Not until 7 August did Howard report to Walsingham his belief that the Spanish were 'past the Isles of Scotland', and the news was not received in London until the 10th at the earliest.[20]

******

On 6 August, when the outcome of the attempted Spanish invasion was still unknown in Edinburgh, William Ashby wrote to Walsingham and Burghley. He tried to justify his actions, admitting to Sir Francis that he had 'passed the bounds' of his instructions but that 'the hazard and danger of ... revolt of this country upon the approach of th[e] Spaniards into the narrow seas made me the bold[er] to descend to these offers to satisfy the King; whereby the best sort will stand firm to him, and keep all Papists and discontented persons from taking arms in favour of the enemy'. Ashby 'craved' instructions from Sir Francis, yet 'in the meanwhile', he would 'feed them [the Scots] with fair promises to pacify the minds of many disco[rdant] persons in these parts'.[21]

The Scots were demanding 'many things', yet the ambassador thought that the King would be satisfied with 'an honourable pension' which might be sufficient to 'quench all the rest' of the concessions sought. Mindful of the smouldering hatred of Elizabeth among the Scottish people for what they believed to be her role in killing their queen, Ashby advised Sir Francis that '[i]t would be thought a most princely part of her majesty to entertain this young king with her gracious bounty in such sort that his subjects and people may think some way'.[22] Betraying some empathy for James, despite the need to 'feed' him with 'fair promises', Ashby said that the King was 'both zealous in [the Protestant] religion, and of nature mild and void of all revenge'.[23]

Ashby commented that Walsingham knew James' character and the state of Scotland better than anyone on the Privy Council, and that the King's good will and an alliance with England against her enemies were not available 'without countenance and help from her majesty'. From long familiarity with Sir Francis' frustration with Elizabeth, Ashby tried to strike a personal chord by stressing how 'dangerous the receiving of strangers [the Spanish] may be to the state of England, I refer to your wisdom to consider: which cannot be avoided, considering the discontented persons in Scotland at this instant, if her majesty have no strong regard, and that presently, to this king'. He ended his first letter to Walsingham by beseeching him to send speedily 'such instructions as may in part answer the expectation of this Prince', stating '[i]t should not be delayed, for great danger must, indeed, ensue in protracting time'.[24]

Next, Ashby wrote to Burghley in a shorter and less personal version of his message to Walsingham. James, he said, was 'ready to hazard his crown and life in [Elizabeth's] defence', but could not do so 'without her bounty'. He similarly 'crave[d] pardon for ... passing the bounds' of his instructions, but felt this was necessary because of the imminent threat and to buy time 'while her majesty and the Council resolve what is to be done'.[25]

Two days later, the ambassador met again with James and Maitland, acting on Walsingham's order to bring pressure to bear by revealing intelligence about the northern lairds' long-term conspiring with Parma. Ashby showed the King a list of names of the traitorous lords, including Huntly, received in a letter from Sir Francis. James was unmoved, refusing to distance himself from Huntly and promising only to be 'vigilant' over the others listed.[26]

By 10 August, Ashby had received confirmation that the Spanish fleet was 'beaten from the narrow seas, and passed the coast of England'. However, he thought it still probable that the Armada would 'bend [its] course to some part of Scotland and join with the northern lords, which are combined together, and have had intelligence a long time with the Prince of Parma'. James was still being solicited by the Spanish agent William Sempill and the Papal agent William Chisholm, Bishop of Dunblane, who had been sent to 'draw the King to the bent of their bow' by offering him the hand of King Philip's daughter, the *Infanta* Isabella, and 'such a dowry as should maintain twenty thousand footmen and ten thousand horse, to revenge the late Queens death and to set the crown of England on his head'.

Like diplomats throughout the ages, Ashby was frustrated with the lack of clear guidance from London. He warned Walsingham and Burghley that James would be imperilled if he agreed an alliance with England without receiving 'an honourable satisfaction made to him' as a sign of Elizabeth's sincerity. Because the King had 'so many malcontents and papists in his realm,' with the Spanish ready to support them, James would 'be in great peril without relief in money from England'. Reflecting Walsingham's admonitions over the years, the ambassador wrote that '[e]very pound her majesty sendeth hither now will save twenty later, and many a life... *mora trahit periculum*' – delay brings danger.[27]

Evidently, Ashby and Maitland had spent the previous ten days negotiating a deal that would be more politically palatable for both parties, apparently with the advice of Walsingham. The ambassador advised that '[m]any things are demanded here, but I guess these two points would content him [James] and his'.

He proposed that a pension of 20,000 French crowns[28] annually be paid to James personally, 'so England would not or her majesty shall be at no charge in feeing [paying] any subject he has'. This was due to concerns about popular opposition to direct English payments for a unit of royal guardsmen and a Scottish border force. Ashby shared Maitland's fear that James' subjects were 'greatly discontented', most of whom were 'stirring him to revenge'.

In addition, the ambassador suggested that James would be content with the 'land descended to him by his grandmother, the Lady Margaret'. This referred to the disputed inheritance of Margaret Douglas, mother of the King's father, Lord Darnley. Maitland may have proposed this long-standing claim as a means of demonstrating the King's succession rights as well as providing an income that would not be a burden on the English Treasury. Ashby hoped that the revised proposal would appeal to Elizabeth's notorious penny-pinching, writing '[t]hese two granted would save her majesty and her subjects a hundred thousand yearly'.

In his more fulsome letter to Walsingham, Ashby added '*concordia parvae res crescunt, discordia maximae dilabuntur*' (literally 'in harmony even small things grow, in contrast even the largest vanish'). This was meant to emphasise a personal bond, unlike his relationship with Burghley, as Ashby knew that Sir Francis would recognise the quote from the Roman historian and politician Sallust, whose works were on the curriculum at their respective colleges. The phrase was quoted whenever there was a need for a call to a spirit of harmony. In this context, it can be assumed to be a form of code indicating Ashby's trust in the Secretary's support.

★★★★★★

Was Ashby acting solely on his own volition? Walsingham had for some time believed that James should be granted the concessions he sought, and had strongly urged the Queen to do so. Conyers Read, Walsingham's preeminent biographer suggested that it was probable that Sir Francis 'whispered in [Ashby's] ear before he left that if occasion seemed to warrant it he had better not scruple to exceed his instructions'. Acknowledging that the content of Ashby's missing instructions are unknown, Read states that judging by the ambassador's 'conduct, it may be presumed that he was directed to entertain the King with words and general fair promises'.

It would have been characteristic for Walsingham to circumvent Elizabeth and the Burghley faction in the interest of national security. He had done so previously, often provoking the Queen's wrath. Ashby had known Walsingham's 'mind and pleasure' for many years and was too seasoned a diplomat to go beyond his brief unless sanctioned by his boss, especially considering the extraordinary sensitivity of his mission as the personal representative of the Queen.

The ambassador was well aware of the fate of William Davison, who was thrown into the Tower as a scapegoat for the execution of Mary Queen of Scots. Ashby knew that Elizabeth would tolerate no meddling in the sensitive subject of her succession, so deftly avoided answering Maitland in this regard. Like Walsingham, though, he was an English patriot and staunch anti-Papist (even though he was not as zealous an Evangelical as Sir Francis). Even at the risk of repudiation by Walsingham, he was willing to take responsibility for his actions in defence of his country, which he genuinely felt was in mortal danger from a Spanish invasion. In the late sixteenth century, 'plausible deniability' was as much a part of the intelligence and diplomatic world as in the twenty-first century.[29]

Further supporting evidence can be found in Walsingham's terse reply to a series of letters sent to him by Archibald Douglas after Ashby's arrival in Edinburgh. The Scottish envoy's copied messages, now fragmentary due to a fire, contain enough surviving text to show that he was pressing

Sir Francis on the issue of his sovereign's list of demands. Walsingham returned Douglas's letters (possibly because he did not want a record of them other than confidential copies), writing in his cover note that he could not resolve 'the matter' until he could 'hear from Mr. Ashby what train the affairs of the country [Scotland] are likely to fall into', after which he would 'confer with him at Barn Elms'- his private residence and intelligence headquarters – rather than at Richmond Palace, where he was writing from.

A letter written to Walsingham from Douglas the following year adds weight to the Secretary's approval of the offers. Following a new round of demands in April 1589 for James to receive his grandmother's lands and financial support, Douglas met with Hatton, the Lord Chancellor, who was sympathetic to the proposal but warned that Elizabeth 'would have none to meddle in that matter but Sir Francis Walsingham, whom she would have to bring that matter to one final point; if he should other deal, meddle, or accept as was offered, it might turn to one hard construction against him'. The Scottish ambassador told Sir Francis that he thought it 'expedient' to share this information with him, which was almost certainly provided to James as well.

Burghley, who often took a contrarian view to Walsingham's policy initiatives, shared his concerns about Scotland. 'If this fire be presently quenched in Scotland', he wrote, 'Her Majesty need fear no offense ... by Spain or Flanders. Otherwise, surely the danger by foreign war will speedily come from thence, where with surety they make wars without any resistance by sea'. True to his cautious nature, though, the Lord Treasurer added '... but herein I cannot nor dare presume to give advice to Her Majesty'.[30]

During the next three weeks, the whereabouts of the Armada was uncertain, and the threat of invasion via Scotland was undiminished. Sir Francis Drake wrote to Walsingham about conflicting reports concerning the Spanish fleet, varying from it returning to link up with Parma's invasion force to the Armada being past Scotland on its way home (which turned out to be correct). Some battered, leaking Spanish ships found havens on the Scottish islands, giving substance to rumours that the entire Armada had arrived. Sir Henry Widdrington, in Berwick, wrote to his friend Hunsdon that 'intelligence was brought to the King how the Spanish fleet is landed in the Firth of Moray, in the Earl of Murray's country, one hundred miles from Edinburgh'. As late as 1 September, the Privy Council believed it was probable that the Armada was about to descend from the north of Scotland back into the Narrow Seas.

Adding to English distrust of James and his favourites, Widdrington also reported that a Spanish pinnace had landed Spanish agent William Sempill at Leith. Sempill was arrested by Carmichael, but freed by Huntly and entertained at Holyrood, where the Earl was living. When James returned from Fife, he ordered a token arrest of Sempill to placate Ashby. Sempill was imprisoned in a house on the Grassmarket in Edinburgh, but easily escaped soon afterwards when his guards were bribed and was harboured by the northern Papist lairds.

Shortly before her departure on 8 August to make her triumphal speech at Tilbury Camp, Elizabeth learned of Ashby's offers to James.[31] In a fury, she ordered Walsingham to immediately repudiate any agreement her ambassador had made with the King of Scotland. Sir Francis wrote two letters to the ambassador before he left with the Queen, sharply rebuking him for his 'great oversight in the offering to the King.'

Although not unexpected, Ashby was mortified to receive the messages, fearing that he had risked his life On Her Majesty's Service and was in danger of being recalled to follow Davison to the Tower.

# 15. A necessary play of penitence

The King felt betrayed.

The usually mild-tempered James was incandescent with fury, red-faced and sputtering. He had gone to considerable political risk, against the advice of his councillors, to prove his support for the English only to be rewarded with 'their inhonest and unthankful mind towards him'. He ordered Douglas, his ambassador in London, to 'insist very earnestly both with the Queen and her Council that they diminish not' Ashby's offers, and remind them 'of the danger like to ensue to them and this whole isle' if James, in his 'miscontentment', broke relations and sided with their enemies.[1]

The King railed against 'this ridiculous sort of proceeding with him, saying one thing this day and the contrary the next'. He was bitter at how 'unthankfully they have dealt with him, who had declared himself party to them against all their enemies, contented to have borne equal fortune with them in the defence of this Isle'.

The English should beware. They should be left in no doubt that 'if they use him so hardly, he has the means to be avenged by joining those who, with the greatest and most advantageous offers, seek nothing but his friendship and concurrence against [England]'.[2]

When James' temper cooled, he realised that he was now more imperilled than the English for being precipitate in siding with them against his own Catholics and the Spanish. He also seemed to think that his hopes of being declared Elizabeth's successor were slipping away. It was not too late to restore a relationship that was near its breaking point. If Elizabeth truly meant 'to deal honestly with him', he proposed that Maitland and Walsingham should, 'with all possible haste … meet upon the offers made unto him, and to conclude the league'.[3]

William Ashby was trying to save his career, and possibly his life, with a series of *Mea Culpa* letters to Walsingham while striving to perform his mission of keeping the Scottish government aligned, if not allied, with England. While acknowledging that 'the danger of the time by the approach of the enemy' made him 'pass the bounds' of his commission, he eloquently argued that this was justified by the extreme danger to both countries:

> What danger and utter ruin must needs follow if the minds
> of these two princes be not firmly knit together, all the world
> doth foresee; their union must needs be the safety of their
> crowns, persons and states; the weal of their subjects and
> daunting of their enemies.[4]

Promising not to 'draw her majesty to no inconveniencies further than she is pleased to allow', the ambassador 'crave[d] pardon and commended [his] life to her majesty'.[5]

The Spanish threat was still apparent, frustrating Ashby and baffling the Scottish Protestants, who continued to 'make all possible preparation of forces to resist all foreigners minded ... to land in this country'. In mid-August, there was still 'no certainty of what is become of this Spanish army naval, except that it is gone northward, neither any certainty of the ... last conflict ... betwixt the two armies in the pass of Calais ...' although it was thought that 'the English have been victorious'.[6]

Ashby escaped blame by James and his most senior advisors, who believed he had acted in good faith. At great personal risk, he continued to advocate for some concessions to be granted to the King to salve his wounded pride and repair the severely strained relationship. Aware that James blamed Elizabeth for renouncing the offers, Walsingham sternly told Ashby 'I do not see, if the King carry an honourable and princely meaning to maintain good friendship with her majesty, why he should take occasion to "dislike" with her majesty for a fault growing out of an error and oversight committed by you'. Sir Francis warned that he was 'very sorry that you cannot so far forth prevail as to have the said offers suppressed, seeing the standing upon them may work your undoing, without any profit to the King'.[7]

Maitland interceded with Walsingham on the ambassador's behalf.[8] Sir Francis continued to admonish Ashby, while assuring him that 'her majesty rests satisfied by my mediation touching your late dealing without any direction. either by instruction or otherwise'. A close reading of Walsingham's letters to Ashby suggests that they were written with an awareness that others – Elizabeth, Burghley or his political enemies – would read them. The Secretary was muted about whether Ashby – widely known at the Court as his protégé – had gone beyond the bounds of *his* instructions. Sir Francis repeatedly emphasised that the ambassador was transgressing the Queen's commission as her representative: 'her majesty having given you no charge to make the said offers … the offers have grown from yourself … without her majesty's liking or privity, some of them being such as no persuasion can draw her to assent unto the same'. Walsingham appears to be deflecting blame from himself while assuring Ashby that he understood his actions as 'growing out of a good zeal'.[9]

The Secretary also disingenuously told Ashby that '[s]ome of the offers by you made were never heard of before, as that to the title of a dukedom there should be any revenue annexed; that there should be entertained at her majesty's charges fifty gentlemen about the King's person; and, lastly, that there should be maintained one hundred horse upon the Borders. So that it appears that these offers having been neither propounded heretofore there nor thought of here'. Walsingham knew that this was untrue – these 'concessions' had been the subject of discussions with various English and Scottish envoys during preceding years.[10] Sir Francis, trained as a lawyer, appears to have carefully nuanced his message, probably for the Queen's benefit considering her denial of sanctioning Mary's execution and other state decisions.[11]

Despite Walsingham's censuring and Ashby's humiliating contrition, it is possible that the concessions were conceived as a stratagem by Walsingham, with the collusion of Maitland and Ashby. Sir Francis could have been a master chess player if his austere nature did not distain games. King James commented that the man he feared as an adversary was 'very Machiavel[lian]' in his religious fervour, and he appears to have grudgingly credited Walsingham for the extraordinary sense of strategic vision and contingency planning ability which he also applied to foreign affairs.[12]

While Sir Francis was far more circumspect about what he wrote in official – as opposed to secret – documents, in a letter to Maitland sent in the same packet as his admonishments to Ashby, he said he 'cannot but make yet known ... that the stay [withdrawing of support]' was not the result of any personal doubt either of the King's 'sound disposition to continue in good friendship and amity with her majesty', or of the Chancellor's careful efforts to 'do good offices between them to that purpose'. Walsingham cryptically said that Maitland would be confidentially briefed in this regard, so that he 'shall more particularly understand', which suggests an unofficial exculpation for Ashby.[13]

Ashby's error – more accurately a miscalculation – was in exercising his discretion to make offers to James too early – i.e., before a Spanish landing which would have roused the Papist lairds into armed rebellion. However, he believed that greater caution could have left things too late, as James was susceptible to the blandishments of Huntly's faction and agents of King Philip and the Pope. Time had never been more 'of the essence' in tipping an increasingly shrewd king to the English side when the fate of England and its sovereign hung in the balance. Ashby told Burghley that his offers to James were meant 'to satisfy him and his nobility while her majesty and the Council resolve what is to be done'.[14]

Ashby's official reprimanding was concluded swiftly; he was not recalled from his post as would have been expected if his alleged transgression had been truly an independent act. Following a show of repentance in his letters to London – which was *pro forma* for those, including Leicester, who Elizabeth deemed to have offended her –he quickly got on with his crucial mission.

After receiving a letter from Walsingham late on the night of 17 August, Ashby met with the King the following day to 'certify' Elizabeth's 'care' for him and report that she was sending Sir Robert Sidney to Edinburgh as her personal representative. The ambiguity of the message was an embarrassment to the ambassador, giving the King and his Chancellor continued hope that Sidney would be able to confirm that at least some of his demands had been acceded to. Although the King expressed his thanks for Walsingham's promise 'that her majesty would send about £3000', scepticism ran deep at the Scottish court, and Ashby was left in no doubt that even if the funds arrived, they would be inadequate to maintain security.[15]

Sir Robert Sidney, younger brother of Walsingham's deceased son-in-law Sir Philip Sidney, was the high-ranking 'gentleman of credit' sought by King James to repair the tattered League of Amity.[16] In addition to his connection to Walsingham, Sidney was the nephew of Leicester, one of the few Englishmen who was popular in Scotland. Ashby told Walsingham that James and his small circle of trusted advisors were pinning too many hopes on Sir Robert's mission, thinking him to be 'the only restorative for the consumption [disease] that reigneth in these parts'.[17]

The 'disease' that Ashby mentioned was indeed serious. While the Armada, 'last seen between Orkney and Shetland about the 10th of August', was thought to have 'bent its course for Spain', the threat from the Papist lairds was undiminished. Protestant noblemen had mustered between ten and twelve thousand men-at-arms and cavalry 'to bridle the attempts of papists and malcontents, who devise how to apprehend [the King's] person. Both Spain and France will seek to cut him off, seeing him zealous in religion and affected to her majesty's amity'.[18] But James' supporters were starting to melt away as he was perceived as weak and vulnerable, without strong English support. Huntly and another Catholic nobleman, David Lindsay, Earl of Crawford, were plotting with Colonel William Stewart, the King's crony, to murder Maitland and Carmichael.[19]

Reflecting the muddled state of English policy towards Scotland in the aftermath of the Armada, Walsingham wrote to Ashby in late August again reproaching him but ending with the tortuously worded sentence:

> And yet for some other points heretofore propounded, as
> the delivery of the tithe,[20] clearing of the King's title, and the
> pension of the 5000l, I do not see but her majesty is well bent
> to assent thereto, so as she shall find the King, as he has often
> given her just cause so to conceive, inclined to concur with
> her in the defence of the country and in the embracing of
> the amity.[21]

While subject to interpretation (which may have been Walsingham's intent), Ashby evidently read this as permission to continue to dangle concessions in return for James' alliance. He suggested to Sir Francis that awarding the Order of the Garter to the King as a substitute for an English 'earldom or suchlike' would restore his pride and allow him to 'pacify the malcontents'. Such a favour, the ambassador said, 'would win time, and keep him in good hope of [Elizabeth's] generous dealing towards him'. Walsingham told Ashby to keep the offer of the Garter 'in silence' for the time being, indicating that it could be used as a negotiating asset if necessary.[22]

******

What Conyers Read called 'Elizabeth's inveterate parsimony and procrastination' were probably the primary factors in the disavowal of Ashby's offers.[23] Even before the battered Armada had disappeared over the North Sea horizon, destination unknown, the government was slashing military expenditures despite consensus that the threat had not ended. On 8 August, when Walsingham was still with the Queen at Tilbury, he told his friend Hatton that 'our half-doings doth breed dishonour and leaveth the disease uncured'.[24] The following day, frustrated with Elizabeth's indifference to a report that the Spanish planned another invasion attempt, he wrote to Burghley (who shared the

Queen's frugality), '[i]t were not wisdom, until we see what will become of the Spanish fleet, to disarm too fast, seeing her Majesty is to fight for a kingdom'.[25]

One captain, who had lost his command when his vessel was commandeered as a fireship against the anchored Spanish fleet, told Walsingham that '[o]ur parsimony at home hath bereaved us of the famousest victory that ever our nation had at sea'.[26] Sir Francis Drake complained that the Queen risked 'hazard[ing] a kingdom for the saving of a little charge [money]'.[27] The outspoken Admiral Howard, who personally paid for victuals for his crews, advised Walsingham that it was 'too pitiful to have men starve after such a service', warning that 'it would be better to open the Queen's Majesty's purse ... to relieve them', because 'if men should not be cared for better than to let them starve and die miserably, we should hardly get men to serve'.[28]

To be fair to Elizabeth and her government, the severe reduction of expenditures was not the result of official indifference to suffering English sailors and soldiers, but due to a severely depleted state treasury, which by the end of 1588 was nearly empty, with only £3,000 in cash and a few bonds worth around £1,200.[29] Walsingham's budget for the Secret Intelligence Service was drastically cut after the Armada, from possibly as much as £30,000 per annum at its peak to around £1,200 in 1589.[30]

At the beginning of September 1588, the Queen didn't have an extra £3,000 (or £5,000) to give to James, especially in the form of an annual pension, although money could be found from other sources if necessary. And despite her flowery salutations 'To our right dear brother the King of Scotland' from 'Your most assurest sister and cousin', Elizabeth R still thought of James R as a troublesome and ungrateful urchin.[31]

★★★★★★

Sidney crossed the Scottish border on 28 August in company with Ashby's friend Arthur Throckmorton. The ambassador was waiting for the entourage at the village of Haddington, where travellers from

Berwick to Edinburgh often spent the night. He briefed Sir Robert on the precarious political and security situation in Scotland, emphasising that James, Maitland and Carmichael were in desperate need of the £3,000 which, by Walsingham's written authorisation, Ashby had told them would be brought by Sidney. Without the money, the King would be unable to 'to levy a strength about him in this dangerous time', leaving him and his Chancellor in mortal danger.[32]

Sidney was deeply troubled by this. He had not brought the money, and his instructions from Elizabeth (drafted by Burghley), had only stated 'that there shall be presently sent unto him the sum of 3000 pounds sterling in gold'. The Scots had been led to believe that Sir Robert would be able to satisfy James' demands in exchange for openly siding with the English, at great risk from his own subjects. The official instructions contained no mention of concessions other than the missing gold. Sidney's orders were to pressure James 'to take some princely and resolute course in restraining' Huntly, Lord Claud Hamilton and other Papist rebels who 'seek the overthrow and destruction both of the religion within his realm and of his person'.[33]

Personal and national honour were prized by all three Englishmen, and they discussed their shame at the unfulfilled promise of funds, especially when Ashby told the others that at James' request he had already written to Elizabeth to thank her for the money. Sidney confided that even though payment for the King had been 'expressly set down' in his instructions, he had not received it.

After concluding the meeting, Sidney hurriedly wrote to Walsingham to express his dismay, saying that unless 'otherwise commanded' he would pretend to have no knowledge of the missing funds. The lack of English financial support could seriously undermine the alliance with James and result in a hostile regime across the northern border, for 'it seems the King doth greatly need it, for neither he nor the Chancellor are in safety without his guard'. Alluding to the frustration that all three men had experienced with their sovereign, Sir Robert added that he hoped

Her Majesty in her sealed private letter to James – which he was carrying – 'hath n[ot] any way specified' the payment.[34] Sympathetic with Ashby's frustration, Sidney told Walsingham he would 'keep within the bounds of my instructions, but if by reason of the violent proceedings of the Papists her majesty think good to pass any fa[vours to James] I beseech your honor that thereafter I may have my instructions enlarged'.[35]

When Sidney and his entourage arrived in Edinburgh on Thursday the 29th, they were advised that the King was away and could not 'have audience' with them until his return on Sunday, 1 September. Sir Robert told Walsingham he hoped 'that in the mean time I should receive farther order from you touching the £3000 ... which the King hath already in conceit received, and as Mr. Ashby told me hath given the Queen thanks for, by him'.

To his consternation, Sir Robert was 'fetched' by 'many of the gentlemen of the court' including Carmichael, who pressed him for immediate payment of the gold. The courtiers confirmed what Ashby had told him, that 'the King hath so reposed himself upon the assurance of the said money that, if he fall from hope of it, it must nearly touch [affect] him'.

Sidney was in a serious quandary as Elizabeth's personal ambassador. He informed Walsingham that James 'and his Council expect with me not only that money but also answer to his other demands'. Failing receipt of clear instructions about responding, he would have to be non-committal, and must 'take knowledge of nothing, and make promise of nothing. They shall not through my speeches have occasion to hope less than hitherto they have done'.[36]

Similar to many other of Elizabeth's envoys, Sir Robert regretted accepting the assignment and, like Ashby and Walsingham before him, worried about being blamed for a mission that seemed doomed from the beginning due to the Queen's whims. He was eager to escape from Scotland, adding in a postscript to Sir Francis: 'I beseech your honour that after I have delivered what I have in mine instructions, it will please you to procure my coming home, for I am here very ill provided to make any long stay'.[37]

He was not the only English diplomat 'very ill provided' for: Throckmorton (who had a penchant for *double-entendre* rhyme), told Walsingham that 'My lord ambassador [Ashby] here maketh good cheer and payeth dear' – referring both to Ashby's unappreciated diplomatic efforts as well as to his chronic lack of funds to maintain the embassy and intelligence network.[38] Ashby begged Sir Francis 'to receive out of the exchequer such money as is due to me for postage and other things, and also for my [maintenance], which is 30 shillings a day in the beggerliest dearest country in Europe for a stranger, to l[ive], as your honour and all such as have proved it can [certify]'. He reminded the Secretary that he arrived in Edinburgh with just £60, and since then had had to rely upon loans.[39]

The King summoned Sidney on Saturday, 31 August, a day earlier than expected. James declined Elizabeth's letter, directing that it be given unopened to Maitland. In an accusatory tone, the King reminded Sir Robert that he could 'have harkened to the offers of Spain' but had instead not only 'carried himself as a neutral … but as an open enemy to the Spaniards … [and] commanded all assistance should be given unto her majesties fleet, and forbidden the same unto the enemies'. No mention was made of Ashby's offers, or the missing gold, and to Sidney's relief the remainder of the audience was spent in an exchange of platitudes and 'open discourses of the [two] fleets'.[40]

The pleasantries soon ended.

After leaving the King, Sidney was escorted to the Chancellor's apartment in Holyrood, where he delivered the Queen's letter. Maitland asked if he was aware of Ashby's offers. Sir Robert replied that 'the Queen took knowledge of them' but that his instructions were only delivered after he left London. From the fragmentary accounts of this meeting, it appears that Sidney did know of the offers but pretended ignorance, telling Walsingham that he 'could not tell him any thing … knowing of them'. When pressed, he told the Chancellor he had 'never heard of them till at Haddington Mr. Ashby told me he had of his own authority made certain offers beyond his commission, and that he was much troubled withall'.[41]

Maitland scoffed at this, saying he thought Ashby had been 'commanded to deny he had made [them] by commission, and reckoned unto me the offers and the manner how they were made'. The exchange became heated, and Sidney lost his composure (and seemingly let slip the truth of the matter). He 'demanded of [Maitland] if the King would take hold of the said offers or no. He answered me that certainly he would, except he might receive some other things that were equivalent and equipolent'[42].

As the meeting grew more acrimonious, Sidney – uncomfortable with his shaky negotiating position – took the diplomatically unorthodox step of 'protesting that what [he said] was not as her majesty's ambassador, but as a private man that wished well to the cause, for in that matter [he] did not know anything of her majesty's intent'. When Sir Robert again tried to blame Ashby and 'gave some reasons why it would be disprofitable for the King to demand such things', the Chancellor interrupted him, aggressively 'touching the point of the dukedom, and the lands which were the King's grandfathers'. In a sign of his own precarious position, Maitland stated that 'the King must be some way pleased, or he will have to change his course, for the factions continue against him, and he [Maitland] stands only by [James'] favour', by which he meant that the English would lose their key ally in the Scottish court if the King turned against him.[43]

Sidney was now under great pressure from the Scottish officials, especially Maitland and Carmichael, whose lives were threatened and who were worried that the King was distancing himself from them. The morning after Sidney's meeting with James and Maitland, Carmichael came to his lodgings at the English embassy, accusing him – and Queen Elizabeth – of duplicity regarding 'the offers made by Mr. Asheby'. Carmichael told him 'that howsoever they were performed there was never a wise man in Scotland that would be persuaded that an ambassador authorised by a prince would or durst make any such offers without having commission for them'.[44]

Sir Robert's weak defence was the same as that used with Maitland – claiming that he knew nothing of the offers until he entered Scotland, and that Ashby had told him that he had made them solely on his own authority. Carmichael refused to believe this. When asked about the £3,000, Sidney was further embarrassed, lamely reverting to his instructions to respond that the money would be sent presently. Carmichael scorned this also. Cautiously shifting blame to Elizabeth, Sir Robert wrote to Walsingham 'if it please [not] her majesty to perform the said sum, the King will be exceedingly galled'.

That afternoon, Carmichael again went to the English embassy, apparently considering it more secure than anywhere else in Edinburgh. He told Sidney that he had met with the Chancellor and that the Scottish government proposed that if the offers made by Ashby were performed, King James 'would make any assurance to her majesty she would desire', that he would not make any 'alliance of foreign princes' other than Elizabeth and 'would bind himself to follow any such course as her majesty should appoint him'.

Carmichael asserted that what 'the King desired was not so much to profit himself, but to stop the mouths of his subjects, among whom all the Papists and many Protestants cry out that the King should show what cause he hath to embrace the alliance of England'. James needed to prove his ties to England with a Dukedom, and did not care if he had any revenues from it. The £3,000 was not for his own use, but to pay for 'the guard about him, if her majesty would have the King at her devotion she must take care to make him master of himself, and not to be ruled as his great men would'. As for the request for the English to cover the expense of 'the one hundred horse and one hundred foot upon the Borders, that it is more profitable for England than for [the Scots] to restrain the thieves, which else will make continual spoils'.[45]

Like Ashby (and probably Walsingham), Sidney personally thought the Scottish requests were reasonable and the benefit to England's security would far outweigh their minimal costs. He told Carmichael that he 'desired that I might think of these things – in order to get time and to [seek Walsingham's guidance]' and promised 'talk again tomorrow with the Chancellor and him'. Sir Robert asked 'what would become of this country if these things were not accorded'. Carmichael answered '[that] the King would be forced to do things [in] spite of his teeth [opposition], and that it would [not] be without the death of him and [of] far greater persons'; by which I think he meant the Chancellor'.[46]

The supposed alliance now hung by a thread. As Ashby had warned, the immediate threat to James and his pro-English advisors was from rebellious lairds, Papist and Protestant, and a fractious populace hostile to England. The only positive note was that Ashby had maintained, and possibly enhanced, his credibility as the King's advisors thought he had acted in good faith. This was to stand him in good stead in the months ahead, and was a key factor in his continuing as Her Majesty's ambassador.

# 16. '...the great ship was blown in the air'

Amidst his other crushing responsibilities, and attendance on the wilful Queen, Walsingham had been working to heed the pleas of Sidney, Ashby and Bowes to salvage relations with Scotland by sending 'some speedy comfort' to James 'to encourage him in his course with her Majesty'.[1]

Sir Francis arranged for the Earl of Huntingdon, a close ally and President of the Council of the North, to deliver £3,000 in gold angel coins to Robert Bowes in Berwick.[2] Bowes told Walsingham that the money was '[a]ccording to my Lord Treasurer's direction', which suggests that it came from Burghley's exchequer, presumably with the Queen's knowledge if not specific approval. However, the payment could have come from the Council's treasury, or from Walsingham's secret funds, similar to modern black budgets – government funds allocated for classified or other secret operations.[3] In late August, Huntingdon had assured the Privy Council that he would 'avoid her Majesty's charges as much as I may'.[4]

Bowes wrote to Ashby and Sidney to inform them that Burghley had directed him 'to receive of the Earl of Huntingdon £3000 in gold to be delivered for the King of Scots'. He wrote a separate letter to Carmichael confirming that he 'was ready to pay and deliver the said sum in gold'. This message was 'sent open to Sir Robert Sidney and Mr Ashby, that upon view thereof, and consideration of the matter, with their own proceedings and course with the King, they might stay or deliver that letter, and fully dispose of the cause, as should most profit her Majesties service, and best agree with their own intentions for the execution of their negotiations'.[5] Bowes therefore left it to the ambassadors' discretion whether the funds could be used for leverage over James, or if relations were so damaged or the King in a hopeless situation, they could decide to withhold the funds and not waste precious English gold.

Agreeing that time was of the essence, Sidney and Ashby gave the letter to Carmichael, who quickly summoned them to a meeting with James at Holyrood. The Scots 'promised that a good part [of the money] shall be employed ... for the guard and safety of the person and estate of the King and others about him that be well affected and stand in danger, and also for the suppressing of the troubles of the Borders'. The 'others about him' – Maitland and Carmichael – were especially grateful, as they had 'lately found themselves in great danger, and that they are still driven to arm themselves against the malice and violence of their enemies'.[6]

Although the King could not turn down the funding, behind flowery expressions of gratitude his bitterness deepened. He angrily complained to Huntly and others that 'the Queen used him like a boy'.[7] Elizabeth, 'the falsest and meanest of women', was reviled as the reneging culprit.[8] 'Of all the golden mountains offered', the Master of Gray wrote to Archibald Douglas, James had 'received a fiddler's wages.'[9]

Ashby knew that gold alone was not enough to assuage James' wounded ego. Before the money was delivered, he wrote a long letter to Queen Elizabeth on 7 September, again craving her pardon for 'pass[ing] the bounds of [his] instructions' and reiterating that he acted 'to satisfy his highness for the present, to qualify the minds of his nobility to keep all in quiet in these parts till your majesty with your honorable counsel do resolve what is to be done herein'.[10]

Evidently, the ambassador, who had been 'much troubled withal' by his official chastisement, felt so strongly about the great strategic threat that he was willing to again risk the Queen's wrath, and his own position if not his life, by writing to her.[11] Having spent the past week with Sidney and Throckmorton, who were favoured courtiers, he may have been emboldened knowing that they shared his awareness of the volatile Scottish political environment. All three diplomats would have thought that Walsingham supported them, despite his apparently contrary messages.

James was 'ready to hazard his crown and life' in the defence of Elizabeth and 'the religion that your majesty hath esta[blished] in your kingdom and in the whole isle', but he was unable to continue without her 'bountiful consideration to enable him ... and to content his nobility', whose support was doubtful without a strong show of material English support. This was imperative 'to keep his papists and malcontents in awe, and to take all hope from the common enemy of finding favour in these parts'.[12] The King had taken enormous risk in committing to an Anglo-Scottish league, but now he 'draweth into great peril without help' from the Queen.

Ashby ended by warning: 'What danger to these two crowns and to the church in Europe must follow if your minds be not knit in amity, all the world doth see'. The ambassador took the precaution of sending the letter to Walsingham 'to censure, to add and take away as shall seem best to your wisdom'. This was a wise move, considering that the Queen 'would not suffer any body to have access unto her, being very much grieved with the death' of the Earl of Leicester when the letter was delivered. Elizabeth probably never read it, although Burghley did after Walsingham shared it with him.[13]

The timing of the payment was indeed critical, as James was apparently close to making a deal with Huntly and other rebellious lairds, and would have reluctantly thrown the Chancellor and Carmichael to the wolves to save himself and his throne. If the two chief royal advisors had been murdered, Scotland would almost certainly have turned into a hostile neighbour, providing a base for a second invasion attempt as proved by subsequent events. The payment simply postponed the crisis.

On the day that the gold – which Ashby drolly called 'the last legion of angels'– was delivered, Sidney received Walsingham's message that his uncle, Leicester, had died suddenly on 4 September. Accompanied by Ashby, Sir Robert called on the King to take his leave. Both Englishmen were puzzled and vexed by James' brusque condolences on the Earl's death; the King seemed more regretful that Sidney would not be able to join him in hunting at Falkland Palace. Ashby told Sir Francis that 'the King [was] marvellous sorry he had such occasion so suddenly to depart, meaning to have killed all his bucks in Falkland if he had tarried'.[14]

Despite knowing that Leicester was the great love of Elizabeth's life, James referred to his death 'very slightingly' in his subsequent letter thanking her for the 'sums of money'.[15] Whether or not this was intended as an insult, or was due to the King's tactless oversight, it increased the Queen's hostility towards him at a time when she was so grief-stricken that she locked herself in her room for several days, requiring Burghley to break down the door. The powerful anti-English faction, including those such as Huntly who remained close to the King, and 'the Romish, Spanish and seditious sort do ... much rejoice ... [at] the decease of the Earl of Leicester'.[16]

Walsingham wrote privately to Sidney while he was *en route* to London, complimenting him on 'the manner of [his] dealing' with the Scots and confiding that 'we hoped here that upon the delivery of the 2000l, wherof it seemeth they have more need [than] of titles, they will not stand so peremptorily upon Mr. Ashby's offers'.[17] Sir Francis suggested that Elizabeth could be 'drawn to yield' in granting James the Order of the Garter, which he 'ought to rest satisfied with'. Exasperated with the King's threats to break with England in favour of her enemies if he wasn't better compensated, the Secretary warned that James would lose any possibility 'that he pretendeth to have to this crown after her majesty's decease by serving Spain or France because there is neither of them both that either can or will bestow the like kingdom u[pon] him'.[18]

This was probably true – while the Spanish and French might have tolerated James as a puppet on the Scottish throne in the event that they conquered both England and Scotland, he would not have been the first choice to succeed Elizabeth. A Catholic sovereign – such as the Spanish *Infanta* – would have been preferred by King Philip. By declaring his

Protestantism and public opposition to his own Papists, James' credibility was doubted by all parties, especially as he kept a secret diplomatic channel open to the Vatican offering 'his subjection to the Pope of Rome so he would confirm the crown to him'.[19] James' claim to the English throne was also in doubt by legal scholars due to the terms of Henry VIII's will, which stipulated that in the line of succession descendants of his sister Mary Tudor would follow immediately after his own children, and which effectively disinherited Scottish sovereigns, descendants of his elder sister Margaret, the King's great-grandmother.

For several months after Sidney's departure, Ashby's relations with James and his councillors were at a low ebb, reduced to desultory negotiations about the League. James was rarely in Edinburgh, and Maitland – who lived in constant fear of assassination by Huntly's faction – found refuge at Lethington Castle, his fortified house near Haddington. Concerned that he would be recalled early, in early November Ashby assured Walsingham that James was no longer pressing him about his offers, and that as the King was 'well accepting of my being here, I crave that I may stay till this good effect [the League] be brought to pass'.[20]

In his dual role as 'station chief' for the Secret Intelligence Service in Scotland, Ashby began devoting more of his time and energy to espionage, which he seemed to prefer to the tedium and deviousness of diplomacy. He expanded the already extensive English infiltration of the Scottish court, merchant community and Kirk by recruiting spies and informants, many of whom were double or triple agents.

One of these was Robert Scott, an Edinburgh merchant, who in turn employed 'a trusty man' who was sent 'to the isles to learn what he can of the Spaniards'. If 'recompensed as he shall deserved', Ashby told Walsingham, Scott could 'discover great matters touching these northern lords and their dealings with the Prince of Parma; the Spanish fleet and their plots, and how to prevent them'. Funds for maintaining the embassy and paying intelligence assets were always meagre, and like Walsingham and other ambassadors, Ashby incurred private debt to support his mission.[21] Another key resource was Sir William Keith of Delny, Master of the King's Wardrobe, who was probably recruited during diplomatic missions to London in 1583 and 1587.

A grave concern was the number of Spanish sailors and soldiers who had found haven in Scottish harbours after separating from the Armada as the main fleet limped back to Spain. Unlike in Ireland, where most shipwrecked Spaniards were hunted down and 'put to the sword' unless they were noblemen who could be ransomed, those who sheltered amidst the remote islands and villages of northern Scotland were usually left alone, especially if they were able to use escudos and pieces of eight to buy food. Survivors who made it home to Spain said they 'found the English even more cruel than the winds and waters, as they had murdered nearly all of them'.[22]

Ashby routinely sent Walsingham reports about the Armada survivors, some of whom he did not consider dangerous. In mid-October, he reported that '... there are escaped out of Ireland and landed in Scotland fifty Spaniards and Italians, poor and miserable, passing through this country towards England who [were] wrecked the 6th September in a ship in the north of Ireland called *La Ballanzara* of 1200 tons .... 500 soldiers and seventy-nine mariners left at their landing; the captains and master taken, divers other put to the sword, saving those which es[caped] into Scotland. The 10th October there came to Edinburgh twenty Spaniards and sixteen Italians; the rest are sick'.[23]

Several of the Spanish ships and their crews were still threats. Sir William Keith reported to Ashby that on '13 of September there arrived a great ship of Spain of 1400 tonnes, having 800 soldiers and their commanders, at an island called Ila [Islay] on the west part of Scotland, thether driven by weather'. The ship was said 'to be furnished with eighty brass pieces [cannon]; she beaten with shot and weather'.[24] Ten days later, another 'great ship of Spain' (which may have been the same vessel) anchored in Tobermory Bay, off the island of Mull.

This ship was the *San Juan de Sicilia*, a refitted, high-sided, commercial trading carrack of 800 tons with twenty-six guns and a complement of sixty-two sailors and 287 soldiers. The *San Juan* was largely undamaged except for her sails, which were in tatters, and she was short on 'victuals'. A deal was struck with Lachlan MacLean, the local chieftain, that in exchange for provisions and materials for repairs, Spanish soldiers would be used to settle feuds against clans on nearby islands. The Mull islanders schemed to take the galleon, but were 'not able to possess her, for she is well furnished with shot and men'. Ashby urged Walsingham 'if there be any ships of war in Ireland they might have a great prey of this ship, for she is thought to be very rich'.[25]

With Walsingham's approval, Ashby conceived and managed one of the earliest known examples of a Secret Intelligence Service 'Black Op' – a covert operation which the English government was able to deny by pinning the blame on others. The ambassador sent John Smollet, an agent working undercover as a Dumbarton merchant, to Mull. Smollet had a chequered history as a double agent. As a servant of the late Duke of Lennox, in 1583 Smollet offered his espionage services to the English and secretly met with Elizabeth and Walsingham, who 'dealt roughly with him'.[26] Smollet was 'subtle, prone to practice, full of words, neither secret nor trusty and greedy of gear [fancy clothing and accoutrements]'. The Secretary decided that, however untrustworthy the Scotsman might be, he could prove useful and was therefore 'shown some favour and promised more'.[27]

In October 1587, Smollet was arrested as a conspirator for plotting to kill the Master of Glamis (Thomas Lyon), Maitland and others. He was carrying a 'letter ... from the King himself to the Earl of Huntly for the killing of the Master of Glamis'– the revelation of which would have resulted in his death sentence. His crime was covered up, apparently by Glamis and Maitland at the instigation of Robert Bowes, who reactivated Smollet as an English agent in exchange for his release.[28] Now serving as one of Ashby's assets, Smollet's mission was to ingratiate himself with the *San Juan*'s officers and crew by providing supplies, especially replacements for her sails, which was a deliberately lengthy process. Over the course of six weeks, Smollet developed 'great trust among the Spaniards'.[29]

Ashby ordered a sabotage operation after Smollet reported that the Spanish soldiers were besieging Mingary Castle on the mainland, thinking that such a large force of nearly 300 well-armed professional soldiers could join the growing albeit undisciplined forces of the Papist lairds. The saboteur 'entered the ship and cast in the powder upon a piece of lint and so departed. Within a short time after the lint took fire' and the 'great ship' was 'blown in the air ... most part of the men ... slain'.[30] Most of the Spanish soldiers were encamped around MacLean's seat, Duart Castle, and nearly two hundred survived, half of whom returned to Spain over a year later while others stayed behind and merged their DNA into the bloodlines of the Inner Hebrides.

Scotland was a neutral country, and a cover story for the operation was required. Ashby informed Burghley that the *San Juan* had been 'burnt by treachery of the Irish, and almost all the men consumed by fire'.[31] This was written to conceal his, and Walsingham's, role in the sabotage, as he separately told Sir Francis that on 24 November, eighteen Spaniards 'saved from the ship burnt in the Isle of Mull' arrived in Edinburgh, adding 'the particularities thereof I think your honour understands by the party that laid the train [the trail of gunpowder to ignite the magazine] ... the man known to your honour and called Smallet [Smollet)'. Ashby spirited the saboteur into England, probably because his life was in danger.[32] The cover story changed over time, possibly due to altered geo-political dynamics; a year later, the ambassador wrote to Walsingham (who knew better) and to Burghley that the *San Juan* had caught fire and exploded 'by casualty' (accident), due to 'mischance of gunpowder'.[33]

Subterfuge was needed because the shipwrecked Spaniards were under the protection of James, who 'took them in for more than thirty days, giving them food and new clothes' and refused to hand them over to the English.[34] Anglo-Scottish relations were so tenuous that blame had to be officially shifted to 'treacherous Irish' so that, as in the execution of Mary Stuart, Elizabeth and Burghley could claim innocence. While James piously proclaimed that his succour was motivated by 'Christian charity, which commands us to be beneficial unto our every enemies', his action was seen as a gesture of amity to Philip and the Papist lairds.[35]

Although the ambassador was able to destroy a Spanish ship and many of its crew and troops, he could do little to prevent the aiding of Armada survivors, most of whom were unarmed, ragged and starving. Ashby told Walsingham of 'fifty-two Spaniards and Italians who escaped out of Ireland and came naked to this country: the town of Edinburgh gave them food and apparel and sent them into Germany, France and the Low Countries'.[36] On James' order, another forty-six Spaniards, 'naked and bare and in a most miserable estate' were clothed, fed, and put aboard Scottish ships bound for France with safe conduct passes.[37]

In late November, over 200 survivors from *El Gran Grifón* were landed at the village of Anstruther in Fife, across the Firth of Forth from Edinburgh. *Grifón*, was the 650-ton, thirty-eight-gun flagship of the Armada's supply squadron of Baltic hulks. Like the *San Juan*, she had a large compliment of forty-three crewman and 234 soldiers, some of whom had been taken off another Armada vessel before it foundered.

On 27 September, the ship was wrecked at Fair Isle in Shetland when her anchors dragged. Most of the men made it ashore, where they were sheltered by the islanders until the approach of winter and limited food supplies forced them to leave, taking their treasure with them. With the help of local chieftains, they were transported in fishing boats around the coast of Scotland. Ashby reported that their captains were in Edinburgh 'meaning to hire a couple of ships to take them into the Low Countries: they saved their treasure and are come hither unspoiled; their captains are looked for in this city. A man-of-war might intercept them'.[38]

Nearly a year later, a man-of-war did intercept them, but not an English ship.

Despite the losses, the number of Spaniards converging on Edinburgh grew to over one thousand, including several hundred who had escaped from Ireland.[39] While most were Armada survivors, some infiltrated from the Netherlands along with Scottish officers serving with Parma's army.[40] Noble Spanish officers, including the nephew of the Armada's commander, the Duke of Medina-Sidonia, had saved sufficient treasure to live in style in Edinburgh, renting houses and entertaining members of the court and lairds while their crews and soldiers 'in their begging state' survived on private alms and public charity.[41] In turn, the *hidalgos* were entertained by Bothwell, Huntly and other leaders of the growing pro-Spanish faction.[42]

To add to Ashby's troubles, a man called Thomas Fowler literally appeared on the ambassador's doorstep in Edinburgh,[43] on the run after barely escaping bailiffs and debtor's prison in London for a large sum owed to the estate of the deceased Earl of Leicester as well as other debts.[44] In the following year of 1589, Fowler would become a major thorn in the flesh for William Ashby.

Ashby was steadfast in his mandate to preserve and strengthen the Anglo-Scottish alliance, which he believed was a patriotic duty to protect England and his Queen. He grew increasingly frustrated with what he perceived as his government's neglectful attitude towards Scotland in the aftermath of what was popularly believed to be England's defeat of the Armada. After mourning Leicester, Elizabeth and her court were busy planning elaborate celebrations for the anniversary of the Queen's coronation and a 'General Day of Thanksgiving for Defeat of the Spanish Armada ... throughout the realm, with sermons, singing of psalms, bonfires, etc, for joy, and a thanksgiving unto God for the overthrow of the Spaniards our enemies on the sea'.[45]

The Scottish government grew more dysfunctional due to poverty. Ashby reported that '[c]ertainly both the King and the Church here are in most miserable state, neither of them able to maintain their households; which must bring ruin to the whole state'.[46] Fearful that London's apparent disinterest in Scotland would result in a hostile Spanish vassal on England's only land border, the ambassador continued to officially support James in his letters to Walsingham, reiterating the King's desire for friendship with Elizabeth while reporting on his need for financial assistance and the chaotic state of his court. A few lairds were reliably faithful to James, including the Master of Glamis, Lord John Hamilton and the Earls of Mar and Errol, 'the best bent of all the nobility', but even these feared the Huntly faction and could switch sides as easily as changing their bonnets.[47]

Pretending to humble himself, Huntly wrote 'a letter to the King of submission, promising obedience in religion and otherwise, craving pardon, and offering submission to the church'. James sent him 'to his house in the north, and there as he shall reform himself in religion, so he shall find his favour towards him'.[48]

Ashby and his agents knew this to be a sham, designed to 'covertly further their intentions with fair words and deeds to serve the time'. The King was either in denial about the machinations of Huntly and the other Papist lairds – who were committed 'to wishing and looking to have power to execute the malice of their minds inwardly and closely carried against her majesty'– or was a fellow schemer, maladroitly thinking that he could fool Elizabeth into maintaining 'amity', funding and the succession.[49] The English intelligence network made disturbing reports about James' duplicity, such as that 'the King of Scots … hath solicited the King of Denmark to trouble the seas and traffic of England, with sundry other evil offices towards her majesty', some of which Ashby thought were fabricated.[50]

The bleak Scottish autumn degenerated into dark winter, which Ashby considered a metaphor for the state of Scotland. He perceived James and English allies such as Maitland to be slipping into hostility. At the end of November, two days after the Armada Thanksgiving Service at St. Paul's Cathedral, he wrote to Walsingham that he found 'the King to conceive some unkindness, and fear, if regard be not had in time, all sorts in his state will urge their prince to a course dangerous to both crowns'. The Chancellor, 'who hath endangered himself among the nobility and malcontents, groweth weary of the course he hath held, finding so cold correspondence from England, and his King so lightly regarded'. The Scots generally were angry about the 'no small indignity to their prince and country'.[51]

In mid-December, Ashby attempted to warm the frosty relations by going to Kinneil House near Falkirk, where James had established his court. He was rebuffed. According to Roger Aston, 'the King and he agreed not very well, for the King is heavily offended thereat, and regretted to me the day before the ambassador came, and said "the more he did to please the Queen the less regard she had of him"'.[52]

Aston, bastard son of the Sheriff of Cheshire who sought his fortune in Scotland, was one of James' courtiers and had been an English intelligencer for a number of years. He had been invited to spend the holidays at Kinneil, where he spent his time playing Maw with the King and spying on him and his cronies.

Aston reported that Philip had sent 'a good store' of gold to the pro-Spanish camp, and that a Spanish ambassador was expected to arrive in Edinburgh in the new year. Despairingly, he found 'all men exceeding cold towards England, and the Chancellor among the rest. I fear if nothing be done for this king it will not be well, for [the necessity] was so great that in some way it must be had'.[53]

By Christmas, 'the Spanish faction' had begun 'to grow in great credit', and it was feared that 'the store of Spanish pistoles'[54] would 'work some mischief here. It appears by the proceedings of this faction they have some great turn to work. All good men grieve in great fear, and ministers begin to speak plainly in the pulpit of these proceedings'. English critics of James said he showed 'great inconstancy', and '[a]ll good men begin to grow weary and will return home till they see how the world will go'. It was feared by the English in Scotland that it would become 'a very evil starred country. Great blame is laid on the King, and the ministers cry out daily that he takes no greater care of his office. He gives all from himself and raises great taxations of his poor people, which brings him in great contempt. It is plainly spoken here he is running to his own destruction, as his mother did before'.[55]

William Ashby had himself grown weary and decided to return home for the Christmas holidays. He gave leave to all of his embassy staff except for a disgruntled pair who had drawn lots to remain in Edinburgh to protect the embassy from robbery. Accompanied by his manservant and other Englishmen, he crossed the border at Berwick and headed south on horseback amidst lancing sleet.

*****

Christmas with his family was a balm for the soul as well as the body.

William Ashby had broken his journey down the Great North Road to spend two days with his half-brother Maurice Berkeley at Wymondham. He sent Peter Haye ahead to open the house in Clerkenwell before following him to London, going directly to Walsingham's home on Seething Lane.

Sir Francis had grown haggard in the few months since they had last met, the circles under his eyes deeper, skin like parchment over the fine bones of his face. After greeting Ashby warmly, they sat by the fire and talked of many things as friends and colleagues. The Secretary conveyed the welcome news that his nemesis, the Duke of Guise, had been assassinated by King Henri III's bodyguard. They raised glasses of Canary and toasted Guise's eternal damnation.

Walsingham described a marvellous new form of writing called Characterie, or 'short hand', invented by a doctor of physic, which he thought could be useful for their espionage work. As aged men in their fifties are wont to do, they compared ailments and nostrums. The Secretary told Ashby that due 'to the indisposition of his body' he planned to take two-months leave from the court.[56] He dreaded having to go to Richmond Palace for Christmas, where the Queen expected him to help pacify a feud between her two new favourites, the Earl of Essex and Sir Walter Raleigh.[57] Nonetheless, Sir Francis said, wrinkling his nose, Richmond was preferable to Greenwich where the stench from the sinks [latrines] was so foul that Hatton and Admiral Howard 'could not abide in their chambers for ill airs'.[58]

Before Ashby took his leave, he presented Sir Francis with a gift, a new edition of Cicero´s *De Legibus*. Walsingham gave him one in return – a thin, cheaply printed volume titled *A Pack of Spanish Lies*. 'Burghley's magnum opus,' he said dryly.[59]

After visiting his brother Francis and sister-in-law Margaret, Ashby returned to Leicestershire on Christmas Eve. Familiar traditions of his childhood dispelled the ambassador's melancholia. The scowling austerity of Puritans was anathema amongst Leicestershire's gentry, and his relatives' halls were decorated with a profusion of greenery – bay, laurel, ivy and holly leaves. On the evening of William's arrival, Christmas candles of prodigious size illuminated the Yule Log as it was hauled into the great hearth at Wymondham Manor. The entire household, including bibulous, red-cheeked servants, then feasted to a late hour upon Yule-dough, Yule-cakes and bowls of frumity, with much music and singing.

After Christmas service at St. Peter's, 'the gentlemen presently repair[ed] into the hall to breakfast, with brawn, mustard, and malmsey'. Christmas dinner was sumptuous, more than compensating for the poor fare in Edinburgh. The pièce de résistance was the peacock pie, 'the cock ... cooked whole, with the head projecting through the crust, beautifully decorated at the serving, and the bill gilded; and the tail set up in all its extended grandeur of coloured beauty'.[60]

On the old feast day of St Stephen, they embarked on the traditional round of visits to relatives, friends and neighbours that would last until Twelfth Night. Revels and dancing followed supper, resurrecting happy memories of Ashby's gambols as a youth. Sellinger's Round and Tom Tiler would have been sneered at as dances fit only for country bumpkins by the glittering courtiers he knew in London and the great continental cities. Shrieking with laughter, the youngsters amused themselves playing Hoodman Blind, Hot-Cockles and Shoe the Mare.

Innocent revelling aside, the ambassador was an introspective observer, always aware of the worldly man he had grown into. This saddened him, for he often considered retiring to Leicestershire but knew this was little more than a dream that had sustained him in his darkest hours. For decades he had been a peripheral player in great affairs of state and now, as Walsingham had told him, he was a leading actor in a great northern drama that was actually the second half of the unfinished Spanish and Catholic threat.

Ashby had confided his disillusionment to the Secretary and his inclination to resign his ambassadorship. Sir Francis commiserated, reminding him of his own years of despair in Her Majesty's Service, and the many times when he was close to the breaking point, wanting only 'to take my leave of foreign service'.[61] Yet, Walsingham told him, God had a higher purpose for them, a duty surpassing themselves to protect their religion, country and queen, despite the latter's often infuriating disinterest and contrariness.

The Secretary assured him that the Privy Council was not heedless about Ashby's numerous warnings regarding Huntly and the Malcontents he led. Return to Scotland, Sir Francis pleaded, and shortly you will have the support you need to counter this threat.

On the day following Twelfth Night, Ashby reluctantly left Leicestershire. Joined by his twenty-five-year-old nephew, Robert Naunton, who would serve as his secretary in Edinburgh, the ambassador and his companions set out on the ancient road north, following in the footsteps of Roman legionaries.

# 17. Ashby reveals to James a plot against him by his own lairds

**January 1589**

Ashby's party arrived in Berwick hours before an epic blizzard closed all roads, rendering the walled border town an island in a sea of snowdrifts. The inns were clogged with stranded travellers, but the ambassador and his nephew Naunton were able to lodge with Bowes, the young secretary sleeping in front of the hearth rolled in a malodorous bear skin.

Bowes updated Ashby on intelligence matters. Scotland's situation was deteriorating, with everything the ambassador had warned about seemingly coming to pass.

The King had spent the holidays at Kinneil with Huntly, Crawford and others. Ominously, Maitland, who until recently was in mortal fear of Huntly, was included in the Christmas assembly. The Chancellor was reportedly ready to join Huntly's faction; 'he had dangered his life for the favour of England, and was hated of his countrymen for favouring that court so long; they thought he was the Queen's pensioner [a paid English agent] ... and her majesty's dealing is such that he will deal no farther that way'.[1] After Christmas, James had gone 'to Dunfermline to be merry for three or four days,' accompanied by Maitland, Huntly, a pair of English Catholics and a Spaniard, where it was 'thought they practise to turn the King from her majesty'.[2]

There were fears of an armed Scottish incursion across the border, poorly defended in the midst of winter and known to be 'much infested with broken men and thieving'.[3] The King was reported to have met with a Scottish colonel 'come from the Prince of P[arma], who hath desired that intelligence may pass between the King and him. The said colonel is very busy labouring such as he knows to be [of] the Prince's faction'.[4] The Papist lairds offered to secure the north of Scotland as a beachhead for Parma's forces to land, which he refused to do unless Maitland was sent to him with authorisation from James to allow the incursion. Huntly was angry that his bed mate James had yet to decisively choose sides, so plans were afoot to seize 'the King and draw him perforce from favoring of England'.

One English spy at the Scottish court reported that 'all hope for the King here is gone', meaning both hope for him with respect to England's wishes, and for his own personal safety.[5] Ashby concurred with this assessment, telling Walsingham (who continued to work while convalescing) that, unlike English obedience to Elizabeth's power, the Scots ignored James' authority, 'which must needs bring the ruin of this state'.[6]

While Ashby thought that the intelligence from his sources was generally credible, it was little more than hearsay. He needed documentary evidence plus unequivocal authority from London to take action.

Walsingham's promise that he would have the support needed to counter the threat was soon proven true. On 26 February, Ashby received a packet from the Privy Council in London accompanied by a five-and-a-half-page cover letter dated 14 February addressed 'To Our Loving Friend Mr. Ashebie, Squire, Her Majestie's Ambassador with the King of Scots'. The letter, probably drafted by Walsingham but written in Burghley's hand, explained that the enclosed letters in cyphers had been 'by some good diligence taken upon … a Scottish man appointed to have carried them to the Duke of Parma' in the Low Countries. Mindful of the debacle resulting from Ashby's ambiguous instructions the previous summer, the letter explained that '[a]fter our heartily commendations, we do send to you by this bearer a certain packet sealed up with our seals, for the better understanding whereof and for your proceeding therein, this you shall understand'.[7]

The letters had been found on Thomas Pringle, a former soldier of fortune who had served on both sides in the Netherlands and was an agent of Colonel Sempill, Spain's principal Scottish intelligence officer.

Pringle was a regular courier for Robert Bruce, Huntly's main liaison to Philip, as well as for Huntly, Errol, Crawford, Bothwell and Lord Claud Hamilton. He had been under surveillance by English intelligencers for some time and was apprehended in early February when known to be carrying especially incriminating messages, possibly after a tip-off from Bruce, who was a double agent and trafficker.[8]

Pringle was 'held in prison' in London in readiness to be sent to Scotland 'to be used for the proof, that it was he which carried these letters'. Burghley, who like Ashby had trained at Gray's Inn, was meticulous in compiling unimpeachable legal evidence for the ambassador's use:

> The letters that was in cipher are deciphered and written in
> [plain text] for to be read; the others are sent in their proper
> [original] nature; and for warrant of the true deciphering of
> them we have caused some few lines of the ciphered letters
> to be superscribed by interlineation with the true and plain
> words in common letters; and to the intent that the rest may
> appear to be also truly deciphered we do send to you the true
> alphabet of the ciphers so as any man skillful therein may
> perceive the letters to be truly deciphered.[9]

The Lord Treasurer explained that the contents of the letters were of 'great weight' and were to be 'used very secretly and substantially', being 'so dangerous both for the Queen's Majesty and [James] and both their realms and faithful subjects', which had been 'cunningly and subtly plotted' for many years. Expecting that James would doubt the authenticity of the documents,[10] the Privy Council had gone to great lengths to prove 'that these ciphered letters come from the parties therein named, and that the contents are not anywise feigned, but certainly containing the minds and purposes of the traitors therein mentioned, the scope of their secret actions, the truth of all circumstances, for the naming of the persons that are in prison, the Jesuits that are there secretly harbored, and the behaviours of the earls and lords now conspired in all their actions, are infallible proves of the truth of all the contents....'

With a profound feeling of vindication, Ashby read the continuation of Burghley's sentence: '... which we do mention to you as not doubting of your judgment so to censure the same, both by reason of the present contents and of your own knowledge of the dependences of a great number of circumstances better known to you there than can be to us'.

The ambassador closed his eyes and heaved a sigh of satisfaction before reading his precise instructions, by 'her majesty's pleasure', indicating that the Queen approved the Council's directions to him. As soon as he had familiarised himself with the letters, he was commanded 'without delay' to meet with James and deliver the personal letter from Elizabeth. He was then to urgently request a 'most secret' (i.e., without courtiers present) meeting to alert him to 'a matter of great weight', of such immediate danger that he needed to act 'secretly, wisely, stoutly and princely' to remedy it. Next, and still in secret, the ambassador was to 'show to him the letters ... whereby his majesty may himself plainly see the truth'.[11]

Walsingham and his fellow councillors knew that James was surrounded by the very people that he was being warned about. It was imperative that the King read the letters 'in secret manner ... for avoiding of suspicion by the standers by', after which Ashby would 'feel his mind' to learn who he planned to tell about the contents. The ambassador would use his 'judgment and opinion' on whether the persons named by James could be trusted, then 'by good persuasions', convince him not to disclose information to those deemed unreliable 'for fear either of discovery of the matter to the persons who are the principal offenders or partners with them'.[12] He was directed to use every effort to make the King take seriously the 'traitorous conspiracies' and move swiftly to imprison the ring leaders simultaneously so as to 'terrify their factious dependants from attempting anything'.

Ashby was to remind James that his toleration of the Jesuits, 'the roots of these conspiracies', and allowing many Spaniards to remain for so long, had 'surely corrupted very many of his subjects, and ... made them very bold to attempt these treasons; and therefore the sooner they be banished [from] the country and committed to the seas the better'. No time could be lost in 'rooting out of such wicked, corrupt members' who, according to their letters, were plotting the 'subversion of the whole state of the realm and ... the destruction or captivity of the King's own person'.[13]

To deflect suspicion from the conspirators until James could act, Walsingham had concocted a cover story by enclosing letters and petitions from a Netherlands representative regarding routine diplomatic matters. The courier Pringle was being transported to Berwick, where he would be kept under maximum security in readiness to be sent to Edinburgh 'to avow from whom he had the letters', but not before the King was ready to receive him, so the plotters would not be alerted. The cover letter ended 'Your loving friends' and was signed by Walsingham, Hatton, Hunsdon and Thomas Heneage.[14]

Forbidding interruption, Ashby closed his chamber door, and cut open the waxed packet stamped with the Queen's seal and those of the four Councillors. Excluding the cover letter and Elizabeth's message, there were seven original letters with accompanying decoded transcriptions and various cypher keys. All were dated between 14 and 24 January 1589. Huddled in his heavy cloak, the ambassador's pulse quickened as he read the documents in the light cast by a candelabrum.

Written in French from Edinburgh, the first letter, from 'Scottish Lords to the King of Spain', expressed 'great regret' that the Armada had passed so near to Scotland where their forces were waiting to support an invasion of England. Offering to provide pilots to guide Spanish ships through the treacherous Caledonian seas, the Lords assured Philip that with 'six thousand of your men here, with money', a levy of a similar number of Scottish troops could be raised 'as freely as in Spain, who will serve you no less faithfully than your natural subjects'. Such a force could divert the enemy to allow Parma's forces to land in southern England 'and within six weeks after their arrival be well advanced ... in order to join and assist the forces which your majesty shall send thither'. This letter was signed 'George Earl of Huntly, etc. in name of the Lords Catholics of Scotland'.[15]

The second letter, from Robert Bruce to Parma, provided further identities of the conspiracy ringleaders.[16] Bruce reported that John Chisholm had arrived from the Low Countries carrying a large sum of Spanish gold with Parma's letters and had gone to Huntly's house, where he gave the Earl one third of the '6272 crowns of the sun, and 3700 pistoles of Spain', after which he delivered the balance of the money to Bruce in Edinburgh.[17] Although James had considered arresting Chisholm, after he met with him, 'the King was quite satisfied with the pretexts put forward by him for his said return', due to Huntly's influence.[18] Bruce told Parma that Huntly, Morton and Claud Hamilton were pressuring him to divide the gold equally among them 'because they were the first who made offer of their service to the King of Spain', but he advised that the money should be given as needed to the large number of Scots who were 'well affectioned to the King of Spain's service and yours'.[19] A *coup d'etat* was evidently near; the gold was hidden in Edinburgh and elsewhere 'to aid, if need be, the Catholic lords who will soon assemble here to resist the designs of those of the English faction'.

Huntly had to remain at court 'for otherwise he cannot please the King, who in appearance loves him above all others after the Duke of Lennox' and it was dangerous 'to converse with him openly'. Although the Earl had publicly disavowed the Church of Rome 'to avoid the manifest dangers of all those who call themselves Catholics ... for all that his heart is in no wise alienated from our cause'. James' secret correspondence with Parma was noted, as well as suspicion that the courier, Thomas Tirrey, was an enemy agent.

Bruce wrote of conspirators, agents and plans, as well as bribes, such as 400 crowns to spring Colonel Sempill from prison. Morton, currently imprisoned, was said to 'matter more for the good of our cause than any one of the others, by reason of his forces being near to England and to the chief town of Scotland and usual dwelling places of our kings, and that he is also the most resolute, steadfast and energetic of all the Catholic lords'. The young Protestant earls Errol and Crawford had been converted to Catholicism by Jesuits, and were 'very desirous to advance the Catholic faith and your good enterprises in this island; which they have resolved to testify to the King of Spain and to your highness by their own letters'.[20]

Bothwell, although a Protestant, was 'nevertheless extremely desirous to aid you against England, having made a levy of some troops of soldiers and maintained them all this summer, under pretext of going to subdue the islands, in order with his ordinary forces to join the whole to yours had they come here'. His support was conditioned on being given ownership of two abbeys 'after the restoration of the Catholic faith'. Bruce's letter gave further proof of James' duplicity, as he stated that Bothwell was 'also to treat in the name of our king with the King of Spain and your highness', for which purpose 'he is procuring a warrant from his majesty, of whom he already has a promise'.

The packet also contained testaments of Catholic faith by Huntly and Errol, as well as letters from John Chisholm and Bruce to Sempill, using the cover names 'John Jamieson' for Chisholm and 'William French' for Sempill. These outlined movements of Spanish agents and funding for the coup.

Ashby immediately requested an audience with the King, who was fortunately at Holyrood, meeting him the next morning, Thursday, 27 February, attended only by Maitland.[21] The ambassador presented Elizabeth's letter, which James opened and read with a stony face.

The Queen did not mince words. Reminding James of her promise to be his 'faithful watch' to provide him with 'assured intelligence' of dangers, she said a messenger had been intercepted that 'carried letters of high treason to your person and kingdom'. She had sent him the 'discovered treason' so that he could see 'as in a glass, the true portraiture of [her] late warning letters', which, had he resolved to follow, as well as read them, he might have crushed [the treason]. Instead, the conspiracy had strengthened and 'grown daily' as a result of James' allowing 'so many practices which, at the beginning, might easily have been prevented'.[22]

Elizabeth's scolding increased with each line. She chastised the King for what she saw as his weakness in 'supposing to deal moderately and indifferently to both factions', and not 'taking or punishing' from the beginning the 'notorious offenders' who dared 'to send to a foreign king for forces to land in your land … the same never punished; but rather [held] … dear and near'.

'Good Lord!' her letter thundered, 'Me think I do but dream: no king a week would bear this! Their forces assembled, and held near your person, held plots to take your person near the sea-side; and that all this wrapped up in giving them offices, that they might the better accomplish their treason!'[23] This was not the form of government that she had learned over many years, and she swore such a disastrous course would never be allowed in her own realm.

Elizabeth exhorted James not to be 'subject to such weakness, as to suffer such lewdness long to root'. His weakness had 'bred the laughter' of conspirators. He needed to pluck up strength and 'take speedy order' to crush the planned rebellion; 'God forbid!' that he would shun her advice after he had 'perused the great packet' she sent him.

As if exhausted from her written tirade, the Queen closed by saying 'I know not how to end, but with my prayers to God to guide you for the best. My agent with you shall tell you the rest'.[24]

The Queen's agent was Ashby, who summarised the contents of the packet before presenting the letters.

James refused to read them or to discuss the ambassador's briefing, probably because of resentment at Elizabeth's harsh message. As Walsingham had anticipated, the King's reaction was that the documents were fabricated and intended to harm Huntly and other lairds. He petulantly told Ashby that 'it might be a matter feigned, and it was dangerous to touch the credit of noble men; if it could not be proved it would breed a feud for ever'. In this he was right; Scottish lairds were powerful entities and not to be lightly insulted. However, 'within an hour', the ambassador 'found means that [James] was better persuaded',[25] probably due to Maitland's intervention.[26]

James sent for Ashby to bring the papers again. After reading them, he called a Council meeting at the Tollbooth, the medieval municipal building located at the northwest corner of St. Giles' Cathedral, a stone's throw from the English embassy. The letters were read aloud (presumably by Maitland). After 'long perusing and debating', Huntly offered to be 'warded'(incarcerated) until he could be tried. James allowed him to choose Edinburgh Castle for his 'place of warding'. Erroll, Montrose and Bothwell, who were not Councillors, had received word of the meeting and were waiting for Huntly in the street outside the Tollbooth. He 'went aside to a [street] with them, and [they had] long conference together in secret', during which he was urged to launch the insurrection immediately. When he hesitated, he was accused of 'feebleness and negligence' by the co-conspirators.[27]

As Huntly was being escorted to the castle,[28] Bothwell went into the Council chamber to argue on his behalf, but was also ordered to be imprisoned in the castle. 'Erroll retired to his lodging, disguised himself and fled that hour. Not long after the King sent for him, but he was gone, and with him two or three principal gentlemen, papists and counsellors to him and Huntly'. James ordered the burghers of Edinburgh to 'put themselves into arms for his defence; for the other party is strong, and [there were] many Spaniards about the city'.[29]

At first, Ashby was heartened by 'the King's resolute proceeding', but he was soon disappointed. Even Maitland, who the ambassador had listed as leader of the small number of those who were 'Protestants and well-affected to the confession of England' in a report to Walsingham, was suspected of duplicity. On the night of the Council meeting, James went to the Chancellor's lodging, where they met for several hours.

The following day, 'the King and the Chancellor went up to the castle, and dined with Huntly. The King kissed him often, and protested he knew he was innocent'.[30] James dined with the Earl daily until 8 March, when he was 'set at liberty and lodged that night in the King's chamber' after dining with Maitland.[31] Like a conquering hero, Huntly clattered down the High Street to Holyrood 'well accompanied by his friends, about two hundred men'.[32]

Ashby's disappointment changed to amazement and then anger. He was unsure whether James was being brazenly deceitful, was in denial, or was very weak as Elizabeth had accused, yet it was obvious that he was taking only token action against the traitors. His 'extraordinary show of favour' made 'Huntly's friends stout, and threatens revenge both to English and Scots'.[33] Ashby was warned that his life and those of other Englishmen were endangered as 'Huntly's friends are in fury'.[34]

The King was wilfully blind to the evidence against Huntly and his co-conspirators, and seemed persuaded by 'evil affected persons [who] believe and constantly give out that [the letters] was feigned in England or by the Lord Chancellor here, and sent of purpose to be intercepted'. Ashby repeatedly begged Walsingham and Burghley to send the courier captured with the letters to testify.[35]

Ashby continued to meet with Maitland, and was willing to concede that the Chancellor's apparent collusion with Huntly was done for self-preservation, as '[w]arning has been given him that he will shortly be in peril of his life'. Apparently referring to an assassination attempt, the ambassador told Burghley that '[t]hey shot at the chancellor to cut him off that they might thoroughly possess the King, which would greatly hazard here the state of religion, and this country made a receptacle for all foreign forces. I see none so fit as [Maitland] to manage the affairs of this country; he hath carried the King hitherto in religion and affecting the amity of her majesty, and is ready to do many good offices if he be backed'.[36]

The faction that Ashby labelled as 'Papists and discontented Earls and Lords' considered Maitland the main obstacle to taking control of the government and making James their puppet, as had happened in previous years. Now, though, the 'contrary faction' constituted a grave threat to England's national security, as they were determined to open the 'northern portal' to the Spanish. Ashby advocated material support for the Chancellor, warning Walsingham:

> ... if her majesty back not the Lord Chancellor, and that
> with speed, the envy and malice that the evil-disposed bear
> him will wreck and cut him off from the King, who carries
> him yet from them all to the daily hazard of his life. If this
> man should be taken away by the practice of the papists, it
> is feared that the discontented would carry the King at their
> will and pleasure.[37]

The 'backing' urged by the ambassador was not just financial. There was a growing notion that the only way to eradicate the menace was for intervention to support a pre-emptive *coup d'etat* by the pro-English, anti-Papist faction. A coup was debated but not carried out. Walsingham considered other schemes, including one propounded by 'a poor gunner of Berwick' to kill 'those traitors now in Scotland'.[38]

From Ashby's espionage network, he was aware of Scottish ships carrying letters to Parma, and 'return[ing] hither with money and direction from the duke to the papists here'. He suggested that an English man-of-war be 'kept about Newcastle and Berwick to intercept five or six captains of the Spaniards'. The warship could also 'apprehend a pirate or two with letters of marque from the prince of Parma and countenanced by Lord Admiral of Scotland [Bothwell]'. The Scottish pirates were intercepting provisions sent to Berwick, with the full knowledge of James, who also failed to 'purge the country of Spaniards'.[39]

The English felt James could not be trusted; evidence was mounting of the King's dealings with Bothwell and other conspirators as well as Parma.[40] An intercepted letter stated that 'his Majesty seemed to be well contented that the correspondence would increase betwixt him and the Duke of Parma, unto whom he promised to give mutual satisfaction in all things he can crave at his hands'.[41]

Scotland had, according to the English, a 'most confused estate
and government that ever was in any country'. The 'poor King [was]
weary of his life';[42] his people blamed him for the turmoil caused by his
'fond dealing, which not any can alter'. The pro-English group 'doubt
him greatly, and are determined that if he dissemble, if they may have
the Queen's support, they will not leave one of the Spanish faction in
Scotland, and yet serve their king the better. And they desire to know
shortly and secretly what her majesty will do, if need be'.[43] Ashby told
Burghley that even though James still promised to abide by Elizabeth's
guidance 'thoroughly to her contentment … few believe this, for he
is fearful and not able to deal as the case requireth,' and without her
support, 'he can no way bridle the insolent and traitorous dealing of his
nobility and the papists'.[44] The King had 'been much afraid of his own life
since this began'.[45]

To say that James was heavily conflicted is an understatement. He
genuinely respected Maitland 'for he manages the whole affairs of this
country. He sees he cannot be without him; he finds his whole care for his
well-doing'. The Chancellor was the only councillor who was unafraid 'to
dealt most plainly and stoutly with the King'. James 'had a special care to
make and keep' the Chancellor and Huntly friends – which was probably
the main reason that Maitland escaped assassination – 'but it never lasted
forty days without some suspicion or jar'.[46] The two passionately hated
each other; Maitland, the Protestant patriot, because he believed the
'Popish earls' would turn Scotland into a Spanish client state, and Huntly
because the Chancellor was the main obstacle to his great ambitions.[47]

Huntly always prevailed over Maitland's advice, even when James had
agreed to it. The King had 'a strange, extraordinary affection to Huntly,
such as is yet unremoveable, and thereby could persuade his majesty to
any matters to serve his own particular or friends'. James would 'yield
and promise much' to maintain amity with England, 'but when Huntly
or his solicitors come in place he forgets all, and many say they doubt him
[not to be] bewitched'.[48]

The Earl was given command of James' guards, allowed to return to the Council, and 'was lodged in the King's chamber'. Mutterings about the King's sexuality, the 'lewdness' mentioned in Elizabeth's letter, became more vocal. It was 'thought that this king is too much carried by young men that lie in his chamber and is his minions'.[49]

The Chancellor was so thoroughly disgusted with the deteriorating situation that he told James 'if he would maintain Huntly in that sort he would not have a Protestant in Scotland to follow or acknowledge him; they would leave him to the papists and would provide securely for themselves'. Maitland was considering whether 'they [his faction] must have the King either with his will or against it'. Yet he thought that they could never prevail if they followed Elizabeth's advice to prosecute Huntly for treason, as his noblemen would rally to free him, and the government would fall to them, benefiting Philip of Spain.[50]

Eight months earlier, during the height of the Armada threat, Ashby had presciently warned that the greatest threat to the northern portal was from the Popish lairds and their allies. Without their support, the Spanish would be unable to establish a secure base for an invasion of England. In the early spring of 1589, he believed the boast of 'a knight of [Huntly's] party' that 'such an alteration in Scotland as was not [seen] this forty years' was imminent.[51]

# 18. The lairds' open insurrection

James' attempts to deceive the English and play all sides were transparent. No one, from Maitland to Huntly to Ashby, took him seriously. While he moaned about 'the wickedness of his nobility and their evil natures, declaring himself weary of his life among them',[1] he was simultaneously issuing a royal license to Bothwell to solicit Parma.[2]

The King became an object of mockery, suffering 'great indignities of some of his unruly subjects'.[3] A popular ditty cruelly likening James ('Jocko') to a monkey was mirthfully recited in Edinburgh taverns and even in the homes of merchants, gentry and nobles of all factions:

> If I have Jocko in my hands, I can make him bite you;
>
> If you have Jocko, you can make him bite me.[4]

The doggerel had a sinister meaning: whoever held the King would control him. The Papist conspirators were now determined to capture James, although there was disagreement about what was to be done with him afterwards. Huntly and Crawford believed it was possible to 'nourish him with the pope or the King of Spain'– to convert him to Catholicism and marry him to Philip's daughter, the *Infanta*. Other Catholic lairds, such as Claud Hamilton and Morton, believed James should be permanently exiled, while the Protestant 'malcontents' advocated an 'alteration of Court', a *coup d'état* that would maintain him as a puppet similar to the short-lived Gowrie regime.[5] Dormant hatred of England for killing Mary Stuart had resurfaced, and many Scots had begun to 'hate their king' for any show of amity. The pro-Spanish faction was united in planning to eliminate Maitland, although its attempts had been unsuccessful so far.

Some lairds who Ashby called 'Protestants and well-affected to the confession of England' supported James – and a pro-English policy – because they hoped he would succeed to Elizabeth's throne, due to 'the greedy desire of a number to be there [England] with him, hoping to better their poor estate'.[6] This was a canny move by some loyalists; for example, the Earl of Mar was granted several English manors and appointed to James' privy council after his accession.

The political situation was so dire that 'every one misliked and stood in fear of others'. Ashby and his colleagues continued the refrain that without speedy English financial support to James and his dwindling number of loyalists such as Maitland, 'the papists will put themselves into arms, for they expect force and money out of Spain, as is here constantly affirmed; and truly their want is such they will take from any prince to the ruin of their King, country and religion'.[7] A second attempt at a Spanish invasion was expected in the summer of 1589, and the ambassador believed that time to prevent this was running out.

Ashby was keenly aware of the perennial 'poverty of this prince and country'. Despite his previous chastisement for overstepping his authority, he saw that his duty, and his legacy, was to prevent a Spanish strategic base in Scotland. Tired and looking forward to retirement, he was emboldened to advise Walsingham and Burghley on solutions to the now acute Scottish problem, which centred as always on money.[8]

Always in a precarious financial situation, James was now in 'miserable poverty'. His massive debts to leading burghers, and 'taxes *alias* subsidies' had reached their limits, and contributed to popular support for his political opponents. He was 'not able to live like a king', having 'neither plate nor stuff to furnish one of his little half-built houses, which are in great decay and ruin. His plate is not worth £100; he has only two or three rich jewels, and his guards are unpaid ... His saddles are of plain cloth ... no bread but of oats', and his clothing was worn and stained. James, it was said, 'never thinks of money nor how [it] should be gotten'.[9]

Having been pressured for several years to find a wife, James thought that a strategic marriage might solve some of his financial problems and put to rest idle gossip about his fondness for men. The King was 'cold about the marriage, and the Chancellor ... opposed to it', but they agreed that an appropriate alliance 'would drive the country into some settled order'. While grappling with his tenuous hold on the throne, he decided to ask the King of Denmark for the hand of his sister Anne, who he believed would bring a dowry of '40,000 crowns, besides jewels and money', and if her brother died, the princess would be heir to 400,000 crowns a year rent.[10]

Maitland was 'the best affected of all towards England', but he could not hold out much longer against the pro-Spanish faction, which alternated between continual death threats and bribery offers to join them. Due to his own poverty, the Chancellor was 'covetous ... and driven to keep a great train [a heavy security detail] to save his life from his enemies'. As one of Burghley's agents alleged: Maitland 'spends much more than his living, and need makes men do that they would not; – and what is it that a Scot will not do for money?'.[11]

Ashby was frustrated that while Elizabeth urged him to prevail upon James 'to purge the country of' Armada survivors, she seemed to ignore that fact that the King and his government were so broke that they were on the verge of succumbing to the 'Popish Earls' and Bothwell. The best way to have the 'country purged of the Spaniards will be', he judged, 'to have some consideration of the lord Chancellor', who 'countenanced by her majesty, will be able to keep the King in this good course, and encourage others to follow in his steps. Some consideration for him now will save her majesty many thousands'.[12] Despite Huntly and Claud Hamilton making 'great means to win the chancellor both by money and friends', Maitland was considered to be the key person in curtailing the papist faction, 'for he it is that does all ... if he perish, farewell Scotland and all good men here'.[13]

James continued to be in denial about Huntly's treason and restored him to command of the household guard at Holyrood, prompting the Chancellor to refuse to go to the palace without a strong contingent of loyal men-at-arms. After a standoff of several days, Maitland gave James an ultimatum: either remove Huntly and discharge his guards, or he would resign and, with fellow Protestants, prepare for civil war. 'This put the King in a great brangle, [quandary] for he had great love to Huntly, yet he agreed to discharge his guard, and Huntly to go home'.[14]

Huntly agreed to banishment to lull James and the Chancellor while he planned his insurrection. He invited James to a farewell hunt and banquet on 13 March. While hunting that morning, Huntly, Errol and Bothwell tried to persuade James to go away with them on a pretext that Maitland's faction planned to launch a coup that afternoon, and the people of Edinburgh were arming themselves against him. With the King sequestered, the plan was for Bothwell to murder the Chancellor at the feast. James refused to go with them and returned to Edinburgh, staying at the Chancellor's house as he feared that the guards at Holyrood were loyal to Huntly.

As Huntly's feast had already been prepared, James and Maitland – probably glad to have a free meal in their impecunious state – went to the banquet anyway that evening without their host and his fellow lairds, who had gone north to assemble an army.

Harsh winter weather delayed travel and communications between London and Edinburgh, requiring nine days in transit for couriers. Ashby received word that Pringle, the traitors' intercepted messenger, had finally arrived in Berwick on 15 March under heavy guard. The ambassador immediately 'sent to the court to have audience to acquaint the King of this man's coming to Berwick, and to understand what order should be taken for his convoy to Edinburgh'. James made excuses for not receiving him, 'being troubled with a pain in his side, which he had taken the day before in hunting',[15] which was probably depression brought on by the troubles in his relationship with Huntly.

Over the next two days, Ashby unsuccessfully tried to meet with the King. He confronted the Chancellor about the urgency of bringing Pringle to Edinburgh so he could testify against the Huntly faction. Sharing the ambassador's vexation, Maitland told him that James refused 'to take knowledge' of the prisoner until Errol surrendered himself, having being 'put on the horn' – denounced as an outlaw.

It was obvious to Ashby that James did not want to hear Pringle's testimony. 'The King carrieth such a fond affection to Huntly as is incredible', he told Burghley in exasperation. 'His young years is greatly abused by the flattery and false oaths of the adverse party and papists in this land, and his lenity emboldens that faction very much'.[16] He was finally able to meet with the King on 21 March, during which he gave him the Queen's scathing letter in which she snidely asked 'what injurious plan against my nearest neighbours reigns with such blindness as suffers them not to foresee their hanging peril and most imminent danger?'[17]

James blithely responded that 'her majesty's letter he liked well of, acknowledging her careful mind for him', and promising that he would 'prosecute [the traitors] most severely'. The King was at this point far beyond where the English would take him seriously; Ashby expected that his 'young years and mild nature will be abused by the papists and malcontents'. Nonetheless he succeeded in obtaining Maitland's agreement to transport Pringle to Edinburgh escorted by a hundred cavalrymen to protect him from Bothwell's men, who were determined to silence the prisoner.[18]

The Chancellor finally persuaded James to 'examine' Pringle. Bizarrely, the interrogation took place in the Holyrood bedchamber of Ludovic Stewart, 2nd Duke of Lennox, the fourteen-year-old son of James' deceased favourite. It was said that '[t]he King loves this Duke as him self; the Duke loves Huntly out of measure'.[19] The King swept in with his current 'best-loved minion' and 'only conceit', Alexander Lindsay, younger brother of the Earl of Crawford, who was James' 'nightly bedfellow' in Huntly's absence but was also 'Huntly's wholly'.[20]

The prisoner was escorted by Maitland, Sir Robert Melville and Alexander Hay, the Clerk of the Register. No English diplomats were present. With the exception of the Chancellor, there was 'not one in the chamber ... but are Huntly's. These men have the King's ear, and work great effect for Huntly, and the Chancellor cannot mend it, for the King will not change his servants, he loves them so well'.[21] Huntly's supporters claimed that Pringle had been suborned and his testimony was of no value. For the record (which was the reason that the Clerk of the Register was present), James voiced suspicion of Huntly, but saw 'no proof against him'. His fate undecided, Pringle was taken in chains to Maitland's house and confined in a cellar under round-the-clock guard.[22]

Amidst the turmoil and unending frustration, Ashby was pleased to be asked by Lord John Hamilton to be godfather – a 'gossip' as the medieval term was still used in England – to his son, James. Lord John, *de facto* Earl of Arran due to his elder brother's 'disordered intellect', was one of the few reliably pro-English noblemen in Scotland. Hamilton's younger brother Claud, a leading member of Huntly's faction, had been named in the packet of treasonous letters, and his sister was Huntly's mother – a prime example of the incestuous nature of Scottish politics, which mirrored the political and social environment in England.

Ashby told Burghley that he had been invited to the christening 'in respect of the place I hold' as the Queen's ambassador, and that the King would attend as the infant's second godfather. Lord John, who would be created Marquess of Hamilton in 1599, was shrewdly demonstrating loyalty to both Elizabeth and James.[23] Due to events that were soon to unfold in April, the child's christening was postponed until late June.

Regardless of urgent pleas to Burghley and Walsingham for assistance to the King's faction, none was forthcoming. James Colville, laird of Easter Wemyss, travelled to London in late March for the purpose of a new round of 'propositions' and to notify Elizabeth of James's intended marriage with the Danish princess Anne, which the Queen opposed.

Wemyss had been ordered to pursue Ashby's repudiated offers, although the Scottish envoy knew not to ask for too much, and James would hopefully be content with whatever Elizabeth deemed reasonable, despite his 'demand for great matters at first'. Knowing that the Scots' dogged determination to obtain the rejected 'concessions' would antagonise the Queen, Ashby warned Burghley that Wemyss would 'demand the lands descended to [James] by his grandmother ... urge her bounty in augmentation of his charge [financial support]' and press 'for the uniting together for defence of religion, and security of these two kingdoms against invasion of strangers'.[24] However unrealistic, in Edinburgh there was 'great expectation of Wemyss's return and that he shall bring satisfaction to the King and good men'.[25] James may have thought pressing for fulfilment of the ambassador's consideration would be accepted as a *quid pro quo* for punishing Huntly, but Elizabeth held a far stronger hand in the great power version of the game of Maw.[26]

The Queen was tired of appeasing James. She was beginning to think that he was a lost cause, not worth wasting any more gold from her depleted coffers on. On 5 April, Elizabeth told Heneage that she was 'fully persuaded of the weakness of that king and of the uncertainty of that alliance'. Heneage 'very plainly' reminded her of the 'needful preventing of the danger imminent' to 'the kingdom by that perilous postern' north of the border, and evidently discussed an English invasion to restore order and eliminate the Catholic faction. Wemyss' renewed demands from James were called 'a conceit', to be responded to in due course.[27]

While Elizabeth fulminated against James, and her Privy Council debated, events in Scotland climaxed. On 7 April, Ashby reported to Walsingham (who had returned to court): 'The smoke is now turned into flame'– the insurrection had begun.

******

Ashby's agents reported that Bothwell planned to attack across the border into the Middle and East Marches, but failed to generate support from local chieftains, who feared English retaliation. Instead, the Earl rode towards Edinburgh with 300 horsemen, intending to link with Huntly's forces descending from the north to 'welter the court [wreak havoc] and dispatch the Chancellor'. Both the King and Maitland narrowly escaped attempts to capture them. Every Edinburgh male 'from sixteen to sixty' was ordered to man the ramparts.

Hearing a great blaring of trumpets and furious drum beats, Ashby buckled on his rapier, donned a heavy cloak and ordered his pair of body guards to go with him to the Netherbow Port.

'Don't speak,' he cautioned. 'They could take us for English spies and hang us or run us through.'

Netherbow was a good vantage point as the stench from rotting heads and body parts on spikes was so foul that the tower top over the gate was deserted except for a quartet of bilious-looking men-at-arms. Holding a gilt pouncet box to his nose to avert the reek, Ashby surveyed Bothwell's force parading haphazardly outside the city walls.

He estimated that there were no more than six hundred cavalry and infantry, and many of the latter appeared to be armed only with broadswords and targets. Through curtains of rain, the ambassador could discern what must have been Bothwell in full armour on a destrier, surrounded by a dozen other lairds. When one of his men began gagging, Ashby motioned for them to go down the winding stone staircase to the doorways exiting onto the Flodden Wall, which was lined with boys and men of every age, including greybeards, wearing ancient sallets and pieces of rusty body armour. As the Englishmen walked along the ramparts with their heads down, a mighty shout launched a wave of cheering, with mutual congratulations and much backslapping.

'He's leavin', the fuckin' coward!' shouted a fat burgher in an oversized morion, 'Bothwell's leavin'. We won!'

Ashby told Walsingham that Bothwell withdrew after seeing what appeared to be a strong force on the city walls. This was fortunate for the Edinburghers, he said, who were largely armed with ancient billhooks, yew bows, crossbows and a few obsolete matchlock hackbuts which were useless in the pelting rain.

******

Bothwell encamped outside Kelso to await Huntly's army, which was believed to number 'five or six thousand at the least'[28] and included Jesuits and priests, who Ashby called 'those caterpillars'.[29] Huntly assembled his sodden men and spoke to them from the back of his warhorse. James had been forced to support the English 'to his and the country's shame', he roared, Maitland was Elizabeth's chief agent 'bought by English money', and an English army of three thousand men was *en route* to the Borders to support the pro-English traitors, with the goal of overthrowing the nobility and bringing Scotland 'into bondage'. He called for all good Scots to liberate the King, 'remove the English faction and deliver this realm from the tyranny of those who murdered the King's mother and have done him all the wrong they can'.[30]

Believing themselves to be outnumbered by the rebel forces, James and the Chancellor were reported to be separately negotiating with the pro-Spanish faction to save themselves. The King was 'in privity' with the plans of Bothwell and Huntly, and was said to have 'turned from the chancellor'. Maitland sent an emissary to Bothwell with the message that 'he was very willing to surrender up his office of chancellorship ... and to leave the court and go home to his own house; and hath offered to give Bothwell ten thousand crowns for his friendship'.[31] It was unlikely that the impoverished Chancellor had 10,000 crowns (£2,500 Scots coinage or roughly £625 sterling), and the 'malcontent' lairds probably wouldn't have allowed him to peacefully retire, as they opposed him more for being an upstart who had usurped their traditional roles at court rather than for political differences.[32]

James confounded his detractors by taking decisive action urged by Maitland. The King was 'exceeding angry' and vowed revenge, especially against Bothwell. He managed to raise a force of nearly 2,000 men with minimal training, of whom less than a quarter carried firearms, with only enough munitions for a few shots each.[33] In his last audience with Ashby before embarking on his counter-insurgency campaign, he told him he was willing to follow Elizabeth's advice, but thought it 'strange that no encouragement comes out of England from her majesty in this dangerous time'.[34]

Joined by Lord John Hamilton and other loyalists, the ragtag royal army left Edinburgh on 9 April 'to join with the earls to prosecute Huntly and his party with fire and sword'. James and Maitland, both in full armour, were in the vanguard. To his regret, Ashby was unable to accompany the force, 'being in physic to shorten a tertian ague'.[35] He sent Thomas Fowler in his place, lending him his gelding, accompanied by a courier to bring daily intelligence reports.

What motivated James to act so decisively, with anger which was uncharacteristic of what Ashby termed 'his mild nature'? Maitland was a key influence as the Chancellor knew that if the coup succeeded, he would be executed. There was general expectation that 'the Spanish succours'[assistance] was 'looked for here daily to come out of the Low Countries' after which the 'Popish' forces would be invincible, and the King would become little more than Philip's puppet, his dream of the English throne vanishing like snow melting on the Cairngorms.[36] Fears that the insurgents would prevail were justified; Parma's gold paid their forces, and Spanish troops were expected to join the more than 1,000 Armada survivors in Scotland, at least half of whom were soldiers.

James was outraged by Bothwell's treachery and disappointed by Huntly, although he would continue to find excuses for the latter's behaviour. He realised that he could expect no material support from Elizabeth unless he obeyed her exhortations to 'awake … out of your long slumber, and deal like a king who will ever reign alone in his own' [right].[37] During the expedition, he was quoted saying 'Think you not that this will be pleasing to the Queen? … she shall see I will do my part so far as I may by any travail or moyen [means]'.[38]

His anger and sense of betrayal at the Queen's refusal to honour Ashby's offers during the Armada crisis were unabated. The King probably always believed that the ambassador had acted in good faith with official approval, from Walsingham if not from Elizabeth and Burghley. It is unlikely that, after his accession to the English throne, James would have shown such a high level of favouritism to Ashby's nephew, Robert Naunton, if he bore a grudge against the ambassador (see Appendix I).

As the King's army marched towards Huntly's castle at Strathbogie in Aberdeenshire, it was joined by other lairds known to favour the rebels, such as the arch-Catholics Lord Seton, who had long conspired with the Spanish, and James Chisholm, whose brother John, named in the Spanish Letters, was with Huntly's forces. Such men wore treachery like a second skin, and would turn on the King's party in an instant if they thought Huntly would prevail.[39]

Hampered by 'want of victual, with evil weather', they struggled across rugged countryside stripped of livestock and oats, watched from the hills by hostile Highlanders. On 17 April, the royalists approached the 'Brig o' Dee' (Bridge of Dee), on the outskirts of Aberdeen, where Huntly, Errol and Crawford with approximately three thousand cavalry and footmen were drawn up for battle. A stalemate ensued. As word spread through the 'malcontents' ranks that the King himself opposed them, desertions began, especially among those who had been falsely led to believe that James was the prisoner of Maitland and the English. By the 20th, Huntly and his co-conspirators had fled to their respective castles, and all their men had scattered. James and his shivering, starving army entered Aberdeen unopposed.

The King and Maitland had been extraordinarily fortunate. By the time they arrived at the Brig o' Dee, they had less than a thousand men, all hungry, cold and wet, with no shelter, the weather like the 'frost and snow as at Christmas'. There was little fodder for the horses, many of which, including James's were lame. As rumour circulated that the King had no money to pay them, disgruntlement raced through the ranks like a plague. If the insurgents had attacked, the royal forces would have been overwhelmed. But true to the nature of the Scottish nobles, feuds and disagreements divided the leadership. For example, the earls of 'Sutherland and Caithness, both papists, fell out ... which prevented them from being with Huntly', and in a bloody clan battle 'at least 300 [were] slain on a day between them'.[40]

James pursued the rebel leaders, 'preparing to raze to the ground the houses of Huntly, Erroll, and Crawford.' He and his army, which was reduced in numbers daily, marched first to Strathbogie with one hundred workmen recruited from Aberdeen to demolish the castle. 'Huntly had caused all the country to be disfurnished of whatsoever might serve for victual or prey, and this his own house nothing left in it but woodwork and some feather beds, without furniture'. Before the destruction began, Huntly 'sent messenger after messenger to offer himself to yield to the King's mercy, under condition to save his life and lands unattainted' [without confiscation]. Late that night 'the captain traitor, like a good goose', surrendered. Crawford and Bothwell followed, while other lairds remained at large knowing that the royal army was too weak 'for want of victual' to pursue them in the mountains.[41]

After the Brig o' Dee campaign, James' martial energy evaporated, along with that of his exhausted army. Huntly and the other rebels who surrendered were accused of treason and tried at the Toll Booth on 24 May. Huntly's examination was described as 'a little garden party' conducted by James and four Council members in the 'pleasance behind the council house'.[42] All were found guilty, but James 'meant no harm to the convicted, for they were soon after set at liberty', much to Ashby's anger.[43] The ambassador was equally disheartened by the return of the Master of Gray, inexplicably 'restored' to court by Maitland, and who immediately began sending intelligence to both Burghley and the Vatican.[44]

Wemyss' 'propositions' on behalf of James were finally answered on 26 April. In a scathing letter probably composed by Burghley, the Queen expressed her irritation that 'answer had been made very often' about 'any right that the King might claim as heir to his mother', as Elizabeth had 'testified under her hand and seal' to him. However, for his 'better satisfaction' he would be provided with an official document signed by 'commissioners both of her Council and judges of the realm to verify his claim'.[45]

She again repudiated 'such overtures as Mr. Ashby the last summer made unto the King,' asserting that the offers:

> … were only matters of his private conceit and not directed
> nor warranted theareto from her majesty nor from any of
> her Council. So as upon the first knowledge thereof to some
> of her Council before her majesty was thereof informed, to
> avoid her high displeasure, the knowledge of his doing was
> kept from her majesty for a good time, and he reprehended
> for the same, until by his own letters to her majesty he
> confessed his offence and craved pardon, alleging that he had
> no evil meaning therein, but thought to show his goodwill to
> the King in seeking to please him with such overtures. And
> for proof that he had no authority to use such speeches, her
> majesty is sure he will take his oath if it be offered unto him.[46]

The ambassador's offers were still a very sore point for Elizabeth, and it is clear that she blamed members of her Council (with Walsingham and Hatton being the likely suspects) for not informing her earlier to avoid her wrath. It is unlikely that Ashby would have perjured himself by taking an oath that he acted on his own initiative.

The Queen also stated that the issue about James' claim to 'the title of those lands of the Earl of Lennox' had been 'often answered'. To put the matter to rest, she said she was 'very certain that such as favour the title of the Lady Arbell have offered to show her title to be very good by the laws of the realm'.[47]

Regarding the languished offensive and defensive league, Elizabeth scolded James, reminding him that in her realm she 'bridle[d] and suppresse[d] all attempts of evil subjects', yet the King had foolishly waited until it was nearly too late to follow her example 'against certain conspirators, being of great countenance and connived enemies with the

Pope and the Spaniards'. The Queen was non-committal about advice for the King's marriage, citing that her 'own example in forbearing marriage' made her unqualified to guide him on such matters, although she offered to give her opinion in secret.[48]

No mention was made of the urgent requests for money.

Some members of the Privy Council disagreed with Elizabeth about support for James' beleaguered regime. Walsingham and Hatton, recognising the disastrous national security consequences if Scotland fell to the pro-Spanish faction, were favourable to Wemyss' propositions, as apparently was Burghley.[49] These senior councillors were afraid of 'meddling' due the Queen's warning of 'a hard construction' against them if they did so.[50]

Nonetheless, once Elizabeth's wrath was vented, Ashby was informed that the Queen had signed a warrant for £3,000 'to be sent to the King for his strength against the rebels'. Although the ambassador was disappointed that the funds were so late, and meagre, he hoped that more material and symbolic support for James would follow. If the insurgents had 'received foreign succour,' he told Walsingham, 'they would have maintained a continual war, and put her majesty to infinite charges before they could have been suppressed: but now their chief taken, and seeing her majesty so ready to assist this prince, the rest will quail and vanish away, some rendering themselves to the Kings mercy, and the rest by fleeing their country'.[51]

# 19. Fowler's defamation of Ashby

By the end of May 1589, William Ashby was thoroughly weary of his service in Scotland. As an experienced diplomat and intelligencer, he knew that duplicity and intrigue were to be expected. But in Scotland the constantly shifting currents of power weighed on his disillusioned soul.

Reluctant to accept the ambassadorship the previous year, he was 'greatly troubled' by having stayed in Edinburgh longer than anticipated. He told Burghley that while he enjoyed *'otium cum dignitate'* (leisure with dignity) – respect as Her Majesty's representative – he was not able to sustain the expenses. He reminded the Lord Treasurer that shortly before his appointment he had confided his poverty and ill health 'which was such as flesh and blood is not able to comport: yet better could I bear it at home, then in this room [place] I now hold of honor and credit'.[1]

Having given up his parliamentary seat and the small income it provided, he had hoped to be granted an extension of his lease of 'the manors of Donington and Thriplow and the parsonage of Hinxton' in 'the bishopric of Ely', which the Queen had granted as a gift. Burghley did not extend the lease, but promised to 'help procure her majesty's liberality some other way'. This had not occurred, causing financial stress, as Ashby's twenty-one-year lease for tithes and profits from manors in Leicestershire, Lincolnshire and Yorkshire had expired shortly before he assumed the ambassadorship.

He wrote that having 'nether land nor lease to sell or pawn' he would be unable to stay in Edinburgh and perform his duties without new manorial grants from the Crown. Edinburgh was excessively expensive, and his official allowance for expenses less by 10 shillings a day than previous ambassadors, all of whom had been 'gentlemen of wealth', whereas his only source of income was from the Queen. A proud man who had already suffered the unjustified indignity of apologising to his two masters and the Queen, Ashby poignantly told Burghley – who was not known for his sympathy – 'I know not which way to turn; without present help I shall hazard my credit, dishonour the place I hold, and be unable to perform any service. Thus want forceth me to pass the bounds of modesty'. As a postscript he added, 'I am ready to stay or to return as shall please her majesty; but without that which she granted me out of Ely, or such allowance as others in this place have had, I shall not be able to remain'.[2]

Ashby's financial difficulties may have been exaggerated. He was certainly not a 'gentleman of wealth', but he was not without resources. Prior to his arrival in Scotland, Walsingham had procured for him the recusancy penalty of a 'Mr. Dratch', who the ambassador had reached an agreement with to keep him from imprisonment. Subsequently, Ashby was informed that Dratch was 'in prison in Shrewsbury and his land extended' [expropriated]. He asked Sir Francis to ensure that he would continue to receive income from the penalty 'according to her majesty's grant', and that Dratch have 'such favour as law and equity will permit'.

Aside from an example of how public servants such as Ashby were remunerated, this is an interesting case as Dratch is possibly a Jewish name, and he may have been one who refused to convert (or pretended to convert) and stubbornly refused to attend Church of England services, thereby committed a statutory offense. The ambassador requested that Dratch 'be delivered out of prison and committed to the custody of my cousin Ashby in Leicestershire, of whose zeal in religion I refer you to the report of Mr. Lisle Cave'. The cousin was probably George Ashby of Quenby – who had accompanied Leicester on his 1585 Netherlands expedition – and Lisle Cave was a prominent Leicestershire lawyer who provided affidavits of adherence to Anglicanism. Dratch, who may have been elderly, was presumably sheltered as an act of charity.[3]

To add to Ashby's unhappiness, his house in London had been ransacked and his 'apparel and household stuff taken away to the value of £200'. Breaking into and robbing unoccupied houses was common, especially in areas such as Clerkenwell that bordered on warrens of criminals. The loss would be equivalent to around £62,000 today.

Ashby's personal problems were compounded as he became aware that Thomas Fowler and his accomplice James Hudson were trying to undermine him with the Scottish court as well as with Walsingham and Burghley.

Fowler was a sycophantic rogue, craving the company of those he considered his social superiors yet suffused with jealousy of them. Based on his writings and the observations of people who knew him, he was a classic paranoiac as well as a liar and murderer.[4] His past was remarkably chequered. A quarter of a century earlier, he had been described as one of the 'Crafty and wily strangers' who, with 'other unworthy persons' including David Rizzio, had wormed his way into the court of Queen Mary Stuart to 'occupy the place of native councillors and manage all weighty affairs'.[5]

A servant of Lady Margaret Douglas, Countess of Lennox, Fowler brokered the 1565 marriage of Mary and Lord Darnley, Lady Margaret's son. He fell out with Darnley, disguised himself and took ship to London, where he was arrested and sentenced to death. Mary begged Elizabeth to spare his life, after which he had a resilient career as a double agent, spying for the English as well as the Scots, and as Leicester's steward. Promising to 'behave myself', he fled to 'this poor country of Scotland' after Leicester's death 'having great enemies and few friends, and having some discontentment', as well as to escape his wife and father-in-law.[6] His letters to Burghley and Walsingham often contained pleas to intercede with creditors and family members.

Despite being an Englishman, Fowler had (and sometimes pretended to have), privileged access to key personages in Scotland, including James and the Papist lairds. Although he sent reports to Walsingham and Burghley individually, Fowler was primarily the latter's agent. In their communications, the Lord Treasurer used the code name 'Fidelis' for Fowler, referring to himself as 'Spectator'.[7]

Walsingham flattered Fowler as the best source of Scottish intelligence since he became Secretary, despite being warned by John Colville in 1583 not to trust him.[8] Sir Francis had no qualms about employing knaves as intelligencers, but he seemed unusually solicitous of Fowler for reasons unknown, promising that 'for your own causes I will have care of you', and using his considerable influence to assist with domestic problems and debtors.[9] The Secretary said he would 'do well hereafter to set down nothing in your letters that may not be showed publicly … If you have any thing of secrecy to be communicated unto me you may do it in a letter apart'.[10]

Although addressed as 'Mr.', which was the usual salutation for university graduates, there is no record of Fowler matriculating at Oxford or Cambridge. His early life is a mystery; he was rumoured to be illegitimate, possibly sired by a high-status member of Lady Margaret's household and raised by his mother's family at Settrington, the Countess' Yorkshire manor. Fowler evidently had a close connection with Lady Margaret as he was appointed sole executor of her estate after she died in 1578, receiving her flock of sheep at Settrington and custody of all her 'clocks, watches and dials'.[11]

Fowler had a tenuous family relationship with Ashby, which was probably a factor in his twisted behaviour. Ashby referred to him as 'my cousin' in writing to his wife, Elizabeth, who he addressed as 'sweet lady', while in one of Fowler's letters to her he referenced 'Your cousin Asheby'. In the Elizabethan era, the term 'cousin' was used much more broadly than in modern English, connoting almost any relative beyond the immediate family, both for blood kin and through marriage. The ambassador was distantly related to Elizabeth Fowler (née Mainie or Venstrie) through Elizabeth Tanfield, wife of his first cousin, John Ashby of Loseby. The family connection is relevant to William Ashby's life because of Fowler's exploitation of it impacting Ashby's reputation.[12]

Hudson's connection to Fowler was through the Lennoxes. He was the third of four brothers, Yorkshiremen like Fowler, who came to Scotland in Darnley's wedding retinue and were employed as viola players to the court. Hudson was recruited by Bowes as an intelligencer in April 1583,[13] and was subsequently "handled' by John Colville, the Scottish courtier, diplomat and erstwhile Presbyterian minister who 'for mercenary motives' in 1578 began 'to furnish private and confidential information for the Court of England'.[14] Hudson was employed by Ashby as both a courier and an intelligencer.

Within weeks of his arrival in Edinburgh, Fowler was conspiring with Hudson to diminish Ashby's credibility and access to the Scottish court. He cautiously opened separate lines of communication to Walsingham and Burghley, telling Sir Francis that he had 'hitherto delivered the ambassador here all my knowledge, and he is so honest a gentleman that I would not offend him. I would be glad to know if it be your pleasure that I deal with him, or write only to yourself'.[15]

Fowler toadied to the ambassador, pretending respect for his position as the Queen's resident representative while telling Burghley and Walsingham that though Ashby was 'able to do such service' as he could not, he was better placed with James and his court, 'being in the King's ear and the Chancellor's'.[16] In his reports to London, he attempted self-aggrandisement by commenting that he had been hunting with the King or had to sign off abruptly because James had called him to join a game of Maw.[17]

The concept of paranoia was unknown in the sixteenth century, yet Fowler's writing indicates that he had symptoms recognised today, especially an apparent persecution complex possibly stemming from his illegitimacy. He told Walsingham that he had been 'very busy in these troubles and have been threatened for my labour'. He believed that an English nobleman was 'very angry' and had 'vowed to discredit him'. After learning that Ashby's friend Sir George Carey would be returning to Scotland as the Queen's special envoy to James, Fowler complained that

Carey had been 'persuaded to deface and discredit me with this king; at least if he can'. The Scots evidently thought that Fowler was a renegade Englishman as he was terrified of exposure as a double agent.[18]

Fowler's resentment expanded. He felt slighted and unappreciated by Ashby. He told Burghley that while the ambassador was honest, he was not giving him credit for his intelligence reports and was using these for his own advantage.[19] Fowler complained that 'the ambassador dare promise nothing', but with the Armada crisis passed, and Elizabeth's vacillating attitude towards Scotland, neither could any other English envoy, such as Hunsdon.[20]

On the contrary, Ashby was initially sympathetic to his fellow countryman and 'cousin', accepting his story of being unfairly persecuted in England. He championed him, writing to Walsingham soon after his arrival that 'hard dealing is used against Mr. Fowler in his absence, as though he had committed some treason; it troubles the gentleman not a little. I beseech your honour vouchsafe such favour as equity will require'.[21] He told Burghley that Fowler was 'ready to perform any good office that lieth in him for her majesty's service'.[22] Attempting to mediate, Ashby wrote a letter to Fowler's estranged wife, which Fowler thought 'would have done much good', but fretted that it had nefariously not been included in the diplomatic pouch.[23]

The defamatory campaign against Ashby increased in May 1589, no doubt adding to his despondency. On Fowler's behalf, Hudson sought to have him replace the ambassador, arguing that Fowler 'does all the service here', and that if he were granted a formal position, he would be 'able to do more service than four such as Mr. Ashby is'. The intelligence network would be strengthened, and Fowler could accomplish more on 20 shillings a day than Ashby could with his per diem of double that amount.[24]

As a relatively impoverished gentleman, Ashby was more vulnerable to enemies than wealthier counterparts. Hudson told Walsingham that the ambassador 'had no gift to persuade or reason with the King or

Chancellor, for they will put him presently to a nonplus'.[25] Fowler and Hudson tried to erode Ashby's reputation by keeping alive the story that his offers of the previous year were his personal initiative, knowing he would not disavow this. Fowler's henchman said that 'Lack of judgement is [Ashby's] want rather than lack of good will'. Their maligning extended to Robert Naunton, implying that Naunton was an unreliable courier and incompetent secretary.[26]

Despite the Yorkshire mongrels nipping at his heels, Ashby was gratified by the arrival of English warships which he had often requested to wipe out an infestation of pirates and 'intercept the Spanish succours which are looked for here daily to come out of the Low Countries'.[27] On 1 June, the Armada hero Sir George Beeston sailed into the Firth of Forth on the thirty-two-gun *Vanguard* and anchored off Leith. He was followed a few days later by the twenty-two-gun *Tiger* and the thirteen-gun *Achates*. While the 'Malcontents' and many Edinburghers were angry about the fleet showing St. George's Cross in their Firth, James welcomed it as a long overdue demonstration of Elizabeth's support, proclaiming that 'the ships of war [were] ready to fulfil and follow his Majesty's direction'.[28]

On the 5th, an incident involving some of the hundreds of Spaniards in Edinburgh nearly set back the improving Anglo-Scottish relations. Three 'trumpeters'[29] from the *Vanguard* were drinking in a sordid ale house on the Leith waterfront when they brawled with drunken Scottish sailors. A crewman was wounded with a dagger. As his mess mates helped him back to the ship's boat, they were followed and attacked by a group of Spaniards, who murdered one of the Englishmen.

Two days later Ashby and Beeston met with James at Holyrood, taking a hard line on finding and punishing the Spanish assailants. With three warships menacing Leith, the King was galvanised into action. Ashby suggested that if the Spaniards who slew the seaman could not be found, Spanish officers living in Edinburgh should be rounded up and handed over to the English until they produced the guilty parties. Fearing that an even greater diplomatic incident would result if well-connected *hidalgos* were captured and delivered to Armada veterans eager to punish their enemy, James commanded that 'two of the principal Spaniards' be imprisoned in the Tolbooth. The murderers were never found, and the pair of Spanish grandees was quietly released after the English fleet sailed.[30]

Fowler falsely claimed credit for the English response. Writing to Burghley that the sailor had been murdered by 'villainous base papists and Spaniards together', he libelled Ashby, writing that as his other prior requests had been disregarded, the ambassador asked him to become 'his secretary and draw him two requests to present to the King and Council'. Fowler boasted that 'it may well be that they may do more good than other ways would, for I have convinced the King to see justice done and the English well used'.[31]

This incident is an example of how Fowler's vendettas and craving for social acceptance resulted in concocted information in his reports. While he was a key intelligence asset within the court, and therefore a useful research source, historians should be wary of taking his writings at face value. He claimed Maitland's authority was so diminished that he was unable to influence James, while he also boasted that he was so close to the King that he followed his advice in any 'public thing touching England'.[32] Yet in a rare admission, apparently after being scolded by James, he told Burghley 'the King prays me not to speak for him nor to deal in his matters'.[33]

James made other efforts to mollify the English naval visitors. On 10 June, 'at the earnest desire of the King's Majesty', an 'honest banquet' was hosted by the burgesses for Ashby and the officers of the warships.[34] The King gave a locket set with diamonds to Beeston, and 100 gold crowns, gold chains and rings to the captains of the other warships. James was too poor to personally sponsor the dinner, and the gifts were provided by Thomas Foulis, an Edinburgh burgess, goldsmith, financier and mining entrepreneur. Relations restored, the warships weighed anchor on the 16th and left on the ebb tide.

The murder was a catalyst for deporting the Armada survivors, as Maitland told Walsingham that the time had come to 'relieve this realm of them, where their remaining longer can do no good'.[35] Parma agreed to pay four shillings a head for the Spaniards' passage, and Ashby began negotiating with Maitland for their transportation. A burgess named William Napier agreed to arrange transport provided that the ambassador obtained safe conduct passes from Elizabeth, which he received in mid-July. Ashby withheld the passports until 'satisfaction be had for the murder of the trumpeter'. He warned that if they failed to comply, 'let them take their hap: if they meet English or Dutch ships without safe-conduct they will get their deserts: they are poor and proud, and unable to resist any force that shall encounter them'.[36]

As subsequent events prove, his comment suggests involvement in yet another stratagem conceived by Walsingham.

Ashby supported a group of Edinburgh merchants that petitioned the Scottish Council to keep some of the *hidalgos* as hostages pending the release of 'diverse Scotsmen detained in the holy house in Spain' – prisoners of the Inquisition.[37] Bowing to diplomatic pressure, as well as that of disgruntled burgesses in Edinburgh, Leith, Burntisland and Kirkcaldy who were tired of supporting hundreds of indigent Spaniards, a compromise was negotiated. The ambassador released the safe conduct passes in exchange for an ordinary Armada sailor left 'with the provost of Edinburgh to be answerable for the malefactor'.[38]

Watched by Ashby's agents, on 25 July, 660 Spaniards embarked from Leith and Burntisland in four Scottish ships bound for the Low Countries. The ambassador told Walsingham that around 400 of the Armada survivors were 'serviceable men, the rest sick, lame, miserable wretches who will never be fit for service'.[39] A number of Spaniards stayed behind 'sprinkled abroad in noble men's houses, choosing rather to lead a serving man's life at ease in this country then to follow the wars in Flanders in want and danger', while others were delayed. The latter included around one hundred soldiers from the *San Juan de Sicilia*, the ship blown up by Ashby's agent in Tobermory Bay, who Lachlan MacLean, the local chieftain, would 'not suffer to come away, but employs them against his neighbours and enemies'.[40] However, these Spaniards providentially arrived in Edinburgh two days after their comrades departed.[41]

With favourable winds, the ships sailed south along the coast, occasionally putting in at English ports, where they were unmolested after showing the passports to local authorities. They turned east across the narrow seas, resurrecting painful memories for the pathetic Spaniards crowded aboard the small ships. Many were on deck rejoicing at the sight of Dunkirk, when a large number of sails appeared rapidly closing on the lumbering Scottish coasters.

The flotilla of thirty shallow-draft Dutch *cromsters* was commanded by the implacably anti-Spanish Justin of Nassau, whose 'Sea Beggars' had played an important role in the defeat of the Armada, taking two galleons. The Netherlanders captured one of the Scottish ships and threw all of its crew and passengers overboard to drown. They pursued the other three ships which deliberately ran themselves ashore and broke up under heavy fire. Three hundred more Spaniards and Scots died, only a handful managing to struggle through the surf to safety ashore.[42]

Like the sabotage of the *San Juan de Sicilia*, this attack appears to be another well-coordinated 'Black Op' against the Spanish with the Sea Beggars serving as English proxies after being alerted by a chain of Walsingham's agents. Similarly, the English were able to claim 'clean hands' and blame the attack on others, in this case the Dutch.

Word of the ambush spread quickly throughout the British Isles and the Spanish Empire. The *San Juan's* soldiers who had missed the boat were so terrified of meeting the same fate as their comrades that they waited several months before arrangements could be made for them to sail to Spain in three small ships via Orkney and Ireland to avoid the Sea Beggars.[43]

A few days after the departure of the English flotilla, James and most of his court travelled to Lanarkshire to attend the postponed christening of James Hamilton. Ashby followed a few days later, feeling honoured to serve as the infant's godfather, along with the King. The ambassador's melancholia was partially dispelled the following month when he received a letter from his nephew, who had gone to the court at Nonsuch Palace. Naunton wrote that the Queen 'rested especially well satisfied and content' at the report of your 'commendable behaviour at the great christening, as well for your present, which she doubted before that the country there would hardly have afforded; and therefore is to provide a second compliment here wherewith to present my Lady Hamilton there'. The 'present' was probably from Lord John Hamilton to Elizabeth rather than from Ashby personally.[44]

Burghley managed Scottish affairs through mid-June due to Walsingham's illness, although the Secretary continued to communicate – and manage intelligence operations – from his homes at Seething Lane and Barn Elms. Sir Francis returned to court at the end of the month, when Ashby congratulated him on the apparent 'recovery of your health'. In the same letter, the ambassador beseeched Walsingham to continue favouring him, and to remember his request for recall. His stay in Scotland 'had been longer than looked for' and his 'poor state is such as I am no way able to sustain the charge without her majesty's gracious consideration some way by gift or larger allowance'.[45] While Ashby had received a positive response from Burghley a week earlier regarding his 'poor estate', the wheels of Elizabethan government turned very slowly, especially when money was concerned.[46]

The ambassador continued to seek his 'revocation'. During one of Naunton's visits to London, he solicited Walsingham and Burghley to expedite the recall, writing to his uncle that he would return to Scotland when he heard 'her majesty's resolution'. Elizabeth's habitual dithering was undiminished; Burghley told him that both he and Walsingham had moved Ashby's petition to the Queen, 'but as yet she was neither of nor on, but remained uncertain, upon the uncertainty of the state there

[Scotland]'. The Lord Treasurer thought that Sir George Carey would be sent again to Edinburgh soon, and would bring Ashby home with him.[47]

Naunton was distressed that his uncle had not received his two previous letters, worrying that if intercepted they would cause trouble. Referring to Fowler's efforts to discredit Ashby, he said that he 'wrote them incensed with such indignities as I saw offered by some whom it least became' because the ambassador's 'service is not better accepted of'. Naunton asked Ashby to write to his other uncle, Francis, to loan him one of William's geldings – which he was stabling in his absence – so he could make a speedy return to Edinburgh.

Naunton was also involved in trying to mediate between Fowler and his wife, perhaps hoping that by doing so Fowler would cease undermining his uncle. He tried numerous times without success to meet 'Mistress Fowler', saying that he and his cousin William Ashby of Loseby,[48] would try 'to sup at the Spittle with her if she be there. Whereof if it hit, I [will] certify you and Mr. Fowler'.[49]

Late summer was unusually hot in Edinburgh. Many, including Fowler, fell ill and feared for their lives. Ashby apologised to James for being unable to personally brief him about the assassination of French King Henri III by a Catholic fanatic, explaining in a note that his 'travail and the heat haith brought a fever upon me, so as I am forced to stay by the way'.[50] While impatiently waiting to receive Elizabeth's approval of his recall, he corresponded with friends and relatives, writing to Arthur Throckmorton:

> I hope soon to see you, that we may philosophise together.
> You will marvel why I seek my revocation, holding a place
> where I enjoy *otium cum dignitate*: you know my mind, you
> know my state; my health will not comport with this climate;
> other particulars I will satisfy you *bocca a bocca*.[51] [52]

Recognising his old friend's despair, Throckmorton tried to cheer him, replying, 'You will come home horsed upon hope, which is never a jade but at his journey's end'.[53]

Expecting to be liberated from Scotland soon, Ashby freely vented his low opinion of the country and its ruling class to Walsingham and other members of the English court: 'These feuds make them poor and divided: want of justice is the cause of barbarous cruelty: the King's miserable state and his lenity will ruin his state'.[54] Using the intellectual wordplay fashionable for classically educated gentlemen of the period, the ambassador criticised James by paraphrasing an ancient quote about Hannibal: '*Vincere scit Rex, sed uti victoria nescit* [the King knows how to win a victory, but not how to use it]; his lenity will occasion greater mischief'.[55] In a further jibe, Ashby compared James and his passion for hunting to the mythological Queen of the Amazons, saying '[t]his young prince, chaste and continent as Hypolites, spending the time in Diana's exercise'.[56]

'I have been so long in this climate,' Ashby wrote, 'as you may see I am grown a tratling [chattering] Scot, gossiping. To cure me of this, hasten my revocation before winter; my health and my want make me weary of this place'.[57]

Meanwhile Fowler, although claiming illness, drafted a letter for Walsingham to use in appointing him *de facto* ambassador on the premise that 'her majesty [was] to call home Mr. Ashby'. There was no need to appoint a new resident ambassador, he asserted, because Fowler 'being here and having little business, may negotiate any matters there is to deal in' on behalf of the English government. He asked that a similarly worded letter should be written to the King and a private letter to Fowler from the Secretary stating that he 'hath persuaded her majesty to trust me in this service, and that she might do it'.

Fowler admitted that he was 'bold to set down his opinion', but that an official appointment was necessary to avoid losing his credit with James. London was unresponsive to his request. Subsequent events demonstrate that Fowler's intrigues were starting to backfire. Walsingham himself was ill during this time, and may have been losing his focus on the intricacies of Scottish policy.[58]

Ashby's spirits and health improved when he finally received Elizabeth's letter in the second week of August granting his request for revocation of his ambassadorship. He told Burghley that he hoped shortly to 'tell him all by word of mouth' and planned to depart for London about the 22nd of the month.

James' marriage caused a change in the ambassador's plans, with unfortunate consequences.

# 20. Ashby tarries in Edinburgh while the King seeks his bride

James became distracted to the point of obsession about his pending nuptials with Princess Anne of Denmark, to the exclusion of most of his governmental duties but not of hunting, a passion occupying half of his time.[1] In mid-June, he sent George Keith, the Earl Marischal, to Denmark to negotiate the terms of the marriage.

The Scottish demands for Anne's dowry, reflecting James' financial desperation, were so ludicrous that even Maitland was embarrassed.[2] Foremost was £1,000,000 ('ten hundred thousand pounds Scots') to be 'transported here together at once and delivered really in our hands immediately after the completing of the marriage'. All Scots were to become naturalised Danes, 'eight thousand footmen and two thousand horsemen' would be sent at the Danish King's expense for 'just defence against a foreign enemy, or the recovery of the possession of foreign titles due unto us by just inheritance' (i.e., the English throne), a fleet of warships was to be granted, the Danes would give up their claim to the Orkneys, and both nations would 'join together in straight league for ... common defence against ... the Pope and his adherents'.[3]

Quoting from Petrarch, Ashby mocked James' financial needs masked as love for his intended Danish bride, telling Throckmorton *'Amor' con amor' si paga'* (*'Love with love if it pays'*). 'The King is but a cold wooer', he wrote Walsingham, initially ambiguous about the marriage, not sure whether to hasten or delay it, but driven 'to match with the Danes to please his boroughs and merchants' who wanted stronger trade links with the Baltics and who perceived Maitland as siding with Elizabeth in opposition to the marriage. At the end of May, Edinburgh's 'provost, bailiffs and many of the burgesses' forced their way into the Chancellor's apartment at Holyrood 'and told him with threats that if the marriage with Denmark went not forward, being crossed by England to keep the King unmarried altogether, he would die for it, and all the English faction here'.[4]

Edinburgh was on the verge of another rebellion, this one possibly a greater threat than that of Huntly's 'malcontents' the previous month, as it was fomented by the Protestant middle class who depended on Denmark for 'their timber for building, shipping, and furnishing, and other needful things' and would have quickly spread to other trading centres such as Aberdeen and Haddington. 'Every man was ready to take arms', threatening that 'if the King would not satisfy them … that he would proceed with his marriage in Denmark, they would shew what they durst do', including freeing the imprisoned Papist lairds and 'making them their party'. The crisis was averted when, under pressure, 'the King declared himself most affectionate to the match with Denmark, and proud to go through with it'.[5]

The Danes quickly rejected the demand for 'the great dower', asserting that 'kings should match for love and alliance, and not expect sums of money' and that the princess could bring only her inheritance of 70,000 dollars.[6] James had no choice but to accept this if the marriage was to proceed, grudgingly telling Ashby that 'he would not be thought a merchant for his wife'.[7] The royal bride and groom were wed by proxy on 20 August. The ambassador wrote Burghley that the unhappy King 'felt he had been abused, and drawn into this match very craftily, which now in honour he cannot refuse'. Nonetheless, the die was cast, and Ashby recommended that the Lord Treasurer persuade Elizabeth to provide more funding. In possible awareness that Burghley and his son Robert Cecil favoured James as the Queen's successor, he added that if the King received any favour 'from her majesty he will account you the worker of it, and always acknowledge your fatherly care'.[8]

Anne and her entourage were expected to set sail for Scotland immediately, causing panic at Holyrood, especially when James learned that his bride had spent a large portion of her dowry on 'plate, fair hangings and household stuff, jewels, horses, and their furnishings' and 'a coach with no iron in it but all silver'.[9] 'Surely Scotland was never in worse state to receive a Queen', Ashby told Burghley, 'for there is neither house in repair but all most ruinous and want furniture; and the time so short as this defect cannot be helped if she come before winter which is looked for'.[10] He advised Walsingham that 'this hasty marriage makes the King half amazed. He knows not which way to turn, having no house ready to receive the Queen, nor his subjects willing to contribute towards her maintenance and that of her train. His only refuge is to her majesty, whose gracious dealing now will bind him more than all that is past'.[11]

James had already spent the full £10,000 levied as a special tax for the marriage, and £1,500 of the last tranche of the English subsidy had been allocated to the Scottish marriage delegation to support itself in the expected courtly style, leaving him so penniless that he couldn't pay for the tailoring of his wedding apparel. The King begged Burghley for assistance, saying 'no hours nor days must be lost, for tempus [time] deals most straitly with me'.[12] Edinburghers were so angry about his taxation and spendthrift ways that he was afraid to spend more than a day in the city, nervously waiting for the arrival of his fifteen-year-old Queen by passing 'his time for ten days in hunting in the islands of Lough Lomond in the west'. Yet he experienced humiliation even in his favourite past-time, having need 'specially for horses and money', petulantly telling cronies that he took it 'unkindly that the Queen will send him none for hunting; he has to borrow of his servants'.[13]

With each passing day, Ashby grew more contemptuous of Scotland, succinctly describing the state of the country to Burghley: 'A young prince so facile and in want, a nobility factious and thirsting the blood of one another and inconstant, the churches spoiled and the ministers overwhelmed with poverty, the boroughs loath to contribute to the King's necessities, doth show this state to be in such miseries as *ipsa si cupiat salus servare non potest hoc regnum*' [even if the goddess of health desired it, she could not save this kingdom].[14]

Expressing Elizabeth's exasperation, Walsingham told Ashby that because the King was 'resolute in his marriage', the Queen was 'disposed to grace it with her allowance' – not out of regard for James, but 'in respect of her friendship with the late King of Denmark'. However, 'if the King expect from hence any great supply of money', he would be very disappointed.[15]

James was indeed disappointed with Elizabeth's wedding 'consideration', which was not what Ashby termed the *aurum potabile*[16] he hoped for but only £1,000 in hard cash plus £2,000 worth of furniture, silk for wedding apparel and 'gilt plate, parcel gilt plate, and white plate' supplied by the London goldsmith Richard Martin. Burghley, who personally pledged to cover the cost of the gifts, was being hounded for payment by the goldsmith and 'sundry persons'. The Lord Treasurer could 'not obtain from her majesty any discharge as yet' because she was peeved that James had not thanked her. He complained to the ambassador that he 'must in honesty pay the ... whole three thousand pounds of her gift, which I will do, though I leave not myself a spoon of silver'.[17]

Ashby hoped to be reinstated in the Queen's favour. John Colville, who journeyed to London to collect Elizabeth's begrudged wedding gifts, advocated for him during an audience with the Queen. Referring to Fowler's attempts to smear the ambassador as ineffectual, the Scottish envoy told him:

> At my first audience I trust – as my duty was – I have done your lordship no harm, and I think her majesty will declare the same at your meeting. I assured her highness that your lordship, seeming to do nothing, had effectuate[d] a good work, considering in what disposition our estate was into at [your] arrival among us, which her highness confessed to be true, with other speeches that passed among us which I om[it], lest you should think I did flatter.[18]

Ashby left his departure too late. Maitland told him that the King was unwilling to have him leave before the formal wedding because 'the rumours of the Queen's dislike of the match would be increased by his departure'. Disappointed, he asked Walsingham 'for direction herein with speed', reasoning that as Queen Anne was expected out of Denmark within days, he thought it 'good to stay, the time being so short, to avoid hard constructions'. To his regret, Elizabeth approved his remaining until after the wedding.[19]

Days stretched into weeks, and the royal consort did not arrive. Ashby described James as like a lover 'distracted with a world of passionate cogitations', having heard nothing since Anne's embarkation on 1 September. His anxiety may have been partly financial; as part of the marriage settlement, the Danes demanded that the Scots execute a bond for repayment of the young Queen's dowry if she died within the year.[20] James, 'passionate with long delay, flies to God, commanding public fast and prayer, hoping for good news'. The King spent his days at Craigmillar Castle on the outskirts of Edinburgh, which had a commanding view of the Firth, 'sighing' as he searched for signs of Anne's fleet or the Scottish ships sent out to find her.[21]

Rumours of disaster and witchcraft abounded, stoked by 'ominous chances' [bad omens]. Ashby took a more pragmatic view, speculating that 'the winds have been so great and so contrary that it is presumed the fleet is driven back into the Sounds of Norway'.[22] This turned out to be the case, and numerous poor Danish women suffered as a result. 'The tempestuous winds drove them upon the coast of Norway.... Which storm of wind was alleged to be raised by the witches of Denmark, as by sundry of them were acknowledged, when they were for that cause burnt'.

While James fretted for his bride, Ashby resumed his ambassadorial duties, dealing with border issues and mollifying disgruntled English dignitaries such as the Earl of Lincoln who had been invited to the wedding but were now cooling their heels in Carlisle and Berwick.

He thanked Burghley for 'his care of him', having received the Queen's 'grant signed and sealed' of the recusancy penalty paid by a 'Mr. Draycote'.[23]

Recusants – Catholics or Protestant dissenters who refused to attend the Church of England – could be charged the considerable sum of £20 per month. Ashby had reached an agreement with Draycote prior to going to Scotland to pay him the penalty directly rather than to the Exchequer and this had fallen in arrears. Draycote was apparently being hounded by tax collectors on the ambassador's behalf. Now satisfied that the payments were up to date, Ashby asked the Lord Treasurer to intervene so that the recusant 'may be no more troubled'. With the Queen's displeasure of the previous year still weighing on his spirit, Ashby also beseeched Burghley 'to employ his endeavours towards her majesty for the qualifying of her misliking hereof and the continuance of her favour'.[24]

Word came on 10 October that the storm-battered Danish nuptial fleet was in such poor condition that Anne's grand entrance to Scotland would be delayed until the spring. James ordered that a convoy of more seaworthy Scottish vessels be outfitted to voyage to Denmark to transport his Queen. Within a few days, Ashby's agents informed him that the impassioned King planned to go with the fleet 'secretly to avoid such disturbance as were likely to arise if his determination were publicly known'.[25]

Gravely concerned that such a move would create greater instability so soon after the recent insurrection, Ashby wrote a carefully worded letter to James, saying that 'a fear crept into many men's minds that your highness is determined secretly to … hazard your person in this fleet'. He remonstrated that committing himself to 'so great hazard and danger' would 'greatly amaze your good and faithful subjects, and make the world judge your grace rather a passionate lover then a circumspect prince'. James could 'nether command the winds, nor rule the raging sea, nor bring hither that young princess the sooner'.[26]

James waited until the following day, 22 October, to send a terse reply from aboard his ship off Leith. He hoped that Elizabeth would have a 'favourable interpretation of this our peregrination', casually adding that he had been too busy to write letters of thanks, and relied on the ambassador to make his excuses to the Queen in the 'most hearty manner'.[27]

Ashby knew that Elizabeth would be infuriated. He wrote to her immediately after receiving the King's letter, which he enclosed to protect himself. 'The King defers his own letters to her majesty', he wrote, 'excusing himself by want of leisure', but the real cause of his negligence was 'a passionate extremity of an impatient affection towards his love and lady', causing James to commit himself and all his hopes 'Leander like to the waves of the ocean, and all for his beloved Eroes sake'.[28]

At midnight on the 22nd, James sailed with Maitland and a 300-strong retinue leaving behind two documents of singular importance to his reign. The first, dated 20 October, written while in solitude at Craigmillar, was a rambling, self-pitying, yet remarkably honest 'Declaration of the Causes of His Departure'. The King had been 'generally found fault with by all men for the delaying so long of ... marriage', the reasons being that he 'was alone, without father or mother, brother or sister, king of this realm and heir apparent of England'. His 'nakedness' made him weak and '[his] enemies strong'. He was distained because his long delay in marrying 'bred in the breasts of many a great jealousy of inability as if I were a barren stock'.[29]

James devoted several paragraphs defending Maitland, who 'had been blamed of putting' ideas in his head, and accused of 'leading [him] by the nose' as if the King 'were an unreasonable creature or a bairn that could do nothing' on his own. He wanted his people to know the reasons for his leaving so he would 'be not unjustly slandered as an irresolute ass who can do nothing of himself, as also that the honesty and innocency of [the Chancellor] be not unjustly and untruly reproached'.[30]

The second document, which was probably largely drafted by Maitland, authorised the Privy Council to rule in James' absence, with the fifteen-year-old Duke of Lennox appointed President and – to the consternation of many – Bothwell to serve as his deputy amidst a coalition of recent rebels such as Maxwell sitting uneasily with Lord John Hamilton and other loyalists.[31]

Ashby found himself in a state of diplomatic limbo. Elizabeth had agreed to the King's request that he remain as English ambassador until after the marriage, yet James and Anne had been legally wed by proxy the previous month, and were formally married in Copenhagen on 24 November. He could not return to London without the issuance of a new 'revocation' by the Queen.

Burghley[32] was in no hurry to recall him due to alarm at court resulting from James' precipitate departure, telling Ashby he was 'sorry that the Duke is made president of the Council, and Bothwell next after him, whereby it is to be feared that some stirs and troubles may be moved in the King's absence by the papists and that faction'. The Lord Treasurer ordered Ashby to 'do what he can to keep things there in as good estate as they were left', and said he should 'deal with the clergy that they may endeavour to stay any mutinies and uproars'. A rare consolation was word that the Queen was pleased with his diligence.[33]

Elizabeth was outraged at the King's behaviour. Ashby was instructed to tell Colville that her wedding largess was not really a gift but a loan, which she would have discharged if he had bothered to thank her. Burghley was being pursued by the merchants and was trying to scrape together the means to pay them, which added to the strains in the diplomatic relationship.[34]

After months of apathy, the Queen was motivated to take a personal interest in Anglo-Scottish relations. She strongly disapproved of the Council being headed by the teenage Lennox, who she feared would become a puppet of Bothwell like James had been under the Duke's father. She commanded Ashby to 'deal inwardly with the rest' of the Council who were committed 'to the maintenance of peace, specially against the Spanish and Popish faction, which is feared will put out their heads at this time of the King's absence'.[35]

However much he personally disliked and distrusted Bothwell, Ashby wisely concluded that the Earl was key to maintaining stability. With a touch of sarcasm, he told Walsingham that this 'noble man is able to offend more than any subject in Scotland.... Without him the malcontents dare attempt nothing, so as the winning of him will be a bridle to the rest: he makes great promises to do good offices towards her majesty'.[36] The ambassador proposed that effort be made to strike an accord with Bothwell, adding that the Earl had offered to share intelligence about Parma.[37]

Sir Francis, who had recovered enough to attend Council meetings, responded that Ashby was to tell Bothwell that 'her majesty received great contentment of his offer' and the Earl should think 'no course so honorable or so profitable for him, as also for both the kingdoms, as to run the course of England'. The ambassador busied himself fostering relations with Bothwell and advising the Council on improving relations with England, including sending 'humble thanks to her majesty for the great present of plate it pleased [her] highness to send to the King'.[38]

With no word from James for weeks, Scotland settled into an uneasy peace at the national level, while interminable petty clan feuds continued. Ashby reported that Bothwell and the Council agreed that 'all quietness might be kept during this interregnum', but 'the Scottish nature is hardly reconciled'. If the King delayed his return until the spring, as the Council now feared, 'the long smothered flames will break out by instigation of the papists and malcontents, as men [were] ready to blow the cool and vigilant for their [own] purpose'.[39]

# 21. Vindication

James' departure coupled with Bothwell's rehabilitation in the eyes of the English were a catalyst in unmasking Fowler's perfidy and unravelling his web of deceit. Consumed by persecutory delusion, he accused his wife and her friends – including Ashby and Naunton – of using their 'uttermost power' to 'discredit him in many ways'.[1] His royal patron gone, fearful of Bothwell, whom he vilified as 'the greatest enemy to England and English men that may be', Fowler fled his lodgings on the Canongate and took refuge in Edinburgh Castle.

Ashby had known for some time of Fowler's defamation and treasonous acts, but as a well-trained product of Gray's Inn, he bided his time while collecting evidence. On the day of James' departure, the ambassador wrote to Burghley warning him not to be 'abused by [Fowler's] crafty dealing', and obliquely accusing him of treason. Although Fowler had led Burghley to believe that his written communications with him and Walsingham were secret, actually he 'follows the Chancellors advice, and acquaints him with his letters, and shows himself a right Scot, for that he dares not return to his country'. He had made so many enemies, and was 'so hate[d] popularly … in the King's absence he dares not come abroad'[go out]. Ashby said that while Fowler may pretend that everything he did was 'for the service of his country', in reality he had 'small regard' for England, about which Ashby would report in detail when he returned to London.[2]

From his frigid chamber in the Castle, Fowler must have felt as if the stone walls were closing on him. On All Hallows Eve, he wrote a long, self-pitying letter to Burghley complaining 'of the cruel dealing of the ambassador Ashby' who he claimed paid him 'not a groat' for 'all the intelligence he had provided, and had relied on him as a secretary and advisor. He blamed Wigmore for turning Ashby against him by revealing that he was sending reports to the Lord Treasurer and Walsingham using the diplomatic pouch. Fowler wrote that Ashby and Wigmore had persuaded Bothwell to intercept Hudson whilst *en route* to London and seize letters he carried.[3]

Ashby had indeed confiscated and opened Fowler's letters proving that Wigmore's allegations were true. Fowler said that the ambassador confronted him with the evidence, calling him 'a perilous fellow' and threatening to expose him to the Scots as an English spy. When asked 'to admit his fault in giving intelligence to the council without [Ashby's] knowledge', Fowler refused. The ambassador 'then raged and said he doubted not to find that I had spoken evil of [Mr.] Secretary to this king'. He also accused him of unlawfully keeping from James 'much riches' that had belonged to Lady Margaret, and would discredit him with the King when he returned from Denmark.

'There was [never] poor gentleman used so despitefully as [I] am', he whinged. 'Wigmore now guides the ambassador [like] a child; and if your lordship knew the man and his life here, you would think him a fit guide for a ruffian or [whore] master, than an ambassador for his lordship'.[4] Wigmore was also the target of Fowler's defamation. He complained to Walsingham, who ordered Thomas Phelippes to ask Archibald Douglas, Scottish ambassador in London, for an explanation about rumours that Wigmore 'had been forced to leave England for certain youthful treacherous courses – evil reports which he attributes to Fowler who has done many things almost as bad'.[5]

Fowler's reckless accusations were jeopardising the mission as well as the life of Wigmore, the English agent sent into Scotland in an elaborate ruse devised by Walsingham to penetrate James' court. A 'great man for hunting and all such sports, to which King James was out of measure addicted', Wigmore's cover story was that he had been forced to leave England 'by reason of certain hard courses intended against [him] at the appetite of the Lady Leighton' and chose to exile himself in Scotland 'as a place of smallest charge [expense], and ... of least offense'.[6]

Sir Francis had persuaded Elizabeth, who loved intrigues, to 'affront' Wigmore publicly 'to give him the more credit' for his cover story. He was given a voluminous set of cyphered instructions 'in all the proper methods to gain upon the King's confidence, and to observe and give account of all that he saw in him' – a top secret operation that Fowler was unwittingly endangering.[7] Wigmore had been sent into Scotland in May 1588, two months before Ashby's arrival, and the ambassador had been briefed on his mission.

In early November, Fowler sent another diatribe to Burghley complaining that he was forced to keep himself a prisoner in Edinburgh Castle by 'the extreme spiteful dealing against' him by Ashby and Bothwell, describing the Earl as 'the man of worst life who lives, a tyrant where he may overcome'. Oblivious to the new English policy of amity with Bothwell, he stormed about being 'very evil encumbered by the Earl Bothwell, who by the ambassador's solicitation' had threatened to kill him.[8]

Burghley seems to have ignored Fowler's complaints, and was apparently pleased with Ashby's diplomacy as the ambassador answered a letter from the Lord Treasurer dated 29 October saying it was received 'to my special encouragement in that I perceive my service acceptable to your lordship'. Wigmore, he wrote, would carry the diplomatic packet to London and personally present a situation report, including the troublesome Fowler's activities.[9]

Fowler's case was taken up by Archibald Douglas, who had been involved in his plots for years. The Scottish envoy wrote to Burghley and Walsingham about Fowler's confinement caused by the 'heavy displeasure' of Bothwell. Douglas – who Wigmore nicknamed 'Archknave' in a play on his first name[10] – said he had been told that Ashby and Wigmore had 'stirred up' Bothwell and that they were trying to smear Fowler, even though he disingenuously asserted that he did not believe this.[11]

With no word from James for over a month after his departure, concern arose in London and Edinburgh. In a letter headed 'The continuance of the Kings silence', Ashby told Burghley 'either [James] must return speedily, or abide on yonder side the sea till the spring, which may breed a world of inconveniences in a people of such turbulent spirits'.[12] Unbeknownst to his subjects or the English, James was in the midst of revels following his marriage, indulging in hunting, making 'good cheer' and drinking 'stoutly',[13] perhaps enjoying true safety and regal dignity for the first time in his life.

Lairds were feuding and failing to consult Lennox or Bothwell. Ashby said that the duplicitous Earl 'soareth daily in the wind, hovering now hither now thither, only expecting – as he would seem – who should reclaim him with the loudest lure'. Bothwell would remain loyal to Elizabeth as long as he had hope to 'procure some real entertainment from her majesty'.[14]

Although still eager to return to England, Ashby was now more contented with his service than at any time over the past eighteen months. He had found purpose in his adept dealings with Bothwell and the Council. He was pleased with the compliments received from Burghley and gratified that Scottish government ministers and others came to him 'for information on foreign affairs'. He thought that, with the help of courtiers such as Wigmore and Throckmorton, he had stamped out the attempts to destroy his reputation.[15]

Ashby's contentment was short-lived. He received a reproving letter from Walsingham containing a copy of a 'Memorandum of William Asheby's conduct towards Thomas Fowler', composed by the latter. While repeating Fowler's earlier complaints, his memorandum declared that Ashby 'railed upon me, calling me knave and other vile speeches too diverse, and brought his gentility in question'. The ambassador was accused of telling 'his best friends' (presumably including Throckmorton, Lord John Hamilton and George Carey) that Fowler was 'a seditious man, marvelling that the King would give him credit or countenance, being a spy in this country'. Ashby's unwarranted investigation, Fowler said, sought evidence of bribery and of jewels that had belonged to Lady Margaret which Fowler had allegedly 'detained from the King'.[16]

Ashby replied in a letter enclosed within a message to Throckmorton, which he knew would be privately delivered to Walsingham. He was 'overwhelmed with grief' upon receipt of the Secretary's letter and requested him 'to suspend judgment till his return', which he hoped would be soon, and continue 'his accustomed favour' meanwhile. It had always been a joy to honour and serve Sir Francis, and he had strived to be *'honori tuo acceptum fero'* (a credit to your credit). His intent had not been to make Walsingham choose sides, but to give warning of a dissembling person 'that feareth nether God nor loveth man, as appeareth both in his word and life past, whereof I see no amendment'.[17]

In his cover letter to Throckmorton, Ashby wrote that he 'doubted not but the storm will be overblown, and hopes to see those make shipwreck that have by their enchantments raised the tempest'. He was baffled and deeply troubled that Fowler had so 'greatly moved against him'. Ashby would appeal, trusting that with patience the truth would prevail, as Throckmorton had counselled, which for the present was 'the only shield to quench the fiery darts of all sycophants'.

The ambassador asked Throckmorton to learn the actual cause of Walsingham's displeasure. If it was, as Fowler claimed, for searching Hudson and taking his letters, Ashby knew nothing of it until Bothwell brought the letters to his house. If it be 'touching' Fowler 'who is retired into the castle of Edinburgh for fear of the Earl Bothwell', he had 'taken sanctuary' before the ambassador 'knew of the Earl's displeasure against him'.[18]

Walsingham's subsequent letter to Ashby bore no hint of admonishment, conveying instructions for diplomatic business as usual, and even trusting him 'to best judge whether the Duke of Lennox or the Lord Hamilton' should first receive a letter from Elizabeth to Bothwell. Knowing of the ambassador's friendship with Hamilton, who was considered a steadfast friend of England, this was a delicate diplomatic move to keep Lord John informed of ties with the treacherous Bothwell.

Sir Francis also enclosed a letter from the Queen to the Scottish Privy Council, which was apparently disgruntled at the delay in her correspondence. Walsingham instructed that if the council seemed to think they should have had answer sooner, Ashby was 'to allege for a cause her majesty's weighty affair of France, the Lord Treasurer's sickness, and the slackness of the posts'.[19]

At the beginning of December, Ashby learned of fresh slander. Normally mild-tempered, he reached his limit of restraint and expressed his wrath in a letter to Fowler. Quoting from the Bible, he wrote '*Veritas no quaerit angulos*' [Truth seeks not concealment]. If you had regard ether to honour or honesty you would not have dealt with me in such sort as you have done, having now I see *aliud in ore, aliud in pectore*' [meaning that while the duplicitous Fowler might say one thing, his heart held a different, more malevolent feeling].

He said that at first he could not believe what others told him of Fowler's perfidy. Ashby had provided him with gratis 'meat and drink and lodging' and had, as requested, recommended him to Burghley and Walsingham. The ambassador had considered him a 'wise and faithful friend', which made his undermining and defamation all the more painful. He could not 'believe you will so far forget both honour and honesty to charge me with such reports as are brought to me, and to breathe such threatenings against him that hath reported better of you then all your friends in England hath done'.[20]

The damage had been done in London. Walsingham and Burghley told Elizabeth about the situation, and she ordered that Robert Bowes go to Scotland 'to continue there until order be taken for the setting of a quietness in that state'. Concerned that what was perceived as a personal feud would impair the effectiveness of the English diplomatic mission, Sir Francis advised Ashby to 'concur with Bowes for his own credit's sake', writing that he had charged Bowes to mediate a reconciliation between

Ashby and Fowler because it was 'very unfit that particular quarrels should reign between her majesty's subjects', since all should join in her service.[21]

Throckmorton had a series of meetings with Walsingham to advocate for Ashby. After his third meeting, he told his friend that he had dealt with the Secretary 'as effectually' as he dared, 'find[ing] him better bending to a milder course then I did the last time'. Throckmorton assured him that Ashby 'would prove more honest than his counter currant' [Fowler]. Sir Francis answered that while he had regard for the ambassador's care and diligence, 'for this matter [he] had taken order with Mr. Bowes to go there and understand the truth of the difference between them; and when he hath advertised me, then will I determine according[ly]'.[22]

Mediation between Ashby and Fowler was secondary to Bowes' primary mission of ensuring that stability was maintained and the Scottish Council remained united while the King was missing.[23] There was fear on both sides of the border that the Spanish and Popish faction would 'put out their heads at this time of the King's absence'.[24] Elizabeth's Privy Council considered Scotland 'so broken an estate' that English military intervention might be necessary as it had been many times before. Bowes was authorised, at his discretion, to tell the Scottish government that a force of 'both horsemen and footmen' had been mobilised on the border 'to be sent into Scotland to join with the King's party if need shall require'.[25]

Alexander Hay, Clerk of the Council and one of Ashby's spies, reported that the Catholic faction was gathering strength for 'some new enterprise' with Jesuits serving as agents of Parma and Philip. Pressed by the ambassador to penetrate the conspiracy and gather more intelligence, Hay told him 'it will be the more difficult to me by reason I have nae cunning to cover me with a papist's garment'.[26]

Ashby wrote to Lord High Admiral Howard that James' return was 'as uncertain as his embarking was sudden. As the heat of his lady's love drew him over the seas, so it and those frozen seas will keep him prisoner till the spring. Meanwhile we are in some fear of the fire of the deadly feuds he left at home'. Referring to the number of Armada survivors still thought to be in Scotland, he said 'There is no lack of fire workers, both Spanish and Italian, as well to blow the bellows to these coals, ready enough to kindle otherwise of themselves, as also to cast in wild fire of their own'.[27]

Unaware of Bowes' mission, Fowler's poisonous letters continued. 'This occasion makes wise men wish for an ambassador of England of good credit', he told Walsingham. 'This man [Ashby] hath no power to speak to his betters here but to their liking, for he is fearful, neither hath he credit nor never will, because they say he spoke and delivered in writing to the King himself that yet was never performed'. Fowler wrote that he was not reporting this because of dislike of Ashby, but 'at the desire of his friends', such as his 'host' the captain of Edinburgh Castle, 'a lover of the amity and religion'.[28]

On 11 December, Ashby received a note from Bowes stating that Elizabeth had chosen him 'to execute her pleasure', asking the ambassador to procure a safe conduct pass. This was delayed by the absence of Bothwell, Lennox and other principal councillors and the 'slackness of their return' to Edinburgh. Upon their return, they approved the passport and ordered Alexander Hay, Clerk of the Council, to 'draw it up with speed'.[29]

When Ashby dispatched Naunton to pick up the documents, Hay sent them back with a cover note saying that although he could not prevent Bowes from entering Scotland, the Council was not pleased about his coming and would meet to decide on what terms, if any, to receive him. Council members thought that the ambassador had 'gotten some advertisements from Denmark' that an 'accident [had] befallen their king', and that an English army led by Hunsdon was massing on the border to back the pro-English faction. Ashby wearily told Bowes 'you know the tumultuous spirits of these people', and asked him to wait at Berwick until the outcome of the Council's meeting was known.[30]

On the 16th, Ashby received a letter jointly signed by Walsingham and Burghley ending his ambassadorship. The formal notification was uncritical, explaining that Bowes was being 'sent into Scotland, in respect of the long experience he hath had of that country and the good opinion and confidence of those that are well affected there to religion and to the maintenance of the amity between these two realms'. Bowes was to become the Queen's resident ambassador 'in these troubled times', and Ashby was instructed to remain in Edinburgh long enough to 'acquaint [Bowes] with such things as may concern her majesty's service', following which he was to return to London 'with convenient speed'.[31]

Bowes was evidently unaware that he had been appointed to replace Ashby as resident ambassador until he arrived in Edinburgh on the day that the revocation was received. Thinking that his mission was to assist Ashby in maintaining equilibrium in the factious Scottish government and mediating the rancour with Fowler, he was 'dismayed' when Ashby showed him the letter from London. Keenly aware of the hostility towards him, and detesting having to live in Edinburgh again, he asked Ashby not to inform the Council that he was to replace him until 'he should understand the Queen's and their honour's final resolution, and be better settled in this place, to the avoidance of such sinister surmises as are too rife here'.[32]

Ashby agreed to this, but felt obligated to inform the Council of his recall without naming his replacement. He told Walsingham and Burghley that the Councillors were content with this and 'some difficulties had been removed'. He was 'not a little glad of so good an occasion to leave this unwieldy nation', and was 'ready to depart at any moment'. Ashby recognised that while Bowes was no more zealous than himself to serve the Queen, he was better qualified to take his place in performing Her Majesty's services.[33]

Bowes told Ashby that Throckmorton had been a faithful friend in his absence, tirelessly working to re-establish his good relationship with Walsingham. Ashby thanked Throckmorton, writing that he was 'sure you will continue the same, that Mr. Secretary may still think of me as ready to serve him faithfully', and that 'when he shall understand the truth his honour will acknowledge that I am most shamefully injured'.[34]

Ashby had other friends and supporters at Elizabeth's court who were actively countering Fowler's betrayal. Arthur Agarde, who had been appointed by Sir Nicholas Throckmorton, Arthur's father, as Deputy Chamberlain of the Exchequer, sent Ashby information about secret Treasury payments made to Fowler through his servant codenamed 'Angouse', who was probably Hudson. As Burghley's agent, Fowler was presumably sent these funds for payment to Scottish spies, although Agarde questioned how the money was used. He hoped that Bowes would accept the truth about the problem with Fowler, and advised Ashby to be circumspect in his personal meetings and correspondence, probably because of Fowler's influence with Burghley. Agarde told him that 'doubtless at his home-coming he can show more than he can conveniently write', and assured him personally that 'Your well-wisher continueth his good affection towards you'.[35]

At Ashby's request, Lord John Hamilton, the most reliably pro-English of the lairds, wrote strong commendations to Elizabeth and to Walsingham. He told Ashby 'in respect of your loving mind towards me … you shall find me ready as your most special and faithful friend to do for you to the uttermost of my power'.[36]

Ashby could not return home until Bowes was accredited as resident ambassador. The Council had scheduled a 'convention' for Monday, 22 December, to debate the government's relationship with England generally and Elizabeth's choice for a new ambassador. Some lairds, well aware that the English embassy was used as much for intelligence activities as for diplomacy, were opposed to having another resident ambassador. Due to the animosity of Lennox and Bothwell towards Bowes, Ashby used his connections among the pro-English nobility to garner support for his acceptance.

Hamilton, respected by both friends and enemies, was key in this regard. At Ashby's urging, he roused himself from his sickbed to attend the convention, promising Ashby to assist 'the rest of the nobility in anything [that] may tend to the benefit of religion and maintenance of the amity betwixt the two crowns'.[37]

The Council failed to reach a decision at the meeting, and the lairds scattered to their castles for the Christmas holidays. Ashby was forced to remain in Scotland pending the outcome of Bowes' accreditation, staying at Hamilton with his 'assured friend', Lord John. With Naunton and his retainers, Ashby braved the snowbound roads to return to Edinburgh shortly after Christmas.

On Hogmanay morning (31 December) a heavily cloaked messenger from the Scottish Council delivered a letter adorned with the heraldic seals of Lennox, Bothwell and other councillors addressed to 'The Queen's Majesty of England'. The letter was left unsealed so Ashby could read it.

The Council acknowledged that the Queen's 'servant Mr. William Assheby, your late resident ambassador here' would be replaced by 'Mr. Robert Bowes, treasurer of Berwick', and formally accredited him 'according to your majesty's recommendation'. After enduring months of stress and depression, Ashby felt as if an oxen team's yoke had been lifted from his shoulders as he read the letter's final sentence:

> And for this gentleman your highness's servant that now returns, we cannot omit to testify unto your majesty that during the time of his remaining and negotiation in this realm, as well before the departing of the King our sovereign lord to Norway as since, he has behaved himself very dutifully and diligently to our knowledge in all respects.[38]

Ashby showed the letter to Bowes, who bowed his head and breathed a prayer of thanks. 'You should thank Lord John Hamilton,' Ashby said.

Ashby sat at the plain oak table he used for a desk and drew a plain sheet of paper from a pile. Dipping a silver pen in the inkwell, he carefully wrote 'May It Please Your Majesty', addressing it to the King.

He told James that being revoked the second time 'he was forced to depart, though to his grief, for the desire he had to see the King's arrival with his Queen.' Yet he rejoiced 'to leave Scotland in amity with England, and settled in peaceable tranquillity.' Ashby 'had hoped on the King's return to utter his zeal and honour towards him,' but that had been frustrated by the necessity of his leaving. He craved James' 'approbation of his carriage [conduct]' in Scotland and asked that he 'vouchsafe a few lines of favour to her majesty'. Familiar with the King's vanity, he ended by professing his readiness to serve him 'before all princes, saving his own mistress'.[39]

Ashby now prepared for his departure. He asked other Scottish friends and acquaintances for help in rebuilding his reputation at the English court. The King's furrier, Thomas Murray, wrote to Walsingham that he had 'almost become a Papist, had not the right worshipful Master Ashby, the Queen majesty's ambassador, prevented the same by his courtesy and liberality'.[40]

No record exists of whether Bowes carried out his instructions to mediate between Ashby and Fowler, and it is doubtful that he did. Fowler remained in Edinburgh Castle between the time of Bowes' arrival and Ashby's departure, and his vitriolic messages to Walsingham and Burghley seem to have ceased.

Accompanied by Naunton, Peter Haye and two body guards, Ashby left Edinburgh on 6 January 1590, riding their horses towards the border, hindered by what Ashby described as 'the badness of the ways, the weather, and my indisposition of body'.[41]

## 22. A last plot foiled before death's gloomy shade

Following his return to London, Ashby was reconciled with Walsingham. On 21 January, he sent Naunton to Sir Francis to notify him of his arrival. Ashby evidently wished to maintain a low profile, as he asked the Secretary to tell his nephew a 'time and place, where they could meet privately and impart such intelligences as my desire is your honour should be first informed of before my return hither be further known'.[1] However, the former ambassador met with Throckmorton before sending his note to ascertain Walsingham's attitude and the mood at court, as on 20 January Throckmorton recorded in his diary that William Ashby 'came out of Scotland and was heard'.[2]

Ashby's 'intelligences' constituted a lengthy debriefing covering the current state of affairs in Scotland and Papist conspiracies as well as a discussion of Fowler's behaviour. Stranded by a snow storm in Morpeth while *en route* to London, Ashby sent a courier ahead with coded copies of letters concerning a Catholic plot against the Queen that he received from an agent the evening before his departure from Edinburgh.[3] He had shared these with Bowes, who gave him 'a disguised alphabet' for encryption, so that Walsingham and Burghley 'may take order to prevent their [the Papists'] designs'.[4]

The letters took four days to reach Richmond Palace from Northumberland. Sir Francis gave the letters to his secretary and recently appointed Clerk of the Signet Thomas Lake, who immediately passed them on to Thomas Phelippes, the code-breaker, for action. Lake explained that Ashby had used 'an old-fashioned cipher, and I have forgotten the rules. I am commanded to send it to you, Mr. Secretary being busy in council in the Lord Treasurer's chamber, and to pray you to do it with speed and return answer'.[5]

The plot was 'a treacherous conspiracy against her majesty's person'.
A meeting of the assassination team was scheduled for 2 February at
an Irish gardener's house near Clerkenwell. The assassins were to be
'four Irishmen to come out of Ireland of purpose, two Frenchmen, and
as many Scots'. Other conspirators were identified: 'Thomas Barkley,
Scot; he dwells at the furthest end of the falburgs of Aldgate,[6] as ye go
to the Mile End Green, besides the church at the sign of the "Bull with
the Golden Horns"'; a grocer, 'name unknown; a glover, a neighbour
of his in Smithfield, red bearded; lately married an old woman. A third
Scotsman, his near kinsman, one for whose security he is careful, as also
for his own'.[7]

Ashby hand-carried the original letters to give to Walsingham, which
may have been done to prove his efficiency and ongoing usefulness as
an intelligence officer. If this was his intention, it worked. The Catholic
agents were arrested, the plot was foiled, and Ashby was given a new role
at court, reporting to both Walsingham and Burghley. In the Elizabethan
era, there was no dividing line between foreign relations and intelligence,
and Ashby continued to combine both, with an emphasis on maintaining
ties with agents in Scotland whom he had personally recruited, without
interfering with Bowes' function as ambassador and *de facto* station chief
of the Secret Intelligence Service.

Due to his service in Northern Europe, Ashby had access to
intelligence from the Continent as well as Scotland. While in Edinburgh,
he had befriended François de Civille, Seigneur de Saint-Mards, a French
soldier and diplomat who arrived in Scotland in March 1589. Civille, a
member of Walsingham's extensive network of informants, had been
sent to Scotland to raise an army of 3,000 soldiers for Henri of Navarre
and attempt to persuade James to marry Henri's sister, Catherine de
Bourbon, who was preferred by Queen Elizabeth.[8]

After returning to France, Civille sent Ashby 'occurrences', which
were reported to Walsingham and Burghley, and copied to Alexander
Hay in Edinburgh, who had become both a friend and an agent.[9] Hay

shared the 'French Occurrences' with 'other good fellows' who were pro-English and Protestants, and in turn provided intelligence from Scotland, including the unwelcome news that by mid-February 1590, the Scottish council had not 'heard or received nothing'[10] but rumours of King James since Ashby's departure.

Ashby also sought to rehabilitate the reputation of Richard Wigmore, who had been equally castigated by Fowler and was in disfavour in London despite his service as a spy in the Scottish court. Wigmore carried on a lively correspondence with Ashby and Naunton (having caroused with the latter in the ale and bawdy houses of Edinburgh). He told Naunton his uncle 'left behind him affectionate regret', having high regard 'in the hearts of the honestest'. He had developed an acquaintanceship with Bothwell, who Wigmore said expressed his friendship to both Ashby and Naunton.[11]

By the beginning of April, Ashby's campaign to obtain supporting affidavits for Wigmore from Lord John Hamilton and other lairds had succeeded, and Bowes became Wigmore's direct handler for his espionage mission.[12]

A few weeks after Ashby's return to London, he was deeply saddened by the death of his brother Francis. The poor sizar at Peterhouse had become a successful lawyer and in his later years made a 'good' marriage with Margaret Browne, the widow of Robert Browne of Walcot, Northamptonshire, who had been closely connected with the Cecils.[13] Having lost his sister Elizabeth a decade earlier, and with no other close family except that of his half-brother Maurice Berkeley, Ashby doted on Robert Naunton, using his connections to advance his nephew's academic and political career. He wrote to his brother-in-law, Henry Naunton,[14] that 'being at length returned from Scotland, he could not return [Robert] without commendation'. The young man had 'carried himself to [Ashby's] good liking, and the spending of his time abroad has been no way prejudicial to his progress in study'.[15]

Walsingham's health deteriorated to the point where he knew he was dying. Although he continued to attend Council meetings until late in March, he began handing over responsibilities and state papers to Burghley and fellow councillors, including Hunsdon, the Lord Chamberlain, who was given some of the Secretary's Scottish portfolio. This was fortunate as Hunsdon's son, George Carey, was a friend of both Ashby and Throckmorton.[16]

On 1 April, Sir Francis suffered a 'fit', prompting Sir Thomas Windebank, Clerk of the Signet and Deputy Clerk of the Council, to meet with Elizabeth the following day and ask her – at Walsingham's request – to appoint his replacement.[17] Four days later, on 6 April, the Secretary died at his home in Seething Lane. Burghley's words in a letter to a friend of Sir Francis certainly would have expressed the thoughts of William Ashby:

> ... the Queen's Majesty and her realm and I and others his
> particular friends have had a great loss, both for the public
> use of his good and painful long services and for the private
> comfort I had by his mutual friendship.[18]

*****

Tuesday, 7 April 1590

Two score mourners gathered in the north aisle of St. Paul's choir, the gloom of the cavernous gothic cathedral barely dispelled by flickering sconces. Ashby stood near the oblong opening in the stone floor close to the grave of the deceased's son-in-law Sir Philip Sidney. The faint stench of putrefaction emanated from the uneven paving stones; some of the courtiers held gilt pomanders to their noses, and Ashby found himself missing the heavy incense that had been outlawed with other Papist paraphernalia.

Hushed conversations fell silent as the great double doors swung open and the funeral cortege moved slowly up the nave, proceeded by the dean with a lantern. The widow, Lady Ursula, followed the simple oak coffin carried on the shoulders of six yeomen of the guard, the only concession to pomp in keeping with the wishes of the deceased, whose will stipulated that he be buried 'without any such extraordinary ceremonies as usually appertain to a man serving in my place, in respect of the greatness of my debts and the mean state I shall leave my wife and heir in'.[19]

After the brief burial service was read from the Book of Common Prayer, the mortal remains of Sir Francis Walsingham were lowered into the dark aperture.

Three weeks later, William Ashby took advantage of the fine spring weather to walk from Clerkenwell to St Pauls to pay private respects to his patron and friend. On the wall above Walsingham's unmarked grave slab was affixed a modest wooden tablet painted with a Latin epitaph. One passage in particular resonated with the former ambassador, and tears blurred his vision as he read:

'... he hereby freed his Country from many apparent Perils,
Preserved the Republique and ratified the peace of the Realm;
And consequently still studied to be beneficial and helpful to all
Especially those who were eminent in the possession of Arts or Arms.
And thus evermore regardless of Himself,
He was ever ready to help and assist others,
Though to the consumption and much impairing
of his own Purse and Person'.[20]

******

After Walsingham's death, Ashby served on Burghley's staff at court, dealing with matters relating to Scotland and, to some extent, France.[21] He was referred to as 'Her Majesty's Servant' as late as July 1593. There is no record of his traveling abroad, probably because of chronic ill health that had plagued him for years.

Within a month of Ashby's return to London, Wigmore reported that Fowler – referred to as 'Sanny' – 'hath left his crow's nest; not that he is delivered of his fear, but in regard of his evil which mightily increaseth: some horrible judgment of God must ensue'.[22] While Wigmore's words may appear prophetic, God's judgement may have been by a human hand.

Fowler left his 'crow's nest' in the Castle in early February and moved as a lodger into the Canongate house of the deceased royal goldsmith John Acheson. Fowler's treachery had been 'vividly painted' [exposed]; he was ill and fearful of Bothwell and others he had intrigued against. He planned to flee to Denmark to seek James' protection, but 'the wind and storm … stayed him' in Edinburgh. One week after Walsingham's death, Fowler died after becoming speechless.[23] Although he had been ill for some time, Fowler had so many enemies that poisoning was a likely cause of his painful death.

Bothwell immediately sent agents to the house to seize all of the dead man's 'jewels, bonds, writings, and apparel', claiming them for the King. This caused a minor diplomatic row in which Burghley was personally involved, as he asked Bowes to intervene to get whatever he could 'for the relief of' Fowler's estranged wife, 'who complains that she is left in hard estate by him', and to recover jewels which 'purportedly belonged to Arbella Stuart'.[24] But James – who returned to Scotland on 1 May – claimed the jewellery was rightfully his as a legacy from his grandmother Margaret Douglas.

Ashby asked for Wigmore's help in getting anything from the estate to ease his 'cousin's' poverty. Wigmore responded that this was hopeless because as Fowler had died intestate, James 'pretended to be his heir'. There was very little money to be had anyway; only twelve shillings were found in the dead man's lodgings, although Wigmore suspected Fowler's servant 'had very handsomely helped himself'.[25]

With satisfaction, Wigmore told Ashby that Fowler's death was surely 'very profane to the world' having behaved himself 'unchristianly' towards a minister who tried to comfort him, and he died 'full of miserable torments'. Wigmore hesitated to speak ill of the dead, but said he could:

... confidently affirm, whatsoever had been hoped for to the contrary, that both her majesty and this king by his death are delivered from a most dangerous instrument ... What his secret course in state matters was cannot appear by any writings left behind him, all of which were either committed by himself to some other trust, or since his death by some handsomely embezzled.[26]

Wigmore was unaware that at least some of the secret writings were given to Burghley, who presumably destroyed them.

In the autumn of 1590, Ashby was in a legal dispute with Sir James Harington, a leading Midlands landowner and brother-in-law of the late Sir Philip Sidney. Ashby's expired lease to the valuable manor called the Bishop's Fee had been renewed by Burghley, but Harington was interfering with his leasehold rights. Asserting that he had been 'most unjustly dealt with', Ashby asked Burghley to intercede 'in the present matter' and 'take order with ... Harington, that he may be permitted to enjoy his lease'.[27] The matter was apparently settled in Ashby's favour by the Lord Treasurer.

Ashby appears to have retired from active foreign and intelligence activities in early 1591. During the following two years he devoted his energies to securing patronage for personal financial security and promotion of his nephew's career. Naunton was already serving on the Continent as an intelligencer under cover as a student, reporting to Elizabeth's new favourite the Earl of Essex.[28] (See Appendix I).

The new year of 1593 began ominously for Londoners. Plague had broken out the previous autumn, killing at least two thousand people by January. Alarmed by the rapidly spreading contagion, the Privy Council forbade 'all manner of concourse and public meetings of the people at plays, baitings of bears and bulls, bowlings and any other like assemblies for sports be forbidden ... (preaching and Divine service at churches excepted) throughout the city and neighbouring counties'.[29] Burghley became 'very dangerously sick', but recovered. The plague was 'so sore' that those who could do so fled into the countryside.[30]

Elizabeth and her court moved from palace to palace as the pestilence flowed towards them like a deadly flood tide, first to Nonsuch, next to Oatlands and then to Windsor. The Queen ordered 'that no citizen of London or other person coming from any place where the present infection may be should resort to the town of Windsor, there to inhabit, make any residence or stay, that they should all forbear that place ... considering how the sickness is now dispersed in sundry towns and villages far and near'. Those who 'obstinately and undutifully refuse to obey' were 'severely to be punished'.[31] On Elizabeth's command, the Council decreed that 'no dung or other filth be laid in any of the highways, being a very great annoyance both to breed infection and to her Majesty riding sometimes in the fields to take air'.[32]

The Parish of All Hallows-on-the-Wall 'Paid to the painter for making red crosses upon the doors when the infection of the plague was, 20d; for red wands or rods, 2d'; at Lambeth, churchwardens were paid sixpence 'For writing a book of them that were visited with the plague', while at St Margaret's Westminster, adjacent to the Abbey, churchwardens made several payments for killing dogs believed to be spreading 'the infection'.

For the Queen and the privileged classes, life continued surreally amidst the omnipresent death and misery of the lower orders. George Gower, 'Serjeant Painter', billed the royal household 13s 4d for work at St James's Palace including 'painting and gilding with fine gold a seat of wainscot for the Queen's Majesty's monkey in the Privy Chamber'.[33] In early April, Burghley was petitioned by 'the Keeper of the Queen's Elephant' for permission to take the beast to Holland because of 'the great expenses of looking after it' ... 'or else they will have to find it another lodging, as it needs a change of air after the winter'.[34] At the same time, Elizabeth complained that the counties were not maintaining 'poor soldiers ... so that they become vagabonds, and the Queen is troubled, whenever she takes the air, with these miserable creatures'.[35]

William Ashby felt that he had finally reached a stage in his life when he could enjoy monetary rewards and a degree of recognition for his decades of service to the Crown. Although his notorious offers to King James made five years previously were still cited as a cause of the Scottish King's resentment against Elizabeth, they apparently did no lasting damage to his reputation or standing at court, which may be further evidence that he had been acting for Walsingham.[36]

He was granted additional land expropriated from recusants. In July 1593, Ashby prevailed in a legal action regarding Charles Waldegrave, a prominent Norfolk Catholic whose father had been Queen Mary Tudor's Master of the Great Wardrobe. Ashby was responsible for Waldegrave being charged with recusancy in London, and initiated a new lawsuit to prevent the undervaluing of the lands, which he claimed was defrauding Elizabeth and himself of rental income. This action demonstrates an extraordinary degree of influence, probably at Burghley's request, as it was in the form of a letter from the Privy Council to the Lord Chief Justice of the Queen's Bench – second only to the Lord Chancellor in the judicial hierarchy – and 'the rest of Her Majesty's Justices, or to any of them'. The letter specifically allowed Ashby to remove any lower court action to the Queen's Bench.[37]

Waldegrave was a victim of the 1593 *Act Against Recusants*, directed against:

> sundry wicked and seditious persons, who, terming themselves
> Catholics, and being indeed spies and intelligencers, not only
> for her majesty's foreign enemies, but also for rebellious and
> traitorous subjects born within her highness's realms and
> dominions, and hiding their most detestable and devilish
> purposes under a false pretext of religion and conscience,
> do secretly wander and shift from place to place within this
> realm, to corrupt and seduce her majesty's subjects, and to
> stir them to sedition and rebellion.

The Act stated that 'every person and persons that shall offend against the tenor and intent of this Act in anything before mentioned, shall lose and forfeit all his and their goods and chattels, and shall also forfeit to the

Queen's Majesty all the lands, tenements, and hereditaments, and all the rents and annuities of every such person so doing or offending, during the life of the same offender'.[38]

With most Church assets such as the Bishop's Fee which had been confiscated during the Reformation no longer available, the Act was a means not only of rewarding royal servants like Ashby, but also augmenting the Treasury, as the Queen received a percentage of all rents and annuities from seized properties.

By early June, the plague had become 'very hot' in London. Ashby's home at Clerkenwell was close to the Fleet Ditch, the capital's most infected area.[39] Like others who could afford to escape from the city, Ashby found refuge from the plague in Leicestershire, staying with relatives at Quenby and Wymondham. While the epidemic was not as lethal as the Black Death of the fourteenth century, it rapidly spread beyond London, killing thousands in provincial cities and towns. Hundreds fell victim at Derby 'not two houses together being free from … the great plague and mortality'. In Leicester, 'a contribution was levied for the plague-stricken'.[40]

For those who had to remain in noisome urban tenements, baking heat added to the misery of illness and fear of death. The summer of 1593 was the hottest and driest of the sixteenth century. In the Tower of London, several prisoners died in their cells from heat exhaustion. In London alone, an estimated eighteen thousand people – a tenth of the population – died during the year, two-thirds from plague.[41]

Unlike in previous centuries, a larger percentage of people who contracted the disease, including Burghley, recovered. The spread of the contagion was contained by enlightened sanitary measures in orders given to 'magistrates and rulers of Cities and towns'. These included 'no stinking dunghills … Suffer not any dogs, cats, or pigs to run about the streets, for they are very dangerous, and apt to carry the infection from place to place' and 'cause all the clothes, bedding, and other such things as were used about the sick to be burned, although at the charge of the rest of the inhabitants you buy them all new'.[42]

Like hundreds of others, Ashby returned to London in the autumn thinking that cold weather would dispel the plague. He was to be fatally mistaken.

One contemporary observed recorded that 'The like plague as is now in England hath not been seen in our age so long continuing and so vehement... In London is great desolation, the greater part of the people fled and dead, and the Mayor is dead of the plague also'.[43] The Lord Mayor, Sir William Roe, died on 23 October, and in the following days, other high-status people who thought they had escaped the plague were struck down.

John Stanhope sent Robert Cecil a description of the death of a young courtier named John Darcy, who had gone with his brother from Greenwich to London in a wherry:

> ... the day being very wet, and the watermen without a tilt
> [canopy], one of the watermen did borrow the coverlet of a
> bed to cast over the boat, which had lain ... over some had
> died of the sickness. That night, Robert Darcy fell sick and
> without hope of life, but took physic [medicine], and God and
> nature wrought his escape. John Darcy, being lightly troubled
> with headache, scorned to take physic ... the marks appeared
> in his neck, and then he went to bed and the next day drank
> eight or nine jugs of cold drink, and died that night. Both the
> watermen sickened ... and the woman that kept them had
> the sickness and escaped.[44]

In November 1593, Ashby was nominated by Lord Lumley to fill the vacant seat caused by the death of Valentine Dale, MP for Chichester, a close friend of Burghley, and Ashby was described as 'a diplomat and friend of Burghley'. Chichester's mayor, John Farrington, hoped that Ashby, 'a mere stranger unto this place and unknown unto us all ... only liked and allowed of' as a mark of respect to Lumley himself, would do what he could 'to further the state of this poor city ... wherein we shall think ourselves greatly beholding unto him'.[45]

Although Ashby was recorded as taking his seat in Parliament, he did not occupy it for long. Weakened by the malaria that had afflicted him for years, he fell ill a few days before Christmas 1593. His nephew, Nicholas Berkeley, summoned Dr Thomas Fryer, an eminent physician and fellow Cantabrigian. Fryer immediately recognised the 'tokens' [symptoms] of an advanced case of the plague – 'cold sweats, vomiting; excrements corrupt ... urine black, or colour of lead. Cramp, convulsion of limbs, imperfection of speech and stinking breath, colic, swelling of the body as in dropsy, visage of divers colours, red spots quickly discovering and covering themselves' – and knew recovery was hopeless.[46] He told Ashby to prepare to meet his maker.

William Ashby dictated his last will and testament to Dr Fryer on Saturday, 22 December. Robert Naunton, Ashby's heir and executor, was not present, and Fryer and Berkeley served as witnesses.

The wording was rambling, suggesting a mind struggling with waves of pain and weakness, as the doctor wrote by candlelight in the dark bedchamber of Ashby's house on Clerkenwell Green. He asked that his body 'be honestly brought to the Sepulcher' (the church of St Sepulchre-without-Newgate) before making a number of bequests to family members. These included £100 for his godson William Ashby, a minor child of William's second cousin George Ashby of Quenby.[47]

Naunton was to receive an annuity of £100 per annum, while members of the Ashby of Loseby family, including a spinster named Ursula Ashby, received small bequests, some of which were to be paid out of rents from the Waldegrave grant. Ashby asked that his friend and neighbour Charles Bedingfield manage the Waldegrave revenues for his heirs, and 'for part of a recompense for his pains he shall take in this matter', Bedingfield was bequeathed 'a Basin and Ewer of silver he hath already of mine in his custody'. William gave Berkeley £20 'for the pains he has taken with me', together with a 'black', which meant black cloth for a funeral cloak or gown. He also bequethed Dr Fryer 'one black'.

William closed his eyes, breathing shallowly. The physician leaned close and asked if he was finished. Ashby nodded, and Dr Fryer helped him sit up and placed a pen in his quivering hand. Berkeley witnessed his barely legible signature.

Tormented by thirst like the young courtier Darcy, his breathing shallow, William rallied enough to whisper that he wished to add more to his will. 'In token of old friendship and kindness', he left William Huninges furniture and asked that 'five marks be given unto him to wear a black cloak for my sake'. After drinking water from a pewter mug the doctor held to his lips, Ashby said that he wished to give his faithful servant Peter Haye 'twenty shillings by year paid him so long as he shall live and at his going away twenty shillings to be given him'.[48]

Ashby lingered, determined to survive until 'the Feast of the Nativity'. He slipped in and out of variegated dreams, sometimes smiling at pleasant memories such as his journey across Europe with Arthur Throckmorton, at other times wincing at remembered humiliation and betrayal during his Scottish sojourn. Shortly after midnight on Christmas day, 1593, William Ashby passed into eternity at the age of fifty-seven.

# Appendix I
# Sir Robert Naunton

William Ashby's life story would not be complete without a short profile of his nephew, Robert Naunton. As one of the more interesting characters of the Elizabethan and Jacobean eras, Naunton deserves his own biography. He was not only the childless William Ashby's heir, but his protégé, whose career followed a remarkably similar trajectory as scholar, spy and statesman. Ashby groomed Naunton for important governmental roles, roles which Ashby may have aspired to himself but failed to achieve. The former ambassador to Scotland would have been immensely pleased, and found it deliciously ironic, to know that his sometimes-wayward nephew was appointed to Walsingham's former post as Principal Secretary of State – and Spymaster – by King James I.

Born *circa* 1563, Robert was the son of Henry Naunton of Alderton, Suffolk, and his first wife Elizabeth Ashby, William's elder sister. Naunton senior had served as Master of Horse to the Dowager Duchess of Suffolk, mother of the two young dukes who died of the sweating sickness after being infected at Cambridge in 1551. Robert attended King Edward VI Grammar School in Norwich before matriculating as a pensioner at Trinity College, Cambridge, during Lent term 1578.

Naunton was a gifted student, having 'addicted himself from his youth to such studies as tended to accomplish him for public employment'.[1] He was awarded a B.A. in 1582, named a Scholar the same year, admitted as a Fellow of Trinity in 1585 and received an M.A. degree in 1586. However, like his uncle, he was frustrated by academic life and determined to follow in Ashby's footsteps. He joined Ashby in Scotland in early 1589, serving as secretary, courier and trainee intelligencer. The ambassador devoted considerable correspondence to advancing the young man's career, writing to Walsingham's secretary Francis Mills to say he was 'greatly pleasured at your hands for the courtesy yow have shewed to my nephew Naunton in procuring Mr. Secretaries letters in his behalf to Mr. Doctor Styll, master of Trinity College in Cambridge',[2] and to his old friend Thomas Byng (a contemporary sizar at Peterhouse who had risen to Vice-Chancellor of the university), who was well-connected at court.[3]

In Edinburgh, Naunton caroused with Richard Wigmore, the charming deep cover agent posing as a self-exiled lover of an angry noblewoman in Elizabeth's court. After Naunton returned to London with his uncle, Wigmore wrote to him about the 'enchantment' Robert had with a lady he had spent a 'last good night' with before departing and who 'continual demands whether' he had heard from him.[4]

Although some sources state that Naunton probably met Elizabeth's last romantic favourite, Robert Devereux, 2nd Earl of Essex, in 1595, he evidently was acquainted with Essex much earlier. Near contemporaries in age, they would have undoubtedly known each other at Cambridge; Essex was admitted as a Fellow-Commoner to Trinity College in 1577 and Naunton the following year. In a letter written to the Earl's secretary in November 1590, Naunton mentions his last correspondence from Florence and reports that he is now studying French in Paris. He refers to previous letters to Essex and says 'he craves a little direction how far I may engage myself now' and hopes 'to receive a kind long letter of modern instructions'. Considering the Earl's connection with Burghley, and Ashby's work with the Lord Treasurer, this is compelling evidence that Naunton was already working as an intelligencer in Europe.[5]

In 1596, Essex sent Naunton to the Continent on a supposedly secret mission to serve as intermediary with Antonio Perez, a former secretary of Phillip II of Spain who was on the run from Spanish agents for the murder of Don John's secretary eighteen years earlier. Naunton operated under cover as tutor to Robert Vernon, a nineteen-year-old ward and cousin of Essex. The mission was unofficial as Queen Elizabeth, Burghley and Sir Robert Cecil (who had assumed Walsingham's role) shunned Perez. Essex lost interest, and the mission was a failure. Following this,

Naunton was expected to 'inform himself what he could in so short a time of in the knowledge of the languages, and the principal places, of France and Italy; and then to return homewards through Germany, if the passage should be free for Englishmen'.[6]

Naunton was embittered by the experience, and frustrated by his ambiguous professional status. Charged with communicating any political intelligence he could gather to Essex, he described himself as 'betwixt a pedagogue and a spy', saying he did not know which trade was more 'odious or base'.[7] He was said to 'have acquired an antipathy to the French only outweighed by his profound Hispanophobia' resulting from this flirtation with espionage. Although Essex frequently referred to Naunton as his friend, he seemed disinterested in finding him a government position after his return to England in 1598.[8]

William Ashby left Naunton assets worth over £1,000, to be managed in trust by his friend Thomas Bedingfield, a gentleman pensioner to the Queen and translator of works including Machiavelli's *Florentine Histories*. An affable scholar, Bedingfield had no business sense and made disastrous investments with Naunton's inheritance.

After his return from abroad, Naunton was horrified to discover that his inheritance from Ashby was lost and irrecoverable despite legal action against the doddering Bedingfield. He was forced to return to Cambridge, 'to live a poor scholar in the university, ... so distracted in my state of mind ... as I could not enter or think of any course for my preferment'.[9] His academic poverty was exaggerated; at Cambridge Naunton held the posts of Senior Proctor and Public Orator. The estrangement from Essex worked to his advantage as Naunton became a loyal supporter of Cecil, and was far removed from Essex's circle by the time the Earl was executed for treason in February 1601.

James' long-sought accession to Elizabeth's throne was a turning point in Naunton's life, catapulting him into a career that would take him into the highest echelon of the English government. In his role as Public Orator of Cambridge, Naunton officially greeted the King on his way to London in May 1603, which was a stroke of good fortune as James remembered him from his service in Edinburgh fourteen years earlier.

Naunton's rise was rapid over the following years, helped by his extensive family connections. Soon after the accession, he accompanied the 5th Earl of Rutland on a delegation to Denmark. William Ashby owed his Grantham parliamentary seat to the Earl's uncle, and Naunton had become acquainted with the young nobleman when he was a Cambridge student. From 1606, Naunton served as a Member of Parliament for various constituencies (including Cambridge University) over a twenty-year period.

By the beginning of 1612, Cecil (now the Earl of Salisbury) had appointed Naunton one of his under secretaries of state, although he was replaced after Salisbury's death in May of that year. Naunton's kinsman, Sir Ralph Winwood, became Principal Secretary in 1614, further benefiting his career.

However, it was the ascent of the King's 'last and greatest lover', George Villiers, that immeasurably boosted Naunton's advancement.

Villiers, from the tiny Leicestershire village of Brooksby, a few miles from Loseby and Quenby, was Naunton's cousin via the Ashby side of his family. Described as Villiers' 'kinsman, his creature, herald and honest man', Naunton's elevation paralleled that of the King's favourite, who was knighted in 1615 as Gentleman of the King's Bedchamber, and subsequently ascended the ranks of the peerage from Baron to Duke of Buckingham in eight years.

Naunton was knighted the same year as his kinsman. The following year, he was appointed Master of Requests and Surveyor of the Wards, with an annual pension for life of £100, holding both posts concurrently. After Winwood's death, he was appointed Principal Secretary of State, serving for five years.

Sir Robert's government service was controversial. As an MP, he was threatened with loss of office 'for speaking his mind freely and honestly'. Known for his dogmatic Protestantism and abhorrence of

Roman Catholicism, he was suspended from the Privy Council in 1621 and placed under house arrest for meddling in plans for the marriage of Prince Charles. However, thanks to Buckingham's patronage, he continued as *de facto* Secretary for another two years, communicating with English diplomats and managing foreign and domestic intelligence operations. After formally resigning as Secretary in 1625, he resumed his seat on the Privy Council.

Naunton took an early interest in English colonisation of America. Among other initiatives, he and his colleague Sir Edwin Sandys, a founder of the Virginia Company, were involved in a scheme to promote indentured servitude for the poor of England who could try to make a better life for themselves in the New World. In January 1620, Sandys wrote to Naunton:

> The City of London have appointed one hundred children, from their superfluous multitude, to be transported to Virginia, there to be bound apprentices, upon very beneficial conditions. They have also granted 500*l* for their passage and outfit. Some of the ill-disposed children, who under severe masters in Virginia may be brought to goodness, and of whom the City is especially desirous to be disburdened, declare their unwillingness to go. The City wanting authority to deliver, and the Virginia Company to transport these children against their will, desire higher authority to get over the difficulty.[10]

In 1619, at what was then considered the advanced age of fifty-six, Naunton married 'with much secrecy' Penelope, daughter of Sir Thomas Perrot and Elizabeth Devereux, the latter a sister of the decapitated Earl of Essex. History is rife with strange twists, and William Ashby would have been pleased that his nephew's wife was an heiress connected (through her half-sister) with one of the most influential Scottish courtiers, James Hay, Viscount Doncaster and subsequently Earl of Carlisle, a kinsman of his friend and intelligence agent, Alexander Hay, Clerk Register of the High Court of Scotland.

Naunton's son, James, died tragically at the age of two-and-a-half in 1624. His only other child, Penelope, survived to marry into the nobility, first to Viscount Bayning and then to Philip, Lord Herbert, who became the 5th Earl of Pembroke.

Towards the end of his life, Naunton wrote a lively account of the Elizabethan Court which is considered one of the best primary sources for the late Elizabethan and Jacobean eras. Unfinished at his death on 27 March 1635, the book was first published in 1641 under the title *Fragmenta Regalia*.

Naunton's line died out after the death of his childless grandson, the 6th Earl of Pembroke.

# Appendix II
## Dramatis Personae

**Acworth, George** (1534–c. 1581). Protestant divine and civil lawyer.

**Agarde, Arthur** (1540–1615). English antiquary and archivist at the Exchequer, Westminster.

**Ainsworth, Ralph** (?–1569). Cambridge academic, Master of Peterhouse 1544–1553.

**Anjou and Alençon, Francis, Duke of** (1555–1584). Military leader and erstwhile suitor of Queen Elizabeth.

**Arran, Earl of** – see Stewart, James.

**Ashby, Everard**. father of William Ashby.

**Ashby, William Sr.**, (c. 1470–1543). MP, grandfather of William Ashby.

**Aston, Sir Roger** (? – 1612). English-born courtier to James VI/I.

**Bellenden, Sir Lewis** (c. 1552–1591). Scottish Diplomat and Lord Justice Clerk.

**Bothwell, Earl of** – see Stuart/Stewart, Francis

**Bowes, Robert** (c. 1535–1597), English diplomat, resident ambassador to Scotland.

**Burghley, Baron** – see Cecil, William.

**Carey, Henry, 1st Baron Hunsdon** (1526–1596). English courtier, soldier and diplomat.

**Carey, Sir George, 2nd Baron Hunsdon** (1547–1603). English diplomat and soldier. Friend of Ashby.

**Carmichael, Sir John** (?–1600). Scottish diplomat and soldier.

**Cecil, William, Baron Burghley** (1520–1598). Elizabeth's Chief Minister. Lord High Treasurer 1572–1598. Organiser of domestic and foreign intelligence network.

**Cecil, Robert, 1st Earl of Salisbury** (1563–1612). Secretary of State of England (1596–1612) and Lord High Treasurer (1608–1612).

**Chisholm, William III, Bishop of Dunblane** (1547–1629). Scottish Papal agent.

**Cobham, Sir William Brooke, 10th Baron** (1527–1597). English diplomat and Lord Chamberlain.

**Colville, John** (c. 1540–1605). Scottish clergyman, judge, politician and author.

**Colville, James, 1st Lord Colville of Culross** (1551–1629). Scottish soldier, courtier and diplomat.

**Davison, William** (1541–1608). English Junior Secretary of State and Privy Councillor (1586–1587). Fined and imprisoned in the Tower of London for the dispatch of the execution warrant of Mary Queen of Scots. Subsequently Clerk to the Treasury.

**Douglas, Archibald** (c,1540–1601). Scottish ambassador in England.

**Douglas, Archibald, Earl of Angus** (1555–1588). Scottish Protestant nobleman.

**Elizabeth I** (1533–1603). Queen of England 1558–1603.

**Fowler, William** (?–1590). English spy. Ashby's enemy.

**Gilpin, George** (1514–1602). English diplomat and intelligencer.

**Gordon, George, Earl of Huntly** (1562–1636). Scottish rebel and soldier. A favourite of King James.

**Gray, Patrick, Master of, Sixth Lord Gray** (?–1612). Confidant of James VI, Scottish ambassador to England 1584–1585 and 1586–1587.

**Grey, Henry** (1517–1554). 1st Duke of Suffolk. Beheaded by Queen Mary I.

**Hamilton, Lord Claud** (c. 1543–1622). Mary Queen of Scots' agent in Scotland. Rebel. Brother of Lord John Hamilton.

**Hamilton, Lord John, 1st Marquess of Hamilton** (1540–1604). Ashby's friend.

**Hatton, Sir Christopher** (1540–1589). Vice-Chamberlain and later Lord Chancellor of England.

**Hay, Alexander** (?–1594). Scottish Clerk of the Council and one of Ashby's spies.

**Heneage, Sir Thomas** (1532–1595). Vice-Chamberlain to Elizabeth.

**Howard, Charles, Second Baron Howard of Effingham** (1536–1624). Lord High Admiral of England.

**Hudson, James**. Member of English family of musicians at the Scottish court. Intelligencer and co-conspirator with William Fowler against Ashby.

**Hunsdon** – see Carey.

**Huntly, Earl of** – see Gordon, George.

**James VI of Scotland, later James I of England** (1566–1625). Son of Mary Queen of Scots. Succeeded Elizabeth to throne of England, 1603.

**John, Don, of Austria** (1547–1578). Illegitimate son of Emperor Charles V, governor and viceroy of the Spanish Netherlands, 1577–1578.

**Killigrew, Sir Henry** (c. 1528–1603). English diplomat and soldier.

**Leicester, Robert Dudley, Earl of** (c. 1532–1588). English Privy Councillor. Queen Elizabeth's favourite and her Master of the Horse.

**Lennox, Duke of** – see Stuart, Esmé.

**Lyon, Sir Thomas, Master of Glamis** (?–1608). Lord High Treasurer of Scotland.

**Maitland, John** (1537–1595). Lord Chancellor of Scotland.

**Malby, Sir Nicholas** (c. 1530–1584). English soldier.

**Mendoza, Bernardino de**. Spanish ambassador in London 1578–1584.

**Mildmay, Sir Walter** (c. 1520–1589). Chancellor of the Exchequer and brother-in-law to Francis Walsingham.

**Orange, William, Prince of** (1533–1584). Chief leader of the Dutch Revolt against the Spanish.

**Ruissingen, Frederic, Baron von**. Dutch-German official and double agent.

**Palavicino, Sir Horatio** (c. 1540–1600). Financier and political agent.

**Parma, Alexander Farnese, Duke of** (1545–1592). Spanish commander in the Netherlands.

**Peverel, William** (fl. 1086). Favourite of King William I, powerful Norman noble, feudal lord of Saffrid.

**Philip II** (1527–1598). King of Spain 1556–1598.

**Pope Gregory XIII** (1502–1585). Pontiff 1572–1585. Supporter of various invasion and assassination plots against England.

**Rogers, Daniel** (c. 1538–1591). Anglo-Flemish diplomat and politician.

**Saffrid (Saxfrith, Sasfrid or Safrid),** (fl. 1086). Norman soldier, ancestor of William Ashby.

**Schenck, Martin** (c. 1540–1589). Warlord in the Netherlands.

**Sempill, William** (1546–1630). Chief Spanish agent in Scotland.

**Stafford, Sir Edward** (1552–1605). English ambassador to France. Alleged traitor and enemy agent.

**Stuart/Stewart, James, Earl of Arran** (?–1595). Scottish Lord Chancellor.

**Stuart/Stewart, Sir William** of Houston (c. 1540–c. 1605). Scottish soldier, politician and diplomat. Cousin of the Earl of Arran.

**Stuart, Lady Arbella** (1575–1615). Possible successor to Queen Elizabeth I for English throne.

**Stuart, Esmé, 1ˢᵗ Duke of Lennox** (1542–1583). Powerful Roman Catholic French nobleman of Scottish ancestry.

**Stuart/Stewart, Francis, 5th Earl of Bothwell** (1562–1612). Scottish rebel. Collaborator with Huntly.

**Sturmius, Johannes** (1507–1589). German educator, Protestant reformer and chief English agent in Germany,

**Sidney, Robert, Earl of Leicester** (1563–1626). English diplomat and soldier.

**Throckmorton, Arthur** (c.1557–1626), English courtier and politician. Close friend of Ashby.

**Wemyss, Laird of Easter** – see Colville, James.

**Wigmore, Richard** (?–1621). English courtier and secret agent.

**Wilson, Thomas** (1524–1581). English diplomat and judge who served as a privy councillor and Secretary of State to Queen Elizabeth.

**Wotton, Nicholas** (c. 1497–1567). English diplomat, cleric and courtier.

# Bibliography

PRIMARY SOURCES

Ashby, W., *Will of William Ashby of Clerkenwell*, National Archives reference PROB 11/82/616.

Ashby, W., *Will of William Assheby of Lowesby, Leicestershire*, National Archives reference PROB 11/29/498.

Bodley, T., *The Life of Sir Thomas Bodley, Written by Himself* (Chicago 1906).

Bowes, R., & Stevenson, J., *The correspondence of Robert Bowes of Aske, esquire, the ambassador of Queen Elizabeth in the court of Scotland.* (London 1842).

Boyd W., & Meikle, H., eds., *Calendar of State Papers, Scotland (CSP-S)*: Vols. 6–10, 1589–1593, (Edinburgh, 1936).

Bray, G., ed., *Documents of the English Reformation 1526–1701* (Cambridge 1994).

Brown, K., Mackintosh G., Mann A., Ritchie P., Tanner R., eds., *The Records of the Parliaments of Scotland to 1707* (St Andrews, 2007–2020).

Bruce, J., ed., *Letters of Queen Elizabeth and King James VI of Scotland*, (London 1849).

Bruce, J., ed., *Correspondence of Robert Dudley, earl of Leycester: during his government of the Low Countries, in the years 1585 and 1586* (London 1844).

Burnet, G., *Bishop Burnet's History of His Own Time* (London 1724).

*Calendar of Border Papers*, i, 1560–95, Bain, J., ed., (London, 1894).

*Calendar of Close Rolls*, England, Court of Chancery, (London 1892–1963).

*Calendar of State Papers, Spain (Simancas)*, Vols 2/4, 1568–1603, Hume, M., ed., (London, 1894).

*Calendar of the Patent Rolls preserved in the Public Record Office: Elizabeth [I]*, (London 1939).

Camden, W., *Annales in the Historie of the Most Renowned and Victorious Princess Elizabeth, late Queen of England* (London 1635).

Camden, W., Vincent, A., Lennard, S., & Fetherston, J., College of Arms (Great Britain). (1870). *The visitation of the county of Leicester in the year 1619.* (London 1870).

Cary, R., *The Memoirs of Robert Cary, Earl of Monmouth* (Edinburgh 1808).

Colville, J., *Original Letters of Mr. John Colville 1582–1603*, (Edinburgh 1858).

Crosby, A., ed., *Calendar of State Papers Foreign (CSP-F): Elizabeth, Vols. 10–23, 1572–1589*, (London, 1876).

https://opendomesday.org/place/SP5690/ashby-magna/

Dasent, J., ed., *Acts of the Privy Council of England*, (London 1901).

*Domesday Book*, https://opendomesday.org/name/saxfrith-of-catesby/ and https://opendomesday.org/place/SP5690/ashby-magna/ accessed 14/09/2021

Dyfnallt, Owen, G., ed., *Calendar of the manuscripts of the Marquis of Bath preserved at Longleat, Wiltshire* (London 1980). Paris, Sir Harris. *Memoirs of the Life And Times of Sir Christopher Hatton, K. G.: Vice-chamberlain And Lord Chancellor to Queen Elizabeth. Including His Correspondence With the Queen And Other Distinguished Persons.* London 1847).

Elizabeth R., & James VI, *Letters of Queen Elizabeth and King James VI. of Scotland: Some of Them Printed From Originals In the Possession of the Rev. Edward Ryder, And Others From a MS. Which Formerly Belonged to Sir Peter Thompson, Kt.* (New York, 1968).

*Egerton Manuscripts*, British Library or available online at https://www.british-history.ac.uk.

Foster, J., ed., *The Register of Admissions to Gray's Inn, 1521–1889* (London 1889).

Foster, J., ed., *Alumni Oxonienses 1500–1714*, (Oxford, 1891).

Gee, H., & Hardy, W., eds., *Documents Illustrative of English Church History*, (New York 1896).

Gibson-Craig, J. ed., *Papers relative to the marriage of King James the Sixth of Scotland, with the Princess Anna of Denmark* (Edinburgh 1828).

Gray, P., *Letters and papers relating to Patrick, Master of Gray: afterwards seventh Lord Gray* (Edinburgh 1835).

Harris Nicolas, N. ed., *Memoirs of the Life and Times of Sir Christopher Hatton, Vice-Chamberlain* (London 1847).

Inderwick, F., ed., *A Calendar of the Inner Temple Records*, (London 1896).

Laing, D., ed., *Original letters of Mr. John Colville, 1582–1603* (Edinburgh1858).

Lamb, J., *A collection of letters, statutes, and other documents from the ms. Library of Corp. Christ. Coll., illustrative of the history of the University of Cambridge, during the period of the Reformation, from A.D. MD., to A.D. MDLXXII* (London 1838).

Laughton, J.K., ed., *State Papers Relating to the Defeat of the Spanish Armada*. Vol. I (London 1894).

Lemon, R., ed., *Calendar of State Papers Domestic (CSP-D): Edward VI, Mary and Elizabeth, 1547–1625*, (London, 1856).

Marwick J., *Extracts From the Records of the Burgh of Edinburgh, 1573–1589*, (Edinburgh 1882).

Melville, J., *The Diary of Mr. James Melville, 1556–1601*, (Edinburgh 1829).

Melville, J., *Memoirs of His Own Life*, (Edinburgh 1827).

Melville, J., *The Memoirs of Sir James Melville of Halhil*, Donaldson, Gordon, (London 1969).

Metcalfe, W., ed., *The Visitations of Northamptonshire Made in 1564 and 1618–19* (London 1887).

Moryson, F., *An Itinerary Written By Fynes Moryson, Gent. Containing His ten yeeres trauels thorovv Twelve Dominions, The First Part*, (London 1617).

Moysie, D., *Memoirs of the affairs of Scotland: from early manuscripts* (Edinburgh 1830).

Muller, J., ed., *The Letters of Stephen Gardiner* (Cambridge 2013).

Murdin, W., & Haynes, S., eds, *Collection of State Papers left by William Cecill, Lord Burghley* (London 1759).

Nashe, T., *The Unfortunate Traveller or The Life of Jack Wilton. Qui audiunt audita dicunt.* (London 1594).

Nichols, J., *The history and antiquities of the county of Leicester* (London 1795).

Robinson, H., ed., *Original Letters Relative to the English* Reformation (Cambridge 1847).

Robinson, H., ed., *The Zurich Letters*, (Cambridge 1842–47).

Rutland, C., *The Manuscripts of His Grace the Duke of Rutland: ...preserved At Belvoir Castle...* (London 1888).

Säenz-Cambra, C., *Scotland and Philip II, 1580–1598: Politics, Religion Diplomacy and Lobbying* (PhD thesis, University of Edinburgh 2003).

Sainsbury, W., ed., *Calendar of State Papers Colonial, America and West Indies*: Vol. 1, 1574–1660, (London, 1860).

Salisbury, R., et al., *Calendar of the Manuscripts of the Most Honourable the Marquess of Salisbury ... Preserved At Hatfield House, Hertfordshire* (London 1883).

Smith, J., *Index of Wills Proved In the Prerogative Court of Canterbury ... And Now Preserved In the Principal Probate Registry, Somerset House, London* (London 1893–1919).

Southey, R., *Journal of a tour in Scotland in 1819* (London 1929).

Stow, J., *Annales, or a general Chronicle of England* (London 1631).

Stow, J., *A Survey of London, Written in the year 1598 by John Stow* (London 1842).

Stowe, J., *Annals of England to 1603* (London 1603).

Strype, J., *Annals of the Reformation and Establishment of Religion ...*, (Oxford 1824).

Stuart, M., *Letters of Mary, Queen of Scots*, Agnes Strickland ed. (London 1842).

Throckmorton, A., *The Diary of Sir Arthur Throckmorton,* held in the Hales Family Collection, Canterbury Cathedral Archives and Library, Ref. U85/38/14. 3 vols 1578–1583

Traheron, B., *A Warning to England to Repent, and to tvrne to God from idolatrie and poperie by the terrible exemple of Calace* (London 1558).

Prerogative Court of Canterbury (PCC), 86 Neville. Will of William Ashby Catalogue reference: PROB 11/82/616

Verstegan, R., & Petti, A., eds., *The Letters And Despatches of Richard Verstegan* (London 1959).

Walsingham, F., *Journal of Sir Francis Walsingham: From Dec. 1570 to April 1583.* Martin, C. ed., (London 1870).

Watson, T., *An Eglogue upon the Death of Sir Francis Walsingham* (London 1590).

Westcott, A., *New poems by James I of England: from a hitherto unpublished manuscript* (New York 1911).

## SECONDARY SOURCES

Acheson, E., *A Gentry Community: Leicestershire in the Fifteenth Century, C.1422–c.1485* (Cambridge 1992).

Adams, R., 'A Most Secret Service: William Herle and the Circulation of Intelligence' in Robyn Adams & Rosanna Cox, eds. *Diplomacy and Early Modern Culture* (London 2011).

Archer, E., Goldring, E., & Knight, S., eds., *The Progresses, Pageants, and Entertainments of Queen Elizabeth I* (Oxford 2007).

Arnade, P., *Beggars, iconoclasts, and civic patriots: the political culture of the Dutch Revolt* (Ithaca 2008).

Ashby, T. 'Walsingham and the Witch' in *History Scotland* Vol. 21 No. 5 September/October 2021.

Baker, R., Clarges, T., & Phillips, E., *A chronicle of the Kings of England: From the time of the Romans government, unto the death of King James, etc.,* (London 1684).

Bucholz, R., & Key N., *Early Modern England 1485–1714: A Narrative History* (Hoboken 2003).

Budiansky, S., *Her Majesty's Spymaster: Elizabeth I, Sir Francis Walsingham, and the Birth of Modern Espionage* (London 2006).

Burton, W., *Description of Leicestershire: containing matters of antiquity, history, armoury, and genealogy,* (London 1777).

Calderwood, D., *The History of the Kirk of Scotland* (Edinburgh 1842–1849).

Chambers, R., *Domestic Annals of Scotland* (Edinburgh 1858).

Collins, A., *The Peerage of England* (London 1756).

Cooper, J., *The Queen's Agent* (London 2011).

Cooper, Charles Henry. *Annals of Cambridge* (Cambridge 1842).

Creighton, C., *A History of Epidemics in Britain from A.D. 664 to the Extinction of Plague* (Cambridge 1891).

Cunningham, G. ed., *Lives of Eminent and Illustrious Englishmen* (Glasgow 1837).

Davies, C., *The History of Holland and the Dutch Republic* (London 1851).

Davies, C., 'Slavery and Protector Somerset; The Vagrancy Act of 1547', *The Economic History Review*, vol. 19, no. 3, 1966.

De Lisle, L., *After Elizabeth* (London 2005).

De Lisle, L., *The Sisters Who Would Be Queen: Mary, Katherine, and Lady Jane Grey: A Tudor Tragedy* (New York 2009).

Digges D., ed., *The Compleat Ambassador or two Treaties of the Intended Marriage of Queen Elizabeth* (London 1655).

Douthwaite, W., *Gray's Inn, Its History & Association* (London 1886).

Duffy, E., *The Church of Mary Tudor* (Aldershot 2006).

Elton, G., *The Tudor Constitution, Documents and Commentary*, (London 1982).

Fisher, P., *The Tombes, Monuments, and Sepulchral inscriptions, lately visible in St. Pauls Cathedral, and St. Faith's under it, etc.* (London 1684).

Fletcher, R., *The Reformation and the Inns of Court* (London 1903).

Fletcher, W., *Leicestershire Pedigrees and Royal Descents* (London 1887).

Foxe, J., *The Actes and Monuments* Cattley, S., Ed., (1563; repr. London, 1839).

Fuller, T., *The History of the University of Cambridge, and of Waltham Abbey* (London 1840).

Garrard, P., Stephenson, J., Ganesan V., & Peters T., 'Attenuated variants of Lesch–Nyhan disease: the case of King James VI/I', *Brain*, Vol. 133, Issue 11, November 2010, 153.

Garrett, C., *The Marian Exiles, a study in the origins of Elizabethan Puritanism* (Cambridge 1936).

Gehring, D., ed., *Diplomatic Intelligence on the Holy Roman Empire and Denmark during the Reigns of Elizabeth I and James VI* (London 2016).

Glover, S., *The History of the County of Derby* (Derby 1829).

Goodare, J., 'The Debts of James VI of Scotland', *The Economic History Review*, 62, iv, (2009),

Guy, J., *Tudor England* (Oxford 1988).

Guy, J., *Elizabeth: The Forgotten Years* (London 2016).

Hammer, P., *Elizabeth's Wars: War, Government and Society in Tudor England, 1544–1604* (Basingstoke 2003).

Haynes, A., *Invisible Power: Elizabethan Secret Services, 1570–1603* (London 1992).

Higueras Rodriguez D., and San Pio Aladren, M., 'Irish Wrecks of the Great Armada: The Testimony of the Survivors', in *God's Obvious Design: Papers for the Spanish Armada Symposium* Gallagher, P., & Cruickshank, D., eds., (London 1990).

Hinds, A., *The Making of the England of Elizabeth* (New York 1895).

Hoskins, W., 'The Leicestershire Farmer in the sixteenth Century,' (*Leicestershire Archaeological Society*, v 22, 1941–2).

Hoskins, W., 'Harvest Fluctuations and English Economic History, 1480–1619', *The Agricultural History Review*, Vol. 12, No. 1 (1964).

Howard, C., *English Travellers of the Renaissance* (Project Gutenberg 2004).

Hutchinson, R., *Elizabeth's Spymaster: Francis Walsingham and the secret war that saved England* (London 2007).

Hutchinson, R., *The Last Days of Henry VIII* (London 2005).

Hume, M., *Philip II of Spain* (London 1911).

James, S., *The Feminine Dynamic in English Art, 1485–1603: Women As Consumers, Patrons and Painters* (Abingdon 2009).

Jortin, J., *The Life of Erasmus* (London 1758).

Kaplan, B., 'Remnants of the Papal Yoke', *Sixteenth Century Journal*, XXVI, 1992.

Keats-Rohan, K., *Domesday People: A Prosopography of Persons Occurring in English Documents 1066–1166* (Suffolk, 1999).

Lang, A., *A History of Scotland from the Roman Occupation, Vol. 2 (Edinbugh 1907).*

Lodge, E., ed., *Illustrations of British History, Manners and Biography*, vol. II (London 1838).

Loomie, A., 'Philip III and the Stuart Succession in England, 1600–1603', *Revue belge de Philologie et d'Histoire* (Brussels 1965).

Mackenzie, A., *History of the Chisholms with genealogies of the principal families of that name* (Inverness 1891).

Malia, Martin., *History's Locomotives: Revolutions and the Making of the Modern* World (New Haven 2006).

Marcus, L., Mueller, J., & Rose, M., eds., *Elizabeth I: Collected Works*, (Chicago 2000).

Martin, C., & Parker, G.., The Spanish Armada (London 1988).

Marshall, P., *Beliefs and the Dead in Reformation England* (Oxford 2002).

Martin, L., *Henry III and the Jesuit Politicians* (Genève 1973).

*Scotland and England 1286–1815*, Mason, R., (ed.) (Edinburgh 1987).

MacCaffrey, W., *Queen Elizabeth and the Making of Policy*, 1572–1588 (Princeton 1981).

Mattingley, G., The Defeat of the Spanish Armada (London 1959).

Matusiak, J., *James I: Scotland's King of England*, (Stroud 2015),

Merewether, H., *The History of the Boroughs and Municipal Corporations of the United Kingdom*, v. ii, (London 1835).

Moore, J., 'Demographic Dimensions of the Mid-Tudor Crisis', *The Sixteenth Century Journal*, Vol. 41, No. 4 (Winter 2010).

Moore, J., 'Jack Fisher's 'Flu': A Visitation Revisited', *The Economic History Review*, New Series, Vol. 46, No. 2 (May, 1993).

Overman, S., 'Sporting and Recreational Activities of Students in the Medieval Universities', *Physical Education* Vol. 1, No. 6, 1999.

Pickstone A., et al, *A Medieval Manor at Main Street, Wymondham, Leicestershire-Post-Excavation Assessment and Updated Project Design* (Oxford Archaeology East 2008), Report Number 1024.

Porter, H., *Reformation and reaction in Tudor Cambridge* (Cambridge 1958).

Pugh, R., ed., *The Victorian History of the Counties of England – A History of Leicestershire* (London, 1958).

Read, C., *Mr. Secretary Walsingham and the Policy of Queen Elizabeth* (Oxford 1925), vols. 1–3.

Read, C., *Lord Burghley and Queen Elizabeth*, (London 1960).

Reid, S., 'Of Bairns and Bearded Men' in Miles Kerr-Peterson and Steven J. Reid (eds), *James VI and Noble Power in Scotland 1578–1603* (London, 2017).

Roach, J., ed., *A History of the County of Cambridge and the Isle of Ely: Volume 3, the City and University of Cambridge*, (London, 1959).

Roelke, N., *One King, One Faith: The Parlement of Paris and the Religious Reformations of the Sixteenth Century* (Berkeley and Los Angeles, 1996).

Rosenberg, E., 'Giacopo Castelvetro: Italian Publisher in Elizabethan London and His Patrons', *Huntington Library Quarterly*, Vol. 6, No. 2 (Feb., 1943).

Rowse, A., *Ralegh and the Throckmortons* (London 1962).

Schmidt, A., 'Thomas Wilson, Tudor Scholar-Statesman', *Huntington Library Quarterly*, Vol. 20, No. 3 (May, 1957).

Stedall, R., *Survival of the Crown*, II, (Sussex 2014).

Steven, L., ed., *Dictionary of National Biography*, (London 1885–1900).

Stewart, A., *The Cradle King, A Life of James VI and I* (London 2003).

Strickland, A., *Life of Mary Queen of Scots* (London 1893).

Strickland, A., & E., *Lives of the Queens of Scotland and English Princesses: Connected with the Regal Succession of Great Britain* (reprint – New York 2010).

Temple, P., ed, *Survey of London: Volume 46, South and East Clerkenwell*, (London, 2008).

Tuchman, B., *A Distant Mirror: The Calamitous 14th Century* (New York 1978).

Thompson, B., & Watts, J., eds., *Political Society in Later Medieval England* (Woodbridge 2015).

Tytler, P., Eadie, J., & Alison, A., *Tytler's History of Scotland: with illustrative notes from recently discovered State documents, and a continuation of the history, from the Union of the Crowns to the present time, including an account of the social and industrial progress of the people; also an essay on Scottish ecclesiastical history Scotland* (Glasgow, 1841–1843).

*Victoria County History – Rutland* (Rut. VCH), (London 1908, 1935).

Wilkinson, J., *Mary Boleyn: The True Story of Henry VIII's Favourite Mistress*.

Walker, T., *Peterhouse*, (London 1906).

Walker, T., *A Biographical Register of Peterhouse Men* (Cambridge 1927).

Webb, A., Beckwith, J., & Miller, G., *The history of Chislehurst: its church, manors, and parish* (London 1899).

Williams, P., *The Latter Tudors, England 1547–1603* (Oxford 1995).

Williams, C., *James I: Biography of a King* (Eugene 1934).

Wilson, C., *Queen Elizabeth and the Revolt of the Netherlands* (London 1979).

Woolfson, J., *Padua and the Tudors: English Students in Italy, 1485–1603* (Cambridge 1998).

# *Endnotes*

## Introduction

[1] John Burke, A Genealogical and Heraldic History of the Landed Gentry, (London 1848), vol IV, 176.

[2] Hastings Robinson, ed., *The Zurich Letters* (ser. 2) (Parker Soc.), ii. (Cambridge 1842–1847), 285.

[3] 22 August 1588, Walsingham to William Ashby, 498 CSP-S, 598–9.

[4] A list of Dramatis Personae with brief biographical details is provided in Appendix II.

## Prologue – 'the benefits conferred on us by our ancestors'

[1] William of Malmesbury, c. 1125.

[2] William Ashby to Walsingham, 9 July 1588, 470, (CSP-S).

[3] The term 'Anglican church' originates from a phrase in the Magna Carta – 'Anglicana ecclesia libera sit'.

[4] William Ashby to Walsingham. [July 30, 1588.] 478 CSP-S, 585.

[5] 9 July 1588, Robert Bowes to Burghley and Walsingham, 471 CSP-S, 579.

[6] Leanda de Lisle, *After Elizabeth* (London 2005), 32, quoting Thomas Phelippes, Calendar of State Papers Domestic (CSPD), 12 addenda, p. 407.

[7] 'Plausible deniability' in modern diplomatic and intelligence terminology, is the practice of people, usually senior officials in a chain of command, to deny knowledge of, or responsibility for, actions committed by others in an organizational hierarchy that can confirm their participation, even if they were personally involved or professed wilful ignorance of the actions.

[8] Also spelled Saxfrith and Sasfrid in the Domesday Book.

[9] https://opendomesday.org/name/william-peverel/ Accessed on 9 December 2019.

[10] *Victoria County History – Rutland* (Rut. VCH), (London 1908, 1935) vol ii., 245.

[11] According to feudal law a vavasour was a tenant or vassal with allegiance to a baron, having his tenancy under a baron, but also having tenants of his own. Henry of Bracton (c. 1210 – c. 1268) ranked the magnates seu valvassores between barons and knights; for him they are 'men of great dignity', and were noted similarly in an 1166 charter of King Henry II. See Henry de Bracton, De Legibus et Consuetudinibus Angliae, lib. i. cap. 8, 2.

[12] https://opendomesday.org/place/SP5690/ashby-magna/.

[13] Ibid.

[14] Robert Catesby, leader of a group of English Catholics who planned the failed Gunpowder Plot of 1605, was a member of the Northamptonshire and Warwickshire Catesby family which also claimed descent from Safrid. See C. Phythian Adams, ed., *Norman Conquest of Leicestershire and Rutland*, (Leicester, 1986), 24.

[15] The moated site of the manor house with nearby carp ponds is extant and undisturbed.

[16] William Burton, *Description of Leicestershire: containing matters of antiquity, history, armoury, and genealogy*, (London 1777), 23–4.

[17] William Farrer, *Honors and Knights Fees*, Manchester University Press (Manchester 1925), 170, citing Cal. Pat. 1266, 606.

[18] Leicestershire: Ashby Magna, Ref. D5336/1/15, Derbyshire Record Office https://calmview.derbyshire.gov.uk/calmview/Record.aspx?src=CalmView.Catalog&id=D5336%2f1%2f15&pos=2. Shukburgh Ashby, a member of the 'senior line' of the Leicestershire Ashby family, was a direct descendant of Ambassador William Ashby's first cousin, Barbara Ashby.

[19] The Ashbys quartered their arms with those of Zouch until the early sixteenth century.

[20] Benjamin Thompson and John Watts, eds., *Political Society in Later Medieval England: A Festschrift for Christine Carpenter* (Suffolk 2015), 70.

[21] *Calendar of Close Rolls*, 14 Edward III, AS 1327–1330, pp 77–8.

[22] Ibid, p. 120.

[23] CPR, 1494–1509, p. 646; Statutes, iii. 84, 115, 169; LP Hen. VIII, i–viii, x, xiii–xv; *Trans. Leics. Arch. Soc.* xvii. 79.

[24] Arthur Collins, *The Peerage of England* (London 1756) 625.

[25] There are discrepancies between the Ashby of Loseby genealogies in *Camden's Visitation of The County of Leicester in the year 1619* (p. 14) and Nichol's *The History and Antiquities of the County of Leicester*, published in 1795. The Camden pedigree is confirmed by the 1543 will of William Ashby of Loseby.

[26] MS, C23, Herald's College, in Arthur Staunton Larken and Arthur Roland Madson, *Lincolnshire Pedigrees*, (London 1902), v. I, 108.

[27] The site of the original manor house, on Main Street, Wymondham, was excavated in 2007 by CAM ARC (Cambridgeshire County Council).

[28] PCC 17, 28 Spert, 72; F. A. Greenhill, *Incised Slabs of Leics. and Rutland* (Leicestershire Archaeological and Historical Society, 1958), 118.

[29] Penbury v Assheby. Records of Equity Side: the Six Clerks, C 1 – Court of Chancery: Six Clerks Office: Early Proceedings, Richard II to Philip and Mary, National Archives, ref. C 1 / 1150 / 37. The elder William Ashby left 500 marks (equivalent to £225,000 in 2022) to his then unmarried daughter, Elizabeth, probably as a dowry to attract a suitable husband.

[30] Grant: George Rithe and Thomas Grantham of Lincoln's Inn, Middlesex, esq. Ref. 44'28 / 149, Leicestershire, Leicester and Rutland, Record Office. These former monastery properties were among those surveyed by Everard Ashby's father, William Ashby.

[31] https://premium.weatherweb.net/weather-in-history-1500-to-1599-ad/ .

[32] Nigel Ramsay quoted https://folgerpedia.folger.edu/Symbols_of_Honor:_Heraldry_and_Family_History_in_Shakespeare%27s_England .

[33] Lay Subsidy 183/26. Poll Tax. 1377. Quenby. Chief Justice Sir Edward Coke (1552–1634) defined 'gentlemen' as those who bore 'coat armour'.

[34] George Nicholls, *A History of the English Poor Law* (London 1854) Vol III, p. 1, 290–4.

[35] Robert Hutchinson, *Elizabeth's Spymaster: Francis Walsingham and the secret war that saved England* (London 2007), 27.

[36] 7 May 1583, court, Manners to Rutland: 'Her Majesty passes over the offence taken with Mr Sidney concerning his marriage'. Sir Philip Sidney (1554–1586), son of Sir Henry Sidney and nephew of the Earl of Leicester, married Frances Walsingham (c.1567–1632), daughter of Sir Francis Walsingham. The Queen became godmother to Sidney's daughter (November 1585).

**Part One – Early Life**

**Chapter 1. Education**

[1] William Ashby's birth year is extrapolated from his matriculation at Cambridge University in 1551. The usual age for new students was fifteen.

[2] 6 March 1536, 427. Dr. Ortiz to the Empress, 'Henry VIII: March 1536, 1–10', in *Letters and Papers, Foreign and Domestic, Henry VIII, Volume 10, January-June 1536*, ed. James Gairdner (London, 1887), pp. 161–81.

[3] Chapuys to Charles V, 21 January 1536, and Di Mons. di Faenza de 26, 27, 28, 'Letters and Papers, Foreign and Domestic, Henry VIII', Vols 10 and 11, January–December 1536.

[4] Benjamin Kaplan, 'Remnants of the Papal Yoke', *Sixteenth Century Journal*, XXVI, 1992, 653.

[5] John Foxe, *The Actes and Monuments* Cattley, S., Ed., (1563; repr. London, 1839). 166, https://www.exclassics.com/foxe/foxe167.htm, accessed 2 January 2020.

[6] John Stowe, *Annals of England to 1603*, 971.https://archive.org/stream/annalsofenglandt00stow#page/n987/mode/1up accessed 2 January 2020.

[7] John Foxe, *The Actes and Monuments* Cattley, S., Ed., (1563; repr. London, 1839). 222, Exclassics.com. Accessed 2 January 2020.

[8] Ibid.

[9] Bradgate, a Leicestershire prodigy house built by Thomas Grey, 2nd Marquis of Dorset, circa 1520, was one of the earliest unfortified mansions in England and among the first since Roman times to be built of brick.

[10] Alexandra Pickstone et al, *A Medieval Manor at Main Street, Wymondham, Leicestershire* – Post-Excavation Assessment and Updated Project Design (Oxford Archaeology East 2008), Report Number 1024.

[11] John Jortin, *The Life of Erasmus* (London 1758), 76.

[12] William Hoskins, 'The Leicestershire Farmer in the sixteenth Century,' (*Leicestershire Archaeological Society*, v 22, 1941–1942) 237, fn 3.

[13] William Ashby senior left twenty ewes and twenty lambs to his granddaughter Elizabeth Ashby, daughter of Everard Ashby, but nothing to his grandsons Francis and William. Elizabeth became the mother of Sir Robert Naunton.

[14] Barbara Tuchman, *A Distant Mirror: The Calamitous fourteenth Century* (New York 1978), 108.

[15] William Fletcher, *Leicestershire Pedigrees and Royal Descents* (London 1887), 113.

[16] https://premium.weatherweb.net/weather-in-history-1500-to-1599-ad/

[17] John Nichols, *The history and antiquities of the county of Leicester* (London 1795–1811) v.2 pt.1., 405.

[18] Eric Acheson, *A Gentry Community: Leicestershire in the Fifteenth Century, c.1422–c.1485* (Cambridge 1992), 177.

[19] 'The Growth of Literacy in Western Europe from 1500 to 1800' (posted on February 18, 2018), https://brewminate.com/the-growth-of-literacy-in-western-europe-from-1500-to-1800/ accessed 16 Dec. 2019).

[20] Gulson's son, William junior, matriculated at Queen's, Cambridge, in 1561, and succeeded his father as rector of Wydmonham in 1584.

[21] Joyce Ashby of Loseby, William's great-aunt, married Geoffrey Sherrard of Stapleford, ancestor of the Earls of Harborough.

[22] Robert Hutchinson, *The Last Days of Henry VIII* (London 2005), Fn 62.

[23] George Ashby (c. 1534–1618) was the son of William Ashby's first cousin, Barbara Ashby (1508–1598), who married Robert Ashby and reunited the Ashbys of Quenby and Loseby. George Ashby matriculated as a pensioner at Trinity College during Easter Term, 1550. He was High Sheriff of Leicestershire in 1601.

[24] Eamon Duffy, *The Church of Mary Tudor* (Aldershot 2006), 47.

[25] Charles Cooper, *Annals of Cambridge* (Cambridge 1842), 58.

[26] John Guy, *Tudor England* (Oxford 1988), 204.

[27] National Archives, Will of William Assheby of Lowesby, Leicestershire, Reference: PROB 11/29/498.

[28] Evidently, the Everard Ashby family moved to Coston after Maurice Berkeley reached his majority and inherited Wydmondham.

[29] Thomas Fuller, *The History of the University of Cambridge, and of Waltham Abbey* (London 1840), 187.

[30] Hastings Robinson, *Original Letters Relative to the English Reformation*, 727. The boys were nephews by marriage of Henry Grey, who was awarded their title after their deaths.

[31] The disease was called the 'English Sweat' as it was commonly believed to infect only the English nationality, attributed to the '… peculiar disposition in the constitution of the English …', either because of 'their peculiar diet, their use of malt liquor, and their manner of living; or from the peculiar disposition of the English air, or from both'. Mr. Kimber, *The History of England* (London 1767) v. 5, 151–2.

[32] In 1548 displaced peasants in Hertfordshire revolted after Sir William Cavendish obtained a royal warrant allowing him to enclose a large area of common land where he planned to farm rabbits for fur. Two thousand of Cavendish's rabbits were killed and their burrows blown up with gunpowder.

[33] Guy, *Tudor England*, 208.

[34] Cliff Davies, 'Slavery and Protector Somerset; The Vagrancy Act of 1547', *The Economic History Review*, vol. 19, no. 3, 1966, pp. 533–49. JSTOR, www.jstor.org/stable/2593162, 534.

[35] Charles Cooper, *Annals of Cambridge*, 52–3.

[36] Harry Porter, *Reformation and reaction in Tudor Cambridge* (Cambridge 1958), 52–3.

[37] Sermon by Thomas Lever, 13 December 1550, in Charles Henry Cooper, *Annals of Cambridge* (Cambridge 1842), 53.

[38] Thomas Walker, *Peterhouse*, (London 1906), 66.

[39] Ibid.

[40] Ibid. 23.

[41] Ibid. 69.

[42] Ibid.

[43] Thomas Walker, *A Biographical Register of Peterhouse Men* (Cambridge 1927), 170–1, 230–1.

[44] In 1567 William Ashby received leases of some value in Leicestershire and Yorkshire from the Crown in compensation for a debt of over £240 owed to his late father by the attainted Duke of Suffolk. https://www.historyofparliamentonline.org/volume/1558–1603/member/ashby-william-1593.

[45] George Cunningham, ed., *Lives of Eminent and Illustrious Englishmen* (Glasgow 1837), 207.

[46] Thomas Walker, *Peterhouse*, 72.

47 Ibid.

48 Information from Dr. Roger Lovatt, Emeritus Fellow and Archivist, Peterhouse College, Cambridge, 20 November 2019.

49 John Lamb, *A collection of letters, statutes, and other documents from the ms. Library of Corp. Christ. Coll., illustrative of the history of the University of Cambridge, during the period of the Reformation, from A.D. MD., to A.D. MDLXXII* (London 1838), 124–5.

50 In mid-sixteenth century academia, 'perspective' meant a specific point of view in understanding or judging things or events, esp. one that shows them in their true relations to one another. Roughly equivalent to the modern subject of Logic.

51 For example 11 August 1589, William Ashby to Burghley, 175 CSP-S.

52 *British History Online* http://www.british-history.ac.uk/vch/cambs/vol3, fn. 96 and 97 [accessed 15 December 2019].

53 Charles Cooper, *Annals of Cambridge*, 68.

54 Ibid.

55 *The Letany and Sufrages, The Book of Common Prayer*, 1549. http://justus. anglican.org/resources/bcp/1549/Litany_1549.htm accessed 10 February 2020.

56 Thomas Walker, *Peterhouse*, 20.

57 Ibid 66–8.

58 Ibid.

59 Ibid. 55.

60 Ibid. 88.

61 https://en.wikisource.org/wiki/Digby,_Everard_(fl.1590)_(DNB00). Accessed 2 January 2020.

62 Steven Overman, 'Sporting and Recreational Activities of Students in the Medieval Universities', *Physical Education* Vol. 1, No. 6, 1999, 28. http://facta. junis.ni.ac.rs/pe/pe99/pe99–03.pdf accessed 03 January 2020.

63 John Roach, ed., *A History of the County of Cambridge and the Isle of Ely: Volume 3, the City and University of Cambridge*, (London, 1959), British History Online http://www.british-history.ac.uk/vch/cambs/vol3 [accessed 15 December 2019].

64 Charles Cooper, *Annals of Cambridge*, 68.

[65] Leanda de Lisle, *The Sisters Who Would Be Queen: Mary, Katherine, and Lady Jane Grey: A Tudor Tragedy* (New York 2009), 110.

[66] Gerald Bray, ed., *Documents of the English Reformation 1526–1701* (Cambridge 1994), 284.

## Chapter 2. Exile

[1] Harry Porter, *Reformation and reaction in Tudor Cambridge* (Cambridge 1958), 75.

[2] Jane was Lady Jane Dudley as a result of her recent marriage to Lord Guildford Dudley.

[3] Harry Porter, *Reformation and reaction in Tudor Cambridge*, 75.

[4] Sources: 'Offering Freedom of Conscience, Prohibiting Religious Controversy, Unlicensed Plays, and Printing', 18 August 1553 in *Tudor Royal Proclamations*, Hughes and Lakin, eds., 3:5–8. *Myth of Bloody Mary* by Linda Porter and Mary Tudor by Anna Whitelock.

[5] The Queen to Bishop Gardyner, Chancellor of the University of Cambridge, and others. Commands that the ancient statutes, foundations, and ordinances of the University be inviolably kept and observed. 20 August 1553. 'Queen Mary – Volume 1: August 1553', in *Calendar of State Papers Domestic*: Edward VI, Mary and Elizabeth, 1547–1580, ed. Robert Lemon (London, 1856), pp. 54–5. British History Online http://www.british-history.ac.uk/cal-state-papers/domestic/edw-eliz/1547–80/pp54–55 [accessed 20 December 2019.]

[6] Thomas Fuller, *Fuller's History of the University of* Cambridge (Cambridge 1840), 251.

[7] Charles Cooper, *Annals of Cambridge,* 80–1.

[8] Ibid, 76–7.

[9] Sidney Lee, *Dictionary of National Biography*, Perne, Andrew 1885–1900, Vol 45, https://en.wikisource.org/wiki/Perne,_Andrew_(DNB00) Accessed 06 January 2020.

[10] Charles Cooper, *Annals of Cambridge,* 84.

[11] Harry Porter, *Reformation and Reaction in Tudor Cambridge* (Cambridge 2015), 76.

[12] Christina Garrett, *The Marian Exiles, a study in the origins of Elizabethan Puritanism* (Cambridge 1936), 3.

[13] James Muller, ed., *The Letters of Stephen Gardiner* (Cambridge 2013), 168.

[14] Richard Baker, Thomas Clarges, and Edward Phillips, *A chronicle of the kings of England: From the time of the Romans government, unto the death of King James*, etc., 325.

[15] John Lamb, *A Collection of Letters, Statutes, and Other Documents from the Manuscript Library of Corpus Christi College: Illustrative of the History of the University of Cambridge* (London 1838),170–1.

[16] Thomas Walker, *A Biographical Register of Peterhouse Men* (Cambridge 1927), 170. On 1 July 1555 Francis Ashby paid £3 for special admission to the Inner Temple and was 'pardoned for all offenses'

[17] Allen Hinds, *The Making of the England of Elizabeth* (New York 1895) 75–6

[18] Harry Porter, *Reformation and Reaction in Tudor Cambridge* (Cambridge 2015), 78. Magdalene was the sole exception.

[19] Ibid.

[20] Thomas Walker, *A Biographical Register of Peterhouse Men*, 170.

[21] Christina Garrett, *The Marian exiles*, 33.

[22] Ibid.

[23] Clare Howard, *English Travellers of the Renaissance* (Project Gutenberg 2004). https://www.gutenberg.org/files/13403/13403-h/13403-h.htm#CHAPTER_I accessed 20 January 2020.

[24] Sir Thomas Bodley, *The Life of Sir Thomas Bodley, Written by Himself* (Chicago 1906), 47.

[25] Ibid, 7–8.

[26] Ibid.

[27] Information from Jacqueline Cox, Cambridge University archives, 13 January 2020. The attrition was so severe that in 1557, the year prior to Mary's death, only 59 students were enrolled throughout the university.

[28] Some sources state that Walsingham matriculated as a Scholar. See Jonathan Woolfson, *Padua and the Tudors: English Students in Italy, 1485–1603* (Cambridge 1998), 280.

[29] Robert Hutchinson, *Elizabeth's Spymaster* (London 2011), 27–8

[30] Ibid.

[31] Joseph Foster, ed, *The Register of Admissions to Gray's Inn, 1521–1889* (London 1889) Folio 490, 72.

[32] Christina Garrett, *The Marian Exiles*, 68.

[33] The strappado (corda) was a form of torture in which the victim's hands were tied behind the back and suspended by a rope attached to the wrists, usually causing the shoulders to dislocate.

[34] Thomas Nashe, *The Unfortunate Traveller or The Life of Jack Wilton. Qui audiunt audita dicunt.* London. Printed by T. Scarlet for C. Burby, & are to be sold at his shop adjoining to the Exchange. 1594. (Modern spelling edition by Nina Green, London 2002), 44.

[35] Thomas Walker, *A Biographical Register of Peterhouse Men*, 170.

[36] Christina Garrett, *The Marian Exiles*, 33.

[37] Linda Taber, 'Religious Dissent within the Parlement of Paris in the Mid-Sixteenth Century: A Reassessment' *French Historical Studies 16.3* (Spring 1990: 684–99), 685.

[38] Nancy Roelke, *One King, One Faith: The Parlement of Paris and the Religious Reformations of the Sixteenth Century* (Berkeley and Los Angeles, 1996), 231.

[39] Allen Hinds, *The Making of the England of Elizabeth*, 73.

[40] Ibid, 78.

[41] Ibid, 73–6. On 7 June 1557 Mary finally declared war on France.

[42] Nicholas Wotton had previously served as resident ambassador in Paris during the reign of Edward VI.

[43] Nicholas Wotton to the Council, 9 January 1555, 46–7. CSP-F, Mary, 1553–1558.

[44] https://specialcollections-blog.lib.cam.ac.uk/?p=15576. Accessed 31 January 2020.

[45] Thomas Walker, *A Biographical Register of Peterhouse Men*, 170, quoting Latin original in MS UA Grace Book Delta, 000-00086-B, 194.

## Chapter 3. Return to an unhappy land

[1] Richard Baker, Thomas Clarges, and Edward Phillips, *A chronicle of the kings of England: From the time of the Romans government, unto the death of King James, etc.* (London 1684), 325–6

[2] William Hoskins, 'Harvest Fluctuations and English Economic History, 1480–1619', *The Agricultural History Review*, Vol. 12, No. 1 (1964), 36.

[3] Ibid.

[4] Richard Baker, Thomas Clarges, and Edward Phillips, *A chronicle of the kings of England: From the time of the Romans government, unto the death of King James, etc.*, 326.

[5] John Moore, 'Demographic Dimensions of the Mid-Tudor Crisis', *The Sixteenth Century Journal*, Vol. 41, No. 4 (Winter 2010), 1039, 1040, 1060.

[6] William Douthwaite, *Gray's Inn, Its History & Association* (London 1886), xii.

[7] Equivalent to a modern moot court, a mock court at which law students argue imaginary cases for practice.

[8] John Stow, *A Survey of London, Written in the year 1598 by John Stow* (London 1842), 29–30.

[9] Joseph Foster, ed., *The Register of Admissions to Gray's Inn, 1521–1889* (London 1889), Folio 512, 26.

[10] William Douthwaite, *Gray's Inn*, xxi.

[11] Bartholomew Traheron, *A Warning to England to Repent, and to tvrne to God from idolatrie and poperie by the terrible exemple of Calace* (Wesel? 1558), 4.

[12] John Moore, 'Jack Fisher's "Flu": A Visitation Revisited', *The Economic History Review*, New Series, Vol. 46, No. 2 (May, 1993), 280.

[13] John Foxe, *The Actes and Monuments* Cattley, S., Ed., (1563; repr. London, 1839), 264.

[14] John Foxe, *The Actes and Monuments* Cattley, S., Ed., (1563; repr. London, 1839), 344.

[15] Ibid.

[16] Reginald Fletcher, *The Reformation and the Inns of Court* (London 1903), 7–8.

[17] Will of William Ashby of Clerkenwell, The National Archives' reference PROB 11/82/616.

[18] William Douthwaite, *Gray's Inn*, 28.

[19] Ibid, 29.

[20] Shoe Lane, or Shoe Alley as it was also called in the sixteenth century, was outside the city wall, in the ward of Faringdon Without. It ran north-south, parallel to the Fleet River.

[21] William Douthwaite, *Gray's Inn*, xii.

[22] Ibid, xix.

[23] Ibid, 98.

[24] Benchers, or Masters of the Bench, were senior members, often judges, who usually held their elective office for life.

[25] William Douthwaite, *Gray's Inn, Its History and Association* (London 1886), 90.

[26] Ibid.

[27] Ibid, 89.

[28] Overly bearded students must have been considered a serious problem, as 40 shillings (£477 in 2022 pounds sterling) was as much as a skilled tradesman could earn in two months, or the price of a good Leicestershire cow.

[29] Ibid.

[30] William Douthwaite, *Gray's Inn*, 97.

[31] Ibid.

[32] Henry Milman, *Annals of St. Paul's* (London 1868), 142.

[33] James Marusek, *A Chronological Listing of Early Weather Events*, https://wattsupwiththat.files.wordpress.com/2011/09/weather1.pdf, 138, accessed 19 February 2020.

[34] Richard Baker, Thomas Clarges, and Edward Phillips, (1684). *A chronicle of the kings of England: From the time of the Romans government, unto the death of King James, etc.* (London 1684), 326.

[35] Amy Blakeway, 'The Anglo-Scottish War of 1558 and the Scottish Reformation', *History, The Journal of the Historical Association*, Vol. 102, Issue 350 (April 2017), 201–24.

[36] Armigal Waad (c. 1510–1568), a former Privy Council clerk, quoted in P. Williams, *The Latter Tudors, England 1547–1603* (Oxford 1995), 229. See also Robert Bucholz and Newton Key, *Early Modern England 1485–1714: A Narrative History (Hoboken 2003)*, 121.

[37] Charles Cooper, *Annals of Cambridge*, 148.

[38] Ibid, 167.

[39] Thomas Walker, *Peterhouse*, 230–1.

[40] Joseph Foster, ed., *Alumni Oxonienses 1500–1714*, (Oxford, 1891), British History Online http://www.british-history.ac.uk/alumni-oxon/1500–1714 [accessed 29 February 2020].

[41] Information from Flora Chatt, Archives Assistant, Oxford University Archives, Bodleian Library, Oxford. 26 November 2019.

[42] Public Record Office, *Calendar of the patent rolls preserved in the Public Record Office: Elizabeth* [I]. (London 1939) (21), 8.

[43] Derek Charman, 'Leicester in 1525', Leicestershire Archaeological Society, 21. The *Valor Ecclesiasticus* was a survey of church finances in England, Wales and English controlled parts of Ireland made in 1535 on the orders of Henry VIII. It was probably not a coincidence that the Bishop's Manor was one of the church properties surveyed by William Ashby senior as one of the Leicestershire commissioners.

[44] Public Record Office, *Calendar of the patent rolls preserved in the Public Record Office: Elizabeth* [I]. (London 1939) (21), 8.

## Part Two – On Her Majesty's Service
### Chapter 4. Walsingham's intelligencer

[1] Robert Hutchinson, *Elizabeth's Spymaster* (London 2996), 33–4.

[2] John Cooper, *The Queen's Agent* (London 2011), 56–60.

[3] Henry Chadwick, *Atlas of the Christian Church* (London 1987), 113.

[4] Bernardo de Mendoza to Zayas, 13 June 1578, 512, *Calendar of letters and state papers relating to English affairs: preserved principally in the Archives of Simancas: Elizabeth, 1568–1579*, Martin A. S. Hume. (London 1894), 595. Hereafter Simancas.

[5] University graduates, such as Walsingham before his knighthood, were addressed as 'Mr'.

[6] References to the Duke of Anjou and the Duke of Alençon often cause confusion. Prior to his accession to the French throne in May 1574, Henri III was styled (among other royal titles) as The Duke of Anjou. Subsequently, his younger brother Francis, Duke of Alençon, as heir to the throne, became Duke of Alençon and Anjou. Both were considered as potential consorts for Queen Elizabeth, with Francis the more serious suitor. Francis was often referred to by Elizabeth, Walsingham and others as 'Monsieur'.

[7] Francois Le Roi, Seigneur de Chavigny.

[8] Walsingham to Lord Burghley, St. Cloud, 11 March 1572 (erroneously catalogued as 1572 when the actual year was 1573), CSP-F, 821.

[9] Ashby did not have a command of Spanish.

[10] Including Sir Nicholas Throckmorton, father of Ashby's close friend, and Walsingham's protégé, Arthur Throckmorton.

[11] The first recorded use of the term 'Intelligencer' was in the 1570s but was probably used earlier.

[12] Bernardino de Mendoza to the King, 19 August 1583, 355 Simancas, 499.

[13] Secret Service Money, A minute of receipts and payments by Sir Valentine Browne, 25 September 1523, CSP-F, 571.

[14] Isaac D'Israeli, *Curiosities of Literature* Second Series vol. 2 (London 1849), 87.

[15] Sir Francis Walsingham and Charles Trice Martin. *Journal of Sir Francis Walsingham: From Dec. 1570 to April 1583.* (London 1870), 71, 77, 82.

[16] The Queen to the Lords of the Secret Council of Scotland, 30 June 1567, CSP-F, 1365.

[17] Frederick Inderwick, ed., *A Calendar of the Inner Temple Records*, vol II (London 1896), 284.

[18] In 1574, fifteen benchers, twenty-three barristers and 151 resident students lived in the Inner Temple.

[19] De Mendoza to Zayas, 15 January 1579, 543 Simancas, 629–30

[20] Letters and Papers, Foreign and Domestic, Henry VIII, Volume 20 Part 2, August-December 1545, https://www.british-history.ac.uk/letters-papers-hen8/vol20/no2, accessed 10 March 2020.

[21] Stephen Budiansky, *Her Majesty's Spymaster: Elizabeth I, Sir Francis Walsingham, and the Birth of Modern Espionage* (London 2006),53, quoting William Camden.

[22] Zurich Letters (ser. 2) (Parker Soc.), ii. 286–87.

[23] La Mothe to Henri III, 17 June 1575, https://folgerpedia.folger.edu/mediawiki/media/images_pedia_folgerpedia_mw/2/20/ECDbD_1575.pdf, Accessed 20 March 2020.

[24] Ibid, 285.

[25] M. de Mauvissière to Walsingham, London 24 Jan. 1578, 610 CSP-F.

[26] Sir Martin Frobisher (d. 1594) led several expeditionary voyages to what is now Canada and served with distinction during the Armada battles in the English Channel.

[27] Miscellaneous, CSP-D, March 1578, 586–7.

[28] Geoffrey Elton, *The Tudor Constitution, Documents and Commentary*, (London 1982), 126, citing Robert Beale.

[29] Cecil, created 1st Baron Burghley in 1571, was Secretary of State 1550–1553 and 1558–1572.

[30] Robert Hutchinson, *Elizabeth's Spymaster* (London 2996), 33–4.

[31] Daniel Rogers to Walsingham, 20 July 1577, CSP-F, 38.

[32] Present day Belgium, the Netherlands, Luxembourg and parts of France and Germany.

[33] Peter Arnade, *Beggars, iconoclasts, and civic patriots: the political culture of the Dutch Revolt* (Ithaca 2008), 232–3.

[34] Edward Chester to Lord Burghley, 20 July 1576, CSP-F, 852.

[35] The Prince of Orange to the Queen, 5 Sept. 1576, CSP-F, 900.

[36] Charles Wilson, *Queen Elizabeth and the Revolt of the Netherlands* (London 1979), 39.

[37] Preface to CSP-F, Vol. 11, 1575–1577.

[38] News from Spain, 6 January 1577, 1165 Simancas.

[39] Walsingham to Randolph, Antwerp, 29 July 1578, CSP-F, 121.

[40] Daniel Rogers to Walsingham, 20 July 1577, CSP-F, 38.

[41] The Queen to the Princes of Germany, 25 May 1578, CSP-F, 911.

[42] Andrew Lang, *A History of Scotland from the Roman Occupation*, vol. 2 (Edinburgh 1907) 246.

[43] Frederic Ruissengen to Walsingham, Frankfurt, 10 April 1577, 1380, CSP-F.

[44] Frederic Ruissingen to Davison, The Hague, 18 December 1584, 196.

[45] Frederic Ruissingen to Lord Burghley, London 22 September 1575 CSP-F, 142.

[46] Daniel Rogers to Burghley and Walsingham, Bruges, 13 March 1575, CSP-F, 664.

[47] Dr. Thomas Wilson to Walsingham, 3 December 1576, CSP-F, 1050.

[48] Reasons for the Arrest of M. de Ruissinghen, 17 January 1577, 1186 CSP-F, 1202.

[49] 'Farther fetch' – A stratagem or trick.

[50] Dr. Thomas Wilson to Walsingham, 10 February 1577, CSP-F 1259.

[51] Albert Schmidt, 'Thomas Wilson, Tudor Scholar-Statesman', *Huntington Library Quarterly*, Vol. 20, No. 3 (May, 1957), pp. 205–18.

[52] http://www.histparl.ac.uk/volume/1558–1603/member/wilson-thomas-1523-81

Accessed 28 March 2020.

[53] Dr. Thomas Wilson to Walsingham, 6 May 1577, CSP-F, 1423.

[54] Articles from Don John to the Estates, 6–13 July 1577, 11.

[55] Wilson to Walsingham, Antwerp, 7 July 1577., CSP-F, 14.

[56] Dr. Thomas Wilson to the Queen, 11 June 1577, CSP-F, 1470.

[57] Ibid.

[58] Daniel Rogers to Walsingham, 20 July 1577, CSP-F, 38.

[59] John Guy, *Tudor England* (Oxford 1988), 283.

[60] Walsingham to Davison, 20 March 1577, CSP-F, 714.

[61] John Guy, *Tudor England*, 283.

[62] Walsingham to Davison, London, 5 April 1578, CSP-F, 770.

**Chapter 5. The Queen's vacillation**

[1] News of the Battle of Gemblours, 4 February 1578, CSP-F, 625.

[2] Ibid.

[3] Laurence Tomson to Thomas Davison, Hampton Court, 2 February 1578, CSP-F, 622.

[4] Thomas Davison to Walsingham, 8 March 1578, CSP-F, 676.

[5] Ibid.

[6] Ibid

[7] Ibid.

[8] Notes on Low Country Matters, for the Council, 22 March 1578, CSP-F, 727.

[9] Bernardo de Mendoza to the King, 31 March 1578, 486 Simancas 485.

[10] Bernardo de Mendoza to the King, 19 March 1578, 483 Simancas.

[11] Bernardo de Mendoza to the King, 12 April 1578, Simancas, 487.

[12] Ibid.

[13] Notes on Low Country Matters, for the Council. Questions, 22 March 1578, CSP-F, 727.

[14] Ibid.

[15] Bernardo de Mendoza to the King, 5 May 1578, Simancas, 493.

[16] Ibid.

[17] Edmund Lodge, ed., *Illustrations of British History, Manners and Biography*, vol. II (London 1838), 97.

[18] Walsingham to Davison. May 11 1578, 854, CSP-F.

[19] Ibid.

[20] Simancas 483.

[21] Jayne Archer, Elizabeth Goldring and Sarah Knight, eds, *The Progresses, Pageants, and Entertainments of Queen Elizabeth I* (Oxford 2007), 135.

[22] Instructions given the 12th day of June, 1578 unto … the Lord Cobham … and Sir Francis Walsingham, sent to the States of the Low Countries, 12 July 1578, CSP-F, 17.

[23] Walsingham to Davison, 16 May 1578, CSP-F, 872.

[24] Daniel Rogers to Walsingham (?) May 1578, CSP-F, 927.

[25] Dr. Thomas Wilson to Davison, 5 June 1578, CSP-F, 6.

[26] Henry Cobham and Walsingham to Davison, 17 June 1578, CSP-F, 24.

## Chapter 6. Low Countries reconnaissance operation

[1] 'Jacks' were made of overlapping square plates of iron sewn within the inner and outer layers of a fabric doublet, covering the upper body and arms.

[2] Jacques Rossel to Walsingham, 16 November 1578, CSP-F, 380.

[3] Instructions given the 12th day of June, 1578 unto … the Lord Cobham … and Sir Francis Walsingham, sent to the States of the Low Countries, 12 July 1578, CSP-F, 17.

[4] Guildford Walsingham, who was aged about 20 in 1578, seems to have been included as a trainee intelligencer.

[5] Instructions to Certain Gentlemen Sent Abroad, (probably written 21 June 1578), CSP-F, 55.

[6] 'The Report of Henry Killigrew to the same instructions given him by Your Honours to be observed in his journey between Dunkirk and Antwerp', 'early in July' 1578, CSP-F, 58–9.

[7] Supporters of Don John.

[8] Report of Captains Cary and Malby, and Mr. Ashby, 'early in July' 1578, CSP-F, 60.

[9] Modern 's-Hertogenbosch.

[10] Report of Captains Cary and Molby, and Mr. Ashby, 'early in July' 1578, CSP-F, 60.

[11] Ibid.

[12] Dr. Thomas Wilson to Walsingham, 29 June 1578, Greenwich Palace, CSP-F, 49.

[13] With fair summer weather, a letter sent from Greenwich on 29 June should have been received in Antwerp by 5 July. The courier who carried Wilson's letter would have returned with the messages written by Walsingham and Cobham.

[14] Walsingham to Sir Walter Mildmay, 5 July 1578, CSP-F, 67.

[15] Walsingham to Lord Hunsdon, 5 July 1578, CSP-F, 66.

[16] Robert Bowes to Leicester, 23 July 1578, CSP-S, 304–5.

[17] Henry Cobham to Burghley, Antwerp, 12 July 1578, CSP-F, 76.

[18] Ibid, and Walsingham to Burghley, 14 July 1578, CSP-F, 81.

[19] Ibid.

[20] The Duke of Anjou to the States, 13 July 1578, CSP-F, 78.

[21] Walsingham to Burghley, 18 July 1578, CSP-F, 87.

[22] The Lords of the Council to Cobham and Walsingham, 18 July 1578, CSP-F, 91.

[23] Such 'plausible deniability' was to be a key feature of Ashby's diplomacy in Scotland a decade later.

[24] The Lords of the Council to Cobham and Walsingham, 18 July 1578, CSP-F, 91.

[25] Burghley to Henry Cobham and Walsingham, 18 July 1578, CSP-F, 93.

[26] Burghley to Henry Cobham and Walsingham, 18 July 1578, CSP-F, 93.

[27] Elizabeth, her retainers and ministers were then at Havering Palace in Essex, where she held court during her 'summer progress' to Great Yarmouth, Norfolk.

[28] Burghley to Henry Cobham and Walsingham, 18 July 1578.

[29] Hatton was Vice-Chamberlain and a Privy Councillor.

[30] Edmund Tremayne to Walsingham, 20 July 1578, CSP-F, 102. Tremayne was a clerk of the Privy Council at this time.

[31] Leicester to Walsingham, 29 July 1578, CSP-F, 103.

[32] Ibid.

[33] Ibid.

[34] Bernardino de Mendoza to Zayas, 8 September 1578, 524 Simancas, 609.

[35] Bernardino de Mendoza to Zayas, London, 19th July 1578. 519 Simancas, 605.

[36] With thanks to Professor John Guy, author of *Elizabeth: The Forgotten Years* (London 2016).

## Chapter 7. Purgatory in the Low Countries

[1] William Davison to Dr. Thomas Wilson, 20 July 1578, CSP-F, 98.

[2] The Estates to the Duke of Alenon (sic), Antwerp, 20 July 1578, CSP-F, 99.

[3] Walsingham to Burghley, 29 July 1578, Antwerp, CSP-F, 119.

[4] Ibid.

[5] Dr. Thomas Wilson to Walsingham, 21 July 1578, CSP-F, 106.

[6] Walsingham to Burghley, 29 July 1578, Antwerp, CSP-F, 119.

[7] The Progresses, Pageants, and Entertainments of Queen Elizabeth I, 135.

[8] Walsingham to Randolph, 29 July 1578, Antwerp, CSP-F, 121.

[9] Bernardino De Mendoza to the King, 30th March 1586, Paris, 431 Simancas, 573.

[10] Sir Francis Walsingham to the Queen, 12 September 1581, Paris, Sir Nicholas Harris Nicolas. *Memoirs of the Life And Times of Sir Christopher Hatton, K. G.: Vice-chamberlain And Lord Chancellor to Queen Elizabeth. Including His Correspondence With the Queen And Other Distinguished Persons.* (London 1847), 195.

[11] Ibid. See also Sir Dudly Digges, ed., *The Compleat Ambassador or two Treaties of the Intended Marriage of Queen Elizabeth* (London 1655), 426–7.

[12] James Ferguson, ed., *Papers Illustrating the History of the Scots Brigade in the service of the United Netherlands, 1572–1782, Vol. 1, 1572–1697*, Scottish History Society volumes, Series 1, Volumes 32, 35 and 38 (Edinburgh 1899), 48–51.

[13] Bernardino De Mendoza to the King, 8 September 1578, London, Simancas 525.

[14] Burghley to Henry Cobham and Walsingham, 29 July 1578, CSP-F, 123.

[15] Leicester to Walsingham, 7 August 1578, CSP-F, 149.

[16] Burghley to Walsingham, 8 August 1578, CSP-F, 178.

[17] Burghley to the Ambassadors, 9 August 1578, CSP-F, 161.

[18] Ibid.

[19] The Queen to the Ambassadors, 9 August 1578, Bury, CSP-F, 159.

[20] Susan Doran, *Monarchy and Matrimony: The Courtships of Elizabeth I* (London 1996), 149.

[21] Bernardino De Mendoza to Zayas, 14 August 1578, London, Simancas, 521.

[22] Ibid.

[23] Treaty between Bussy, acting as deputy for the Duke of Anjou … and the Estates, 13 August 1578, CSP-F, 163.

[24] Henry Cobham did not accompany him, for reasons unknown.

[25] George Carey and Nicholas Malby having returned to England.

[26] Walsingham to Burghley, 17 August 1578, Antwerp, CSP-F, 170.

[27] Walsingham to Gastel, 26 August 1578, Louvain, CSP-F, 191.

[28] The substance of the speech sent to Don John by Jean Gastel, 'about August 25', CSP-F, 185. Jean Marmier de Gastel was Don John's agent who met with the English ambassadors prior to their formal meeting with the Governor-General and conveyed their terms.

[29] Walsingham to Jean Gastel, 26 August 1578, Louvain, CSP-F, 191.

[30] William Davison to Wilson, 22 August 1578, CSP-F, 178.

[31] John Digges to Burghley, 4 September 1578, CSP-F, 227.

[32] Duke Casimir to the Queen, 6 September 1578, CSP-F, 231.

[33] Walsingham to Leicester, 2 September 1578, CSP-F, 217.

[34] Walsingham to Davison, 27 August 1578, Louvain, CSP-F, 195.

[35] The Ambassadors to the Lords of the Council, 27 August 1578, CSP-F, 194.

[36] Davison to Burghley, 1 September 1578, Antwerp, CSP-F, 211.

[37] Walsingham to Wilson, 2 September 1578, Antwerp, CSP-F, 213.

[38] Daniel Rogers to Walsingham, 15 September 1578, CSP-F, 254.

[39] Walsingham to Burghley, 2 September 1578, CSP-F, 215.

[40] Walsingham to Hatton, 2 September

[41] Leicester to Walsingham, 10 September 1578, CSP-F, 248.

[42] Walsingham to unknown recipient, early September 1578, CSP-F, 223.

[43] Walsingham to Sir Thomas Heneage, 2 September 1578, Antwerp, CSP-F, 221.

[44] Sir Harris Nicolas, Walsingham to Hatton, Antwerp, 29 July 1578, *Memoirs of the Life and Times of Sir Christopher Hatton, Vice-Chamberlain* (London 1847), 76.

[45] Burghley to Walsingham, 29 August 1578, CSP-F, 200.

[46] Walsingham to Burghley, 2 September 1578, CSP-F, 218.

[47] Walsingham to Burghley, 20 September 1578, CSP-F, 260.

[48] Possibly shingles.

[49] Davison to Burghley, 12 September 1578, CSP-F, 302.

[50] Walsingham to Burghley, 28 August 1578, Louvain, CSP-F, 196.

[51] Walsingham to Randolph, 29 July 1578, Antwerp, CSP-F, 121.

[52] Sir Francis Walsingham to Sir Christopher Hatton, 9 October 1578, Richmond, *Memoirs of the Life and Times of Sir Christopher Hatton*, 94.

## Chapter 8. Brigands on the Rhine

[1] Arthur Throckmorton, *The Diary of Sir Arthur Throckmorton*, 3 vols, held in the Hales Family Collection, Canterbury Cathedral Archives and Library, Ref. U85/38/14.

[2] Ashby to Walsingham, 1 August 1582, Augsburg, CSP-F, 660.

[3] Alfred Rowse, *Ralegh and the Throckmortons* (London 1962), 58.

[4] Both families had Burdett and Catesby antecedents, and convoluted connections via intermarriages.

[5] Alfred Rowse, *Ralegh and the Throckmortons*, 58.

[6] Ibid, 83.

[7] Ibid, 84.

[8] Alfred Rowse confused him with his uncle, Ludovico Castelvetro, the neo-classical scholar, who died in 1571.

[9] Henry Cobham to Walsingham, 4 October 1580, 448 CSP-F, 441–2.

[10] Eleanor Rosenberg, 'Giacopo Castelvetro: Italian Publisher in Elizabethan London and His Patrons', *Huntington Library Quarterly*, Vol. 6, No. 2 (Feb., 1943), 119–48.

[11] *Dictionary of National Biography*, 1885-1900, Vol. 43, https://en.wikisource.org/wiki/Dictionary_of_National_Biography,_1885-1900/Palavicino,_Horatio. Accessed 21 November 2020.

[12] Henry Cobham to Walsingham, 6 January 1581 and 13 March 1582, CSP-F, 5 and 607. Ashby's name was mis-transcribed as 'Mr. Ashle' and 'Mr. Ashley'.

[13] Alfred Rowse, *Ralegh and the Throckmortons*, 86.

[14] Ibid, 92.

[15] Published in Sir Dudly Digges (ed.), *The Compleat Ambassador or two Treaties of the Intended Marriage of Queen Elizabeth* (London 1655), 392; see also CSP-F 1581–1582, 293.

[16] Walsingham to Somers, 19 July 1581, CSP-F, 274.

[17] John Strype, *Annals of the Reformation and Establishment of Religion* ..., (Oxford 1824), Vol. V, 2–4.

[18] Robyn Adams, 'A Most Secret Service: William Herle and the Circulation of Intelligence' in Robyn Adams & Rosanna Cox, eds. *Diplomacy and Early Modern Culture* (London 2011), 63–81.

[19] Ashby to Walsingham, 1 August 1582, Augsburg, 660 CSP-F, 548. Ashby referred to Augsburg by the city's Roman name, Augusta.

[20] Ibid.

[21] Ashby to Walsingham, 3 July 1582, Augsburg, CSP-F, 646

[22] Henry Cobham to Walsingham, 11 September 1582, CSP-F 314. Scotland.

[23] David Gehring, ed., *Diplomatic Intelligence on the Holy Roman Empire and Denmark during the Reigns of Elizabeth I and James VI* (London 2016), 17.

[24] Antonio de Guaras to Zayas, 5 December 1574, Simancas Vol. II, 406, 490.

[25] Maarten Schenck van Nydeggen.

[26] Daniel Rogers to the Secretaries, last of Oct. 1580, CSP-F, 476

[27] Ibid.

[28] Bernardino de Mendoza to the King, 19 February 1582, London, Simancas, 216, 295–6.

[29] Daniel Rogers to the Secretaries, last of Oct. 1580, CSP-F, 476.

[30] Ashby to Walsingham. 1 August 1582, Augsburg, CSP-F, 660.

[31] George Gilpin, *Dictionary of National Biography*, https://en.wikisource.org/wiki/Index:Dictionary_of_National_Biography_volume_21.djvu, accessed 26 May 2020.

[32] William was the brother of Anne of Cleves, fourth wife of King Henry VIII.

[33] George Gilpin to Walsingham, 22 Aug. 1582, Augsburg, CSP-F, 667.

[34] William Ashby to Walsingham, 8 September 1582, Cologne, CSP-F, 316

[35] Ibid.

[36] Wallace MacCaffrey, *Queen Elizabeth and the Making of Policy, 1572–1588* (Princeton 1981), 237.

[37] Ibid.

[38] Martin Malia, *History's Locomotives: Revolutions and the Making of the Modern World* (New Haven 2006), 126.

[39] Daniel Rogers to Walsingham, 24 Oct 1582, CSP-F, 416.

[40] William, Duke of Cleves to the Queen, 13 June 1584, Dusseldorf, CSP-F, 657.

[41] Steven Le Sieur to Walsingham, Wesel, 27 September 1584, CSP-F, 80.

[42] Charles Maurice Davies, *The History of Holland and the Dutch Republic* (London 1851), 233.

[43] Henry Cobham to Walsingham, 11 Sept. 1582, CSP-F, 323.

[44] 'Petition of the Merchants Adventurers touching the slander of monopoly their traffic is charged withal'. 1582 (exact date unknown), CSP-F 550.

[45] Will of William Ashbye, The National Archives' reference PROB 11/83/154. As Ashby did not leave the house to his heirs, he probably leased it.

[46] 'Clerkenwell Green', in *Survey of London: Volume 46, South and East Clerkenwell*, ed. Philip Temple (London, 2008), pp. 86–114. British History Online http://www.british-history.ac.uk/survey-london/vol46/pp86-114 [accessed 1 June 2020].

[47] Now Turnmill Street.

[48] Walsingham to Archibald Douglas, 22 July 1588, 703 Salisbury, R. Cecil, et al., *Calendar of the Manuscripts of the Most Honourable the Marquess of Salisbury ... Preserved At Hatfield House, Hertfordshire* (London 1883), 339.

[49] John Lyly, *Euphues*, (London 1580), Title Page, http://www.luminarium.org/renlit/lylyadd.htm.

[50] Robert Hutchinson, *Elizabeth's Spymaster* (London 2006), 44.

## Part Three – Scotland
## Chapter 9. Anglo-Scottish animosity

[1] Timothy Ashby 'Walsingham and the Witch' in *History Scotland* Vol. 21 No. 5 September/October 2021.

[2] William Camden, *Britannia, or, A Chorographical description of the most flourishing kingdoms of England, Scotland and Ireland.* (London 1586), 114.

[3] Timothy Ashby 'Walsingham and the Witch' in *History Scotland* Vol. 21 No. 5 September/October 2021.

[4] Hunsdon to the Privy Council, 4 April 1581, 4 *Calendar of State Papers, Scotland* (CSP-S), 2-3.

[5] Robert Bowes and Joseph Stevenson. *The Correspondence of Robert Bowes of Aske, Esquire, the Ambassador of Queen Elizabeth In the Court of Scotland* (London, 1842), 160.

[6] Sir Nicholas Harris Nicolas, *Memoirs of the Life and Times of Sir Christopher Hatton, K. G.* (London, 1847) 67. See also Walsingham to Burghley, 2 September 1578, CSP-F, 215. See also Timothy Ashby 'Walsingham and the Witch' in *History Scotland* Vol. 21 No. 5 September/October 2021.

[7] Martin Sharp (ed.), *Archivo General de Simancas [Simancas]*. (189299). *Calendar of letters and state papers relating to English affairs [of the reign of Elizabeth] preserved principally in the archives of Simancas*, (London 1892), 429.

[8] Objections made against Lennox and Arran, 12 September 1583, 634 CSP-S, 610.

[9] Alan Stewart, *The Cradle King, A Life of James VI and I* (London 2003), 55.

[10] Timothy Ashby 'Walsingham and the Witch' in *History Scotland* Vol. 21 No. 5 September/October 2021.

[11] Bernardino De Mendoza to the King, 7 November 1581, Simancas, 158.

[12] Hunsdon to Walsingham, 5 June 1581, 29 CSP-S, 24.

[13] Hunsdon to Walsingham, 6 June 1581, 30 CSP-S, 26.

[14] Sir Henry Wodrington (Widdrington) letters, 15 May 1582, 142 CSP-S, 149.

[15] Charges Against Lennox, August 1582, 144 CSP-S, 151.

[16] Timothy Ashby 'Walsingham and the Witch' in *History Scotland* Vol. 21 No. 5 September/October 2021.

[17] The Privy Council to Hunsdon, 10 April 1581, 7 CSP-S, 4.

[18] Simancas, 429.

[19] Geriant Dyfnallt Owen (ed.), *Calendar of the manuscripts of the Marquis of Bath preserved at Longleat, Wiltshire* (London 1980) v, 39.

[20] David Calderwood, *The History of the Kirk of Scotland* (Edinburgh 1842–1849) iii, 576.

[21] Sir Henry Wodrington to [Walsingham], 19 July 1582, 135 CSP-S, 142.

[22] Steven Reid, 'Of Bairns and Bearded Men' in Miles Kerr-Peterson and Steven Reid (eds), *James VI and Noble Power in Scotland 1578-1603* (London, 2017), 46.

See also Timothy Ashby 'Walsingham and the Witch' in *History Scotland* Vol. 21 No. 5 September/October 2021.

[23] Ibid., p. 39.

[24] David Calderwood, *History of the Kirk of Scotland* (Edinburgh 1842–1849), iii, 637–8.

[25] Julian Goodare, 'The Debts of James VI of Scotland', *The Economic History Review*, 62, iv, (2009), 926–52, 930.

[26] In Scottish pounds, equal to around £11,350 English pounds, roughly £3 million in 2022.

[27] Steven Reid, 'Of Bairns and Bearded Men', 46.

[28] Statement of Offences Committed by Lennox, 17 September 1582, 173 CSP-S, 173.

[29] Robert Bowes to Burghley, 8 September 1582, 160, 174 CSP-S 161, 175.

[30] Timothy Ashby 'Walsingham and the Witch' in *History Scotland* Vol. 21 No. 5 September/October 2021.

[31] Steven Reid, 'Of Bairns and Bearded Men', 40.

[32] Sir George Carey to Elizabeth, 14 September 1582, 169 CSP-S, 170.

[33] Simancas, 317. See also Timothy Ashby 'Walsingham and the Witch' in *History Scotland* Vol. 21 No. 5 September/October 2021.

[34] Ibid., 438.

[35] Steven Reid, 'Of Bairns and Bearded Men', 40.

[36] Simancas, 444–5.

[37] Ibid., 436–7.

[38] The Colonel's and his relative's names were alternatively spelled 'Stewart' and 'Steward' in contemporary documents.

[39] Steven Reid, 'Of Bairns and Bearded Men', 40.

[40] Simancas, 400.

[41] Walsingham to Cobham, 31 August 1582, 298 CSP-F, 291.

[42] Money Sent to Scotland by the Queen of England, September 1582, 186 CSP-S, 184–5.

[43] The mark was 'money of account' worth 2/3 of a pound (13s 4d).

[44] Sir Francis Walsingham to Burghley, 29 January 1583, 33 CSP-D, 93.

[45] Keith Brown, 'A financial burden' & 'The Price of Friendship – The "Well Affected" and English Economic Clientage in Scotland before 1603,' in *Scotland and England 1286–1815*, Roger Mason (ed.) (Edinburgh 1987), 146–7.

[46] *Original Letters of Mr. John Colville 1582–1603*, (Edinburgh 1858), iv. Colville, a Scottish clergyman, judge, politician and author, was a supporter of the Earl of Gowrie and had taken part in the Ruthven Raid. One of Walsingham's chief spies in Scotland, he possibly spied for the French as well.

[47] Mr. John Colvile to Walsingham, May 1583, 451 CSP-S, 444.

[48] Earl of Leicester to Walsingham, 5 September 1582, 46 CSP-D, 69.

[49] Austin Lynn Martin, *Henry III and the Jesuit Politicians* (Genève 1973) 67.

[50] Simancas, 345.

[51] Ibid.

[52] Steven Reid, 'Of Bairns and Bearded Men', 39.

[53] *Letters of Queen Elizabeth And King James VI. of Scotland: Some of Them Printed From Originals In the Possession of the Rev. Edward Ryder, And Others From a MS. Which Formerly Belonged to Sir Peter Thompson, Kt.* (New York, 1968), 4–5.

[54] Concepcion Säenz-Cambra, *Scotland and Philip II, 1580–1598: Politics, Religion Diplomacy and Lobbying* (PhD thesis, University of Edinburgh 2003), xvi.

[55] Ibid. The Scottish commander told the Spanish that he would only give up Dumbarton to Lennox; after the latter's death, the Spanish and French suspended the 'enterprise'.

[56] Simancas, 351

[57] Austin Lynn Martin, *Henry II and the Jesuit Politicians*, 74.

[58] Ibid.

[59] Simancas, 345. See also Timothy Ashby 'Walsingham and the Witch' in *History Scotland* Vol. 21 No. 5 September/October 2021.

[60] Bertrand de Salignac Fenelon, seigneur de la Mothe (1523–1589). De la Mothe was a special envoy to Scotland and England from 1582–1583.

[61] Patrick Tytler, John Eadie, and Archibald Alison, *Tytler's History of Scotland: with illustrative notes from recently discovered State documents, and a continuation of the history, from the Union of the Crowns to the present time, including an account of the social and industrial progress of the people; also an essay on Scottish ecclesiastical history* Scotland (Glasgow, 1841–1843), viii, 154.

[62] *Letters of Queen Elizabeth And King James VI*, 46, 6.

[63] Simancas, 343.

[64] Ibid, 338.

[65] Ibid.

[66] Ibid.

[67] The Queen's erstwhile suitor, Francis, Duke of Anjou and Alençon.

[68] Simancas, 338.

[69] Ibid.

[70] *Letters of Queen Elizabeth And King James VI*, 7.

[71] Robert Bowes to Walsingham, 17 June 1583, 532 CSP-S, 506. See also Timothy Ashby 'Walsingham and the Witch' in *History Scotland* Vol. 21 No. 5 September/October 2021.

## Chapter 10. Walsingham's failed diplomatic mission

[1] Ibid, 545.

[2] Stewart was considered 'the principal instrument of the King's liberation', *Simancas*, 348.

[3] Robert Bowes to [Walsingham], 3 July 1583, 549 *CSP-S*, 522.

[4] Simancas, 349.

[5] *The Correspondence of Robert Bowes*, 494.

[6] Ibid., 509.

[7] James VI to Elizabeth, 2 July 1583, 548 CSP-S, 521.

[8] *The Correspondence of Robert Bowes*, 512.

[9] Robert Bowes to [Walsingham], 16 July 1583, 565 CSP-S, 540.

[10] [Walsingham] to Robert Bowes, 10 July 1583, 557 CSP-S, 531–2.

[11] Simancas, 355.

[12] Ibid. See also Timothy Ashby 'Walsingham and the Witch' in *History Scotland* Vol. 21 No. 5 September/October 2021.

[13] 'England Under the Tudors', Luminarium Encyclopedia Project, http://www.luminarium.org/encyclopedia/hunsdon1.htm, accessed 18 November 2019.

[14] Earl of Leicester to the Queen, July 1543, 46 CSP-D, 116.

[15] Simancas, 351.

[16] Elizabeth to James VI, 7 August 1583, 595 CSP-S, 577.

[17] The 'Master of Glamis', a murderer, proposed to King James that in return for clemency 'and other favours' he would invite the Ruthven lords to his house and 'cause them all to be apprehended and committed'. [Walsingham] to Robert Bowes, 12 June 1583, CSP-S, 497–8.

[18] Conyers Read, *Mr. Secretary Walsingham and the policy of Queen Elizabeth*, ii, 205.

[19] Timothy Ashby 'Walsingham and the Witch' in *History Scotland* Vol. 21 No. 5 September/October 2021.

[20] 4 October 1580, Cobham to Walsingham, 448 CSP-F, 441–2.

[21] Richard Douglas to Archibald Douglas, 10 July 1588, 692, *Calendar of the Manuscripts of the Most Honourable the Marquess of Salisbury*, v. III, 336–7.

[22] Instructions for Walsingham by Elizabeth, 3 August 1583, CSP-S, 572–3.

[23] Simancas, 355.

[24] For example, Nicholas Leclerc, French ambassador Castelnau's secretary, who provided copies of the ambassador's secret correspondence in the diplomatic pouch.

[25] James Melville wrote that Walsingham had 'viii score horse in train' which was probably an exaggeration as the Scots would have seen 160 armed Englishmen as a threat. Sir James Melville and Archibald Francis Steuart. *The Memoirs of Sir James Melville of Halhill, 1535–1617* (London 1929), 309.

[26] Ibid.

[27] [Walsingham] to Robert Bowes, 20 August 1583, 607 CSP-S, 589.

[28] Walsingham to Robert Bowes, 28 August 1583, 616 CSP-S, 594–5.

[29] Conyers Read, *Mr. Secretary Walsingham*, II, 209.

[30] Ibid., 31.

[31] Nicolas, *Memoirs of the Life and Times of Sir Christopher Hatton*, 340. Hatton was a favourite courtier of Elizabeth, a member of the Privy Council, and was named Lord Chancellor in 1587.

[32] Ibid., 339.

[33] Robert Stedall, *Survival of the Crown*, II, (Sussex 2014), II, 172.

[34] Walsingham to Mr. Robert Beale, 30 August 1583, 619 CSP-S, 596.

[35] *The Correspondence of Robert Bowes*, XIV, 532. See also Timothy Ashby 'Walsingham and the Witch' in *History Scotland* Vol. 21 No. 5 September/October 2021.

[36] Robert Bowes to Walsingham, 25 August 1583, 609 CSP-S, 591.

[37] Robert Bowes to Walsingham, 27 August 1583, 613 CSP-S, 593.

[38] Walsingham referred to Perth by its old name, St. Johnstone (St. John's Toun).

[39] Walsingham, etc., to Elizabeth, 11 September 1583, 628 CSP-S, 603.

[40] Conyers Read, *Lord Burghley and Queen Elizabeth*, (London 1960), 287.

[41] Gilbert Gifford to Walsingham, 5 September 1588, 35 CSP-D, 525.

[42] Walsingham to Burghley, 11 September 1583, 629 CSP-S, 604–5. See also Timothy Ashby 'Walsingham and the Witch' in *History Scotland* Vol. 21 No. 5 September/October 2021.

[43] Walsingham to Burghley, 11 September 1583, 629 CSP-S, 604–5.

[44] Memorial for Mr. William Ashby from Walsingham, 11 September 1583, 630 CSP-S, 605.

[45] Joseph Haydn, '1791 – The Year part 6 – The Year Ends – Triumph & Tragedy'. https://www.fjhaydn.com/my-blog/2016/02/1791-the-year-part-6. html. Retrieved 7 June 2020.

[46] Robert Chambers, *Domestic Annals of Scotland* (Edinburgh 1858), v. 1, 153.

[47] Ibid.

[48] James Melville, *Memoirs*, 308–11.

[49] George Seton, seventh Lord Seton, was appointed Scottish ambassador to France in December 1583.

[50] Lord Seton to Mary, 16 September 1583, 642 CSP-S, 614–15. The message, sent in code, was intercepted and deciphered by English intelligence. See also Timothy Ashby 'Walsingham and the Witch' in *History Scotland* Vol. 21 No. 5 September/October 2021.

[51] Agnes Strickland, *Life of Mary Queen of Scots* (London 1893), ii, 75–8.

[52] Francis was a cousin of Ashby's friend Arthur Throckmorton.

[53] *The Manuscripts of His Grace the Duke of Rutland: ...preserved At Belvoir Castle...* (London 1888), v 1, 156.

[54] Later in 1584 Mendoza was appointed Spanish Ambassador to France where he continued his plotting for an invasion of England. There was no Spanish ambassador in London for the remainder of Elizabeth's reign.

[55] *Calendar of Border Papers*, i, 1560–1595, Joseph Bain (ed.) (London, 1894), 175.

[56] Walsingham to Robert Bowes, 13 December 1583, 716 CSP-S, 680.

[57] Walsingham to Stafford, 26 October 1583, 194 CSP-S, 172.

[58] M. de Mauvissière to Henry III, November 1583, *Letters of Mary, Queen of Scots*, Agnes Strickland ed. (London 1842), v 2, 66.

[59] Ibid.

## Chapter 11. Universal miscontent in the country

[1] Roger Williams to Walsingham, 12 October 1583, 146 CSP-F, 124

[2] Robert Bowes to Walsingham, 20 January 1584, Berwick, 12 CSP-S, 12–13.

[3] Juan Bautista De Tassis to the King, 18 April 1584, Paris, 377 Simancas, 521.

[4] Robert Bowes to Walsingham, 1 January 1584, 2 CSP-S, 3.

[5] Walsingham to Stafford, 26 October 1583, 194 CSP-F, 172.

[6] Extracts of Letters, January 1584, 9 CSP-S, 8.

[7] The King of Scotland to the Duke of Guise, 19 Feb. 1584, 'From our palace of Holyrood', 370 Simancas.

[8] The King of Scotland to the Pope, 19 February 1584, 'the palace of Holyrood', 371, Simancas, 517–19.

[9] Dr. William Parry to Burghley, 17–27 August 1583, 91 CSP-F, 75.

[10] Stafford to Walsingham, 19 November 1583, 251 CSP-F, 222.

[11] Juan Bautista De Tassis to the King, 18 April 1584, Paris, 377 Simancas, 521.

[12] Ibid.

[13] Ibid.

[14] Ibid.

[15] At that time Mary was held at Sheffield Manor Lodge, South Yorkshire.

[16] Juan Bautista De Tassis to the King, 18 April 1584, Paris, 377 Simancas, 521.

[17] Ibid.

[18] Gordon Donaldson, ed., *The Memoirs of Sir James Melville of Halhill* (London 1969), 125.

[19] Andrew Land, *The History of Scotland – Volume 2: From Mary Stuart to James V*, (Charleston 2015), 219.

[20] Walsingham to Angus and Mar, 5 May 1585, 100 CSP-S, 113.

[21] John Bruce, ed., *Letters of Queen Elizabeth and King James VI of Scotland*, (London 1849).

[22] Charles Williams, *James I: A Biography of a King*, (Eugene 2007), 66.

[23] Walsingham to Mr. William Davison, 2 August 1584, 231 CSP-S, 246–7.

[24] Andrew Lang, *History of Scotland*, 222.

[25] Burghley to Hunsdon, 20 August 1584, 258, CSP-S, 286.

[26] Mary to Sir Francis Englefeld, 9 October 1584, 333 CSP-S, 360. Englefield was a Roman Catholic exile who was a pensioner of Philip.

[27] Andrew Lang, *History of Scotland*, 219.

[28] [Mr. William Davison] to Walsingham, 4 August 1584, 236 CSP-S, 251.

[29] Memoranda Concerning the Master of Gray, October 1584, 356 CSP-F,

[30] The Master of Gray to Sir Francis Walsingham, 12 February 1585, London, Patrick Gray, *Letters and papers relating to Patrick, Master of Gray: afterwards seventh Lord Gray* (Edinburgh 1835), 64–5.

[31] Andrew Lang, *History of Scotland*, 220.

[32] [Mary] to the Master of Gray, October 1584. 364 CSP-S.

[33] Mary to the Master of Gray, 1 October 1584, 321 CSP-S.

[34] James Melville, 127–8.

[35] Mr. Secretary Walsingham to the Earl of Leycester, 20 May 1586, CSP-F, 275.

[36] John Bruce, ed., *Correspondence of Robert Dudley, Earl of Leicester: during his government of the Low Countries, in the years 1585 and 1586* (London 1844), vi.

[37] Walsingham to Stafford, 22 March 1585, CSP-F, 369–70.

[38] Susan Doran and Norman Jones, eds, *The Elizabethan World* (London 2013), 11.

[39] Roger Howe to Alderman George Bond, 15 June 1585, Seville, CSP-F, 528.

[40] Walsingham to Stafford, 20 July 1585, CSP-F, 618.

[41] Instructions to Sir John Smith, Sent to the Prince of Parma, 22 August 1585, CSP-F, 671.

[42] Simancas, fn 1, 583.

[43] Bernardino de Mendoza to the King, 8 November 1586, 501 Simancas, 644–6.

[44] Lord Burghley to the Earl of Leicester, Correspondence of the Earl of Leycester, 52.

[45] Charles Williams, *James I: Biography of a King* (Eugene 1934), 88.

[46] Procedure: accusations against Patrick, master of Gray for the raid at Stirling Castle, James VI: Translation 10 May 1587, Holyrood, Convention, *The Records of the Parliaments of Scotland to 1707*, K.M. Brown et al, eds (St Andrews, 2007–2020), date accessed: 15 July 2020.

[47] John Ballard to Walsingham, 6 March 1587, 494, Calendar of Border Papers: Vol. 1, 1560–1595, ed. Joseph Bain (London, 1894), pp. 247–53. As Conyers Read noted in *Mr. Secretary Walsingham*, vol. II, the letter was actually written by Maliverny Catlyn, having been wrongly attributed to Ballard, who had been executed in September 1586.

[48] 31 July 1587, Roger Aston to [Burghley?], 165 CSP-S.

[49] Burghley to Sir Robert Carey, 3 April 1587, 333 CSP-S, 393–4.

[50] Discourses between Elizabeth and Mr. Archibald Douglas, October 1587, 407 CSP-S, 496–7.

[51] Extracts of Letter of Robert Carvill, 22 Sept. 1587, 396 CSP-S, 485–6.

[52] The Duke of Guise to Bernardino De Mendoza (Document accompanying the aforegoing letter), 16 July 1586, 451–453, Simancas, 589–90.

[53] State of Scotland 1588, 573 CSP-S, 664.

### Chapter 12. The Armada cometh

[1] Sir Edward Stafford to Walsingham, 27 March 1586, CSP-F, 492. Stafford referred to Ashby as 'Mr. Vice-Chamberlain's man', but this is doubtful unless Walsingham sent him on a mission on behalf of Sir Christopher Hatton, who was an ally of the Principal Secretary on the Privy Council and who similarly suspected the ambassador of being a Spanish agent.

[2] Henry Merewether, *The History of the Boroughs and Municipal Corporations of the United Kingdom*, v. ii, (London 1835), 1344–1345.

[3] James VI to The Earl of Rutland, 5 July 1586, 558, CSP-S, 504.

[4] https://www.historyofparliamentonline.org/volume/1558–1603/member/bagnall-sir-henry-1556-98, accessed 12 August 2020.

[5] Robert Bowes to Burghley and Walsingham, 9 July 1588, 471 CSP-S, 579.

[6] Walsingham told Burghley that 'Mr. Robert Carye was quite recovered, and was the most fit man to be sent into Scotland'. Walsingham to Burghley, 19 June 1588, 36 CSP-D, 490.

[7] Robert Cary, *The Memoirs of Robert Cary, Earl of Monmouth* (Edinburgh 1808), 69.

[8] Robert Bowes' Account, September 1588, 527 CSP-S, 620.

[9] Robert Carey to Mr. Carmichael and the Chancellor of Scotland, 22 June 1588, 466 CSP-S, 575–6.

[10] William Ashby to Walsingham, 20 July 1588, 473 CSP-S, 582–3.

[11] Walsingham to William Ashby, 22 August 1588, 498 CSP-S, 598–9.

[12] Richard Douglas to Archibald Douglas, Edinburgh, 10 July 1558, 691, MSS Hatfield v. iii, 337–8.

[13] William Ashby to Walsingham, 9 July 1588, 470 CSP-S, 579.

[14] Conyers Read, *Mr. Secretary Walsingham*, vol III, 342.

[15] Intelligence from Berwick, 28 June 1588, 467, CSP-S, 576–7.

[16] Sir Robert Sidney to Walsingham, 1 Sept.1588, 509 CSP-S, 608.

[17] Thomas Staynton to Walsingham, 23 Oct–2 Nov. 1587, CSP-F, 386.

[18] Admiral Charles Howard to Walsingham, 27 January 1588, John Knox Laughton, ed., *State Papers Relating to the Defeat of the Spanish Armada*. Vol. I (London 1894), 48–9.

[19] Admiral Charles Howard to Walsingham, 1 February 1588, 'aboard her Majesty's ship the White Bear', *State Papers Relating to the Defeat of the Spanish Armada*, Vol. I, 56–7.

[20] Martin Andrew Sharp Hume, *Philip II of Spain* (London 1911), 204.

[21] Ibid, 58.

[22] Paul Hammer, *Elizabeth's Wars: War, Government and Society in Tudor England, 1544–1604* (Basingstoke 2003), 145.

[23] Colonel William Sempill of Lochwinnoch.

[24] Unknown agent (signature erased) – to M. de Villiers, 4 May 1588, CSP-F, 349. De Villiers – Pierre l'oyseleur Dit de Villiers – was a Calvinist minister, an ally of the English but evidently not one of Walsingham's actual intelligencers.

[25] Cobham to Burghley, 4 May 1588, Ostend, CSP-F, 352.

[26] Walsingham to Burghley, 19 June 1588, 36 CSP-D, 490.

[27] Lord Burghley to Walsingham, 24 June 1588, 56 CSP-D, 493. Allen took part in planning the invasion and would probably have been named Archbishop of Canterbury if it had been successful.

[28] Lord Admiral Howard to Walsingham, 22 June 1588, 'Aboard the Arke', 46 CSP-D, 492.

[29] Lord Admiral Howard to The Queen, 22 June 1588, 'Aboard the Arke', 50–1 CSP-D, 492.

[30] Ibid, 209.

[31] Sir Henry Woddrington to [Walsingham], 20 June 1588, 465 CSP-S, 575.

[32] Juan Everye to John Bird and John Watts, merchants, 29 June – 9 July 1588, CSP-F, 531.

[33] Duke of Parma to the King, 21 July 1588, Bruges, 351 Simancas.

[34] William Chatto, *Facts and Speculations on the Origin and History of Playing Cards* (London 1848).

[35] The letter took eight days to be carried by courier on a series of post horses.

[36] Richard Douglas to Archibald Douglas, Edinburgh, 10 July 1558, 691, MSS Hatfield v. iii, number 2, 337–8.

[37] See Chapter XX. This refers to Thomas Fowler, a renegade Englishman with a murky background, who was a double agent serving both Burghley and Walsingham as an intelligencer. He was not 'a near kinsman' of Ashby, which would have meant 'very near in consanguinity' (a blood relationship), whereas his second wife was distantly related by marriage. Fowler turned against Ashby and sought to undermine him during his ambassadorship. He is sometimes confused with William Fowler (1560–1612), an unrelated Scottish makar (royal bard or poet) and courtier, who had been spying for the English since 1581.

[38] Report of Mr. Randolph's Last Journey into Scotland, July 1586, 603 CSP-S, 533.

[39] Richard Douglas to Archibald Douglas, Edinburgh, 10 July 1558, 691, MSS Hatfield, 337–8.

[40] Martin Andrew Sharp Hume, *Philip II of Spain* (London 1897), 215.

[41] Henry Killigrew to Walsingham 'News of the Spanish Fleet', 31 July 1588, 92 CSP-F.

[42] The declaration of John Bonde, of Kenton near Exeter, 5 June 1588, 486 CSP-D.

[43] Certificate of the whole number of horse and foot furnished by the clergy of the diocese of Ely, June 1588, 82 CSP-D.

[44] The Deputy Lieutenants of Surrey to the Council, 9 July 1588, 26 CSP-D, 500.

[45] The true report of George Wod, June 1588, 97 CSP-D, 497.

[46] Robert Bowes to Burghley and Walsingham, 9 July 1588, 471 CSP-S, 579.

[47] Robert Bowes to Burghley and Walsingham, 9 July 1588, 471 CSPS, 579–80.

[48] Ibid. 580.

[49] Ibid.

[50] William Ashby to Walsingham, Berwick, 9 July 1588, 470 CSP-S, 579.

[51] Ibid.

[52] David Moyse, *Memoirs of the Affairs of Scotland*, James Dennistoun ed., (Edinburgh 1830), 69.

[53] Conyers Read, vol II, 170.

[54] *Elizabeth I: Collected Works*, Leah Marcus, Janel Mueller and Mary Rose, eds., (Chicago 2000), 197, fn. 1.

## Chapter 13. Ashby's ambassadorship to Scotland

[1] *An Itinerary Written By Fynes Moryson, Gent. Containing His ten yeeres trauels thorovv Twelve Dominions, The First Part*, (London 1617), 274.

[2] Anent the Sick Infants, 16 October 1583, J D Marwick ed., *Extracts From the Records of the Burgh of Edinburgh, 1573–1589*, (Edinburgh 1882), 300.

[3] Proclamatio, beggares, 4 December 1588, Ibid, 533.

[4] Trinitie College, vnlawes of fornicatours, 7 March 1589, Ibid, 624.

[5] Life in Blackfriars Wynd, https://lynnesfamilies.wordpress.com/2012/08/08/life-in-blackfriars-wynd-edinburgh/ accessed 13 August 2020.

[6] http://gillonj.tripod.com/quotableedinburgh/ Accessed 11 August 2020.

[7] Robert Carvyle to Robert Scott, 23 November 1587, 615, *Calendar of the Manuscripts of the Most Honourable the Marquess of Salisbury* (London 1883), 298.

[8] Hunsdon to Walsingham, 26 March 1581, 772 CSP-S, 679–80.

[9] Robesoun Banished, 2 May 1578, Marwick, *Extracts From the Records of the Burgh of Edinburgh, 1573–1589*, 73. The ambassador's wife was probably Eleanor (né Musgrave), wife of Thomas Bowes.

[10] Robert Southey, *Journal of a tour in Scotland in 1819* (London 1929), 13.

[11] Robert Chambers, *Domestic Annals of Scotland form the Reformation to the Revolution*, (Edinburgh 1848), 436.

[12] Andrew Lang, *A History of Scotland*, 338–9.

[13] Proclamatio, turblance in the kirk, 21 March 1589, Marwick, *Extracts From the Records of the Burgh of Edinburgh, 1573–1589*, 539.

[14] The two William Stewarts (Stuarts) – cousins – are often confused with one another. Sir William Stewart 'the sticker' of Monkton and Carstairs murdered

by Bothwell, was the younger brother of the Earl of Arran. Sir William Stuart of Houston (c. 1540–c.1605), known as 'Colonel Stuart', was captain of the King's guard and accompanied Colville on the 1583 delegation to London. I have used the two spellings of the surname to distinguish them.

[15] William Ashby to Walsingham, 20 July 1588, 473, CSP-S, 562.

[16] Ibid.

[17] Allan Westcott, *New poems by James I of England: from a hitherto unpublished manuscript* (New York 1911), 47–52.

[18] William Ashby to Walsingham, 20 July 1588, 473, CSP-S, 562.

[19] Instructions for Sir Richard Wigmore, May 1588, 460 CSP-S, 562.

[20] Andrew Lang, *A History or Scotland*, 339.

[21] 14 November 1587, Archibald Douglas' Project Touching the troubles in Scotland, 611, Salisbury, R. Cecil, et al. *Calendar of the Manuscripts of the Most Honourable the Marquess of Salisbury* (London 1883), 295.

[22] Ibid, 296.

[23] Ibid, 333.

[24] The Substance of that was delivered me by the Ambassador of Scotland upon the Report made by me of Majesty's answer to His Propositions, 12 April 1587, 514, *Calendar of the Manuscripts of the Most Honourable the Marquess of Salisbury*, 243.

[25] Richard Douglas to Archibald Douglas, 3 July 1588, 687, Ibid, 332–4.

[26] Ibid.

[27] State of Scotland, 1588, 794 Ibid, 385.

[28] The King composed 'a poetic entertainment with speeches from Mercury, a group of nymphs, Agrestis, and some comedy' for Huntly's wedding in Edinburgh on 20 July 1588. Allan Westcott, *New poems by James I of England: from a hitherto unpublished manuscript* (New York 1911), 47–52.

[29] John Matusiak, *James I: Scotland's King of England*, (Stroud 2015), 90–1.

[30] Justice Clerk to Mr. Archibald Douglas, 24 October 1587, CSP-S, 491.

[31] *Tytler's Historie of Scotland*, 231.

[32] Monsieur Fontenay to Mary (Secret Letter 'to Nau'), 14 August 1584, 247 CSP-S, 260.

[33] Ibid.

[34] Richard Douglas to Archibald Douglas, 3 July 1588, 687 *Calendar of the Manuscripts of the Most Honourable the Marquess of Salisbury*, 333.

[35] Ibid.

[36] Peter Garrard, John Stephenson, Vijeya Ganesan, Timothy Peters, 'Attenuated variants of Lesch-Nyhan disease: the case of King James VI/I', *Brain*, Vol. 133, Issue 11, November 2010, 153. https://academic.oup.com/brain/article/133/11/e153/311186 accessed 20 08 2020.

[37] Elizabeth to James, around 1 July 1588, John Bruce, ed., *Letters of Queen Elizabeth and King James VI. of Scotland* (London 1849), 49–50.

[38] Ibid.

[39] Richard Wigmore was the protagonist in an elaborate plot to convince the Scots that he was a double agent. See Chapter XXII.

[40] 16 July 1588, Instructions by Elizabeth to Mr. Richard Wigmore sent to James VI, 472, CSP-S.

[41] William Ashby to Walsingham, 21 July 1588, 474 CSP-S, 583.

[42] Andrew Lang, *A History or Scotland*, 342.

[43] [Mr. Archibald Douglas] to Walsingham, 26 July 1588, 477 CSP-S, 585.

[44] 27 July 1588, Mr. Secretary Walsingham to Archibald Douglas, William Murdin and Samuel Haynes, eds, *Collection of State Papers left by William Cecill, Lord Burghley* (London 1759), v ii, 631–2.

[45] William Ashby to Walsingham, 30 July 1588, 479 CSP-S, 587.

[46] Ibid.

## Chapter 14. Offers from Ashby to James VI

[1] William Ashby to Walsingham, 30 July 1588, 478 CSP-S, 587.

[2] Maitland may have been receiving payments from the English. See Lord Burghley to John Wolley, Latin Secretary to the Council, in which he suggests sending 'some portion of money … for defence of the Chancellor', 11 April 1588, 658, *Calendar of the Manuscripts of the Most Honourable the Marquess of Salisbury* (London 1883), 319.

[3] Ibid.

[4] Ibid.

[5] William Ashby to Walsingham, 3 August 1588, 484 CSP-S, 589.

[6] Ashby seems to have used a boating metaphor – 'strike a stroke' – to indicate that Maitland was taking the lead in formulating policy towards England. The 'stroke' is a rower who sits closest to the stern of the boat and is responsible for the rating and rhythm of the vessel.

[7] Walsingham to the Lord Chancellor of Scotland, 17 August 1588, 496 CSP-S, 598.

[8] Lord Hunsdon to the Queen, 24 October 1587, William Murdin and Samuel Haynes, eds, *Collection of State Papers left by William Cecill, Lord Burghley* (London 1759), v II, 591.

[9] Points of Letter from Robert Bruce to the Duke of Parma, 6 Aug 1588, 367 Simancas.

[10] Ibid.

[11] William Ashby to [Walsingham], 6 August 1588, 486, CSP-S, 590.

[12] Ibid.

[13] William Ashby to Walsingham, 3 August 1588, 485 CSP-S, 589.

[14] Richard Douglas to Archibald Douglas, 14 August 1588, 716 *Calendar of the Manuscripts of the Most Honourable the Marquess of Salisbury* (London 1883), 349–50.

[15] William Ashby to Walsingham,10 August 1588, 491, CSP-S, 594.

[16] James VI to Elizabeth, 1 August 1588, *Letters of Queen Elizabeth and King James VI of Scotland*, 51–2.

[17] James VI to Elizabeth, 1 August 1588, *Letters of Queen Elizabeth and King James VI of Scotland*, 51–2.

[18] Garrett Mattingley, *The Defeat of the Spanish Armada* (London 1959), 304.

[19] Lord Admiral Howard to Walsingham, 'Aboard the Arke', 29 July 1588, 64, CSP-D, 516.

[20] Howard to Walsingham, 7 August 1588, John Knox Laughton, *State papers relating to the defeat of the Spanish Armada, anno 1588*, (London 1894), 54.

[21] William Ashby to [Walsingham], 6 August 1588, 486, CSP-S, 590.

[22] Ibid.

[23] Ibid.

[24] Ibid.

[25] William Ashby to Burghley, 6 August 1588, 487 CSP-S, 591.

[26] William Ashby to Walsingham, 8 August 1588, 489 CSP-S, 592.

[27] William Ashby to Burghley and William Ashby to Walsingham, 10 August 1588, 490 and 491, CSP-S, 593–4.

[28] The French crown or *ecú,* which circulated throughout England and Scotland, was worth about six shillings and four pence, therefore the proposed payment was approximately £5,500 in English currency.

[29] Plausible deniability. See note 7, prologue.

[30] Lord Burghley to John Wolley, Latin Secretary to the Council, in which he suggests sending 'some portion of money … for defence of the Chancellor', 11 April 1588, 658, *Calendar of the Manuscripts of the Most Honourable the Marquess of Salisbury,* 319.

[31] The Queen later claimed that 'some of her council' had not informed her of the offers 'for a good time' to 'avoid her high displeasure'. However, the dates of the series of messages between London and Edinburgh indicate that this was erroneous. 'A Summary of that may be answered to the Propositions presented by the Lord of Weymes, Ambassador to the King of Scotland', April 26, 1589, *A Collection of state papers relating to the Reign of Queen Elizabeth … left by William Cecil Lord Burghley,* William Murdin ed., (London 1759), 635–6.

### Chapter 15. A necessary play of penitence

[1] Richard Douglas to Archibald Douglas, 14 August 1588, 716, *Calendar of the Manuscripts of … the Marquess of Salisbury,* 319–21.

[2] Ibid.

[3] Ibid.

[4] William Ashby to Walsingham, 12 August 1588, 493 CSP-S, 596.

[5] William Ashby to Walsingham, 12 August 1588, 493 CSP-S, 596.

[6] Richard Douglas to Archibald Douglas, 14 August 1588, 716, *Calendar of the Manuscripts of … the Marquess of Salisbury,* 319–21.

[7] Walsingham to William Ashby, 22 August 1588, 498 CSP-S, 598–9.

[8] Ibid.

[9] Ibid.

[10] Instructions to Colonel William Stewart, April 1583, 417 CSP-S, 411–12.

[11] Ibid.

[12] Conyers Read, *Mr. Secretary Walsingham* (Oxford 1925), II, 221.

[13] Walsingham to the Lord Chancellor of Scotland, 17 August 1588, 496 CSP-S, 598.

[14] William Ashby to Burghley, 6 August 1588, 487 CSP-S, 591.

[15] William Ashby to Walsingham, 18 August 1588, 497 CSP-S, 598.

[16] Sir Philip Sydney was mortally wounded at the Battle of Zutphen in 1586 during Leicester's disastrous Netherlands campaign.

[17] Walsingham to William Ashby, 22 August 1588, 498 CSP-S, 598-9.

[18] Ibid.

[19] Sir Robert Sidney to Walsingham, 27 August 1588, 502 CSP-S, 601.

[20] In this context, 'tithe' probably refers to revenues from the estates in Northern England claimed by James.

[21] Walsingham to William Ashby, 22 August 1588, 498 CSP-S, 598–9.

[22] William Ashby to Walsingham, 1 September 1588, 508 CSP-S, 606.

[23] Conyers Read, *Mr. Secretary Walsingham*, III, 325.

[24] Walsingham to the Lord Chancellor, 8 August 1588, *State Papers relating to the Defeat of the Spanish Armada*, II, 69.

[25] Ibid, 84.

[26] Captain Henry Whyte to Walsingham, 8 August 1588, 43 CSP-D, 526.

[27] Sir Francis Drake to Walsingham, 8 August 1588, 47 CSP-D,527.

[28] Howard to Walsingham, 29 August 1588, State papers relating to the defeat of the Spanish Armada 183.

[29] Paul Hammer, *Elizabeth's Wars: War, Government and Society in Tudor England, 1544–1604* (Basingstoke 2003), 153.

[30] Robert Hutchinson, *Elizabeth's Spymaster* (London 2006), 101.

[31] Elizabeth to James, 1 July 1588, *Letters of Queen Elizabeth and King James VI of Scotland*, 49.

[32] [William Ashby] to Walsingham, 30 August 1530, 506 CSP-S, 603–4.

[33] Instructions for Sir Robert Sidney, [27] August 1588, 507 CSP-S, 604–5.

[34] Elizabeth's letter, fulsome in its condemnation of Philip and the Spaniards, contained no mention of the £3,000 or any other concessions. Elizabeth to James, August 1588, *Letters of Queen Elizabeth and King James VI of Scotland*, 52–3.

[35] Sir Robert Sidney to Walsingham, 28 August 1588, 503 CSP-S, 602.

[36] Sir Robert Sidney to Walsingham, 30 August 1588, 505 CSP-S, 602.

[37] Ibid.

[38] Arthur Throckmorton to Walsingham, 30 August 1588, 504 CSP-S, 602.

[39] William Ashby to Walsingham, 1 September 1588, 508 CSP-S, 606.

[40] 1 September 1588, Sir Robert Sidney to Walsingham, 1 September 1588, 509 CSP-S, 607.

[41] Ibid.

[42] Equipollent – equal or equivalent in power, effect, or significance.

[43] Ibid.

[44] Sir Robert Sidney to Walsingham, 2 September 1588, 510 CSP-S, 608–9.

[45] Ibid.

[46] Ibid.

## Chapter 16. '… the great ship was blown in the air'

[1] Robert Bowes to Walsingham, 20 August 1588, 628, *Calendar of Border Papers* (CBP): Volume 1, 1560–1595, ed. Joseph Bain (London, 1894), 330–1.

[2] The Council of the North was a Yorkshire-based administrative body charged with representing the Crown in Northern England and defending the Borders.

[3] Alan Haynes, *Invisible Power: Elizabethan Secret Services, 1570–1603* (London 1992), 48–9.

[4] Huntingdon to the Privy Council, 17 August 1588, 625, CBP, 329.

[5] Robert Bowes to Burghley, 10 September 1588, 633 CBP, 332.

[6] Ibid.

[7] Thomas Fowler to Walsingham, 29 December 1588, 563 CSP-S, 655. James meant that he was being treated like a child.

[8] Andrew Lang, *History of Scotland*, 342.

[9] Master of Gray to Mr. Archibald Douglas, 14 December 1588, 556 CSP-S, 649

[10] William Ashby to Elizabeth, 7 September 1588, 512 CSP-S, 610–11.

[11] Sir Robert Sidney to Walsingham, 1 September 1588, 509 CSP-S, 607–8.

[12] Ibid.

[13] William Ashby to Elizabeth, 7 September 1588, 512 CSP-S, 610–11

[14] William Ashby to Walsingham, 12 September, 517 CSP-S, 614.

[15] James to Elizabeth, [12] September 1588, *Letters of Queen Elizabeth and King James VI of Scotland*, 54–5.

[16] Robert Bowes to Walsingham, 12 September 1588, 634 CBP, 334.

[17] Walsingham was mistaken in the latter amount delivered to the Scots, which was actually £3,000.

[18] James was finally awarded the Garter three weeks after Walsingham's death in 1590.

[19] Albert Loomie, 'Philip III and the Stuart Succession in England, 1600–1603', *Revue belge de Philologie et d'Histoire* (Brussels 1965), 502.

[20] William Ashby to Walsingham, 6 November 1588, 537 CSP-S, 627–8.

[21] William Ashby to Walsingham, 19 September 1588, 521 CSP-S, 616.

[22] Between 6,000 and 7,000 Spaniards died after being shipwrecked in Ireland and Scotland, including 1,100 who were executed by English soldiers commanded by the brother of Sir Richard Bingham, governor of Connacht.

[23] The ship was probably the *Trinidad Valencera*.

[24] William Ashby to Walsingham, 23 September 1588, 524 CSP-S, 618.

[25] William Ashby to Walsingham, 6 November 1588, 537 CSP-S, 627–8.

[26] Cobham to Walsingham, May 1583, 344 CSP-F, 381.

[27] Conyers Read, *Mr. Secretary Walsingham*, II, 193.

[28] Lord Hunsdon to [Walsingham], 25 November 1587, 414 CSP-S, 507. Bowes had served as Smollet's handler since at least the early 1580s.

[29] Roger Aston to James Hudson, 8 November 1588, 538 CSP-S, 628–9.

[30] Ibid.

[31] William Ashby to Burghley, 13 November 1588, 542, CSP-S, 635–6.

[32] William Ashby to Walsingham, 26 November 1588, 545 CSP-S, 637–8.

[33] William Ashby to Burghley and Walsingham, 11 and 18 November 1589, 277 and 281 CSP-S.

[34] Maria Higueras Rodriguez and Maria de San Pio Aladren, 'Irish Wrecks of the Great Armada: The Testimony of the Survivors', in Peter Gallagher and Don William Cruickshank, eds., *God's Obvious Design: Papers for the Spanish Armada Symposium* (London 1990), 160.

[35] Pass for Spaniards, 28 October 1588, 532 CSP-S, 624.

[36] William Ashby to Walsingham, 6 November 1588, 537 CSP-S, 627–8.

[37] Pass for Spaniards, 28 October 1588, 532 CSP-S, 624.

[38] William Ashby to Walsingham, 30 November 1588, 547 CSP-S, 640–1.

[39] Maria Higueras Rodriguez and Maria de San Pio Aladren, 'Irish Wrecks of the Great Armada', 160.

[40] Sir Henry Woddrington to Walsingham, 29 December 1588, 564 CSP-S, 655–6.

[41] Thomas Fowler to Walsingham, 588 CSP-S, 680–681.

[42] 15 January 1589, 20 February 1589, Thomas Fowler to Walsingham, 578 CSP-S, 669.

[43] William Ashby to [Burghley], 13 November 1588, 542 CSP-S, 635–6.

[44] Certificate by Elizabeth Fowlar that Mr. Edward Barker used all mildness in the search of the house of her husband, Thomas Fowlar, in St. Mary Spittle. Note of the sums due on Mr. Fowlar's account, 6 December 1588, 12 CSP-D, 563

[45] John Stow, *Annales, or a general Chronicle of England* (London 1631), 813.

[46] William Ashby to Walsingham, 30 November 1588, 547 CSP-S, 640.

[47] William Ashby to Walsingham, 6 November 1588, 537 CSP-S, 627–8

[48] Ibid.

[49] Intelligence from Scotland, 13 November 1588, 541 CSP-S, 635.

[50] Ibid.

[51] William Ashby to Walsingham, 26 November 1588, 545 CSP-S, 637–8.

[52] Roger Aston to James Hudson, 30 December 1588, 565 CSP-S, 656.

[53] Roger Aston to James Hudson, 1 December 1588, 549 CSP-S, 642.

[54] A pistole was a double gold escudo, more famously known as a doubloon.

[55] Roger Aston to Walsingham, 13 December 1588, 554 CSP-S, 646–7.

[56] Walsingham to Thomas Fowler, 14 February 1589, 586 CSP-S, 679.

[57] Advices from England, 12 January 1589, 499 Simancas.

[58] Thomas Windebank to Walsingham, 17 December 1588, 31 CSP-D, 566.

[59] Lord Burghley to Walsingham, 30 December 1588, 45 CSP-D, 567.

[60] Henry Stephenson, *The Elizabethan People* (New York 1910) 169.

[61] Walsingham to Sir Thomas Heneage, 2 September 1578, Antwerp, CSP-F, 221.

## Chapter 17. Ashby reveals to James a plot against him by his own Lairds

[1] Thomas Fowler to Walsingham, 29 December 1588, 563 CSP-S, 654.

[2] 29 December 1588, Sir Henry Woddrington to Walsingham, 564 CSP-S, 655.

[3] Robert Chambers, *Domestic annals of Scotland* (Edinburgh 1858), v. 1, 170.

[4] Roger Aston to James Hudson, 1 December 1588, 549 CSP-S, 642.

[5] [ ] to James Hudson, Late December 1588, 570 CSP-S, 662–3.

[6] 15 February 1589, William Ashby to Walsingham, 587 CSP-S, 679.

[7] A Letter from the Counsell to the English Ambassador, 14 February 1589, David Calderwood, *History of the Kirk of Scotland* (Edinburgh 1842), 8.

[8] Andrew Lang, *History of Scotland*, 343.

[9] Andrew Lang, *A History of Scotland*, 343.

[10] The Scots believed that the evidence against Mary Stuart had been embellished if not completely fabricated, and there were claims (possibly originated by Elizabeth) that the English Queen's signature on Mary's death warrant had been forged. Agnes and Elizabeth Strickland, *Lives of the Queens of Scotland and English Princesses: Connected with the Regal Succession of Great Britain* (reprint – New York 2010), vol. 7, 465.

[11] Privy Council to the English Ambassador in Scotland, 20 February 1589, 589 CSP-S, 682.

[12] Ibid.

[13] Ibid.

[14] Notably, all four of the Councillors who signed the letter were friends of Walsingham; Burghley did not sign even though he drafted the document. This was probably not the result of a formal Privy Council meeting, the last of which was attended by Walsingham on 15 February before taking leave for his illness.

[15] The other two 'Lords Catholics' were subsequently identified as Morton and Claud Hamilton. David Calderwood, *The History of the Kirk of Scotland* (Edinburgh 1842–1849), 14.

[16] Huntly, Morton and Claud Hamilton. *Calderwood's Historie*, 14.

[17] The gold coins were in French *écus au soleil* and Spanish *pistoles*, the latter worth two *escudos*.

[18] John Chisholm was the youngest brother of William Chisholm III, Bishop of Dunblane, and James Chisholm, Laird of Cromlix, a family of arch-Catholics. See Alexander Mackenzie, *History of the Chisholms with genealogies of the principal families of that name* (Inverness 1891), 198–200.

[19] Privy Council to the English Ambassador in Scotland, 20 February 1589, 589 CSP-S, 682.

[20] Ibid.

[21] William Ashby to Burghley, 27 February 1589, 591 CSP-S, 698–9.

[22] Queen Elizabeth's Letter to the King, February 1589, *Calderwood's Historie*, 7–8.

[23] Ibid.

[24] Ibid.

[25] William Ashby to Burghley, 2 March 1589, 594 CSP-S, 701.

[26] Thomas Fowler to Walsingham, 1 March 1589, 593 CSP-S, 700.

[27] 'Huntlie and Lord Claud Wairded', 27 February 1589, *Calderwood's Historie*, 36.

[28] By the Earl of Montrose, a fellow conspirator.

[29] William Ashby to Burghley, 2 March 1589, 594 CSP-S, 701.

[30] 'Huntlie and Lord Claud Wairded', 27 February 1589, *Calderwood's Historie*, 36.

[31] William Ashby to Walsingham, 8 March 1589, 600 CSP-S, 706.

[32] 'Huntlie and Lord Claud Wairded', 27 February 1589, *Calderwood's Historie*, 36.

[33] William Ashby to Burghley, 2 March 1589, 594 CSP-S, 701.

[34] Thomas Fowler to Walsingham, 1 March 1589, 593 CSP-S, 700.

[35] William Ashby to Burghley, 5 March 1589, 596 CSP-S, 702.

[36] William Ashby to Burghley, 10 March 1589, 605 CSP-S,

[37] William Ashby to Burghley, 55 March 1589, 97 CSP-S, 703.

[38] William Fowler to Walsingham, 23 April 1589, 55 CSP-S.

[39] William Ashby to Walsingham, 8 March 1589, 600 CSP-S, 705–6.

[40] 'A Letter from Robert Bruce to Colonel Sempill', 24 January 1589, *Calderwood's Historie*, 33.

[41] 'The Copie of Thomas Tyrie's Letter to Robert Bruce', Undated, probably January 1589, *Calderwood's Historie*, 36.

[42] Thomas Fowler to Walsingham, 6 March 1589, 598 CSP-S, 703–4.

[43] Thomas Fowler to Walsingham, 1 March 1589, 593 CSP-S, 700.

[44] Ashby to Burghley, March 1589, 610 CSP-S, 709.

[45] Thomas Fowler to Walsingham, 6 March 1589, 599 CSP-S, 704.

[46] Thomas Fowler to [Burghley], 14 March 1589, 3 CSP-S.

[47] *Tytler's History of Scotland*, 232.

[48] Thomas Fowler to [Burghley], 14 March 1589, 3 CSP-S.

[49] Thomas Fowler to Walsingham, 1 March 1589, 593 CSP-S, 700

[50] Ibid.

[51] Fowler to Burghley, 23 March 1589, 16 CSP-S.

## Chapter 18. The lairds' open insurrection

[1] Thomas Fowler to Burghley, 20 March 1589, 10 CSP-S.

[2] [Thomas Fowler] to Walsingham, 8 March 1589, 602 CSP-S, 707.

[3] William Ashby to [Burghley], 18 March 1589, 8 CSP-S.

[4] Andrew Lang, *A History of Scotland*, 345.

[5] 'A whole discourse of the designs against the realm and Scotland', Early February 1589, 590 CSP-S, 697. The correspondents' names were deleted but this report was probably sent from Maitland to Walsingham.

[6] Thomas Fowler to Walsingham, 6 March 1589, 599 CSP-S, 704.

[7] William Ashby to Walsingham, 5 March 1589, 597 CSP-S, 703.

[8] William Ashby to Walsingham, 8 March 1589, 600 CSP-S, 705–6.

[9] Thomas Fowler to Burghley, 28 March 1589, 19 CSP-S.

[10] Richard Wigmore to Walsingham, 18 May 1589, 92 CSP-S.

[11] Ibid.

[12] William Ashby to Walsingham, 8 March 1589, 600 CSP-S, 705–6.

[13] Roger Aston to James Hudson, 15 March 1589, 9 CSP-S, 702.

[14] Ibid.

[15] William Ashby to [Burghley], 18 March 1589, 8 CSP-S.

[16] Ibid.

[17] *Letters of Queen Elizabeth and King James VI of* Scotland, 16 March 1589, 161–3.

[18] William Ashby to Burghley, 23 March 1589, 15 CSP-S.

[19] In this context, 'measure' apparently meant measuring out justice; young Lennox, a Catholic, hated the English, blaming them for his father's early death, and believed that Huntly was the means of vengeance.

[20] John Matusiak, *James I, Scotland's King of England*, (Stroud 2015), 95.

[21] Thomas Fowler to Burghley, 28 March 1589, 19 CSP-S.

[22] Ibid.

[23] William Ashby to Burghley, 2 April 1589, 22 CSP-S.

[24] William Ashby to Burghley, 20 March 1589, 12 CSP-S.

[25] Thomas Fowler to Walsingham, 5 April 1589, 26 CSP-S.

[26] Maurice Lee, *John Maitland of Thirlestane and the Foundation of the Stewart Despotism in Scotland*, (Princeton 1959), 185.

[27] Sir Thomas Heneage to Walsingham, 5 April 1589, 25 CSP-S.

[28] Woddrington to Walsingham, 7 April 1589, 642 Border Papers, 337.

[29] William Ashby to Walsingham, 15 April 1589, 44 CSP-S.

[30] [Thomas Fowler] to Burghley, 7 April 1589 27 CSP-S.

[31] Ibid.

[32] Andrew Lang, *A History of Scotland*, 345.

[33] [Thomas Fowler] to Burghley, 7 April 1589 27 CSP-S.

[34] William Ashby to Walsingham, 15 April 1589, 44 CSP-S.

[35] Malaria, known as tertian ague in the sixteenth century. 'Being in physic' meant under medical care or taking medicine.

[36] William Ashby to Burghley, 11 April 1589, 38 CSP-S.

[37] Elizabeth to James, 16 March 1589, *Letters of Queen Elizabeth and King James VI*, 161–3.

[38] Fowler to William Ashby, 28 April 1589, Thomas 61 CSP-S.

[39] Thomas Fowler to [Walsingham], 23 April 1589, 54 CSP-S.

[40] Thomas Fowler to [Walsingham], 23 April 1589, 54 CSP-S.

[41] Thomas Fowler to [Walsingham.], 27–28 April 1589, 60 CSP-S.

[42] Andrew Lang, *A History of Scotland*, 347.

[43] *Calderwood's Historie*, 58.

[44] Andrew Lang, *A History of Scotland*, 347.

[45] 'A Summary of that may be answered to the Propositions presented by the Lord of Wemyss, Ambassador for the King of Scotland, to Her Majesty', April 26, 1589, *A Collection of State Papers in the Reign of Queen Elizabeth 1571 to 1596*, ed. W. Murdin (London 1759), v ii, part 2, 635–6.

[46] Ibid.

[47] At this time, Lady Arbella Stuart was considered one of the natural candidates to succeed her first cousin twice removed, Elizabeth, not least because of the Queen's dislike for King James.

[48] 'A Summary of that may be answered to the Propositions presented by the Lord of Wemyss, Ambassador for the King of Scotland, to Her Majesty', 26 April 1589, 636.

[49] Mr. Archibald Douglas to Walsingham, 15 May 1589, 88 CSP-S.

[50] Mr. Archibald Douglas to Walsingham, 20 April 1589, 50 CSP-S.

[51] William Ashby to Walsingham, 2 May 1589, 67 CSP-S.

## Chapter 19. Fowler's defamation of Ashby

[1] William Ashby to Burghley, 20 May 1589, 93 CSP-S.

[2] Ibid.

[3] William Ashby to [Walsingham], 15 March 1589, 6 CSP-S.

[4] Articles against Margaret, Countess of Lennox, 7 May 1562, 26 CSP-F, 15

[5] Information to Elizabeth and her Council, 22 September 1563.

[6] Thomas Fowler to Burghley, 29 October 1588, 534 CSP-S, 626.

[7] Thomas Fowler to Lord Burghley, 7 October 1589, Salisbury, R. Cecil, et al. *Calendar of the Manuscripts of the Most Honourable the Marquess of Salisbury ... Preserved At Hatfield House, Hertfordshire ...* (London 1883), 436.

[8] Colville to Walsingham, 25 June 1583, David Laing, ed., *Original letters of Mr. John Colville, 1582–1603. To which is added his Palinode, 1600* (Edinburgh 1858), 35.

[9] [Walsingham] to Thomas Fowler, 22 December 1588, 559 CSP-S, 650–1.

[10] Walsingham to Thomas Fowler, 5 December 1588, 552 CSP-S, 645–6.

[11] Susan E. James, *The Feminine Dynamic in English Art, 1485–1603: Women As Consumers, Patrons and Painters* (Abingdon 2009), 100.

[12] Thomas Fowler to his Wife, 12 August 1589, 176 CSP-S.

[13] Robert Bowes to Walsingham, 29 April 1583, 435 CSP-S, 430.

[14] David Laing, *Original letters of Mr. John Colville, 1582–1603* (Edinburgh 1858), xv.

[15] Thomas Fowler to Walsingham, 18 December 1588, 558 CSP-S.

[16] Thomas Fowler to Burghley, 14 May 1589, 86 CSP-S.

[17] Thomas Fowler to [Burghley], 14 March 1589, 3 CSP-S.

[18] Thomas Fowler to Walsingham, 14 March 1589, 4 CSP-S.

[19] Thomas Fowler to Burghley, 20 March 1589, 10 CSP-S.

[20] Thomas Fowler to Walsingham, 26 March 1589, 18 CSP-S.

[21] William Ashby to Walsingham. [Nov. 26 1588. 545 CSP-S,

[22] William Ashby to Burghley, 20 March 1589, 12 CSP-S.

[23] Thomas Fowler to [Burghley, 22 December 1588, 560 CSP-S,

[24] James Hudson to Walsingham, 22 May 1589, 95 CSP-S.

[25] Not to be taken seriously.

[26] James Hudson to Walsingham, 22 May 1589, 95 CSP-S.

[27] William Ashby to Burghley, 11 April 1589, 38 CSP-S.

[28] *National Records of Scotland, Treasurer's accounts*, June 1589.

[29] In the Elizabethan Royal Navy a trumpeter meant a sailor who signalled with a horn.

[30] William Ashby to Burghley, 8 June 1589, 117 CSP-S.

[31] Thomas Fowler to Lord Burghley, June 1589, Gray, *Letters and papers relating to Patrick, master of Gray*, (Edinburgh 1835), vol. 51, 164.

[32] James Hudson to [Walsingham], 21 June 1589, 130 CSP-S.

[33] Thomas Fowler to Burghley, 24 June 1589, 131 CSP-S.

[34] James David Marwick ed., *Extracts From the Records of the Burgh of Edinburgh, 1573–1589*, (Edinburgh 1882), 544.

[35] Maitland to Walsingham, 18 June 1589, 128 CSP-S.

[36] William Ashby to Walsingham, 22 July 1589, 156 CSP-S.

[37] William Ashby to Walsingham, 14 July 1589, 149 CSP-S.

[38] William Ashby to Burghley, 26 July 1589, 157 CSP-S.

[39] William Ashby to Walsingham, 22 July 1589, 156 CSP-S.

[40] William Ashby to Burghley, 26 July 1589, 157 CSP-S.

[41] William Ashby to Burghley, 31 July 1589, 163 CSP-S.

[42] Colin Martin and Geoffrey Parker, *The Spanish Armada* (London 1988), 249.

[43] Ashby to Walsingham, 11 November 1589, William 277 CSP-S.

[44] Robert Naunton to William Ashby, 13 July 1589, 148 CSP-S.

[45] William Ashby to Walsingham, 28 June 1589, 136 CSP-S.

[46] William Ashby to Burghley, 20 June 1589, 129 CSP-S.

[47] 13 July 1589, Robert Naunton to William Ashby, 148 CSP-S.

[48] William Ashby of Loseby (1561–?), was the son of Ambassador William Ashby's second cousin, Thomas Ashby of Loseby. He matriculated at Balliol College, Oxford, 1578, and was admitted to the Inner Temple.

[49] Robert Naunton to William Ashby, 19 July 1589, 44 CSP-S. 'the Spittle' was Spitalfields in the East End of London.

[50] William Ashby to James VI, 5 August 1589, 170 CSP-S.

[51] William Ashby to Arthur Throckmorton, 1 August 1589, 166 CSP-S.

[52] Ibid. *Bocca a Bocca* – Mouth-to-Mouth, meaning to speak face-to-face.

[53] Arthur Throckmorton to William Ashby, 20 July 1589, 155 CSP-S. In this context, 'jade' meant wearied.

[54] William Ashby to Walsingham, 22 July 1589, 156 CSP-S.

[55] Attributed to the third century BC Numidian general Maharbal after Hannibal failed to conquer Rome after his victory at the Battle of Cannae.

[56] William Ashby to Arthur Throckmorton, 1 August 1589, 166 CSP-S.

[57] Ibid.

[58] Thomas Fowler to Walsingham, 8 August 1589, 879 CSP-S.

## Chapter 20. Ashby tarries in Edinburgh while the King seeks his bride

[1] Alan Stewart, *The Cradle King* (London 2003), 176.

[2] Thomas Fowler to Burghley, 7 June 1589, *Letters and Papers Relating to Patrick, Master of Gray*, 162.

[3] Instructions to the Commissioners for Denmark, [?] June 1589, 124 CSP-S.

[4] William Ashby to Walsingham, 22 July 1589, 156 CSP-S.

[5] 28 May 1589, Thomas Fowler to Burghley, 107 CSP-S.

[6] This currency was the *daler*, a large silver coin used in Sweden, Denmark, and Norway.

[7] William Ashby to Burghley, 31 July 1589, 163 CSP-S.

[8] William Ashby to Burghley, 16 August 1589, CSPS-189.

[9] Thomas Fowler to Walsingham, 5 August 1589, 169 CSP-S.

[10] William Ashby to Burghley, 11 August 1589, 175 CSP-S.

[11] William Ashby to Walsingham, 31 August 1589, 201 CSP-S.

[12] James VI to Burghley, 15 August 1589, 179 CSP-S.

[13] William Ashby to Burghley, 16 August 1589, CSPS-189.

[14] William Ashby to Burghley, 11 August 1589, 175 CSP-S. The quote is from a play by the third century BC Roman playwright Titus Maccius Plautus.

[15] Walsingham to William Ashby, 20 August 1589, 187 CSP-S.

[16] Literally, 'drinkable gold', but Ashby was wittily using the term for its double meaning as cash for wedding entertainment or 'alchemist's gold', hinting at the King's foolishness.

[17] Burghley to William Ashby, 12 October 1589, 241 CSP-S.

[18] Mr John Colvile to William Ashby, September 1589, 227 CSP-S.

[19] William Ashby to Walsingham, 1 and 8 September 1589, 203 and 209 CSP-S.

[20] William Ashby to Walsingham, 26 August 1589, 195 CSP-S.

[21] William Ashby to Walsingham, 8 September 1589, 209 CSP-S.

[22] Ibid.

[23] Probably a member of the Staffordshire Draycott family, which was connected to the Babingtons.

[24] William Ashby to Burghley, 12 October 1589, 239 CSP-S.

[25] William Ashby to [Burghley], 15 October 1589, 243 CSP-S.

[26] [William Ashby] to [James VI], 21 October 1581, 251 CSP-S.

[27] James VI to Ashby, 22 October 1589, 252 CSP-S.

[28] William Ashby to Elizabeth. 23 October 1589, 256. Ashby alluded to the Greek myth of Leander and Hero (Eroes), impatient lovers who met untimely deaths. Leander drowned after losing his way whilst swimming the Hellespont.

[29] James Thompson Gibson Craig, ed., The King's Majesty's Declaration Upon the Causes of His Departure, 20 October 1589, *Papers relative to the marriage of King James the Sixth of Scotland, with the Princess Anna of Denmark* (Edinburgh 1828), 12–16.

[30] Ibid.

[31] The King's Declaration Made at his Departure, *Papers relative to the marriage of King James the Sixth of Scotland, with the Princess Anna of Denmark* (Edinburgh 1828), 22 October 1589, 3–11.

[32] Walsingham was evidently ailing and away from court.

[33] Burghley to William Ashby, 29 October 1589, 260 CSP-S.

[34] Burghley to William Ashby, 30 October 1589, 261 CSP-S.

[35] Ibid.

[36] [William Ashby] to [Walsingham], 11 November 1589, 276 CSP-S.

[37] [William Ashby] to [Walsingham], 11 November 1589, 277 CSP-S.

[38] William Ashby to Burghley, 21 November 1589, 286 CSP-S.

[39] William Ashby to Burghley and Walsingham, 18 November 1589, 281 CSP-S.

## Chapter 21. Vindication

[1] Thomas Fowler to Archibald Douglas, 20 October 1589, Salisbury, R. Cecil, et al, *Calendar of the Manuscripts of the Most Honourable the Marquess of Salisbury, Preserved At Hatfield House, Hertfordshire* ... (London 1883), part iii, 440.

[2] [William Ashby] to Burghley, 22 October 1589, 254 CSP-S.

[3] Sir Richard Wigmore, a Secretary to Burghley, is best known for writing an eyewitness account of the execution of Mary Stuart.

[4] [Thomas Fowler] to [Burghley.], 31 October 1589, 264 CSP-S.

[5] Thomas Phelippes to Archibald Douglas, 9 November 1589, Salisbury, R. Cecil, et al, *Calendar of the Manuscripts of the Most Honourable the Marquess of Salisbury ... Preserved At Hatfield House, Hertfordshire* ... (London 1883), 460.

[6] Elizabeth Knollys, the Queen's cousin and Gentlewoman of the Privy Chamber, who also enjoyed intrigues.

[7] Burnet, *Bishop Burnet's History of His Own Time* (London 1724), vol. I, 7. Wigmore's instructions from Walsingham dated May 1588 can be found at Instructions for Sir Richard Wigmore, 460 CSP-S, 561.

[8] Thomas Fowler to Lord Burghley, 8 November 1589, *Calendar of the Manuscripts of the Most Honourable the Marquess of Salisbury etc.*, (London 1883), 442–3.

[9] Ashby to Burghley, 7 November 1589, William 272 CSP-S.

[10] Richard Wigmore to [William Ashby], 10 February 1590, 354 CSP-S.

[11] Mr. Archibald Douglas to Burghley, 10 November 1589, 275, CSP-S.

[12] William Ashby to Burghley, 21 November 1589, 286 CSP-S.

[13] Sir James Melville, *Memoirs of His Own Life* (Edinburgh 1827), 277.

[14] [William Ashby] to [Burghley.], 28 November 1589, 296, CSP-S.

[15] William Ashby to Burghley, 24 November 1589, 288, CSP-S.

[16] [Memorandum of William Ashby's conduct towards Thomas Fowler), 28 November 1589, 298 CSP-S.

[17] William Ashby to Walsingham, 28 November 1589, 300 CSP-S.

[18] William Ashby to Arthur Throckmorton, 28 November 1589, 299 CSP-S.

[19] Walsingham to William Ashby, 29 November 1589, 301 CSP-S.

[20] William Ashby to Thomas Fowler, 3 December 1589, 305 CSP-S.

[21] Walsingham to William Ashby, 3 December 1589, 306 CSP-S.

[22] Arthur Throckmorton to William Ashby, 8 December 1589, 315 CSP-S.

[23] By mid-December – two months after his departure – James had yet to communicate with his Council or anyone else in Scotland.

[24] Burghley to William Ashby, 30 October 1589, 261 CSP-S.

[25] A memorial for Robert Bowes, esquire, being presently sent into Scotland, 3 December 1589, 307 CSP-S.

[26] [Alexander Hay] to [William Ashby], 4 December 1589, 308 CSP-S.

[27] William Ashby to Lord Charles Howard, 8 December 1589, 312 CSP-S.

[28] Thomas Fowler to Walsingham, 7 December 1589, 311 CSP-S. *The Calendar of State Papers incorrectly attributes this letter to Calendar of the Manuscripts of the Most Honourable the Marquess of Salisbury etc., iii, 446.*

[29] Alexander Hay subsequently became James VI/I's Secretary for Scottish Affairs and Secretary of State.

[30] [William Ashby] to Robert Bowes, 14 December 1589, 320 CSP-S.

[31] Burghley and Walsingham to William Ashby, 10 December 1589, 317 CSP-S.

[32] William Ashby to Burghley and Walsingham, 17 December 1589, 323 CSP-S.

[33] Ibid.

[34] [William Ashby] to [Throckmorton], 19 December 1589, 325 CSP-S.

[35] Arthur Agard to William Ashby, 19 December 1589, 326 CSP-S.

[36] Lord John Hamilton to William Ashby, 23 December 1589, 330 CSP-S.

[37] Lord John Hamilton to William Ashby, 20 December 1589, 328 CSP-S.

[38] The Council of Scotland to Elizabeth, 31 December 1589, 331 CSP-S.

[39] William Ashby to James VI, 31 December 1589, 332 CSP-S.

[40] Thomas Murray, James VI's furrier, to Walsingham, 6 January 1590, 340 CSP-S.

[41] William Ashby to Burghley and Walsingham, 9 January 1590, 341 CSP-S.

**Chapter 22. A last plot foiled before death's gloomy shade**

[1] [William Ashby] to [Walsingham.], 21 January 1590. 345 CSP-S.

[2] Arthur Throckmorton, *Diary of Sir Arthur Throckmorton*, Canterbury Cathedral Archives, U85/38/14, 20 January 1590.[3] Evidently The Master of Gray, who was a quadruple agent for the English, Spanish, French and Scots. See postscript Thomas Lake to Thomas Phelippes, 13 January 1590, 343 CSP-S.

⁴ William Ashby to Burghley and Walsingham, 9 January 1590, 341 CSPS.

⁵ Thomas Lake to Thomas Phelippes, 13 January 1590, 343 CSP-S.

⁶ Possibly 'faubourg' referring to a suburb of Aldgate.

⁷ William Ashby to Burghley and Walsingham, 9 January 1590, 341 CSPS

⁸ Henri, the first Bourbon king of France, was crowned as Henri IV in August 1589.

⁹ William Ashby to Alexander Hay, 24 January 1590, 346 CSP-S.

¹⁰ Alexander Hay to William Ashby, 10 February 1590, 352 CSP-S.

¹¹ Richard Wigmore to Robert Naunton, 10 February 1590, 353 CSP-S.

¹² Robert Bowes to Walsingham, 3 April 1590, 371 CSP-S.

¹³ Walter Metcalfe, ed., *The Visitations of Northamptonshire Made in 1564 and 1618–1619* (London 1887), 167.

¹⁴ Henry Naunton of Alderton, Suffolk, had served as Master of Horse to the Dowager Duchess of Suffolk, mother of the two young dukes who died of the sweating sickness in 1551.

¹⁵ William Ashby to [Henry Naunton.], 31 January 1590, 349 CSP-S.

¹⁶ Walsingham to Archibald Douglas, 27 January 1590, CSP-S, 238.

¹⁷ Thomas Windebank to Sir Francis Walsingham, 2 April 1590, 62 CSP-D, 657–8.

¹⁸ Conyers Read, *Mr. Secretary Walsingham and the Policy of Queen Elizabeth* (Oxford 1925), vol III, 448, quoting undated latter from Burghley to Count Figliazzi.

¹⁹ Alfred Webb, John Beckwith, George Miller, *The history of Chislehurst: its church, manors, and parish* (London 1899), 384.

²⁰ Payne Fisher, *The Tombes, Monuments, and Sepulchral inscriptions, lately visible in St. Pauls Cathedral, and St. Faith's under it, etc.* (London 1684), 7–10.

²¹ William Wylie to William Aschebye, 'Late Resident Ambassador for Her Highness in Scotland', 24 September 1591, *Calendar of the Manuscripts of the Most Honourable the Marquess of Salisbury*, part iv, 138.

²² Richard Wigmore to Robert Naunton, 10 February 1590, 353 CSP-S.

²³ Robert Carlyle to Archibald Douglas, 17 April 1590, *Calendar of the Manuscripts of the Most Honourable the Marquess of Salisbury*, part iv, 29.

²⁴ Burghley to Robert Bowes, 30 May 1590, 408 CSP-S.

[25] The servant, John Montgomery, was sent to London by Bowes where he delivered to Burghley 'such of his master's writings as have come to his hands' and informed 'him as to Fowler's affairs'.

[26] Richard Wigmore to William Ashby, 15 June 1590, 428 CSP-S.

[27] William Ashby to Lord Burghley, October and November 1590, CSP-D 696 and 700.

[28] Robert Naunton to Mr. Reynolds, Secretary to the Earl of Essex, 8–16 November 1590, *Calendar of the Manuscripts of the Most Honourable the Marquess of Salisbury*, part iv, 74.

[29] The Plague in London, 28 January 1593 (incorrectly entered as 1592), John Dasent ed., *Acts of the Privy Council of England*, (London 1901), vol. 24, 1592–1593, 31–2.

[30] R. Robinson *alias* William Sterrell to Thomas Phelippes, [?] January 1593, 26 CSP-D, 312.

[31] A Letter to the Mayor of Windsor, 5 June 1593, *Acts of the Privy Council*, 284.

[32] A Letter to the Lord Mayor of London, 5 April 1593, *Acts of the Privy Council*, 163–4.

[33] Treasurer of the Chamber's Accounts, 23 February 1593, https://folgerpedia.folger.edu/mediawiki/media/images_pedia_folgerpedia_mw/1/1a/ECDbD_1593.pdf, accessed 13 November 2020.

[34] Ibid, 6 April 1593.

[35] Thomas Phelippes to William Sterrell, 7 April 1593, 124 CSP-D, 342.

[36] Robert Bowes to Burghley, 20 June and 12 November 1593, 71 and 170 CSP-S.

[37] The Penalties of Recusancy, 5 July 1593, Acts of the Privy Council 363.

[38] The Act Against Recusants (1593),35 Elizabeth, Cap. 2, Henry Gee & William Hardy, eds, *Documents Illustrative of English Church History*, (New York 1896), 498–501.

[39] Charles Creighton, *A History of Epidemics in Britain from A.D. 664 to the Extinction of Plague* (Cambridge 1891), vol. 1, 352.

[40] Ibid, 357.

[41] John Guy, *Elizabeth: The Forgotten Years* (London 2016).

[42] Charles Creighton, *A History of Epidemics in Britain from A.D. 664*, 355–6.

[43] Richard Verstegan and Anthony Petti, *The Letters And Despatches of Richard Verstegan* (London 1959), 185.

[44] John Stanhope to Robert Cecil, November 1593, *Calendar of the Manuscripts of the Most Honourable the Marquess of Salisbury*, part iv, 425–6.

[45] Peter Hasler, Chichester Borough Published in The History of Parliament: the House of Commons 1558–1603, (London 1981), http://www. historyofparliamentonline.org/volume/1558–1603/constituencies/chichester, accessed 12 November 2020.

[46] Charles Creighton, *A History of Epidemics in Britain*, 365.

[47] The namesake William Ashby (d. 1635) matriculated as a Pensioner at Trinity College, Cambridge, in 1605, received his BA in 1608/9, and was awarded an MA in 1612, when he was listed as a Fellow. He was appointed Taxor (a university representative who exercised the University's rights to intervene in trade in the town) in 1631. His father, George Ashby of Quenby, was the son of Barbara Ashby of Loseby, William's first cousin.

[48] Will of William Ashby of Clerkenwell, The National Archives' reference PROB 11/82/616.

### Appendix I. Sir Robert Naunton

[1] *Memoirs of Sir Robert Naunton, Knt., author of 'The Fragmenta regalia', (London 1814), 2.*

[2] John Still (c.1543–26 February 1608), Bishop of Bath and Wells.

[3] William Ashby to Thomas Mills, 15 July 1589], 151 CSP-S.

[4] Richard Wigmore to Robert Naunton. [10 Feb. 1590], 353 CSP-S.

[5] Robert Naunton to Mr. Reynolds, Secretary to the Earl of Essex, 8–16 November 1590, Calendar of the Manuscripts of the Most Honourable the Marquess of Salisbury, part iv, 74.

[6] *Memoirs of Sir Robert Naunton, Knt., author of 'The Fragmenta regalia'.* (London 1814), 6.

[7] Ibid, 4.

[8] Thomas Birch, *Memoirs Of the Reign of Queen Elizabeth: From the Year 1581 Till Her Death*, (London 1754) vol. 1, 369.

[9] Paul Hammer, 'Essex and Europe: Evidence from Confidential Instructions by the Earl of Essex, 1595–6', *The English Historical Review*, Vol. 111, No. 441 (Apr., 1996), 365.

[10] Sir Edwin Sandys to Sec. Sir Robt. Naunton, 28 January 1620, 'America and West Indies: January 1620', *Calendar of State Papers Colonial, America and West Indies*: Volume 1, 1574–1660, ed. William Sainsbury (London, 1860), 23.

# Index